"In the course of years of writing on imagination, hospitality, and touch, Richard Kearney has shown, in ways both philosophical and poetic, what it is to meet the world in a spirit of open-handed generosity. In this beautiful collection, we see a group of thinkers meeting strangers and horses, gods and trees; they encounter the living and the dead in the written word and the moving image, on the seashore and in the digital classroom, in the history of philosophy and in life lived in the flesh, all in that open spirit that reaches for empathy without presuming understanding. Thinking across generations and in the midst of many orders of being, they show us all over again that the world is not just before our eyes but at our fingertips. If we are paying attention, the extraordinary shines through the ordinary. This is an exercise in thinking together. Be warned; you will find yourself thinking with these writers long after you have closed the book."

Anne O'Byrne, *Philosophy, Stony Brook University, USA*

"If too many philosophers have colluded with a civilization out of touch with the lives, the bodies, the earth that make it up—this collection manifests an enlivening transdisciplinary alternative. Inspired by Richard Kearney's body of work—in its adventures in embodiment, its refusal of the culture of discarnation, its revelatory 'anacarnation' and its oh-so-needed ecology—this conversation brilliantly unfolds the flesh of a radically hospitable hermeneutics."

Catherine Keller, *George T. Cobb Professor of Constructive Theology, Drew University, The Theological School, USA*

I0092132

Anacarnation and Returning to the Lived Body with Richard Kearney

This edited collection responds to Richard Kearney's recent work on touch, excarnation, and embodiment, as well as his broader work in carnal hermeneutics, which sets the stage for his return to and retrieval of the senses of the lived body.

Here, fourteen scholars engage the breadth and depth of Kearney's work to illuminate our experience of the body. The chapters collected within take up a wide variety of subjects, from nature and non-human animals to our experience of the sacred and the demonic, and from art's account of touching to the political implications of various types of embodiment. Featuring also an inspired new reflection from Kearney himself, in which he lays out his vision for "anacarnation," this volume is an important statement about the centrality of touch and embodiment in our experience, and a reminder that, despite the excarnating tendencies of contemporary life, the lived body remains a touchstone for wisdom in our increasingly complicated and fragile world.

Written for scholars and students interested in touch, embodiment, phenomenology, and hermeneutics, this diverse and challenging collection contributes to a growing field of scholarship that recognizes and attempts to correct the excarnating trends in philosophy and in culture at large.

Brian Treanor is Professor of Philosophy and Charles S. Casassa SJ Chair at Loyola Marymount University in California, USA.

James L. Taylor is Professor of Philosophy and Peacemaking and Director of International Programs at the European Center for the Study of War and Peace.

The Psychology and the Other Book Series

Series editor: David M. Goodman

Associate editors: Brian W. Becker, Donna M. Orange, and Eric R. Severson

The Psychology and the Other book series highlights creative work at the intersections between psychology and the vast array of disciplines relevant to the human psyche. The interdisciplinary focus of this series brings psychology into conversation with continental philosophy, psychoanalysis, religious studies, anthropology, sociology, and social/critical theory. The cross-fertilization of theory and practice, encompassing such a range of perspectives, encourages the exploration of alternative paradigms and newly articulated vocabularies that speak to human identity, freedom, and suffering. Thus, we are encouraged to reimagine our encounters with difference, our notions of the "other," and what constitutes therapeutic modalities.

The study and practices of mental health practitioners, psychoanalysts, and scholars in the humanities will be sharpened, enhanced, and illuminated by these vibrant conversations, representing pluralistic methods of inquiry, including those typically identified as psychoanalytic, humanistic, qualitative, phenomenological, or existential.

Recent titles in the series include:

misReading Plato
Continental and Psychoanalytic Glimpses Beyond the Mask
Edited by Matthew Clemente, Bryan J. Cocchiara, and William J. Hendel

Neoliberalism, Ethics and the Social Responsibility of Psychology
Dialogues at the Edge
Edited by Heather Macdonald, Sara Carabbio-Thopsey and David M. Goodman

Anacarnation and Returning to the Lived Body with Richard Kearney
Brian Treanor and James L. Taylor

For a full list of titles in the series, please visit the Routledge website at:
https://www.routledge.com/Psychology-and-the-Other/book-series/PSYOTH

Anacarnation and Returning to the Lived Body with Richard Kearney

Edited by Brian Treanor and James L. Taylor

Routledge
Taylor & Francis Group

NEW YORK AND LONDON

Cover image: "Song of Amergin/I Am The Wave (#1)," 2018, Simone Kearney.

First published 2023
by Routledge
605 Third Avenue, New York, NY 10158

and by Routledge
4 Park Square, Milton Park, Abingdon, Oxon, OX14 4RN

Routledge is an imprint of the Taylor & Francis Group, an informa business

© 2023 selection and editorial matter, Brian Treanor and James L. Taylor; individual chapters, the contributors

The right of Brian Treanor and James L. Taylor to be identified as the authors of the editorial material, and of the authors for their individual chapters, has been asserted in accordance with sections 77 and 78 of the Copyright, Designs and Patents Act 1988.

All rights reserved. No part of this book may be reprinted or reproduced or utilised in any form or by any electronic, mechanical, or other means, now known or hereafter invented, including photocopying and recording, or in any information storage or retrieval system, without permission in writing from the publishers.

Trademark notice: Product or corporate names may be trademarks or registered trademarks, and are used only for identification and explanation without intent to infringe.

Library of Congress Cataloguing-in-Publication Data
Names: Treanor, Brian, editor. | Taylor, James, 1975- editor.
Title: Anacarnation and returning to the lived body with Richard Kearney / edited by Brian Treanor and James L. Taylor.
Description: New York, NY : Routledge, 2023. | Includes bibliographical references and index. |
Identifiers: LCCN 2022015713 (print) | LCCN 2022015714 (ebook) | ISBN 9781032259215 (hardback) | ISBN 9781032259192 (paperback) | ISBN 9781003285649 (ebook)
Subjects: LCSH: Kearney, Richard. | Touch. | Human body (Philosophy) | Hermeneutics. | Continental philosophy.
Classification: LCC B945.K384 A53 2023 (print) | LCC B945.K384 (ebook) | DDC 128/.6--dc23/eng/20220810
LC record available at https://lccn.loc.gov/2022015713
LC ebook record available at https://lccn.loc.gov/2022015714

ISBN: 978-1-032-25921-5 (hbk)
ISBN: 978-1-032-25919-2 (pbk)
ISBN: 978-1-003-28564-9 (ebk)

DOI: 10.4324/9781003285649

Typeset in Times New Roman
by MPS Limited, Dehradun

Contents

Contributors

Daniel O'Dea Bradley is Assistant Professor of Philosophy at Gonzaga University. While valuing the intellectual asceticism and iconoclastic rigor that marked 20th-century thought, Bradley's research project attempts to nurture a renewed appreciation of the beauty and sacredness of being, thereby allowing for dialogue with liturgical and sacramental religion, environmental philosophy, and Native American thought.

Eileen Brennan studied Philosophy in Dublin and Paris and is a lecturer in Philosophy and Education at Dublin City University. She has written widely in the field of hermeneutics with particular concentration on the work of Paul Ricoeur. A former editor of *Études Ricoeuriennes/ Ricoeur Studies*, she has translated a number of books and papers by contemporary French thinkers.

Matthew Clemente is a husband and father of four. He lives and writes in Boston, Massachusetts where he holds teaching appointments at Boston College and Boston University. He has published seven books, most recently *Eros Crucified: Death, Desire, and the Divine in Psychoanalysis and Philosophy of Religion* (Routledge 2020), and is the Assistant Editor of the *Journal for Continental Philosophy of Religion*.

Neal DeRoo is Canada Research Chair in Phenomenology and Philosophy of Religion and Professor of Philosophy at The King's University in Edmonton, Canada. He is the author of *The Political Logic of Experience* (2022) and *Futurity in Phenomenology* (2013), and has co-edited several volumes at the intersection of continental philosophy and the philosophy of religion.

Melissa Fitzpatrick received her Ph.D. in philosophy from Boston College in 2019 and is Assistant Professor of the Practice in Ethics in the Carroll School of Management at BC. She teaches business ethics, environmental ethics, animal ethics, social and political philosophy, and philosophy of religion. She is the co-author (with Richard Kearney) of *Radical Hospitality: From Thought to Action* (2021).

Brian Gregor is Associate Professor in the Philosophy Department at California State University, Dominguez Hills. He is the author of numerous articles in continental philosophy of religion, ethics, and aesthetics, and his books include *Ricoeur's Hermeneutics of Religion: Rebirth of the Capable Self* (2019) and *A Philosophical Anthropology of the Cross: The Cruciform Self* (2013).

Christina M. Gschwandtner teaches continental philosophy of religion at Fordham University. She is the author of six books, most recently *Welcoming Finitude: Toward a Phenomenology of Orthodox Liturgy* (2019) and *Reading Religious Ritual with Ricoeur: Between Fragility and Hope* (2021), as well as many articles and translations at the intersection of phenomenology and religion.

Tamsin Jones is Associate Professor of Religion at Trinity College, CT, where she teaches courses in the history of Christian thought, gender and religion, and the philosophy of religion. She is the author of *A Genealogy of Marion's Philosophy of Religion: Apparent Darkness* (2011) as well as many articles in continental philosophy of religion and political theology.

Richard Kearney holds the Charles Seelig Chair of Philosophy at Boston College. He has published many works in continental philosophy, with particular emphasis on narrative imagination, hospitality, and embodiment. His most recent works include *Touch: Recovering Our Most Vital Sense* (2021), *Radical Hospitality* (with Melissa Fitzpatrick 2021), and *Carnal Hermeneutics* (edited with Brian Treanor 2015). He is also a published novelist and director of the Guestbook Project—Hosting the Stranger.

Sarit Larry holds a Ph.D. from Boston College and is a lecturer at Sapir College in Israel. She is interested in activism and social change as they echo in continental philosophy. She was the Co-Director of Mahapach-Taghir, a grassroots Palestinian-Israeli feminist social change organization and is now leading The Diversity and Inclusion in Academia Project at aChord Center in Israel.

M.E. Littlejohn is a professor of philosophy at the University of New Brunswick. He is an invited researcher at the Sorbonne University.

James L. Taylor is Co-Director and Professor of Philosophy and Peacemaking at the European Center for the Study of War and Peace. He specializes in the ethics of transformation through philosophy, politics, and religion, and is the editor, with Richard Kearney, of *Hosting the Stranger: Between Religions* (2011).

Brian Treanor is Professor of Philosophy and Charles S. Casassa SJ Chair at Loyola Marymount University, where he also holds affiliate appointments in environmental studies and Irish studies. His books include *Melancholic Joy* (2021), *Emplotting Virtue* (SUNY 2014), and *Aspects of Alterity* (2006), as well as a number of edited collections, including, with Richard Kearney, *Carnal Hermeneutics* (2015).

Christopher Yates teaches philosophy at James Madison University and is an Associate Fellow at the Institute for Advanced Studies in Culture, the University of Virginia. He is the author of *The Poetic Imagination in Heidegger and Schelling* (2013). His research concentrates primarily on the phenomenological and hermeneutic traditions, the period of German Idealism, and the intersections of these with currents in the visual and literary arts.

Acknowledgments

This project was developed prior to and during the COVID-19 pandemic. Over three years, from 2018 to 2021, former students and scholars of Richard Kearney wrote contributions that engage Kearney's work through a myriad of lenses and scholarly applications. The original plan was for the contributors to meet in person and discuss chapter drafts at a workshop on the island of Vis, Croatia in June of 2020; for obvious reasons, this proved impossible, and our gathering was postponed. However, the contributors continued to correspond with each other and discuss their ideas during the long, dark months of the pandemic. In January of 2021, another unanticipated but fortuitous event took place: the publication of Richard Kearney's latest book, *Touch: Recovering Our Most Vital Sense*. With many of the contributors already engaging themes of carnality, the publication of *Touch* inspired us to focus the volume on touch and our other senses, incarnation and excarnation, and our sensory immersion in our environment, among other related themes.

This project would not have been possible without the hospitality extended by the European Center for the Study of War and Peace, a groundbreaking organization that, in addition to facilitating study abroad opportunities for colleges and universities in the United States, hosts or facilitates a variety of events and symposia. ECSWP was the organizer and host of our 2021 workshop, during which some contributors were able to gather on Vis, while others "Zoomed" in from around the world to discuss the papers. Particular thanks are due to Petra Belković Taylor, the co-director of ECSWP, who in addition to helping organize and coordinate the workshop, substantively engaged a number of the authors and papers during the development of the volume. A number of the essays were improved on the basis of her input. We are indebted as well to Ana Pavković, ECSWP's administrative and editorial manager, who contributed her expertise to the project by compiling and formatting the manuscript for submission.

We are grateful to David Goodman, Director of Psychology and the Other and the founder of the Psychology and the Other series at Routledge. His early enthusiasm for the project and unwavering support during pandemic-related delays were deeply appreciated. Thanks are due as well to the incredibly responsive and efficient team at Routledge—particularly Amanda Devine, Zoe Meyer, and Jana Craddock—whose dedicated work helped to ensure that the publication process was trouble-free.

An earlier version of "Thinking Like a Jaguar" appeared in the *Journal of the Pacific Association for the Continental Tradition*, vol. 4 (2021); we appreciate the journal's policies and structure, which allow for the republication of a modified version of that essay here.

An earlier version of the first two parts of "Kearney's Journey between Imagination and Touch—in Dialogue with Ricœur" appears in *Études Ricœuriennes/Ricœur Studies*, Vol. 12, No. 2 (2021).

Introduction: Re-touching Philosophy with Richard Kearney

Brian Treanor and James L. Taylor

Richard Kearney is the author of dozens of books, from *Poétique du possible* (1984) to, most recently, *Touch* (2021). Alongside these monographs, we find a long list of edited collections, countless articles and book chapters, three novels, as well as interdisciplinary artistic collaborations, interviews, radio and television programs, and more. One can only guess as to how many other projects are currently in various stages of development. These works are so numerous and so diverse that it is difficult to keep them all in view. Do we read Kearney as a hermeneut? A philosopher of narrative? Of religion? Of imagination? As a distinctively Irish philosopher? Or one of the prominent voices in contemporary "continental" philosophy? Any one of these labels would be true, and each is inadequate.

Although any attempt to succinctly summarize or neatly categorize such a prolific scholar is bound to come up short, given that the present volume is inspired by and engaged with Kearney's recent work on embodiment and on touch, it is possible to give some account of his general intellectual itinerary, and how it brought him to reflecting on embodiment, excarnation, and touch.[1]

The Ana-Structure of the Fourth Reduction

Kearney first deploys the "ana-structure" of his diacritical hermeneutics—as well as coining the term "anatheism"—in the 2006 essay "Epiphanies of the Everyday: Toward a Micro-Eschatology" (Manoussakis 2006). The essay opens with the question, "what if we were to *return* to epiphanies of the everyday?" In it, Kearney proposes a fourth, "micro-eschatological" phenomenological reduction, supplementing the transcendental reduction of Husserl, the ontological reduction of Heidegger, and the "dosological" reduction of Marion.[2] This fourth reduction leads us *back to the everyday*: that is, back to the natural world of simple, embodied life where we may confront again the other 'face-to-face'" (Manoussakis 2005, 6). That is to say, this reduction is a return to our communal, incarnate, lived experience of the world.

DOI: 10.4324/9781003285649-1

But this is no mere return, a retreat back to naive realism, as if we could dismiss the first three phenomenological reductions; it is, rather, a creative "repetition forward" that returns to the everyday *in a new way*. As such, it recalls Kearney's mentor, Paul Ricoeur, who described how the loss of innocent faith could lead, at least in some circumstances, to a new faith, a "second naivete" voluntarily adopted in the wake of critique or doubt. A return to faith after wandering in the wilderness or a dark night of the soul. But the faith of second naivete is not a simple return to the faith of first naivete, which would be impossible. Wrestling with difference and doubt makes simple return impossible, or at least pathological. Once we lose the naivete of innocence, it is gone forever. The faith of second naivete is, rather, a voluntary repetition forward of faith—in God, in another person, in a way of life—that takes account of both the initial faith and the trouble or critique that cast doubt on it. Thus, we can see that while in "Epiphanies of the Everyday" Kearney places a marker of sorts on the *ana*-structure of his hermeneutic project, this wager is not without precedent. First, while the essay coins the term "anatheism," in some sense it is simply giving name to a methodological commitment that had long characterized Kearney's work. Second, Kearney himself observes that he is directing our attention to something that other thinkers have also described or done, but without having thematized it. He sees allies and fellow-travelers in diverse figures including Ricoeur, Duns Scotus, Paul Cézanne, Gerard Manley Hopkins, Patrick Kavanaugh, and Wallace Stevens, to name only a handful.

In drawing our attention to the ana-structure of his hermeneutics, Kearney emphasizes ana-theism, a vision he would develop much more thoroughly four years later in a book of the same name. "Epiphanies of the Everyday" appears in *After God* (2005), a volume dedicated to Kearney's work in philosophy of religion; so, it is no surprise that he draws our attention to the "religious" character of the fourth reduction. However, the ana-structure of Kearney's philosophy is not limited to religion, and there are intimations, even in this early essay, that his thinking was becoming more and more incarnate, embodied, and tactile. This is evident not only in the emphasis on the everyday, or even incarnation. He writes of "touching beyond the tangible (*ana-pathos*)" and a "new way of saying, seeing, and feeling over again—of sensing otherwise, anew, for a second time." It's clear not only that incarnation is an essential aspect of ana-theism, but also that incarnation itself—enfleshment, tactility, contact—is a theme of ongoing, and growing, importance to Kearney. In the years immediately following "Epiphanies of the Everyday," he further developed the religious nature of the fourth reduction in *Anatheism* (Kearney 2011a) and *Reimagining the Sacred* (Zimmerman and Kearney 2015). However, more recently, Kearney's work has turned to focus squarely on the carnal and tactile nature of the fourth reduction in *Carnal Hermeneutics* (Kearney and

Treanor 2015) and *Touch* (Kearney 2021). It is the latter two texts that are the provocation for and focus of the current volume.

Hospitality and Healing

If Kearney's diacritical hermeneutics is characterized by the ana-structure of "repetition forward," both before and after its explicit thematization in 2006, what is the focus or goal of such a retrieval-remembering-repeating forward? That is to ask, are there themes that unify Kearney's diverse body of work, from the *Poétique du possible* (1984) to, most recently, *Touch* (2021)? Or, again, what is it that motivates Kearney's thinking? There are, to be sure, many ways to answer such questions, as attested to by the wide ranges of scholarship taking up or commenting on some of the abiding foci of Kearney's work. Imagination (Littlejohn 2020), the sacred (Zimmerman 2015), possibility (Kearney 2001), and otherness (Veldsman and Steenkamp 2018) all offer themselves as legitimate possibilities; and there are others besides. However, we would not be far from the mark if we identified *hospitality* as the center of gravity around which orbit the diverse satellites of Kearney's philosophical concerns. By "hospitality," we mean that act or "moment when the self opens to the stranger and welcomes what is foreign and unfamiliar into its home" (Kearney and Taylor 2011, 1).[3] This commitment to hospitality and healing informs the treatment of a wide range of subjects in Kearney's published work.

Carnal Hermeneutics, published in 2015, was a collaborative project that gathered together contributions from a range of philosophers, proposing that—despite their diverse agendas and foci—they shared a certain concern with the lived body that marked them out from some of their contemporaries. This collection was part of larger trends in contemporary philosophy working to correct what was increasingly felt to be an over-emphasis on the linguistic, constructed nature of reality in late 20th-century continental philosophy. But the philosophers brought together under the banner of carnal hermeneutics were, and are, not of a single mind. It's clear, for example, that thinkers like Emmanuel Falque and Ted Toadvine, or Julia Kristeva and Emmanuel Alloa, are pursuing substantially different projects. Some contributors to *Carnal Hermeneutics* were motivated by religious questions about the body, others by questions of ethics and vulnerability, and yet others by environmental concerns. Carnal hermeneutics is, at best, a kind of broad genus in which we find diverse philosophical species.

What, then, is distinctive about Kearney's own approach to carnal hermeneutics when compared with Falque, Nancy, Kristeva, or any of the other contributors to *Carnal Hermeneutics*? What themes orient his thinking? What questions is he trying to answer? To what realities is he bearing witness? Clearly, one way we must answer these questions is to say that Kearney's thinking is concerned with the primacy, and reversibility, of *touch*. In the early and programmatic "What is Carnal Hermeneutics?" Kearney makes clear that touch is his preferred way of thinking through incarnation and materiality, something he developed in significantly more detail in his follow-up monograph, *Touch: Recovering Our Most Vital Sense* (Kearney 2021b). So, one thing we can say about Kearney's particular approach to carnal hermeneutics is that it is focused on touch. Well and good. However, his treatment of touch is not an abstract, neutral, disinterested account of tactility; rather, touch itself serves to sharpen the focus on additional themes that Kearney finds significant. It would be very difficult to read Kearney's most recent work—indeed, to read extensively any of his work—and fail to come away with a deep appreciation for the role that hospitality and healing play in framing and forming his thinking.

This is evident, first, in *Carnal Hermeneutics* itself. While "The Wager of Carnal Hermeneutics" includes a careful analysis—both historical and phenomenological—of the sense of touch, otherness, reversibility, double sensation, and intertwining, it also develops these themes as they relate to host and guest, hospitality and hostility, and therapeutic hermeneutics. Second, in his work after *Carnal Hermeneutics,* Kearney has focused even more clearly and overtly on hospitality and healing. Fully one third of *Touch* is explicitly devoted to trauma, tactile healing, and recovery; and themes like tactful touching, handshakes, caressing, empathy, forgiveness, and the like leap from every other chapter and section. *Radical Hospitality* makes this emphasis even more clear. More, in looking retrospectively at Kearney's body of work, hospitality proves a useful framework for thinking about many of the other overt foci of his philosophy: narrative hospitality (Kearney 2002b), religious hospitality (Kearney 2011a), cultural hospitality (Kearney 2002a), and national hospitality (Kearney 1996), as well as carnal hospitality (Kearney 2021; Kearney and Fitzpatrick 2021). Finally, we can look to Kearney's work as a public intellectual, in which he argued for postnationalist forms of identity in which people could identify as "British, or Irish, or both," insisted that interreligious hospitality is the way forward in thinking about our widely shared experiences of the sacred, and founded the international Guestbook Project, which is dedicated to "turning hostility into hospitality" through the exchange of narratives. Thus, without being reductive or simplistic, it seems clear that hospitality is one appropriate thread with which we might link the diverse ethical, political, religious, and incarnational themes at work in Kearney's thinking.

Richard Kearney is then, at heart, a philosopher of radical hospitality.[4] This is evident not only in his scholarship. Many of the contributors to this volume were Kearney's students at one point or another in their own intellectual development. From those he taught early in his career at University College Dublin, to his first doctoral students at Boston College, to more recent students at a number of different institutions. Each of these philosophers benefited from Kearney's availability, openness, and care, a kind of attention that launched a number of successful philosophical careers. There are many other students who moved on to influential positions in diverse, non-academic spheres—in the arts, in politics, in law and business—and who are no less indebted to his generosity and hospitality. And, of course, to these groups we could add the countless people who have been influenced by Kearney through his public scholarship and written work, and his tactful engagement with diverse people across the world. Thus, this volume is a celebration not only of Kearney's recent work on touch, which is already being taken up and widely discussed in periodicals both academic and popular, or on his career-long focus on hospitality; it is also a celebration of the influence Kearney has had through teaching and mentoring several generations of philosophers.

Anacarnation

But, if the ana-structure of the fourth reduction and a commitment to diverse forms of hospitality are core characteristics of Kearney's philosophy as a whole, it is his work on the carnal and tactile that orients the present engagement with his thinking. Clearly, given what has been said about the fourth reduction above, concern with the carnal, the tactile, the everyday *hereness* and *thisness* of things is not new for Kearney. Nevertheless, the explicit thematization of and emphasis on the carnal and tactile in *Carnal Hermeneutics* and *Touch* represent a new stage in his thinking.

Touch is written "for any interested reader concerned with the crisis of touch in our time"; it asks whether we are "losing touch with our senses" in an age of "excarnation" in which "flesh becomes image" (Kearney 2021, 2). We find ourselves confronted with a crisis of touch, a point in history in which accelerating technological innovation (e.g., the fascinating power and allure of the Internet) and circumstance (e.g., a global pandemic, necessitating "social" distancing) conspire to occlude our primary, tactile, sensuous insertion in the world. We are increasingly out of touch with our bodies, with each other, and with the wider world.

But Kearney's work is no one-sided polemic against the evils of technology and virtuality. He acknowledges the "magical, fabulous, otherworldly" benefits of virtuality, and recognizes that it allows us "to exchange culturally, socially, and commercially with all kinds of people in all parts of the world" (3). He concedes the benefits associated with the democratization of and accessibility to information. But he also recognizes the downside of hyperreality, the possibility that, in the process of expanding the options for connectivity we are losing a certain kind of carnal contact, that we live our lives at a distance, so to speak, from the world and from ourselves.

According to Kearney, the prescription for this malady is not some form of neo-Luddism in which we consign the Internet and associated technologies to the bonfire. It is, rather, a *"new commons of the flesh"* (2021, 7) that, in a now-familiar pattern, returns again (and *again*) to our incarnate being-in-the-world in a way that repeats forward its possibilities in the context of our present age. A return to the body that accounts for, and includes, the otherwise excarnating technologies of the Internet, social media, virtual reality, and so on. What Kearney calls, in his essay for this volume, *"anacarnation."* His goal, then, is not merely to critique, or to set up a binary between the carnal and the virtual, or the body and the image, but rather to understand, and recover, the myriad joys of incarnation (Kearney 2021, 6).

The Essays

This volume came together in partnership with the European Center for the Study of War and Peace (ECSWP), a non-governmental organization based in Zagreb, Croatia that is focused—both by sponsoring immersive "study abroad" opportunities for universities in the United States and by hosting conferences, symposia, and workshops for scholars from Europe and North America—on pressing questions of war, violence, peacemaking, and reconciliation. ECSWP had planned to host a workshop on Kearney's *Touch* in June of 2020, plans that were, unfortunately, scuppered by the COVID-19 pandemic. Nevertheless, the contributors began work on their essays with the hope of convening a workshop to discuss and revise the completed work in 2021. In the summer of that year, a workshop did take place on the island of Vis, a relatively isolated location and one little affected, at the time of our gathering, by the pandemic. For several days, spirited discussion of Kearney's work took place over presentations, walks, and meals. Some contributors were able to be present on Vis, while others joined via Zoom video link to participate. The irony and provocation of discussing the meaning and significance of incarnation, excarnation, and touching via video teleconference was not lost on our group; but the resulting conversations, questions, and critiques improved all the essays, and was followed by ongoing discussion and commentary over the subsequent weeks and months. The result is the volume before you, divided into four sections: touching earth, touching the sacred, touching imagination, and touching flesh.

The first group of essays engage Kearney's nascent interest in the more-than-human world of nature. Gestures in this direction have, to be sure, appeared in Kearney's work for some time; however, sustained attention to non-human nature is often a promissory note that is just beginning to come due—for example, in Kearney's essay for this volume. Melissa Fitzpatrick sees, in Kearney's account of touch, the possibility of a more certain ground for empathy and compassion, one that can help orient an ethico-moral sensibility more attuned to non-human animals. The promise of carnal hermeneutics for illuminating human/non-human relationships is also taken up by Brian Treanor, who argues that over-reliance on human language distances us from empathy with the more-than-human world, which is more reliably accessible to us in carnal and tactile experiences that are more widely shared among animals. Crina Gschwandtner also sees promise in Kearney's budding interest in the more-than-human world; she seeks to supplement the rich hermeneutic accounts of tactile encounters with nature by introducing phenomenological and ontological analyses of nature in the work of Hedwig Conrad-Martius. Reading Conrad-Martius alongside Kearney will, Gschwandtner argues, give us a fuller and deeper sense of how human embodiment allows us to be "in touch" with the world. All three argue that Kearney's development of a carnal and tactile hermeneutics shows a great deal of potential for grounding ecological empathy and hospitality, and work to engage and develop this aspect of his work.

The next section links Kearney's more recent work on the carnal with his longstanding interests in philosophy of religion and the sacred. Neal DeRoo argues that the fourth reduction is a methodological principle that applies more broadly than the *persona*-person distinction that is the focus in *After God*. Using the reduction to assess the sacred-carnal distinction, DeRoo argues that carnal hermeneutics is a mere prolegomenon to "carnal sacrality" in which we are poietically attuned to the sacred in and through our everyday interactions with the world. Dan Bradley observes that the metaphor of depth plays a crucial role in Kearney's work, from his earliest publications on imagination to his most recent work in carnal hermeneutics, and that this approach allows him to avoid a number of conceptual traps that are common to other modern and postmodern philosophies. However, Bradley also warns that the horizontal and reciprocal aspects represented in tactility must be balanced with the vertical and asymmetrical features of "depth," present elsewhere in Kearney's thought, in order to safeguard a holistic understanding of reality. Finally, Brian Gregor uses Kearney's work to develop a "carnal hermeneutics of the demonic." Contrary to caricature, it is demonic imagination, not Christianity, that is committed to a disfigurement of carnality. Drawing on examples from Milton's *Paradise Lost* to William Peter Blatty's *The Exorcist*, Gregor describes how the demonic is characterized by a withdrawal of the self that distorts the concrete corporeality of the human being.

The third section considers the role of carnal hermeneutics and touch in various forms of artistic expression and imagination. Murray Littlejohn shows that while early Greek imagination lost sight of the incarnate flesh, viewing soul as separate from body, Judaic imagination kept close to the ground and viewed the human as a body drawn from the earth. Through the lens of Kearney's retrieval of flesh and double sensibility, Littlejohn demonstrates that these two traditions are integrated in the anacarnational approach of St. Augustine. Chris Yates reads Kearney's longstanding interest in the arts, as well as his recent work on the carnal and tactile, in his consideration of Terrence Malick's *A Hidden Life*. He argues that the aesthetic achievements of Malick's film are best appreciated when understood in the terms of Kearney's philosophy, and that the film provides a compelling way to link Kearney's early work on imagination with his more recent work on carnality. Through a chronological overview of Kearney's work—from his early interest in imagination in narrative to his recent work on carnal hermeneutics—Eileen Brennan claims that Kearney's philosophy is unified by his focus on the possible. This focus attests to Kearney's fidelity to Ricoeur; but Brennan finds in Kearney's recent turn to the carnal a deepening interest in the real that takes him beyond the more orthodox hermeneutic concern with the possible.

The final group of essays takes up broadly ethical issues having to do with carnality and touch. James L. Taylor argues that Kearney's turn to touch can help us resist the coercive effects of power relations and retrieve an experience of our bodies as flesh. Foregrounding the ana-structure of Kearney's work as a repeating forward and emphasising the reversibility of sensation, Taylor frames Kearney's work as an art of living carnally, through our acting and sensing bodies, rather than as docile and obedient subjects. Sarit Larry explores the role played by female nudity in various forms of protest. Although nudity is often thought of in reductive forms focusing on violence or the potential for violence, Larry argues that female nudity also contains a specific ethical call in a protest environment saturated with the possibility of unwanted, untactful touch. Because of the volatile possibility presented by female nudity, it harbors the possibility of serving as a focal point for awareness and care that can transform the protesting arena. Matthew Clemente argues that Kearney's work on touch, carnality, and the body helps to return philosophy to its fundamental task: the search for self-understanding expressed in the Delphic maxim *know thyself*. Only by recognizing ourselves as fundamentally, not accidentally, embodied beings can we pursue self-knowledge in earnest. Tamsin Jones concludes this section with an essay reflecting on how our experience of the world is digitally mediated in a way that exacerbates the absence of touch. She focuses, in particular, on the way in which our visual consumption of other people's suffering via digital images poses certain ethical challenges in a particularly harsh light. Jones then considers ways in which the relational model of carnality in Kearney's diacritical hermeneutics might help us to develop a more incarnational gaze when confronted with suffering.

Finally, Kearney himself concludes the volume with an essay outlining his vision of "anacarnation." Tracing the philosophical and poetic roots of the return to the lived body and the interconnectedness of all things, he describes how the ana-structure of time and space shape our engagement with the world, as well as how awareness of this makes possible an "authentic seeing" in which—following the fourth, micro-eschatological reduction—the extraordinary shines forth in the ordinary. Kearney further develops this analysis with several "ecological" examples or case studies highlighting human/nonhuman tactile reversibility, including personal anecdotes of symbiotic relationships with dogs, horses, and other animals. In the spirit of the volume as a whole, Kearney's essay repeats forward themes he has explored previously, but now with a deepening emphasis on hosting those strangers—the earth, animals, our carnal bodies—that we have neglected through a more exclusive focus on mental phenomena and linguistic mediation. Along with the other essays in the volume, Kearney's contribution both signals a present interest and opens new possibilities for thinking in and living through our sensing and touching.

Notes

1 Murray Littlejohn's excellent *Imagination Now* (Littlejohn 2020) is perhaps the best attempt to give the reader a sense of the totality and diversity of Kearney's work.
2 "Dosological," from *dosis* (givenness). See *After God* (Manoussakis, 2005, 5, 21).
3 Although in *Radical Hospitality* (Kearney and Fitzpatrick 2021), a more radical and capacious account of hospitality is offered, one that bleeds into "prioritizing the needs of the other over oneself" (107) or "bearing witness" and "respecting" the other (109). Think of these as the *narrow* (tied to welcoming an other into a home) and *wide* (coextensive with respect) accounts of hospitality.
4 This is not a claim unique to our reading of Kearney's oeuvre. A variety of contributions to this volume—Treanor, DeRoo, Gschwandtner, Fitzpatrick, and others—make the same, or a similar, observation.

References

Kearney, Richard. 1996. *Postnationalist Ireland: Politics, Culture, Philosophy*. London: Routledge.
Kearney, Richard. 1998a. *The Poetics of Imagining*. New York: Fordham University Press.
Kearney, Richard. 1998b. *The Wake of Imagination; Toward a Postmodern Culture*. London: Routledge.
Kearney, Richard. 2001. *The God Who May Be: A Hermeneutics of Religion*. London: Routledge.
Kearney, Richard. 2002a. *Strangers, Gods, and Monsters: Interpreting Otherness*. London: Routledge.

Kearney, Richard. 2002b. *On Stories*. London: Routledge.
Kearney, Richard. 2011a. *Anatheism (Returning to God after God)*. New York: Columbia University Press.
Kearney, Richard. 2011b. "What Is Diacritical Hermeneutics." *Journal of Applied Hermeneutics*. (December 10): 1–14. doi:10.11575/jah.v0i0.53187
Kearney, Richard. 2015. "What Is Carnal Hermeneutics?" *New Literary History* vol. 46, no. 1 (Winter): 99–124.
Kearney, Richard. 2019. "Double Hospitality: Between Word and Touch." *The Journal for Continental Philosophy of Religion*, vol. 1: 71–89.
Kearney, Richard. 2020. "Carnal Hermeneutics." In *Imagination Now*, edited by M.E. Littlejohn, 99–119. Lanham: Rowman and Littlefield.
Kearney, Richard. 2021. *Touch: Recovering Our Most Vital Sense*. New York: Columbia University Press.
Kearney, Richard and Matthew Clemente. 2017. *The Art of Anatheism*. New York: Rowman and Littlefield.
Kearney, Richard and Melissa Fitzpatrick. 2021. *Radical Hospitality: From Thought to Action*. New York: Fordham University Press.
Kearney, Richard and James Taylor. 2011. *Hosting the Stranger: Between Religions*. New York: Continuum.
Kearney, Richard and Brian Treanor. 2015. *Carnal Hermeneutics*. New York: Fordham University Press.
Littlejohn, M.E. 2020. *Imagination Now: A Richard Kearney Reader*. Lanham: Rowman & Littlefield.
Manoussakis, John. 2006. *After God: Encountering Richard Kearney*. New York: Fordham University Press.
van Hoogstraten, Marius. 2020. *Theopoetics and Religious Difference - The Unruliness of the Interreligious: A Dialogue with Richard Kearney, John D. Caputo, and Catherine Keller*. Tübingen: Mohr Siebeck.
Veldsman, Daniël and Yolande Steenkamp. 2018. *Debating Otherness with Richard Kearney: Perspectives from South Africa*. Durbanville: AOSIS Publishing.
Zimmerman, Jens and Richard, Kearney. 2015. *Re-Imagining the Sacred: Debating God with Richard Kearney*. New York: Columbia University Press.

Part I

Touching Nature

Chapter 1

Thinking Like a Jaguar: Carnal Hermeneutics, Touch, and the Limits of Language

Brian Treanor

Thinking Like a Jaguar

In *On Stories* (2002), Richard Kearney writes that

> the narrated action of a drama ... solicits a mode of sympathy more extensive and resonant than that experienced in ordinary life. And it does so not simply because it enjoys the poetic license to suspend our normal protective reflexes ... but also because it amplifies the range of those we might empathize with—reaching beyond family, friends and familiars to all kinds of foreigners. (138)

He goes on to offer specific examples from fiction including Oedipus, Anna Karenina, and Julien Sorel; but then, in a remarkable leap, citing J.M. Coetzee, he extends the claim to include the eponymous jaguar of Ted Hughes's poem: "His stride is wildernesses of freedom: / The world rolls under the long thrust of his heel. / Over the cage floor the horizons come" (Hughes 1968, 4).[1] Building on a claim made by Coetzee's Elizabeth Costello—"there is no limit to the extent to which we can think ourselves into the being of another. There are no bounds to the sympathetic imagination" (Coetzee 1999, 35)[2]—Kearney goes so far as to venture that "we can even transport ourselves into the skin of a 'non-rational' animal. What is impossible in reality is made possible in fiction" (Kearney 2002, 139).[3]

Kearney is in good company when suggesting narrative and metaphor can span the gap between species and connect us with our non-human kin. In addition to Hughes and Coetzee, we might look to figures like Jack Turner, Annie Dillard, Doug Peacock, or Robin Wall Kimmerer.[4] Others extend our imaginative sympathy further still, suggesting that we can transport ourselves into the "experience" or being of abiotic entities, or that we can hear the "speech" of the more-than-human world. For example, Thomas Merton writes of rain as "a whole world of meaning, of secrecy, of silence, of rumor. Think of it: all that speech pouring down, selling nothing,

DOI: 10.4324/9781003285649-3

judging nobody ... " (Merton 2003, 139–140). And Aldo Leopold's call to "think like a mountain" is one of the more famous aspirations in anglophone environmental literature (Leopold 1949, 129–133).

Nevertheless, claims like these—let's keep Coetzee's admiration for Hughes's "The Jaguar" as our guiding example—seem questionable given the profound difficulties we have in sympathizing and empathizing with even human others.[5] Seen in this light, the aspiration to imaginative or narrative empathy with the more-than-human world seems incredibly ambitious, and the claim that there are "no bounds" to the sympathetic imagination warrants further reflection. In what follows, I aim to show that traditional forms of hermeneutics are limited by their commitment to "the metaphor of the text"—rooted in narrative, metaphor, language, and the like—and that lived and embodied forms of hermeneutics offer an alternative, supplementary route to understanding.

Thinking Like a Human Thinking Like a Jaguar

Those of us with highly-developed powers of imagination are likely to find the claim that there is no limit to narrative rapport both attractive and plausible. But while there may well be no bounds to imagination, I suspect that there are indeed bounds to imaginative understanding, as well as to sympathy and empathy. This is especially true with regard to empathy for the more-than-human world when that empathy is rooted in an all-too-human faculty like reason, language, or imagination. This, however, is a distinction that Coetzee's Elizabeth Costello seems to ignore:

> Despite Thomas Nagel, who is probably a good man, despite Thomas Aquinas and René Descartes, with whom I have more difficulty in sympathizing, there is no limit to the extent to which we can think ourselves into the being of another. There are no bounds to the sympathetic imagination. If you want proof, consider the following. Some years ago I wrote a book called *The House on Eccles Street*. To write that book I had to think my way into the existence of Marion Bloom. Either I succeeded or I did not. If I did not, I cannot imagine why you invited me here today. In any event, the point is, *Marion Bloom never existed*. Marion Bloom was a figment of James Joyce's imagination. If I can think my way into the existence of a being who has never existed, then I can think my way into the existence of a bat or a chimpanzee or an oyster, any being with whom I share the substrate of life. (Coetzee 1999, 35)

The problems with this 'proof' are readily apparent. First, given that Molly Bloom is indeed a fiction, there is no sense to an assertion that one has, or has not, "thought oneself into her mind" accurately. I can say anything I want to about the mind of Molly Bloom, but what would it mean to be "right" or "wrong" about what was going on there? Second—bracketing the fictionality of the characters—the ability of Elizabeth Costello to think herself into the existence of another white, Western, English-speaking, heterosexual woman is hardly a strong reason to suppose that she can think herself into the being of bivalve mollusk, a being with which she shares membership in the taxonomic kingdom *animalia*, but with which she does not share a phylum, class, order, family, genus, or species—much less a history, culture, or language.

Given how difficult it is for humans to empathize with each other, we might well be skeptical as to whether the horizons of Hughes's caged jaguar may ever be ours. Can we actually empathize with (feel *as if*), not just sympathize with (feel *with* or *alongside*), the jaguar? What about the curlew? The salmon? The redwood tree? And, when we empathize, how accurate or appropriate is the "as if" of our *pathos*? The power and scope of imagination virtually guarantee that the vast majority of our projections will be very far from the mark. After all, one might imagine Hughes's jaguar or Coetzee's oyster engaging in all sorts of behaviors, directed at all sorts of ends, consumed by all kinds of thoughts and emotions; but that does not mean these imaginings are in fact faithful representations of the inner life of either animal or that empathy rooted in those imaginings is well-(in)formed. If the "power of empathy with living things other than ourselves—the stranger the better—is a major test not just of poetic imagination but of ethical sensitivity," it is arguably a test that we fail with alarming regularity, especially in the case of "stranger" beings (Kearney 2002, 139).[6]

Hughes is, after all, projecting when he imagines that the jaguar, unlike the other animals in the zoo, looks beyond the bars of his prison to imagine wider and wilder horizons; and his projections are full of cultural anthropocentrism of the most obvious sort. What makes the jaguar distinctively wild or mysterious in that English menagerie? Are the apes—who Hughes says, "yawn and adore their fleas in the sun"—any less out of place in the London Zoo simply because their behavior does not appear restless to Hughes's gaze? What about the parrots he compares to "cheap tarts"? Or the tiger and lion he finds "indolent"? Speaking more broadly of our tendency to project, what makes the spotted hyena craven and vicious?[7] The doe peaceful and innocent? The snake sinister? It should come as no surprise that characterizations like these are almost entirely the result of biased cultural narratives (Eaton 1998, 152). Especially in the modern idiom—increasingly detached and alienated from nature—our casual application of human characteristics to the non-human world often has little to do with reality and everything to do with cultural judgments. People speak casually about sharks as "man-eaters" or "killing machines" and dogs as "man's best friend," but dogs injure and kill many more people each year in the United States.[8]

***

These issues present real problems for hermeneutics as traditionally conceived. While it has been some time since hermeneutics has been restricted to literal texts, the vast majority of hermeneutic accounts remain captivated by the metaphor of the text, the idea that 'reading a text' is somehow *the* fundamental model for interpretation (Treanor 2019a, 2019b). But if hermeneutics has taught us anything it is that every "seeing" is always already a "seeing as," an engagement with the world from a particular perspective that reveals some things and conceals others. If so, we must acknowledge that the view that hermeneutics is somehow essentially reading—even when the "reading" and the "text" are metaphorical—will reveal and highlight certain truths while missing or occluding others. This, I think, is particularly evident when we think about more-than-human nature, the otherness of which is significantly more profound than that of human-to-human encounters.

Language is a curious thing. In the hands of skilled wordsmiths, it *can* get us closer to, deeper into, the natural world. Rich poetic description opens up reality, as does rich scientific description. But at some point, the proximity brought about by imagination doubles back on itself, crosses an event horizon in which the near suddenly becomes the far, and we find that poetic fancy has actually placed authentic animal experience even further out of reach. The strangeness of the non-human world eludes us in part *precisely because of its non-linguistic otherness.*

Carnal Hermeneutics and the Limits of Language

While I've framed these concerns in the context of Kearney's work on narrative, they are broadly applicable to all human engagement with the non-human world. As "speaking apes," all of us are caught up in anthropomorphic and anthropocentric engagement with nature to one degree or another. Indeed, one might argue that language itself is structured by anthropocentric bias; and to use it, even skillfully, to describe the inner lives of animals is to engage in anthropomorphism. Of course, in one sense, human language exists on a continuum with other forms of animal—and, indeed, plant—communication (Wohlleben 2016; Simard 2021).[9] We all evolved on the same planet, from the same common ancestral pool; and human languages are as natural as whale songs or plant mycorrhizal networks. However, sometimes a difference in degree is so extreme as to constitute a difference in kind; and this seems to be the case with human language (Chomsky 1975). Language, in the hermeneutically relevant sense, is not mere communication; it is *poiesis*—that is, *creation,* the making of something. Animals clearly communicate; they do not, so far as we can tell, poeticize, fantasize, fictionalize, or dramatize.[10] And these latter metaphorical uses are, arguably, the heart of human language. Certainly, they are at the heart of the hermeneutic "seeing as."

The difference between human language and animal experience should make us question the degree to which the linguistic paradigm can help us actually empathize with a jaguar or 'think' like a mountain.[11] Fortunately, over the last decade, environmental hermeneutics has begun to reassess how philosophy might engage the more-than-human world (Clingerman et al. 2013). Carnal hermeneutics (Kearney and Treanor 2015), including Kearney's work on touch (Kearney 2021), can make contributions to this important work.

Kearney's Hermeneutic Arc

Kearney is a prolific writer, and his work touches on a great many topics. However, he has not, as yet, taken up the environment or non-human nature in a sustained way.[12] There are many ways in which one might summarize his philosophical itinerary; but we would not be far off if we located the pole star of his thinking in something like *hospitality*, which plays a major role in his thinking from his earliest work on imagination to his recent treatment of touch (Kearney 1998a, 1998b, 2001, 2011a, 2021).[13] Nevertheless, in his latest work, there are intriguing gestures toward thinking about the non-human world, and important resources for those who want to push his hermeneutic thinking even further. To see how, we should begin with Kearney's primary focus: the account of hospitality.

Kearney argues that there are (at least) two modes of hospitality: linguistic and carnal; and he claims both are necessary for genuine hospitality (Kearney 2019, 71). I want push that observation a bit further and suggest that what he says explicitly of hospitality we can infer regarding hermeneutics itself. In the linguistic mode, translation is the paradigm because it serves a mediating function between two dialects while attempting to remain faithful to both. This comes, of course, with the risk of a double betrayal in which the "guest" language is forced to conform to words, grammar, and syntax of the "host" language, and the "host" language receives the original meaning of the "guest" language only imperfectly. It has been observed that all translation is interpretation; but perhaps we should add that every translation is both a murder and a reincarnation. Because of this tension between hospitality and hostility, every guest language calls out both "translate me" (i.e., understand me) and, at the same time, "don't translate me" (i.e., don't change what I am, which would be to misunderstand me). As Kearney says, "take me, incorporate me, but leave something of me to myself" (Kearney 2019, 73). But, because language is distinctive to humans, when we apply the linguistic paradigm to 'capture' and 'translate' the meaning of the more-than-human world, the danger of distortion is particularly acute. Here we must remain especially respectful of otherness, keenly aware of the gap between what we encounter and how we speak of it. "Communicate with me! Commune with me! But do not domesticate me; do not reduce my wild essence to your human language." In the case of nature, we must remain attentive to both our kinship with it and its profound otherness and wildness, its irreducible mystery.[14]

Carnal hermeneutics, however, makes a useful foil for the more popular linguistic mode. If the linguistic mode asserts that "to be human is to interpret and to interpret is to translate" (Kearney 2019, 73), the development of carnal hermeneutics calls this identification into question. While translation remains *a* paradigmatic example of hermeneutics, hermeneutics is about more than translation and transcription; it includes transactions, transpositions, translocations, and transformations worked out in perception, orientation, directionality, and similar non-linguistic modes. "Before words, we are flesh, flesh becoming words for the rest of our lives" (Kearney 2015, 99). Kearney observes that Merleau-Ponty argues that meaning is given as a "mobile interaction of signs involving intervals, absences, folds and gaps (*écarts*)," and, further, that "this is not just a function of language ... but the very structure of perception itself" (Kearney 2011b, 6). This indicates that hermeneutics is not, in the broadest sense, reducible to metaphor, narrative, language, or even interpretation. There are multifarious ways to "[sense] another sense beyond or beneath apparent sense," which means hermeneutics is concerned with the "polysemy of language and life" (Kearney 2011b, 1). The *savoir* of hermeneutics is linked to and expressive of all three connotations of the French *sens*: "sensation, direction, meaning," which is why Kearney speaks not only of interpretation or translation but also of "body mapping, orientation and negotiation" (Kearney 2011b, 4). How might this help us to empathize with the jaguar or think like the mountain?

Touch

Kearney's own work in carnal hermeneutics is closely tied to his interest in touch, which he develops in two senses: the narrow and more literal sense of tactile contact with things, and the broader and more metaphorical sense of tactful relationships. Indeed, in *Touch*, he demonstrates persuasively that touch is, in one way or another, operative in all our engagement with the world. Here and elsewhere, he explores the ways in which touch and animal savvy might help to bridge the gaps between humans and our fellow creatures.

First, he argues that *tact*—"the ability to detect subtle differences" in things and in others—is, in the broadest sense, an essential element of all our senses (Kearney 2021, 10, 17–31). Tact is found in the "savviness" of good taste, the carnal know-how that allows us to understand what is required, and what is appropriate, in a given situation. The "flair" of "good nose" helps us to distinguish between the helpful and the harmful, the ripe or comestible and the spoiled; it is tied to arousal, and to memory. Here Kearney draws our attention to the dog Argos, who is one of only two compatriots to recognize Odysseus on his return to Ithaca after his 20-year absence (Kearney 2021, 23, 62). Insight, foresight, and hindsight are manifestations of tact that contribute to having good "vision," the ability to see what others cannot, including that which is invisible to the physical eye. And tact allows those with a "good ear" to perceive the resonance and rhythmic musicality at the heart of things (including, I would argue, nature).

Tact's skill in discrimination is also at play in ethics, helping us to discern differences and to understand which ones are relevant and which are not. In this sense it is not unlike a kind of carnal *phronesis*, the wisdom that helps us to understand what matters in a given situation. It is therefore involved in how we choose to expose ourselves to others, helping us to differentiate between danger and sanctuary, friend and foe. More importantly, however, it is crucial in helping to inform our treatment of others. Tact is what helps us to understand when to touch, and how, as well as when not to touch.

Moving beyond this broader account of tactfulness, Kearney is interested in touch itself, that is, our tactile engagement with others and with the world. Historically, at least in the West, touch has often been framed as one of the "lower" or more "animal" senses, concerned with the material world and, therefore, subject to its pressures and distortions. In contrast, sight, removed from its objects, became the model for the disinterested intellection that would help us to grasp truth. However, following Aristotle in the *De Anima*, Kearney maintains that touch is mediated by the membrane of flesh (*sarx*). Therefore, to touch is not to have direct, unmediated experience of things; rather, touch is a mediated engagement with the world that is always-already a "seeing [or in this case feeling] as" (Kearney 2021, 42). Moreover,

> precisely because it mediates between a self carnally located "here" and an other located "there," touch is what enables empathy. *Empathein*—feeling oneself as one with the other. Which is why touching finds its social beginnings in the handshake: open hand to open hand—the origin of community. War and peace are skin deep in this sense.[15]

Here Kearney makes a claim that will have direct bearing on the question of empathy with the more-than-human world, suggesting that in liminal experiences of otherness—experiences where language, stretched beyond even the expansive range and powers of *poiesis*, begins to fail us—there is the possibility of turning to an alternative hermeneutic mode, and this mode might have some particular role to play in empathy. More on this in a moment.

Note, however, that moving from the book to the body does not, on its own, get us beyond anthropocentrism. "Civilization," Kearney observes, "begins with the handshake" (Kearney 2019, 78). It's only once we shake hands, rather than draw swords, that we stop to ask how someone else understands the world: "it is in touch [not translation] that the most basic act of exposure to others occurs" (Kearney 2019, 78). All well and good; and illustrative of the significance of carnality. But note how talk of handshakes risks giving carnal hermeneutics a subtle anthropocentric spin. Kearney's account of Pumla Gobodo-Madikizela and Eugene de Kock is one of his more powerful examples of carnal connection; however, it is described in terms of their "common *humanity*" and the things that are "common among us fellow *human* beings" (Kearney 2019, 83). If we are to avoid transcending the anthropocentrism of language for the anthropocentrism of the distinctively human body, we must supplement examples centered on handshakes and the breaking of bread with something more.[16]

Kearney does take up animals or animal bodies in various places—drawing on authors including Louv, De Wall, Van der Kolk, and others—and, given his interests in hospitality and healing, he is particularly interested in the topic of human-animal somatic therapy (Kearney 2021, 109–111).[17] In such therapeutic relationships, dogs, horses, or other animals work with humans experiencing the effects of PTSD, autism, and other conditions. Critically, Kearney notes, research also shows that in many of these relationships, the benefit is *reciprocal*; that is, the non-human animal also experiences observable benefits from the embodied interaction. In other words, the tactile contact between human and non-human establishes a relationship that allows each being to feel, and help ameliorate, the woundedness of the other. A kind of embodied empathy made possible by tactful contact; not one that allows us to "say" or "name" what the other feels, but one that goes some way toward meaningful experiencing-with the other.

Not Speaking, Like a Jaguar

Can hermeneutics get beyond human biases? In what sense it is possible, or even desirable, to do so? Returning to our guiding example, the questions are whether we can feel "like" a jaguar, how close that "like" or "as if" can get, and what criteria we might use to know whether our "as if" feelings and experiences are closer to or farther from the truth. How can hermeneutics get us to identify more readily and more accurately with non-human animals? Or with the being of the more-than-human world more broadly? My suggestion is that if we hope to get closer to empathy with our non-human kin, we must bracket or suspend, as much as possible, our all-too-human linguistic engagement with the world. More-than-human nature does not experience the world through the filter of language. Whatever it means to "empathize with a jaguar" or "think like a mountain," it is going to require that we deemphasize the role of language. For it is language (in the sense of *poiesis*) that distinguishes us and separates us from the non-human world.

Silence

Any effective listening to the earth is going to have to begin with silence. This should come as no surprise. Kearney observes that, "learning to be silent in order to listen more keenly to the call of others—human, animal or divine—is a first principle of almost every wisdom tradition" (Kearney 2021, 28). This will require a literal silence, of course, a willingness to stop talking and stop making noise, a willingness to be in the world in a quieter way. But the silence I have in mind is more profound than simply the absence of human vocalization and human noise; we need to efface or disrupt the very tendency to engage the world linguistically, to impose our categories upon it.

Narrative imagination, at least commonly, is so busy describing things that it often fails to adequately listen to them. When it comes to the natural world, we must strive, as Thoreau says, to hear "the language in which all things and events speak without metaphor"—that is, directly, in their own ways and on their own terms, not "as" or according to some human measure (Thoreau 1971, 111). Or, as Michel Serres puts it, "to listen to the things freed of [words], the way they presented themselves before finding themselves named" (Serres 2012a, 38). We must give up our natural—and in other circumstances salutary and even blessed—tendency to narrate and poeticize. The Genesis story of creation, in which God gave Adam the opportunity to name the animals (Genesis 2:19–20) testifies to our obsession with describing the world in human terms, which too often has been closely associated with dominion over it (Genesis 1:28). What were the Leviathan and the Behemoth before Adam named them? What was the jaguar before it became an image for Hughes's own feelings of confinement, or a metaphor for the limited scope of modern, urban life, in which we are separated from the earth, the sky, and our wild origins?

How much of the world do we misunderstand, or miss entirely, because "nature loves to hide" (Heraclitus), and how much do we miss simply because we are just too loud, too presumptuous, too self-absorbed? When ordinary language fails us, we rightly fall back on poetry; but, eventually, we reach the limits of language itself, a point at which words are not just inadequate, they are misleading.[18] Hermeneutics, writes Kearney, "invigilates the limits of the sayable and the tangible" (Kearney 2019, 86). Hear! Hear! But if this applies, as it does, to hospitality and matters of interpersonal boundaries (e.g., social relations, sexual relations) and faith (e.g., Christ's *noli me tangere*), I want to insist that it applies with equal or greater force to our encounters with the more than human world.[19] Don't speak; don't grasp. Be quiet. Be still. Observe rather than classifying or judging or ordering. Watch, listen, smell, feel. *Be.*

Of course, silencing language does not mean silencing the world, which is full of its own particular forms of expression. To hear these voices, it is not enough to stop our chatter, silence our machines, and stop cataloging. Listening to what the world has to say, on its terms, requires that we become receptive to meaning that is expressed in ways other than the natural languages. Poet Denise Levertov reminds us that the world is awash with meaning, but that we are too self-involved and self-absorbed to recognize it: "how naïve, / to keep wanting words we could speak ourselves, / English, Urdu, Tagalog, the French of Tours ... " (Levertov 1999, 53).[20] Rather than listening to (and *feeling*) what the more-than-human world has to say for itself and to us—which it does constantly in its own *inhuman* ways—we anthropomorphize, trying to teach chimpanzees sign language and dolphins Morse code.[21]

Indeed, becoming receptive to what nature is expressing—a necessary first step in trying to understand or empathize with it—requires more than just attending to its sounds. Here is where carnal hermeneutics, including Kearney's rich account of *touch*, offers another option. The more-than-human world first expresses itself to us not through words, sentences, metaphors, or stories, but through sights, sounds, smells, tastes, and textures.

Bodying Forth

To empathize well with the jaguar—indeed, even to sympathize with it—we are going to need more than the standard tropes of narrative imagination. First, we'll need to supplement narrative with other modes of knowing: experiential, empirical, ecological, biological, and so on. However, even these supplements leave us narrowly confined to distinctively human categories and ways of understanding. Thus, second, we are going to need to supplement narrative and other linguistic modes with alternative hermeneutic schemes that reveal some of what is concealed by the metaphor of the text. These alternative approaches should try to get us beyond, behind, or under language—which is the human trait *par excellence*—to explore other forms of expression that are shared more widely with more-than-human nature. We need tools that are more *zoon* and less *logon*, experiences that reconnect us with bodies and with the earth.

In the course of evolution, our bipedalism was a decisive development; our hands became free for tool-making, which in turn may have influenced the development of language (Wilson 1999). And, influencing language, it fundamentally shaped the way we inhabit the world. In standing upright, we also distanced our nose and mouth and hands from the earth—where they remain for our quadruped kin—leading us to disparage the 'animal senses' of taste and touch.

> The word *anthropos* implies that man not only sees but looks up at that which he sees [and, I'd add, 'looks down' on the rest of nature], and hence he alone of all animals is rightly called *anthropos* because he looks up at (*anthropei*) what he has seen. (Plato 1989, 229c)

As Kearney notes, Western philosophy instituted a dichotomy between the "intellectual," which since Plato has operated on a visual metaphor, and the "animal," which remains rooted in touch, taste, and smell.

Perhaps, then, it is time to un-yoke the body, our beast of burden, to give it a sabbath from toiling in the fields (or, more accurately, at the scribe's desk or viewer's screen), and let it run wild. We will, of course, remain human, marked by both the *logos* and the *polis* that characterize our species; but we will cease to insist that being fully human means rejecting our animality. Cease to think that the only way of understanding something requires that we name it, classify it, domesticate it, and control it. Cease to think of the body or the earth as a prison, remembering it as our natal home.

Returning to the example with which we began, Hughes's jaguar, we might observe that Coetzee's Elizabeth Costello contends that humans can "think" their way into animal experience through narrative and poetic imagination. She points to Hughes, Rilke, and others who, in their poetry, provide sufficiently rich accounts to induce something like sympathy, perhaps even empathy. But the language Costello employs is revealing. She speaks of *"bodying* forth the jaguar" and observes that Hughes shows us that we can *"embody* animals" by a process of poetic imagination that "mingles *breath* and *sense* in a way that no one has explained and no one ever will" (Coetzee 1999, 23).[22] Here, I think, we have an implicit recognition that the way to get closer to the jaguar is not quite the same as the imaginative leap that helps us identify with Molly Bloom.

Kearney writes that "carnal hermeneutics may be said to have two patron saints—the god Hermes and the dog Argos. For if Hermes discloses hermetic cyphers from above, Argos brings animal savvy from below" (Kearney 2020, 101).[23] Of course, these two modes—imaginative and embodied—can work in parallel. Indeed, for us they always will. We have a share of both *zoe* and *logos*, and are immersed in both nature and culture.[24] The point is not to become a non-human animal, but to better understand and empathize with them. However, taking a cue from Argos, we might recognize that empathy with a jaguar or dog is better served by emphasizing the carnal frame we share rather than the linguistic frame we do not.

One might well object that many animal senses are either so different (e.g., the echolocation of dolphins, octopuses 'smelling' via their tactile tentacles) or so much more powerful (e.g., the canine sense of smell) as to constitute a difference in kind. I have suggested that human language exists on a continuum with animal forms of communication, but that the difference in degree is so large as to constitute a difference in kind; and perhaps the same should be said of certain animal senses. Fair enough. However, while many animal species have some particular trait that is so alien to human experience as to present an insurmountable barrier to imaginative empathy, they often have other attributes that are less foreign. I might have difficulty imagining accurately what it is like to experience the environment like a dolphin, in part because I lack a sophisticated sense of echolocation; however, I share many other characteristics with the dolphin: being air-breathing, and warm-blooded; being part of a social species; and being disposed to play. So, rather than imposing human *logos* or *poiesis* on the dolphin, and rather than assuming I can accurately imagine the dolphin's experience of perception-via-echolocation, perhaps the thing to do is to start with what we share more broadly. If I want to understand something of what it is to be like a dolphin, perhaps I will do better to reflect less on our divergent vocalizations and more on our common experience of non-purposive play in the surf.[25]

Will there be errors in such an approach? Absolutely. Just as there are errors and misjudgments and infelicities when I try to empathize with another human. But the carnal route to empathy with the more-than-human world is more promising than the linguistic route. As Kearney observes, there are myriad examples of mutual human-animal healing via carnal being-with. And he offers a personal anecdote about his own experience of depression and the role of the landscape and non-human animals in recovery:

> I ultimately discovered modes of 'embodied' healing to be more effective, profound and long-lasting. In my case, these included Iyengar Yoga practice, Shiatsu massage therapy, pranayama deep breathing and regular physical exercises like swimming and fishing in the Irish sea, planting trees and shrubs in the garden and spending as much time as possible with animals (especially horses and dogs). The more I walked the Wicklow hills with my retriever, Bella, the more the Black dog slipped away. In all this I followed the advice of a wise friend: "Enough talk, back to the body." (Kearney 2021, 106)[26]

This is a moving personal account. Could we expand these reflections on human-animal interactions (and those of Haraway, Oliver, and others), which are largely focused on companionship or therapy with domesticated animals, to consider the wider, and wilder, more-than-human world? I think so, although at this point such an account must be deferred.

"Back to the body" is, perhaps, one alternative way to pursue the phenomenological commitment "to the things themselves."[27] And, again, Kearney is in excellent company here. Thoreau writes of seeking "thoughts which the body thought" and of "returning" to his senses "like a bird or beast," during his daily treks. Nan Shepherd is even more direct. Of her life among the elemental realities of her beloved Cairngorms, she writes:

> Here then may be lived a life of the senses so pure, so untouched by any mode of apprehension but their own, that the body must be said to think ... Walking thus, hour after hour, the senses keyed, one walks the flesh transparent. But no metaphor, *transparent*, or *light as air*, is adequate. The body is not made negligible, but paramount. Flesh is not annihilated but fulfilled. One is not bodiless, but essential body. It is therefore when the body is keyed to its highest potential and controlled to a profound harmony deepening into something that resembles trance, that I discover most nearly what it is *to be*. I have walked out of the body and into the mountain. (Shepherd 2011, 105–106)[28]

I am unsure if Shepherd was aware of Leopold; but I know of no better account of how to "think like a mountain." If the inhuman world speaks to us, its language is material, and we hear it bodily: touching, tasting, walking, swimming, climbing, being.

Conclusion

Almost all of Kearney's work has been devoted to bridging gaps between the self and the other in service of healing or hospitality. Much of that work has tended to focus on themes that lend themselves to the metaphor of the text (e.g., inter-religious hospitality, narrative identity), and which highlight encounters with human otherness (e.g., examples of handshakes, the breaking of bread, and other distinctively human acts). There is nothing wrong with that. God knows and history shows those gaps are in dire need of traversing; thus, sharing narratives, swapping stories, proffering open hands, and breaking bread remain essential, and urgent, human tasks. But these are not the only human tasks, as the current environmental crisis—and the profound alienation from the more-than-human world that underlies it—makes abundantly clear. Carnal hermeneutics, including Kearney's recent work on touch, holds significant promise in terms of developing non-textual and non-linguistic modes of understanding otherness. Thus supplemented, the scope of hermeneutics can do justice to both our humanity and our animality, to that which distinguishes us from the rest of reality and that which entangles us in it.[29]

Notes

1 Of course, Hughes was aware of, and perhaps responding to, Rilke's "The Panther" (Rilke 2014). J.M. Coetzee has his character Elizabeth Costello reference this poem favorably in *The Lives of Animals* (Coetzee 1999, 50 ff.).

2 *The Lives of Animals* and *Elizabeth Costello* are commonly thought of as metafictional works that use the eponymous character as a kind of stand-in for Coetzee himself, through which he can make various philosophical and ethical arguments. As I cannot consider the complexities of metafiction or pseudonymous authorship here, in what follows I will not make a strong distinction between the opinions of J.M. Coetzee and those of the fictional Elizabeth Costello.

3 Erazim Kohák makes a similarly bold claim, and in a book committed to a careful phenomenological account of the human relation to the natural world: "The miracle of verbal communication virtually abolishes all limits on the range of empathy" (Kohák 1984, 100).

4 Kimmerer has a fine account of struggling with the complexities of metaphorical empathy and anthropocentrism in a chapter on "the grammar of animacy" (Kimmerer 2013). Turner writes, "I don't think we can say why [certain animals do what they do] without using analogies and metaphors from human emotional life" (Turner 1996, 78). Doug Peacock makes a similar observation: "Humans are so strongly discouraged from comparing their lives with those of other animals. Yet everything I had experienced taught me that metaphor is the fundamental path of imagining, a first line of inquiry into the lives of other creatures that sheds light on our own" (Peacock 1996, 143). This is no doubt true in some sense. Nevertheless, hermeneutic encounters with the more-than-human world must be *especially* aware of the "double betrayal" that Ricoeur sees at the heart of all translation (Ricoeur 2006).

5 The attentive reader will note the slippage between "empathy" and "sympathy" in the matter under consideration. Kearney says "it amplifies the range of those we might *empathize* with" (Kearney 2002, 138), but Costello claims "there are no bounds to the *sympathetic* imagination" (Coetzee 1999, 35). This slippage is the result of the fact that empathy and sympathy are used in a variety of overlapping ways in the English language. I will use sympathy to indicate "shared" or "parallel" feelings with another. Thus, we may sympathize with another who experiences a loss, and can do so even if we have not experienced a similar loss ourselves, even if we cannot imagine experiencing such a loss very well. Empathy, however, implies a more powerful identification with the other; and it is more philosophically and hermeneutically significant because it suggests the power to feel "as if" another, which is at the very heart of what Kearney and others have in mind when thinking of narrative imagination.

6 On our inability to "know what it is to be like" non-human animals, consider Thomas Nagel's famous essay "What Is It Like to Be a Bat?" (Nagel 1974). On "thinking like a mountain," see Leopold's *Sand County Almanac* (Leopold 1949). *What's It Like to Be a Bird?* (Sibley 2020), *The Hidden Life of Trees* (Wohlleben 2016) and *The Inner Life of Animals* (Wohlleben 2017) are recent, more popular engagements with similar themes.

7 Along with sharks and snakes, the spotted hyena is one of the animals most consistently misrepresented by cultural prejudices—both in the West and in their native Africa (Glickman 1995). Or, consider the corvids, the subject of another famous collection of poems by Hughes: *Crow* (Hughes 2001). The crow symbolizes everything from death, discord, and strife (many European

stories) to creation (the Tlingit), from vanity and credulousness (La Fontaine's *Le corbeau et le renard*) to wisdom (the ravens Huginn and Muninn in Norse mythology).

8 Obviously, there are many more dogs in the United States than sharks. Nevertheless, for one comparison of data, complied by the Florida Museum of Natural History, see https://www.floridamuseum.ufl.edu/shark-attacks/odds/compare-risk/dog-attack/. Accessed June 19, 2020.

9 Kearney briefly mentions the kingdom *plantae* in his account of haptic virtual reality mimicking the experience of being a tree.

10 I recognize the hermeneutic biases influencing this claim, and the possibility that I could be in error about the *poietic* possibilities of non-human animals. However, while animals have many of their own excellences, while some of our powers are shared more broadly with others in our animal family (e.g., emotions, problem solving, communication), and while I myself am quite willing to ascribe personhood to non-human beings (cf. Kohák 1984), suggesting that non-human animals *poeticize* seems too anthropomorphic. Animals are not humans "in furry costumes" (Kimmerer 2013, 57); and we should not relate to them in that way. They have their own being and their own dignity. In this essay, I will often use "language" to mean "human language," that is, "language as *poiesis* ." I cannot emphasize strongly enough that this is not meant to imply that non-human entities—animals and plants—do not communicate. They obviously do. They obviously have a "language" of sorts, and we can obviously decode or translate aspects of it. Nevertheless, non-human communication does not, as far as we can see, poeticize or fictionalize; and this difference is significant.

11 Kearney writes that "perception operates like language in that it does not confront an object head on, but senses things which speak to it laterally, on the side, provoking one's 'complicity'" (Kearney 2011). However, he clarifies: "to compare carnal perception to linguistic structure is not to reduce the latter to the former (naturalism), nor to reduce the former to the latter (structuralism)" (ibid.). Perception discovers, receives, and co-constitutes meaning not because it is somehow "mimicking language," which is the error of a narrow fidelity to language and the text. Rather, the similarity is the consequence of the fact that both language and perception—as well as other forms of carnal engagement with the natural world—create and discover meaning in the way they leap across gaps between the world and our understanding.

12 In this volume, Dan Bradley notes that Kearney has not yet really addressed wilderness in his work. Cristina M. Gschwandtner makes a similar observation regarding non-human animals. The present essay, as well as the chapters by Melissa Fitzpatrick and Cristina M. Gschwandtner, seek to turn Kearney's work more explicitly toward the more-than-human, building on his engagement with human-animal therapeutic relationships. And, notably, Kearney has begun to explore these themes, both in the present volume—consider his evocative reflection on human/dolphin anacarnation—as well as in a forthcoming volume entitled *Gods and Dogs* and a 2022 Guestbook conference on "Hosting Earth."

13 In addition to these publications, see Kearney's development of the Guestbook Project, which is aimed a peacemaking and reconciliation through narrative exchange (http://guestbookproject.org/). In this volume, Neal DeRoo also observes that "healing" is the guiding concern and interest in Kearney's work.

14 Kearney notes that there is an ethical element to translation and to narrative hospitality: "one nation's narrative of glory is often another's narrative of

suffering and defeat" (Kearney 2019, 77). That is no doubt true in innumerable cases of historical memory; but if this narrative mismatch is a problem in the history of Ireland, the United States, or the Balkans, how much more would it be the case in the history of human interaction with the non-human world? How does the Enlightenment narrative of progress and the "advancement of humankind"—or, even more anthropocentrically, "the world"—square with the Anthropocene and the advent of the 6th Mass Extinction?

15 It is the reversibility of touching/being-touched that makes it so relevant for empathy, and so useful for providing a non-linguistic grounding for empathy. Chris Yates and James Taylor, in their chapters for this volume, also emphasize the reversible connection of touch, as contrasted with the more unidirectional engagement of vision.

16 Christina M. Gschwandtner also points out the importance of considering "beings without hands" in her essay for this volume.

17 Kearney cites Richard Louv (2019), Franz de Waal (2016, 2019), and Bessel Van der Kolk (2015).

18 Just when and why language fails us is a complex question. I suspect that the supposed ineffability of experience is often not the result of the gap between language and life, but rather a stunted vocabulary (Serres 1997, 72). In other cases, the issue is not lack of facility with language, but rather that language itself is becoming more homogenized, less attentive to particularity (Macfarlane 2016; Lopez and Gwartney 2013). Both these trends can be resisted; and it might be that we can still recover a language that does justice to hard, inhuman reality. However, even if skilled poets and wordsmiths extend the reach of language, there will be limits. I don't mean to suggest we should abandon or disparage language, or minimize the enormous good it does. I merely want to mind the gap between words and things.

19 Tact helps us to both close gaps and respect them, and to understand which is appropriate in a given situation. Thus, tact includes knowing when not to speak or touch. For example, the present defense of carnal hermeneutics is not to suggest that literal touch would be appropriate with the jaguar. The tragic case of Timothy Treadwell—eaten alive by a grizzly bear after what many people believe to be a history of inappropriate behavior anthropomorphizing the bears in Katmai—is an illustrative cautionary tale.

20 As Thoreau says of meaning in the natural world, "much is published, but little printed" (Thoreau 1971, 111). Marjolein Oele and I have used the phrase "expressive content" to encompass both human language and the wide range of expression coming from the more-than-human world (Oele and Treanor 2022).

21 Coetzee's Costello mocks the anthropocentrism and abstraction of many animal experiments: "If I as a human being were told that the standards by which animals are being measured in these experiments are human standards, I would be insulted. It is the experiments themselves that are imbecile. The behaviorists who design them claim that we understand only by a process of creating abstract models and then testing those models against reality. What nonsense. We understand by immersing ourselves and our intelligence in complexity. There is something self-stultified in the way in which scientific behaviorism recoils from the complexity of life" (Coetzee 1999, 62–63).

22 Emphases mine. Costello associated the spirit of Hughes's poem with a kind of "primitivism." Another intriguing perspective here would be the account offered in Eduardo Kohn's *How Forests Think: Toward an Anthropology Beyond the Human* (Kohn 2013). Kohn's work is a sustained engagement with

Peirce's semiotic theory and the worldview of the Runa people of the upper Amazon basin. Coincidentally, the jaguar plays a central role in Runa experience of the world; they speak of shape-shifting "were-jaguars" (Kohn's translation of *runa puma*) that traverse human-jaguar boundaries and can experience something of both perspectives. Kohn's account argues that selfhood, communication, thinking, signifying, and the like are not distinctive to human beings, but are widely distributed among living beings. He argues that life, per se, is "constitutively semiotic" (ibid., 9), though his account focuses a bit more on animals than plants. And he raises the intriguing possibility of "trans-species" pidgin communication. Of course, much hinges on what one means by "thinking," "language," and the like; and Kohn's work deserves its own in-depth study. However, for the present essay, I'll stick with Coetzee, in part because that is the interlocutor Kearney himself has chosen in his earlier work (see above).

23 Argos, of course, was Odysseus's dog. Other than Euryclea—who also recognized Odysseus by a carnal mark—Argos was the only one to recognize Odysseus when he returned to Ithaca 20 years after leaving to wage war on Troy.

24 Different authors attach different meanings to *zoe* and *bios*. For clarity, here, by *zoe*, I mean animal life. By distinguishing between nature and culture, I do not mean to imply a sharp nature/culture dualism.

25 Although peripheral to my point here, it is worth noting that Gadamer suggests that play is hermeneutically significant because, among other things, it reveals the open-ended, incomplete nature of the activity—art being the example that concerns Gadamer, though he also mentions sports, dance, music, and the poetic aspects of language (Gadamer 2003, 101ff.).

26 One early reader of this essay wondered what the fish might have thought of Kearney's therapeutic journey. That's an important question, essential even; however, it is beyond the scope of this chapter.

27 "Go, run, faith will come to you, the body will sort things out" (Serres, 2012b, 78). And, to "back to the body," I would add "back to the earth." We need to reconnect to the elemental materiality of our natal home—humus, soil, is related to *homo*, human.

28 Note that it is walking—not reading or writing—that connects Shepherd to the mountain. The involvement of the body is essential.

29 An earlier version of this essay appeared in the *Journal of the Pacific Association for the Continental Tradition*, vol. 3 (2021).

References

Chomsky, Noam. 1975. *Reflections on Language*. New York: Pantheon.

Clingerman, Forrest, Brian Treanor, Martin Drenthen, and David Utsler, eds. 2013. *Interpreting Nature: The Emerging Field of Environmental Hermeneutics*. New York: Fordham University Press.

Coetzee, J.M. 1999. *The Lives of Animals*. Princeton: Princeton University Press.

de Waal, Frans. 2016. *Are We Smart Enough to Know How Smart Animals Are?* New York: Norton.

de Waal, Frans. 2019. *Mama's Last Hug*. New York: Norton.

Eaton, Marcia Muelder. 1998. "Fact and Fiction in the Aesthetic Appreciation of Nature." *The Journal of Aesthetics and Art Criticism* vol. 56, no. 2 (Spring): 149–156.

Florida Museum of Natural History. "Sharks vs. Dogs." https://www.floridamuseum. ufl.edu/shark-attacks/odds/compare-risk/dog-attack/. Accessed June 19, 2020.

Gadamer, Hans-Georg. 2003. *Truth and Method*. Translated by Joel Weinsheimer and Donald G. Marshall. London: Continuum.

Glickman, Stephen E. 1995. "The Spotted Hyena from Aristotle to the Lion King: Reputation Is Everything." *Social Research* vol. 62, no. 3 (Fall): 501–537.

Hughes, Ted. 1968. *The Hawk in the Rain*. London: Faber and Faber.

Hughes, Ted. 2001. *Crow*. London: Faber and Faber.

Kearney, Richard. 1998a. *The Poetics of Imagining*. New York: Fordham.

Kearney, Richard. 1998b. *The Wake of Imagination*. London: Routledge.

Kearney, Richard. 2001. *Strangers, Gods, and Monsters*. London: Routledge.

Kearney, Richard. 2002. *On Stories*. London: Routledge.

Kearney, Richard. 2011a. *Anatheism: Returning to God after God*. New York: Columbia.

Kearney, Richard. 2011b. "What Is Diacritical Hermeneutics." *Journal of Applied Hermeneutics* (December): 1–14. doi:10.11575/jah.v0i0.53187

Kearney, Richard. 2015. "What is Carnal Hermeneutics?" *New Literary History* vol. 46, no. 1 (Winter): 99–124.

Kearney, Richard. 2019. "Double Hospitality: Between Word and Touch." *The Journal for Continental Philosophy of Religion* vol. 1: 71–89.

Kearney, Richard. 2020. "Carnal Hermeneutics." In *Imagination Now: A Richard Kearney Reader*, edited by Murray E. Littlejohn, 99–120. Lanham: Rowman and Littlefield.

Kearney, Richard. 2021. *Touch: Recovering Our Most Vital Sense*. New York: Columbia University Press.

Kearney, Richard and Melissa Fitzpatrick. 2021. *Radical Hospitality*. New York: Fordham.

Kearney, Richard and Brian Treanor, eds. 2015. *Carnal Hermeneutics*. New York: Fordham University Press.

Kimmerer, Robin Wall. 2013. *Braiding Sweetgrass*. Minneapolis: Milkweed.

Kohák, Erazim. 1984. *The Embers and the Stars*. Chicago: University of Chicago Press.

Kohn, Eduardo. 2013. *How Forests Think: Toward an Anthropology Beyond the Human*. Berkeley: University of California Press.

Leopold, Aldo. 1949. *Sand County Almanac*. Oxford: Oxford University Press.

Levertov, Denise. 1999. "Immersion." In *This Great Unknowing: Last Poems*, vol. 53. New York: New Directions.

Lopez, Barry and Debra Gwartney, eds. 2013. *Home Ground: A Guide to the American Landscape*. San Antonio: Trinity University Press.

Louv, Richard. 2019. *Our Wild Calling*. Chapel Hill: Algonquin.

Macfarlane, Robert. 2016. *Landmarks*. New York: Penguin.

Merton, Thomas. 2003. *When the Trees Say Nothing: Writings on Nature*. Edited by Kathleen Deignan. Notre Dame, IN: Sorin Books.

Nagel, Thomas. 1974. "What Is It Like to Be a Bat?" *The Philosophical Review* vol. 83(4): 435–450.

Oele, Marjolein and Brian Treanor. 2022. "Michel Serres and Ecological Crisis: Listening to the World's Expressions." In *Continental Philosophy and the*

History of Thought, edited by Antonio Calcagno and Christian Lotz. Lanham: Lexington Press.

Peacock, Doug. 1996. *Grizzly Years: In Search of the American Wilderness*. New York: Holt Paperbacks.

Plato. 1989. "Cratylus." In *The Collected Works of Plato*, edited by Edith Hamilton and Huntington Cairns, 421–474. Princeton: Princeton University Press.

Ricoeur, Paul. 2006. *On Translation*. Translated by Eileen Brennan. London: Routledge.

Rilke, Rainer Maria. 2014. *The Poetry of Rilke*. Translated by Edward Snow. New York: Farrar, Straus and Giroux.

Serres, Michel. 1997. *The Troubadour of Knowledge*. Translated by Sheila Faria Glaser with William Paulson. Ann Arbor: University of Michigan Press.

Serres, Michel. 2012a. *Biogea*. Translated by Randolph Burkes. Minneapolis: Univocal.

Serres, Michel. 2012b. *Variations on the Body*. Translated by Randolph Burkes. Minneapolis: Univocal.

Shepherd, Nan. 2011. *The Living Mountain*. Edinburgh: Cannongate.

Sibley, David Allen. 2020. *What's It Like to Be a Bird?* New York: Knopf.

Simard, Suzanne. 2021. *Finding the Mother Tree*. New York: Knopf.

Thoreau, Henry David. 1971. *Walden*. Princeton: Princeton University Press.

Treanor, Brian. 2019a. "Lateralization and Leaning: Somatic Desire as a Model for Supple Wisdom." In *Somatic Desire: Recovering Corporeality in Contemporary Thought*, edited by Sarah Horton, Stephen Mendelsohn, Christine Rojcewicz, and Richard Kearney, 25–40. Lanham: Lexington.

Treanor, Brian. 2019b. "Thinking after Michel Serres." *SubStance* vol. 48, no. 3: 3–44.

Turner, Jack. 1996. *The Abstract Wild*. Tucson: University of Arizona Press.

van der Kolk, Bessel. 2015. *The Body Keeps the Score*. New York: Penguin.

Wilson, Frank R. 1999. *The Hand: How Its Use Shapes the Brain, Language, and Culture*. New York: Vintage.

Wohlleben, Peter. 2016. *The Hidden Life of Trees*. Vancouver: Greystone.

Wohlleben, Peter. 2017. *The Inner Life of Animals*. Vancouver: Greystone.

Chapter 2

Sensing the Call of Other Animals: Carnal Hermeneutics, and the Ethico-Moral Imagination

Melissa Fitzpatrick

This contribution explores Richard Kearney's new frontier: hosting, and being hosted by, the other-than-human world. His work on carnal hermeneutics and carnal hospitality are already pointing in this direction, reminding us (human beings) about the animals that we always and already are—at our core, deeply in touch with and attuned to the world around us, if we pay attention—ultimately calling us back to the body and its most universal sense: *touch*.[1] This is, as Kearney reminds us in his most recent book, *Touch*, the most vital sense that in some sense grounds all of the other senses (2021, 9–10).[2] Touch even grounds sight, which has enjoyed a seat of privilege in a particular strain of Western philosophical discourse. Kearney rightly labels our age the age of excarnation, in which digital clips and sound bites reign supreme, further removing and dissociating us from the flesh of others and ourselves. The question I want to ask is: to what extent has the excarnation affected our relationship to other animals? Though we all too often forget, we are, of course, animals ourselves.

It perhaps goes without saying that the age of excarnation runs parallel to our current ecological crisis, no doubt fueling it as our exploitation of the world (other animals included) has disconnected us from the Earth. The loss of the common world, as Kearney puts it, involves a failure to relate to what is beyond our own psychical and physical boundaries. Untouched by others. Isolated by our private interests (whether we realize it or not). Devoid of values grounded in sensibility—sensibility always being attuned to our shared vulnerability. Kearney writes in *Carnal Hermeneutics*, "flesh … is where the struggle of the heart first takes place—where basic wagers of hostility and hospitality unfold" (2015, 29). Repugnance, leading to hostility, and attraction, leading to hospitality, are not simply subjective affects, varying from person to person, but may in fact have normative force—at least in the case of suffering, whether small scale or large, resulting from the exploitation of animals. The trouble with the digital age, as Kearney puts it in *Touch*, is that empathy has become a "problematic passion" (2021, 120). More connected than

DOI: 10.4324/9781003285649-4

ever, not only are we physically distanced from each other, but we are at the mercy of the images various algorithms produce for us. The optical is no doubt bent in the direction of profit, carefully designed by various mythmakers in society.

Kearney stresses that one of the aims of carnal hermeneutics is to revisit the "deep and inextricable relationship between sensation and interpretation," as there are ethical evaluations at stake (2015, 20–23). I want to build on that dimension of his project in regard to the space other animals occupy in our ethico-moral imagination, i.e., the dimension of the imagination that considers our responsibility to others.[3] My claim is that Kearney's work on carnal hermeneutics provides a much-needed bridge between the realm of aesthetics (involving what is beautiful and repugnant) and ethics-morality (the realm of goodness, justice, right and wrong). In the true spirit of Kearney's work, it should not be either/or, but both/and, further liberating us from problematic dualism. This bridge between aesthetics and ethics opens up a space for a sensitivity to other animals, grounded in our immediate (albeit carnally mediated) compassion toward them when we witness not only their pain but also their joy. This compassion is not exclusively grounded in the "intellectual" or "purely rational" dimensions of ourselves, but (also) in the carnal or "animal" that we always and already are. The age of excarnation, which is the absurd end of a long history of favoring the optical as handmaid to the intellectual, has further dissociated us from any notion of ourselves as animals and, most importantly, the ethical savvy we possess simply by virtue of being carnal.

What Constitutes One as Another?

What constitutes one as another? And why? And beyond this, why does being constituted as another matter? It is indisputable that the first "type" of other that comes to mind is the human other, a person who is at least somewhat like me. And of course, personhood matters because once one is considered a person, they are (at least in theory) guaranteed a certain degree of political recognition: entitled to life, liberty, the pursuit of happiness; allowed to vote; granted a voice; given a seat at the table; provided a space from which they can appear.

In Mary Midgley's "Persons and Non-person" (1985), she brings the question of what constitutes someone to the fore through the question of what makes a person a person. (The presupposition being that in order to count as someone, one needs to be considered a person.) She opens her piece by asking: is a dolphin a person? And describes a case in which two men at the University of Hawaii were convicted of theft because they decided to set two dolphins free from university experimentation to promote their well-being, as the dolphins were displaying signs of anxiety, depression, and were even attempting suicide. The judge ruled that the true offense in the case was not mistreatment of the animals, but theft from the university (i.e., the dolphins were property), and that there could be no appeal to the 13th amendment in the case of dolphins (as the two men were trying to do) because dolphins are simply not persons. Midgley quickly points out that the presupposition fueling the judge's ruling was that persons must be humans (that is, animals *like us*); but she quickly dismantles the idea that persons are so obviously human, considering the fact that many believe that the trinity consists of persons, and that corporations, cities, colleges, pieces of land are all, legally speaking, persons, too.

What then grants privileged access into the sacred category of "person"? As Midgley rightly underscores, intelligence simply cannot be the criteria because we know that dolphins, for example, rival us in intelligence. Is it simply being conscious, sensitive, and endowed with emotions? It certainly seems like animals have these qualities too. What are the roots of a view by which we not only fail to see ourselves as animals, but in fact see ourselves as above, beyond, outside of nature: superior in both intelligence and capacity? We understand ourselves as special, free agents, thanks to rationality. The important question is *why*.

Genesis and Modernity

The influence of the story of creation on our understanding of ourselves in the West (whether one is a practicing Christian or not) in relation to other animals and nature more broadly has been covered extensively.[4] The gist of the genealogy is that man was made in the *image of God* on the sixth day of creation, and was granted *dominion* over all of the other animals—even given the job of naming all of the other animals; and this has evolved into an understanding of man as dominating, i.e., *ruling*, over the animals. This is inevitably linked to the fall of mankind; prior to the fall, all of the animals peacefully coexisted with each other in Eden, but after Eve ate from the tree of knowledge, enmity among the various species on earth became the new normal, and human beings shifted from a vegetarian or perhaps even vegan existence to that which includes a taste for blood and flesh. This is to say that rather than understanding dominion as shepherding—being responsible for, caring for all of the other animals—we have taken it to mean domination: using the other animals and nature more broadly for whatever we please, and understanding the world as raw material meant to benefit or be in perpetual service to humanity. Our understanding of a "natural" hierarchy among the creatures on earth stems from this.[5] We sit at the top of the "food chain" as special, *gods among nature*. Uniquely rational, uniquely free.

In Crispin Sartwell's piece in the *New York Times*, "Humans are animals. Let's get over it," he illuminates the history of separation in the arts and sciences, and sheds light on what is at stake for human beings when refusing to recognize or acknowledge an affinity we have with squirrels or any other animal for that matter. Quoting Sartwell (2021):

> If one were to read through the prefaces and first paragraphs of the canonical works of Western philosophy, one might assume the discipline's primary question to be this: What makes us humans so much better than all the other animals? Really, it's astonishing how relentless this theme is in the whole history of philosophy. The separation of people from, and the superiority of people to, members of other species is a good candidate for the originating idea of Western thought. And a good candidate for the worst.

And why is philosophy in particular so obsessed with this distinction? By Sartwell's account, freedom, rationality, consciousness, and (perhaps most controversially) *being made in the image of God* are at stake. Quoting Sartwell on Kant, "The moral law reveals to me a life independent of animality." Sartwell goes on to point out that the ethical repercussions are clear: our treatment of animals in the West—from use in entertainment to fashion to factory farms—makes it obvious that our understanding of ourselves in relation to other animals is distinctly modern (though the Christian roots suggest that this way of thinking is much older). As Lynn White stresses in the often cited, "The Historical Roots of the Ecological Crisis," Christianity is the most anthropocentric and voluntarist religion humanity has witnessed to date, notably distinct from more "pagan" religions that truly saw God in all things—human and animal alike. This "pagan" orientation also understood that rather than being nature-dominating "free" agents, we are in fact deeply subjected to nature and her will (White 1967).

So, to return to the question opening this section: what constitutes one as another? As things currently stand, from a legal perspective (deeply informed by the prejudice of Christianity and the Enlightenment), only human persons are considered others, though various animal rights groups are advocating for chimps, elephants, and other animals (e.g., cetaceans) who possess cognitive capacities similar to our own, insisting that they ought to have legal personhood as well.[6] Kearney's account suggests that the loss of touch is a symptom of a tradition that favors the ocular, analogically equating sight with reason. But the deeper alienation from our animal, fleshly, touching nature disassociates us ever further from nature and animal others, limiting our perception of who counts as another to the rational human. Though it goes without saying that not every human other makes it into the coveted category of full personhood. The rationality versus animality distinction has been used to justify slavery, colonialization, and exploitation (of more "savage" existences) in general. Only the supremely rational enjoy the privilege of profit; fortunate are those who can overcome their carnality.

Compassion as Carnal: Animals in the Ethico-Moral Imagination

The question that follows from here is: on what grounds do we make this value judgment? Reasoned reflection? Is it really that obvious? Or is this simply the narrative we have been told by those who intend to maintain their privilege? What can carnal hermeneutics—that is, interpretation through the fleshly, non-thetic dimension of ourselves—reveal to us in regard to the incontrovertible value—or better, *dignity*—of other animals? Are other animals not vulnerable in many of the same ways we are? Are they not also striving for a life free from suffering?

Midgley (1985) poses an interesting question that I think directly relates to Kearney's work on carnal hermeneutics. She asks if cruelty to animals is merely a matter of aesthetics, rather than something pertaining to morality proper (is *foie gras*, for example, just something done in bad taste, rather than something morally wrong). In light of the way society functions now, animal cruelty only *occasionally* falls into the moral realm—and typically because animals, more often than not, belong to someone or some corporate entity, so cruelty to them is violating someone's right to property. David Foster Wallace poses a similar question in the controversial piece he wrote for *Gourmet Magazine* in 2004, "Consider the Lobster." After giving an extraordinary analysis of the lives of lobsters and the horror that's involved in eating them, he brings up the point that there is something intrinsically troubling about animal suffering—nobody likes to think about it. He, too, points toward the tensions between taste and what is right and wrong, wondering under which category our treatment of animals fall.

What can or should we make of this troubling dimension of animal suffering? Is there a chance that our instinctive revulsion to suffering is a neglected tact that we ought to make sense of—and thereby "elevate" to ethico-moral status? What place does empathy, compassion, or respect for animals have in the moral imagination?[7] Kearney opens *Carnal Hermeneutics* by asking the crucial question: "How do we interpret the world with our bodily sense, especially those long neglected in Western philosophy—taste and touch? How, in other words, do we discern the world as this or that, as hospitable or hostile, as attractive or repulsive, as tasty or tasteless, as living or dying?" (2015, 15). The question of what repulses us (i.e., what we reject or are disgusted by) is key. In what follows I want to explore the case of animal suffering—utter exposure to the face of their suffering, their vulnerability as living beings—as a revulsion that is pre-thetic, non-rational, carnal.[8] Carnal hermeneutics suggests that touch and tactility more generally may provide the proximity-as-distance that allows for hermeneutic mediation. And what I want to suggest here is that carnality is in fact a crucial entrée to moral imagination, bridging the gap between revulsion and our ethico-moral point-of-view.

To do this, I will briefly turn to an account that I take to be an important moment in the story of carnal hermeneutics and its relation to our ethico-moral sense: Jean-Jacques Rousseau's *Discourse on Inequality*, which was a source of inspiration for Kant's hugely influential and controversial moral project. Ernst Cassirer notes that Rousseau was the thinker who woke Kant up from his *moral* slumber—pushing him to be the thinker of universal human rights that he was. Unlike Kant, however, Rousseau was a friend of environmental ethics (calling us to return to nature and the *laws* of nature); he was one of the few thinkers of the 18th century who was not only a lover of animals, but who was also willing to say that our moral sense extended to them. Quoting Nathaniel Wolloch, "If one seeks a late enlightenment intellectual figure who had a broad influence on the rise of a sentimental, early romantic, consideration of nature and animals, Rousseau is undoubtedly the most prominent candidate" (2008, 294). Rousseau criticized cruelty to animals and the desire to utilize them for self-interested pursuits or understand them as outside the realm of human concern.

Rousseau on natural pity (compassion). Rousseau begins his *Second Discourse* by delineating two key principles that are prior to reason. Or as he understands them, "pre-political" principles present in the state of nature. The first is that we have a natural interest in our own self-preservation (this is the "right" kind of self-love/concern for our own welfare); and the second is our natural repugnance to seeing other sentient beings suffer. This is what he calls pity, but can be understood as compassion—I will use these terms interchangeably. For Rousseau, natural rights flow from these two precepts. What is noteworthy about these precepts, especially the second one, is that our duty to the other is not a lesson of wisdom. Compassion is basic, self-evident, it is how we most naturally relate to the world. As he notes, *contra* Descartes, animals share some of our nature (sentience), so it seems like we have a duty to them, too:

> [Man's] obligations are not dictated to him merely by the slow voice of wisdom; and as long as he does not resist his internal impulses of compassion, he never will do any harm to another man, nor even any sentient being, except in those lawful cases where his own preservation happens to come in question, and it is of course his duty to give himself the preference. But this means too we may put an end to the ancient disputes concerning the participation of other animals in the law of nature.; for it is plain that, as they want both reason and

free will, they cannot be acquainted with that law; however, as they partake in some measure of our nature in virtue of that **sensibility** with which they are endowed, we may well imagine they ought likewise to partake of the benefit of natural law, and that man owes them a certain kind of duty. In fact, it seems that if I am obliged not to injure any being like myself, it is not so much because he is a reasonable being, as because he is a sensible being; and this quality, by being common to men and beasts, ought to exempt the latter from any unnecessary injuries the former might be able to do to them. (Rousseau 2002, 84)

At the time, this position was unpopular. This in mind, Rousseau's call to action in the *Second Discourse* is for us to return to (or at least remember) the state of nature—above all, because for him, the state of nature is not, *contra* Hobbes, a state of war. What Hobbes missed, according to Rousseau, is our natural inclination toward compassion, a key dimension of human beings in their natural state. For Rousseau, the state of civil society is a state of war, fueled by comparison and competition: we live in a capitalist, dog eat dog world, in which the desire to get ahead is, whether we like to admit it or not, a desire to subordinate not only our neighbor, but all of the living world around us. But pity is a *natural* virtue, which is to say that it is self-evident, intuitive, prior to civil society. According to Rousseau, we instinctively feel an aversion to suffering and want to take care (in commiseration). He does not use the language of dignity and respect, but what those terms come to mean are without question latent in his account. Quoting Rousseau:

Pity is a disposition suitable to creatures weak as we are, and liable to so many evils; a virtue so much the more universal, and withal useful to man, as it takes place in him before all manner of reflection; and so natural, that the beasts themselves sometimes give evident signs of it ... with what reluctance are horses known to trample upon living bodies; one animal never passes unmoved by the dead carcass of another animal of the same species; there are even some who bestow a kind of [burial] upon their dead fellows; and the mourning lowing of cattle, on their entering the slaughter-house, publish the impression made upon them by the horrible spectacle they are there struck with. (2002, 106)

He goes on to point out that pity should not only be understood as wishing for the other to not suffer, but actually wanting them to be happy, to be well, to thrive (2002, 107). We commiserate, and this is a pre-cognitive experience, i.e., not the product of reflection. It is the immediate result of encountering the vulnerability of another. Contrary to standard discourse in the history of Western thought, for Rousseau, reason creates a second, potentially perverse kind of self-love (*self-worth, egoism*), and reflection ultimately strengthens it (2002, 107). As he puts it:

> … it is reason that makes man shrink into himself; it is reason that makes him keep aloof from everything that can trouble or afflict him; it is philosophy that destroy his connections with other men [and other creatures]; it is in consequence of her dictates that he mutters to himself at the sight of another in distress, You may perish for aught I care, I am safe. Nothing less than those evils, which threaten the whole community, can disturb the calm sleep of the philosopher, and force him from his bed. One man may with impunity murder another under his windows; he has nothing to do but clap his hands to his ears, argue a little with himself to hinder nature, that startles within him, from identifying with the unhappy sufferer. Savage man lacks this admirable talent; and for want of wisdom and reason, is always ready foolishly to obey the first whispers of humanity. (2002, 107)

The important point for Rousseau is that we do not need to look to arguments to find compassion. And our species (and others) would have ceased to exist long ago if the instinct was not present within all of us (though anthropogenic climate change is truly testing that hypothesis). The crucial claim is that if we are able to truly perceive the suffering, pity does its job. True perception here involves tactility—an immersive experience that touches us by way of permeating our being. As Kearney describes it in *Radical Hospitality*, touch is a "threshold crossing," during which we are thrown into an utterly new experience, as "carnal performance" overtakes "conceptual calculation" (Kearney and Fitzpatrick 2021, 52). With Kearney's reciprocity principle in mind (touch as "double sensation"), when touching, we cannot help but be affected; we are inevitably touched when we touch, "sharing sensibility" (2021, 52). But we have of course become masters at *not* perceiving suffering, and large scale suffering is actually hidden from plain sight (and the examples within society, as we know it, are abundant, e.g., the way we hide the elderly, the location of factory farms, the walls of prisons, etc.). We know full well how to ignore the call for respect, and profit-makers know that visible suffering in the process of production is not conducive to consumption.

In *Emile*, Rousseau stresses that an essential part of human education involves bearing witness to suffering in order to cultivate pity before it becomes deaf to reason. As Rousseau puts it, it is not sufficient to simply tell young people, conceptually, about calamities (e.g., climate change, extreme poverty, etc.). These are abstract ideas that need to be rooted in something concrete, something affective. Paraphrasing Rousseau, let them *see*, i.e., let them *feel* the human calamities: "Unsettle and frighten [the student's] imagination with the perils by which every man is constantly surrounded" (Katz 2005, 205). This is precisely how we learn compassion for the other, which is only partially constructed by a fear of becoming the one who suffers. Compassion, which wholly affects us, also sheds all concerns one has over oneself (in the sense of self-preservation), and one is moved to be for, be with, *help* the other in need so that they can *stop suffering and be happy*. For Rousseau, compassion is self-evident, but can of course be reasoned away. The replacement of the first kind of self-love with self-worth diminishes our compassion for others. It is therefore important to let young people face (watch and thus feel) injustices and the suffering of others, as this effectively sharpens compassion. The mistreatment of animals ought to be on this list. One should experience a factory farm, be it seeing the raw footage of what happens in concentrated animal feeding operations, or perhaps more effectively, smelling the stench of death that permeates the air when you are in the general vicinity of one. This would help us understand what goes into making the plates of food that we eat and the clothing that we wear, facing reality head on. This is how we truly learn to hear the diverse voices of those who suffer, and let our moral instinct do its work. *Facing qua listening* to suffering is the way in which we foster the virtue of hearing, perceiving, looking out, thinking beyond ourselves, and putting the others into the equation.

Unnatural Born Killers

To turn to a more contemporary depiction of natural pity or compassion, I want to briefly look at Harvard psychologist Melanie Joy's account in *Why We Love Dogs, Eat Pigs, and Wear Cows*. The book is meant to expose the cruel, invisible, dominant ideology of carnism: the ideology that condones eating animals. Anatomically, we are not carnivores, but could be considered carnists—or as Foster Wallace puts it, *carnophiles*. This is to say that we do not eat meat because we have to. The interesting question to Joy is this: why do we eat animal flesh? And she chocks it up to carnism, which, like other dominant ideologies (e.g., white supremacy), is one that you cannot see, and therefore cannot name, and therefore cannot talk about, and thus cannot *question* (2010, 32). The most disturbing dimension of carnism is that it is organized around violence—meat cannot be procured without slaughter, something needs to be killed (Joy 2010, 32–33). And the process is so horrific that most people are not willing to witness it themselves; those that do become seriously disturbed (Joy 2010, 33). Although billions of animals are killed every year, the general public never witnesses it. And according to Joy, there are obvious reasons for this. There is a strong argument to be made that if we truly experienced the pain involved in animal slaughter we simply would not consume the product that companies want us to continue consuming, which gives us a kind of prima facie reason to accept Rosseau's belief in natural compassion. Thus, it is in the best interest of big agriculture to hide their operations, keep them private, and prevent anyone from entering or seeing what happens behind closed doors. Quoting Joy:

> Why do we hate to see animals in pain? Because we feel for other sentient beings. Most of us, even those who are not "animal lovers" per se, don't want to cause anyone—human or animal—to suffer, especially if that suffering is intensive and unnecessary. It is for this reason that violent ideologies have a special set of defenses that enable humane people to support inhumane practices and to not even realize what they are doing. There is a substantial body of evidence demonstrating humans' seemingly natural aversion to killing. Much of the research in this area has been conducted by the military; analysts have found that soldiers tend to intentionally fire over the enemy's head, or not to fire at all ... in order to get soldiers to shoot to kill, to actively participate in violence, the soldiers must be sufficiently desensitized to the act of killing. In other words, they have to learn to not feel—and to not feel responsible for their actions. They must be taught to override their own conscience. Yet these studies also demonstrate that in the face of immediate danger, in situations of extreme violence, most people are averse to killing ... as Marshall concludes, "the vast majority of combatants throughout history, at the moment of truth when they could and should kill the enemy, have found themselves to be 'conscientious objectors.'" (2010, 33–35)

Our default (at least for the most part) is that we prefer to do no harm. But, as Rousseau argues, a certain form of thinking—specifically, competitive calculation and consumption—can desensitize us from our carnal revulsion to suffering, and, as a result, lead us to disregard our own vulnerability and the vulnerability of others.

The takeaway here is that ethico-moral sense is something that at least appears to always and already be the case because it is carnal. Ethico-moral sense is something that we (as animals) feel straightaway (or better, *have carnally understood straightaway*)—an instinct, similar to self-preservation. It is something that, in order to ignore, requires either habituated desensitization to stop feeling or a general lack of exposure. In Kearney's terms, there is a carnal interpretation that happens before reflective cognition kicks in. That carnal interpretation is ethical in its orientation in the sense that it not only insists that we do no harm, but confirms that at our core, we prefer for the other to be well. As Rousseau points out, competition and the desire to get ahead help us ignore the call of the other, deaf to their suffering, so we can pursue our self-interest without guilt and remorse.

In terms of the world as we understand it today, embedded in the age of excarnation, capitalism—fueled by competition—and the speed at which we need to move to keep up makes us callous early on. We are less attentive to what is beyond ourselves, less stifled by the pain of the other, less empathetic all together. I do not think it would be too much to say that carnal hermeneutics is a necessary condition for the possibility of ethical behavior altogether because compassion in general is visceral, animal, of the flesh. Our attunement to the other is first mediated by tactility. Not just seeing the pain of the other, but sensing it, facing it, witnessing their vulnerability, and in turn remembering our own. Ethico-moral sense is precisely the inclination we have to stop that pain from happening—to help the other in their vulnerability in whatever way, shape, or form we can, *flourish*. The carnal experience of compassion involves what I would call self-disruption: *a moment of forgetting oneself in being called by the other*, a releasing of reflective reason, a surrender or divesting of the ego's agenda—and, perhaps most importantly, *a risk of transformation*.

Carnal Ecology: Humans and Other Animals

The trouble of course is that we—at least human beings in the West—are part of an ecological orientation that all too often inhibits us from responding to carnal compassion. Or put differently, we have an ecological orientation that is almost wholly numb to the call of other animals, despite the imminent anthropogenic ecological crisis. We have been trained to not disrupt our self-interested pursuits, because if we do, we will fall behind, miss out, or worse, find ourselves unable to support ourselves.

Our ecological sense, i.e., the way we understand ourselves in relation to other living things and our physical environment (White 1967), has been ordered at least in some sense by both Christianity and the rise of Reason that fueled the industrial and scientific revolutions in modernity, meaning that we have come to understand ourselves as superior to other animals, condone mass killing of animals for our consumption, and in fact most regularly encounter animals in the form of food on our plates—masked by names that conceal the singularity of the individual *person* on our plates (e.g., "pork" instead of a particular pig). Ecological sense, on White's account (which is useful for these purposes), is determined by

> beliefs about our nature and destiny, meaning that there is a clear understanding of human nature and our destiny, i.e., religion. Whether or not one is religious, we all have a sense of where we fall in the big picture and where we are headed. The only way to get rid of a particular religious orientation is to replace it with a new one (White 1967).

White offers the orientation of St. Francis of Assisi as a viable alternative, as it actualizes a radical equality among all of God's creatures and a strong sense of humility before nature—admonishing the idea that we are *not* part of the natural process, and that our natural impulses are indeed part of our "lesser" nature. We can of course imagine a host of alternate orientations beyond St. Francis that would insist on our inter-connectedness with every aspect of creation: animal, vegetable, and mineral.

I propose that this is where carnal ecology finds its place, which I understand to be an extension of Kearney's understanding of the "primal embodied wisdom operating in the three senses of sense—sensation, orientation, and meaning—that mark every genuine encounter between self and stranger" (Kearney and Fitzpatrick 2021, 53). A return to sense, tact, and touch as a source of wisdom opens the door to a new form of listening—one that is, without question, ethical in its orientation, as it is attuned to what lies beyond the imagined borders of the ego. With Kearney in mind, this involves (1) the risk of allowing tactility to play a much larger role in determining our orientation toward the world, and with that, (2) coming to terms with our own vulnerability-as-skin, which is a vulnerability we share with every other living creature. Quoting Kearney, "when this carnal power of savvy is at work, it is not impossible for enemies to become friends, for strangers to become guests. In short, for hostility to be transformed into hospitality" (Kearney and Fitzpatrick 2021, 54). We might add it is not impossible for us to become one with the natural world again.

When we suspend calculation and truly *pay attention*—that is, carnally pay attention by and through all five of our senses even if "at a distance" (Kearney and Fitzpatrick 2021, 55)—to what is outside of ourselves, it seems like we are less likely to ignore the call of other animals. Or at least more likely to be more attuned to the call of other animals. This would be the necessary condition to overthrow carnism (at least as its practiced today in the industrialized world) as a dominant ideology, and would heed the United Nation's call for us to consume less animals (fish included, of course—they, too, feel and respond to pain, contrary to popular belief)[9] and rely on a plant-based diet for the sake of the health of our planet. It is interesting to consider that if, perhaps, we listened more closely to our ethico-moral instinct, the ecological crisis in which we find ourselves would be less of a crisis. Carnal ecology would no doubt eradicate a speciesist understanding of human dominion as domination, thereby recognizing that the singularity that grants a person personhood extends beyond human animals, and understanding that our destiny hinges on whether or not we take compassion seriously—and refuse to be deaf to the suffering of others. Echoing Rousseau in the *Second Discourse*, natural difference does not imply or necessitate the type of moral hierarchy that privileges a select few at the expense of all others.

With all of this in mind, the difficult questions that remain are: how, specifically, do we foster this ethico-moral sensibility (or carnal hospitality) to other animals in those who have been habituated into being blind and deaf to the face of human and animal others? How do we fit animals into the moral imagination? Especially in light of the claim that morality is not something we can argue ourselves into. (I am limiting my analysis here to the hidden slaughter that takes place at large-scale concentrated animal feeding operations, though I recognize that the case of the local farmer, whose daily life involves a notably different orientation toward animals, poses important challenges.)

While fully addressing these questions exceeds the scope of this chapter, it seems like the somewhat controversial answer would involve exposing people to the reality of what is behind the deaths of billions of animals each year and let our embodied wisdom—that is, moral sense—do its work, thereby bridging the gap between revulsion (aesthetics) and something that is morally problematic. These difficult questions become even more difficult when we consider the politics of sight (and concomitant *culture of invisibility*) silently governing what we do and do not see—that is, the meticulous industrial regulation of "who has visual access" to the horrific stages of various production processes (Cronin and Kramer 2018, 81–83). This is even further complicated when we consider the passive consumption of graphic images and videos, as Tamsin Jones does in Chapter 13 (this volume, pp. XXX). At what point is the imagery simply too much? And is that type of shock (or even paralysis) necessary to truly hear the call of the other, and prompt a real transformation in values? Does it have to be graphic? And are there limits to who should face it? As Joy (2010, 33) points out:

> In my classes, when I show a film on meat production, I have to take a number of measures to ensure that the psychological environmental is safe enough to expose students to footage that inevitably causes them distress. And I have personally worked with numerous vegetarian advocates who suffer from post-traumatic stress disorder (PTSD) as the result of prolonged exposure to the slaughter process; they have intrusive thoughts, nightmare, flashbacks, difficult concentrating, anxiety, insomnia, and a host of other symptoms. In close to two decades of speaking and teaching about meat production, I have yet to see a person who doesn't cringe when faced with images of slaughter. People generally hate to see animals suffer.

J. Keri Cronin and Lisa Kramer do an excellent job describing how visual imagery has been instrumental in creating a culture of invisibility in regard to the widespread violence toward animals inherent in our food production systems in their piece, "Challenging the iconography of oppression in marketing: confronting speciesism through art and visual culture." This is of course true for fashion systems as well. From the corporate perspective, it is important that violence toward animals remains invisible because the sight (e.g., the inner world of slaughterhouses) would trigger our ethico-moral sense—we would be affected, touched—and we would inevitably struggle to consume the products that companies want us to consume. As displayed above, we do not (for the most part) have a taste for blood, and we do, for the most part, have a taste for the well-being of other sentient beings. But in order to attune ourselves to that ethico-moral taste, we need to stop and pay attention to the savvy that is always and already with us—that is, returning to Kearney, the carnal knowing, *the instinctual compassion*, that knows better than to exploit and harm the other.

To foster natural compassion toward other animals, and thereby allow aesthetics to inform ethics, it is vital that we listen when we are repulsed and self-disrupted, hear the pain we feel when we witness animal suffering and the joy we feel when we witness animals thriving. In the spirit of carnal hermeneutics, this involves allowing ourselves to first feel what we see, and not to immediately rationalize, intellectualize, or thematize it. Echoing Cronin and Kramer, images have the ability to challenge the status quo because of the unique way in which they foster what ecofeminist Lori Gruen calls *entangled empathy*: that is, "a type of caring perception focused on attending to another's experience of wellbeing. An experiential process involving a blend of emotion and cognition in which we recognize we are in relationships with others and are called upon to be responsive and responsible in these relationships by attending to another's needs, interests, desires, vulnerabilities, hopes, and sensitivities" (Cronin and Kramer 2018, 87). It is important to stress that this type of empathy is not limited to bearing witness to images of animal suffering that lets us into the singularity of a given living creature, thus shifting them into the status of a "person" who *deserves better*, but also images that reveal the endless list of qualities that other animals share with human animals: joy, love, curiosity, ingenuity, familial bonds, etc. Within this vein, in his chapter "Thinking Like a Jaguar: Carnal Hermeneutics, Touch, and the Limits of Language," Brian Treanor explores tools that might help foster empathy between us and other animals—tools that are "more *zoon* and less *logon*," "bodying forth" the relatable non-linguistic experiences of other animals (pp. XXX).

Crucial to the development of carnal ecology is safeguarding a space for carnal evaluations like these to take place—and, with Rousseau in mind, not allowing ourselves to rush to justifications, rationalizations, or worse, dangerous hierarchical power relations, but to instead attend to our distaste for violence toward other animals. It is worth considering how our behaviors would change if we regularly visited animal sanctuaries to experience the peace and livelihoods of animals rescued from horrifying conditions, or if factory farms were not completely hidden from the public eye—or if they had glass walls. For instance, could we stomach eating cheese if we knew that in order for dairy products to show up in grocery stores, a calf must be deprived of her mother's milk and shipped to a veal farm before she is even able to walk? The sights and sounds are incredibly difficult to swallow (they are ugly, horrifying, and monstrous). Even if one might understand the final product (e.g., a leather bag, a "fine" cut of steak, bacon, etc.) as beautiful or tasty, is its beauty and tastiness not tainted by a horrifying process? Is the process itself not part of the product? It seems like a carnal hermeneutic of the means of production would reshape our overall interpretation of the final product, exposing the absent-referent (i.e., animal individual or person) that actually constitutes the product.

In the spirit of Kearney's innovative work on carnal hermeneutics, taste carries ethical significance in regard to our treatment of other animals. Carnal hermeneutics is, without question, a tool for animal welfare, revealing the way in which carnal savvy is ethically bent if we are willing to listen, refusing to be deaf to what is self-evidently and non-thetically morally problematic. Or put differently, *to consider other animals as persons to which we have a responsibility*. Our relationships with them could in fact be more beautiful, and thereby lead to not only their flourishing but also ours (and the Earth's). The ecological turn here would involve a deep recognition of the inter-dependence among ourselves, other animals, plants, and the atmosphere—and would also involve, perhaps above all, a deep recognition that the Earth's vulnerability in the Anthropocene is an echo or iteration of our own.

Notes

1 In particular, see Richard Kearney, "Reconnecting with the Animal" and "Coda" in *Touch* (Kearney 2021, 109–111, 129–132).
2 Kearney is careful to delineate the distinction between touch itself, as in physical touch by way of the skin (hands, etc.), and tactility, which describes the way in which touch is present in all of the senses: "Tactful taste we call *savvy*; tactful smell we call *flair*; tactful sight we call *insight*; and tactful sound we call *resonance*."
3 Richard Kearney, "Narrative imagination: between ethics and poetics" (1995). I am borrowing the useful term, "ethico-moral," from Paul Ricoeur, as it encompasses both the realm of ethics (well-being) and morality (normativity, duty).
4 See Pope Francis, *Laudato si* (2015); Lynn White, "The historical roots of our ecological crisis" (1967); and John Passmore, *Man's Responsibility for Nature* (1980).
5 Ibid.
6 Here I have in mind Steven Wise's extraordinary legal fight for animal rights (in particular, securing the status of personhood for chimpanzees, and eventually elephants and cetaceans) in the 2019 documentary, *Unlocking the Cage*, by Chris Hegedus and D.A. Pennebaker.

7 Kearney's work on reconciliation between the self and the (human) other relies on the ethico-moral imagination (grounded in narrative imagination), which, as Kearney points out, is markedly distinct from poetic imagination in the sense that it involves our responsibility to others—hosting as many standpoints as possible. Exercising our moral imagination is precisely attempting to put ourselves in the shoes of the other, while recognizing that we do not, of course, wear the exact same size. To exercise moral imagination is to exercise empathy. Ethical imagination is not the same as narrative imagination, but does in fact need it. As Kearney puts it, narrative imagination is a necessary, albeit not sufficient condition for ethics. It cannot guarantee the movement to responsibility, but it allows the other to impinge on the imaginative self, or one's understanding of themselves (see Richard Kearney, "Narrative imagination: between ethics and poetics").

8 I understand that what is meant by "rational" or "reason" is problematic, and always determined by a particular metaphysical framework. The reason of Kant is very different from the reason of Spinoza—and the reason of Spinoza extends to modes of being that are not "traditionally" understood to be rational, e.g., plants. I loosely have in mind the reason of the Enlightenment, which is a reason that in many instances is capable of being free from sentimentality. Whether or not reason can truly be free from sentiment is beyond the scope of this chapter—but an important question to ask in relation to carnal hermeneutics and the complex interplay between the carnal and the "intelligible." Kearney's aim of course is to detach ourselves from dualistic understandings like this; in the spirit of Aristotle, we never find one without the other—at least not entirely.

9 See Kenny Torrella, "The Next Frontier for Animal Welfare: Fish" (2021).

References

Cassirer, Ernst. 1945. "Kant and Rousseau." In *Rousseau-Kant-Goethe: Two Essays*, 1–60. Princeton: Princeton University Press.

Cronin, J. Keri and Lisa A. Kramer. 2018. "Challenging the Iconography of Oppression in Marketing: Confronting Speciesism through Art and Visual Culture." *Journal of Animal Ethics* vol. 8, no. 1 (Spring): 80–92.

Joy, Melanie. 2010. *Why We Love Dogs, Eat Pigs, and Wear Cows*. San Francisco: Conari Press.

Katz, Claire. 2005. "Teaching the Other: Levinas, Rousseau, and the Question of Education." *Philosophy Today* vol. 49, no. 2 (Summer): 200–207.

Kearney, Richard. 1995. "Narrative Imagination: Between Ethics and Poetics." *Philosophy and Social Criticism* vol. 21, No. 5/6: 173–190.

Kearney, Richard. 2021. *Touch: Recovering Our Most Vital Sense*. New York: Columbia University Press.

Kearney, Richard and Melissa Fitzpatrick. 2021. *Radical Hospitality: From Thought to Action*. New York: Fordham University Press.

Kearney, Richard and Brian Treanor. 2015. *Carnal Hermeneutics*. New York: Fordham University Press.

Midgley, Mary. 1985. "Persons and Non-persons." In *In Defense of Animals*, edited by Peter Singer. New York: Blackwell.

Passmore, John. 1980. *Man's Responsibility for Nature*. 2nd edition. London: Duckworth Press.

Pope Francis. 2015. *Laudato Si*. Vatican City: Vatican Press.

Rousseau, Jean-Jacques. 2002. *The Social Contract and the First and Second Discourses*. Edited by Susan Dunn. New Haven: Yale University Press.

Sartwell, Crispin. 2021. "Humans Are Animals. Let's Get Over It." *New York Times* February 23, 2021.

Singer, Peter, ed. 1985. *In Defense of Animals*. New York: Blackwell.

Torrella, Kenny. 2021. "The Next Frontier for Animal Welfare: Fish." *Vox*, online, March 2, 2021.

White, Lynn. 1967. "The Historical Roots of Our Ecological Crisis." *Science* vol. 155, no. 3767 (March): 1203–1207.

Wolloch, Nathaniel. 2008. "Rousseau and the Love of Animals." *Philosophy and Literature* vol. 32, no. 2 (October): 293–302.

Chapter 3

The Embodied Human Being in Touch with the World: Richard Kearney, and Hedwig Conrad-Martius in Conversation

Christina M. Gschwandtner

In his recent work, Richard Kearney emphasizes the importance of our embodied existence, focusing especially on the way in which touch provides hermeneutic access to the world. Not only in his contribution to *Carnal Hermeneutics* and the essays collected in *Radical Hospitality*, but even more fully in *Touch*, he develops a notion of "carnal hospitality" that takes seriously the ways in which we are situated by and know through the body. He also argues against our current predilection with disembodied existence that experiences reality increasingly in primarily virtual ways, which focus heavily on the visual dimension and ignore the other senses, especially that of touch. He calls this contemporary neglect of corporeality and deficiency of touch *excarnation*. Although Kearney frequently points to places in the history of philosophy—especially Aristotle and Merleau-Ponty—where touch, flesh, and body were analyzed (2015, 19–56; 2021, 33–60), an even fuller phenomenological grounding for an analysis of the human in terms of embodiment or enfleshment would be desirable. Furthermore, he gestures at times to the importance of attentiveness to the environment and of understanding the human within the world rather than separate from it, yet this dimension, also, deserves a more substantive exploration. The present contribution draws on some elements of the philosophical writings of Hedwig Conrad-Martius, one of Husserl's earliest students and a crucial voice in the Göttingen school of phenomenology, for a more robust account of embodiment fully "in touch" with the world to provide a deeper phenomenological grounding for Kearney's important intuitions on matters of touch and human embodied existence.

Kearney's interests in regard to touch and the senses are primarily ethical (carnal *hospitality*) and hermeneutic (carnal *discernment*). This is evident already in his contribution to *Carnal Hermeneutics*, where he traces the legacy of the philosophical tradition regarding touch and embodiment for its hermeneutic potential—"how do we interpret the world with our bodily senses, and especially ... taste and touch"—yet almost immediately gestures to the ethical dimension: "touching well is living

DOI: 10.4324/9781003285649-5

well" and therefore "hostility and hospitality are at stake from the outset" (2015, 15–17). He posits this as a way to bring phenomenology and hermeneutics back together (2015, 16–17, 55). In *Radical Hospitality*, he explores the ethical dimension more fully, stressing again the two-fold dimension of text and body: "In short, an ethical play of word and flesh is necessary for real hospitality to happen. We need linguistic *and* carnal hosting for wounds to be healed, strangers to be welcomed and peace to take place" (Kearney and Fitzpatrick 2021, 57, his emphasis). This is pushed further in *Touch*, which is both about how we know or discern within our sensory existence and about the possibilities this may open for healing wounds and overcoming trauma. For obvious reasons, the emphasis throughout is on *human* touch as a way of "discerning" and "healing." Both hermeneutics and hospitality are thus thought of primarily in regard to the *human* other.[1]

Conrad-Martius provides neither an ethical nor a hermeneutic account. Her interests are primarily phenomenological and ontological. Yet, her phenomenology is profoundly attentive not only to human embeddedness in the natural world but also to the shared embodiment of all living creatures. Reading Kearney's account of hospitality together with her phenomenological analysis of living beings might allow for the development of an *ecological hospitality* grounded in a phenomenology of lived embodiment. Furthermore, her phenomenological analysis of specifically human embodiment might deepen Kearney's account of "carnal discernment" by providing a substantive phenomenological foundation for our ways of living in the world, which have tremendous implications for the possibilities of our knowing of this world and discerning meaning within it. Thus, putting the two thinkers in conversation may give us a fuller and deeper sense of how human embodiment allows us to be "in touch" with the world. Although in regard to touch and embodiment Kearney's hermeneutic emphasis precedes his ethical explication to some extent (1999, 2008, 2011), we will begin with the broader phenomenological account of all living beings before moving to specifically human being, thus first gesturing to the possibility of an ecological hospitality, then to that of an embodied hermeneutics. In both cases, it will be a matter of opening the conversation, rather than developing a full-blown ecological ethics or phenomenologically grounded hermeneutics.

Excarnation and Incarnation: For an Ecological Hospitality

In their introduction to *Radical Hospitality*, Kearney and Fitzpatrick suggest that an "ethics of hospitality" can provide "novel options" for a host of pressing contemporary problems including "the looming ecological challenge" by "hosting the environmental stranger" (2021, 1). Yet, the book does not go on to explore this topic further or provide an account of how our own "carnality" is part of the broader ecological substructure of our bodies within the local and cosmic environment. *Touch* (2021) is focused primarily on recovering our connectedness to our senses and combatting a virtual culture in which sensory awareness goes by the wayside.[2] In the introduction, Kearney contends that "we need to evolve beyond the Anthropocene—marked by our technological domination of the planet—to a Symbiocene" that would involve a kind of "companionship" or "an ecology of mutualism" toward "a renewed interaction with nature" (2021, 6). Such a companionship would require affirming "the interconnection between human life and all tangible sentient beings" and move away from "human exceptionalism" (6). The book, he says in the final line of the introduction, "is written in praise of the desire for tactile proximity with our fellows on this earth" (7). Yet, those "fellows," at least within the pages of this text, turn out to be almost exclusively human. Aside from the repeated mention of dogs (2015, 18; 2012, 180; 2021, 23, 62, 109–110)—maybe the most "humanized" of animals (and so overbred as to be barely "natural")—so far there is not much of an account of other-than-human creatures in Kearney's work. Although Conrad-Martius also does not develop any sort of environmental ethics, partly because she lived before these became pressing issues, explicating a phenomenology of nature in interaction with the natural science of her day is one of her central concerns (,1938, 1961, 1964). Her account of body (*Leib*)—not only of human but also of plant, animal, and spirit embodiment—is firmly situated within that context and thus can provide phenomenological detail for Kearney's stated but unexplored desire to consider all sentient beings.

Conrad-Martius examines in detail the ways in which living beings (including plants) are embodied. She shows how a different phenomenological account must be given of the embodied nature of plants than of that of animals, even when they might be outwardly similar (like the amoebae and a creeping plant or like a polyp and a mimosa).[3] Animals inhabit their bodies in a way that plants do not. Phenomenological thought experiments and imaginative variation enable her to parse those differences in phenomenological terms. Living beings clothe themselves with bodies, dwell within them, and envelop themselves with them. They are able to direct these bodies in specific ways—propelling self-directed movement and action—when they inhabit their bodies in a particular way from a center or core (via a "soul"). A plant is fully enveloped by its body and is phenomenologically defined in its nature or kind by its form or shape without any additional relation to this bodily form (plants are what she calls *Gestaltswesen*). Animals, in addition, are able to have a relation with their body, to direct it, to own it, and even to be free from it in some form. They are able to enter deeply within the body and to operate from its core, radiating from this core out into all facets of the body. The soul in her view is not, as in Aristotle or the later scholastic tradition, the "form" of the body, but rather its inner core that allows it to dwell and inhabit this body in such a way as to act through it. Animals have a certain "mastery" over the body and are thus, phenomenologically speaking, beings of action (*Aktionswesen*) in their nature or kind. Body and soul thus are not "things" but ways of being, manners of living embodiment. In fact, she often employs these terms in a verbal sense (*leiben, seelen, geisten, wesen*) that is impossible to render into sensible English (e.g. Conrad-Martius 1921, 136–137), but conveys their lived reality.

All of this also applies to the human being who in addition lives through its spirit (*Geist*) in an elevating movement that allows it to relate not only to its body (*Leib*) but also to its soul (*Seele*). While the soul allows a being to sink into and dwell in its body, the spirit permits a rising movement within and from the body (but not *without* the body). The human spirit is the breath that animates its living body; it is itself a form of embodiment. This is particularly vivid in her consideration of dis-embodied spirits to which the *Metaphysical Conversations* devote a sig-nificant amount of time, despite one of the interlocutors' hesitations and even ridicule (Conrad-Martius 1921, 26–27, 121–166). Fairies, nymphs, wood sprites, demons, and angels are spirits (rather than having spirits), but because they have no body, they are "hollow" (and some of them are insatiable in their futile search for embodiment).[4] Humans can be "naked," but not hollow in this specific sense, because their existence and nature is embodiment (1921, 80–82, 129). As we will see shortly in more detail, they *are* not spirit or soul or body; they *have* spirits and souls and bodies—both in the sense of inhabiting them and possessing them (1921, 169–172, 216–231). Concrete ways of embodiment thus highlight various modes of sentient and corporeal existence.

In her later work, Conrad-Martius will complicate this account further by speaking of the structural embodiment of the human, partly shared with other living beings, in a four-fold way. The human personal self (*das personalgeprägte menschliche Seelenselbst*) lives "excarnately" (*ex-karnativ*)—like the plant—out into its body (*Leib*), "incarnately" (*in-karnativ*)—like the animal—within into its psyche (1949, 134–137). This "incarnate" relation to the soul or psyche has three dimensions: from the inside out into the body (*leib-seelisch*, again like all animals), the un-folding within the self in affective fashion (*affektiv seelisch*, like many but not all animals), and the objective-subjective relation within the psychic self (*geist-seelisch*). In a different context, she summarizes the three types of body-soul relations as follows: first, the soul-self is fully given into the body and expands into it in the case of plants; second, the self dwells in its body and can govern it actively and sense what happens to it in the case of animals; third, the soul-self is formed into itself, widened into an inner affective space in the case of higher animals and the human (1965, 136–137). It should be noted that the term "excarnation" is used positively (or, more precisely, neutrally) by Conrad-Martius to designate our living within our bodies, an embodied living that is shared by all other living beings, not negatively as a lack of relation to body or disconnection from tactile contact in a cyber-technical, virtual, immaterialized world, as Kearney employs it (2021, 4–5). The human being via soul and spirit thus relates to its body in at least three-fold fashion, a far more complex account than the dualistic Cartesian distinctions of much of the tradition.[5] She calls the four dimensions (*leiblich, leib-seelisch, affektiv seelisch,* and *geistig*) "areas of realization" (*Verwirklichungsbereiche*) of the "soul-self" (*Seelenselbst*) that are incarnated and manifested in these ways.[6] The self, she points out, does not have its standpoint or locus in the body (*Leib*), as if it were some entity within it, but is manifested and realized within and through the body. This provides a complex and differentiated phenomenological account for Kearney's insistence on the centrality of embodiment.

For Conrad-Martius, any embodied being, including plants, practices *excarnation*, namely an unfolding out into its body. She defines *excarnation* as the "leibhaft selbstlose Hinausgestaltung des Ursprungsselbstes in der Form einer arttypischen Stoffsubstanz" (1960, 51). Incarnation, in contrast, refers to the further ability to live into one's body, as is the case for all animals, albeit not for plants, partly because it requires the ability to initiate movement in active, but not necessarily conscious, ways. She defines *incarnation* as the "leibhaft selbsthafte Hineingestaltung des Ursprungsselbst in sich selbst" (ibid.). Thus, both are embodied (*leibhaft*), but one is without an explicit self or detached from it (*selbstlos*), the other attaches to or lives as a self (*selbsthaft*).[7] The former moves or develops out (*hinaus*) into the bodily members, the latter moves and develops deeply into them (*hinein*) so as to dwell within them. Incarnation allows the self to assume a "center" within the body (*Leib*) from which to shape its own dwelling (*in sich selbst*) as its embodied existence. This is how it can be truly "there" (*da*) and become an "aktuelles *Da*sein" (1960, 52, her emphasis). She speaks of these as forms of manifestation and potencies that allow a working out (*werkzeuglich*), rather than static entities.

Conrad-Martius strongly opposes Heidegger's limiting the notion of *Dasein* to human existence alone.[8] While she applauds his broadening of Husserl's account of human consciousness for a return to "being," she firmly insists that many other beings in the world also exist and are not mere objects in the way Heidegger suggests. Only divine being is its own existence. She particularly objects to his strong divisions between *Zuhandenheit, Vorhandenheit,* and *Existenz/Dasein.* Animals and plants are not simply "present" but also maintain relationships with their own bodies. Although she employs the traditional language of "body," "soul," and "spirit," her account of plant, animal, and human existence is deeply phenomenological in its depiction of how those bodies are inhabited and lived without collapsing all distinctions between beings. Thus, although Conrad-Martius certainly distinguishes among the various kinds of living beings, her account also allows for significant continuity and similarity between them, without assimilating their forms of embodiment into a single version, even as it seeks to identify the phenomenological nature (*Wesen*) of body. Tactile and spatial being is shared by all animals and yet lived somewhat differently by each kind, depending on their particular constitution and environment.[9] She also does not simply lump all animals together, but outlines significant differences between one-celled organisms, insects, mammals, and so forth. This does not simplistically oppose the human to the animal, as in so much of the philosophical tradition, but shows continuity of development and forms of embodiment, informed by insights from biology and other relevant sciences. Although Conrad-Martius herself does not take her insights in an ecological direction, her phenomenological explorations of nature do open the possibility of providing a broader account of ecological embodiment that is not limited solely to the human and thus holds promise for Kearney's wish for greater inter-species connection.

Unlike Kearney, for whom the hospitable dimensions of touch are at the forefront, she does not draw out any ethical implications of her analysis of sensory being. In his various discussions of "carnal hermeneutics" Kearney focuses especially on the hands and the mouth, showing how handshakes and the sharing of food express and even embody a hospitable welcome to others that is sometimes able to overcome hostility and trauma (Kearney and Fitzpatrick 2021, 50–57). His account of "embodied hospitality" similarly stresses the handshake and the importance of "tact" in terms of an emphasis on the "tactile."[10] Even more fully, his discussion of touch points to the possibilities of tactile therapies as ways of fostering healing and other forms of healing touch, including in cases of trauma. Without touch we lose our connection to the world and are unable to reconnect to it after traumatic experiences: "If we lose touch with ourselves, we lose touch with the world" (Kearney 2021, 101). Children have to be touched, held, and caressed to flourish. Tactile therapies can help in cases of physical, mental, and emotional illness. Walking may contribute to the "reintegration of head and heart, mind and body, spirit and flesh" (2021, 106). Kearney stresses the need for "healing contact" in response to hostility and marginalization: "we need to replace handguns with handshakes" (2021, 106). While all this shows the crucial ethical contribution touch and other forms of sensory attentiveness can make to human wellbeing, it says very little about ethical implications for non-human creatures.[11] Can beings without hands offer hospitality? Can we extend ethical hospitality to creatures we are accustomed to eat?

Conrad-Martius' phenomenological account of embodiment reminds us that embodied touch goes far beyond the human use of the hand, as evident already in the reaching up of plants and the movements of animals. We share sensory substructures with many other creatures that allow us to experience life in vibrant and vivid ways. Could this enable a more hospitable welcome to them that recognizes our shared, yet different, forms of embodiment? Kearney worries about the technology that makes a virtual world more real than the physical world and has us interact primarily with disembodied surrogates rather than actual human beings (Kearney 2021, 113–140). Yet this technology also removes us increasingly from our other-species kin, not to speak of the fact that its manufacture—especially digging for rare earth metals, disposing of rapidly obsolete technological gadgets, etc.—leads to widespread destruction of habitat and the wholesale elimination of species at an absolutely unprecedented rate. This constitutes not only an "eclipse" of the "human stranger" (2021, 123), but often entails the complete annihilation of many other earthly "strangers." As Kearney notes, it impacts our lives profoundly, makes them much less "natural" and healthy, but also leads to profound consequences for many other living beings.[12] Can a "carnal hospitality" give us an ethics of and for all creatures, an ethics "in touch" with the world and all its inhabitants?[13] A phenomenological account of the many and varied ways of dwelling in the world and within the self, such as that proposed by Conrad-Martius, wedded to Kearney's ethical concerns but broadened significantly beyond their focus on the human, may well play an important role in such endeavor.

Transcendence and Retroscendence: For an Embodied Hermeneutics

Kearney initially explores the importance of embodiment and especially the notion of touch in the context of hermeneutic discernment. Diacritical hermeneutics is "carnal" hermeneutics, inasmuch as it is embodied and linked to "sense" or "savvy," to "taste" or "tact" (Kearney 2011, 4; 2012, 182). He insists that such a hermeneutic approach goes "all the way down" by referring to how our bodies discern at the most basic level (2012, 181; 2015, 15). Indeed, it is "both sacred and terrestrial," reaching up and down (2011, 3; 2012, 180). He frequently points out that touch is the most universal sense and that our bodies are both sites of exposure—thus showing our fragility and vulnerability—and of knowledge, because it is through them that we experience and explore the world (Kearney 2015, 15–19; 2021, 9–32; Kearney and Fitzpatrick 2021, 50). He calls taste "the most primordial sense of carnal hermeneutics" as exemplified also by the many narratives of food and eating so central to accounts of hospitality in many traditions (2012, 182–184; 2021, 20–21). In *Touch* (2021), he explores various dimensions of touch as tact in sensory fashion, including savvy, flair, insight, and resonance (10–31). All are sensory forms of knowing; they both require and enable discernment. Merleau-Ponty serves as a guide for this discriminating perception lodged in our bodily existence and its sensory capacities (2012, 185–187; 2021, 33–60).[14] Kearney's interest here is primarily hermeneutic, not phenomenological, although he does sometimes express the hope that such carnal hermeneutics might bridge the gap between the two by opening "a door where phenomenology and hermeneutics might cross in the swing door of the flesh" (2015, 55).[15] Conrad-Martius' phenomenology could provide an additional interlocutor and some further phenomenological substance to the account of human embodiment that might enable us to walk more deliberately through this hermeneutic door.

It is obviously not sufficient simply to point to our embodiment or the importance of touch, but one must also unfold phenomenologically how this allows for a fully embodied constitution of the self. This requires an account of our relationship to our bodies that neither leaves them behind nor reduces us purely to body or flesh.[16] The assumption in much of the phenomenological tradition, from at least Heidegger onward, is that we *are* bodies rather than having bodies. Conrad-Martius strongly insists otherwise: we are not reducible to our bodies. All animals, including the human animal, *have* bodies and are able to establish relations with them as selves.[17] Despite all the crucial phenomenological insights about our sensory embodiment, especially through the notion of touch, we do not experience the world *only* through physical touch, but—as Kearney frequently points out—also linguistically, narratively, and reflectively. These cannot be wholly separated from touch and other sensory experience; we cannot leave our bodies behind, but we are also not only a purely physical manifestation of bodily processes or firing neurons.[18] This is sometimes forgotten or suppressed in all the eagerness to overcome strict Cartesian mind-body distinctions and to provide a postmodern account of the flesh against the modern overemphasis on a disembodied intellect (sometimes read back into the sources, which are rarely as simplistically dualistic or inattentive to the body as they are often caricatured as being). Conrad-Martius maintains this carefully calibrated tension in her phenomenological account of embodiment that does not reduce the human to "mere" body.

As already noted repeatedly, she establishes significant continuity between human and non-human animals. Let us now turn to some of the distinctions she draws between them in order to explore the specific ways in which humans live their embodiment. Conrad-Martius insists that every animal being (*animalisches Wesen*) is able to form and inhabit its own body, which turns a "körperliche Ausgestaltung" (bodily fashioning) into a true "Leiblichkeit" (embodiment or bodiliness). All animals, including the human, inhabit their bodies, dwell within them, and make them their own (via the soul). In the human—in contrast to both non-human animals and disembodied spirits—this relation "back" is doubled (what she calls *Retroszendenz*); it is an "*absolute* inner form of backward transcendence" that is fully "immanent" (1960, 10; her emphasis). We are *within* our bodies but also relate to them as *Leib* by living them. Animals do this in a "sichhaft" way while humans are able to do it in an "ichhaft" way. That is to say, animals experience themselves as a self (*sich*) that allows them to "own" their bodies or be attached to them (*haften*), but humans in addition experience their own I (*ich*) in a fuller sense than is the case for other animals. We live our psyche or soul in "sichhaft" fashion, our Geist in an "ichhaft" manner (1960, 59). Animals are able to be sad, joyful, angry, depressed, fearful, etc., but the human can establish a relation to or take a position in regard to feeling sad, joyful, angry, depressed, fearful, and so forth (1960, 59–60). The animal has recognition and a measure of transcendence—the dog realizes that the owner's picking up hat and leash means a walk outdoors—but this recognition and self-transcendence involves no distance, no relation to the fact "as such" (1960, 60). The human does not only have affects, but is able to establish a relation to these affects (1960, 61). She is clear, however, that the distinction between *sichhaft* and *ichhaft* does not run within the human in some sort of schizophrenic fashion, but that the human *ichhaft* nature always already shapes its affective expressions (ibid.). The human "excarnates and incarnates" in an "ichhaft" manner (1960, 62). This can help us to unfold phenomenologically how human touch is lived in "tactful" and discerning ways that might differ from those of other species.

Similar to her claims about body and soul, she points out that it is not correct to say that the human *is* spirit, but rather that humans *own* their spirit. She insists that "this is something wholly different" (1960, 11). Humans can raise themselves from their own embodied depth to themselves and thus become a true "I-self" (*Ichselbst*) (ibid.). Yet in no way is the body left behind in this experience of the self as I. She is quite emphatic that Heidegger's account of Dasein is phenomenologically insufficient because it treats our affective embodied being as a mere "appendix" to our spirit and does not "build it up from" our embodied nature (*von der Leiblichkeit her auferbaut*) (1960, 12). Conrad-Martius distinguishes four foundations of usable potencies (*werkzeugliche Potenzgrundlagen*) for human embodiment, which here she calls physical material (*das Urmaterielle* or *Subphysische*), physical ethereal (*das Urätherische* or *Superphysische*), affective-psychical (*das Urpsychische* or *Subpsychische*), and spirited/geistig (*das Urgeistige* or *Superpsychische*) (1960, 19–20). A self only has a psyche if it can draw within itself and has an inner "space" in which it can dwell and which it can fashion. Embodiment thus is literally an in-bodiment (*Innerung*). This is an absolute inner space that allows all animals to own and inhabit their bodies, although different species of animals do so differently and the "inner space" (*Innenraum*) is more fully expressed and fashioned in more complex animals. The human "affect-soul" allows for the same kind of inner embodiment.

Analogously, the soul can realize or actualize (*verwirklichen/aktualisieren*) itself also in two-fold fashion: one more passive and material, the other more active and guiding its own process of actualization. She refers to the first with the term psyche (*das Urpsychische*) and the second with that of spirit (*das Urgeistige*). Phenomenologically speaking, the first "sinks down" into itself (it manifests in a *Versenkungsdynamis*), while the latter rises up from itself (it manifests as an *Enthebungsdynamis*). It is important to stress that this does not entail a separation of the soul or spirit from the body, but ways of dwelling within and inhabiting the body. Even the spirit's "rising" is a rising in, with, and for the body, not an artificial separation from it. The body is never left behind, but continues to operate as our most fundamental dwelling place, even if humans are able to dwell in it and inhabit it in ways that can be distinguished phenomenologically from the modes of indwelling or inhabiting that other beings exercise or manifest (and these distinctions are not absolute but proceed along a spectrum of increasing complexification). She stresses that these are forms of actualization and manifestation. The spirit is experienced via its rising and relating; it is not some "thing" separate from these forms of manifestation and self-realization (1960, 21). This is precisely an account of how activities of the spirit—such as discernment or flair—might be concretely embodied in tactile and sentient ways.

For example, she describes in several places psychosomatic manifestations of joy or fear. Someone who has an experience of sudden joy may clap, jump up and down, have a radiant expression, feel chest and heart broaden or enlarge, spread arms as if to embrace the whole world. A sudden shock can "turn someone to stone," arms are crossed with hands turned inward, one's eyes seem to expand and almost start out of one's head, hair is standing on end, and the blood drains from the cheeks. Fear is expressed through holding one's breath, becoming tense, pulling one's eyebrows together, and so forth (Conrad-Martius 1965, 127). Thus, she concludes, "one shrinks in fear internally *and* externally, is widened and lifted by joy internally *and* externally, is moved by affect internally *and* externally" (ibid., her emphases). She stresses that the inner affect is clearly expressed in these bodily physiological manifestations and yet not reducible to them, because one may suppress one's bodily expression of anger (such as a clenched fist or facial expressions) or other emotions (1965, 127–128). We are fully embodied and experience ourselves through bodily responses and processes, yet we *are not only* body, but *have* body, are in relation to it yet never without it. The physical realities serve as foundation or condition: although we can think about and wish to lift our arm, we cannot actually do so if it has been paralyzed by an accident or is impeded by other physical limitations. She speaks of our "Selbstdurchwohnung des eigenen Leibes," that is, the "living throughout" (or permeating) as a "self" of one's own body (1965, 131). Thus, the soul's relation to the body is not some artificial connection to be laboriously established, but so fully wrapped up in the body that thinking them separately becomes almost impossible (1965, 131–132).[19] In a sense this is the other "side" of Kearney's emphasis on the embodiment of savvy or insight, stressing their physical and neuronal substructure.

These "inner" and "outer" relations to the body are not relative to each other, but of a different kind: the interiority of the self she describes is an "absolute" or "independent" inner space, yet not in a radically different sense of spatiality than the corporeal manifestations (Conrad-Martius 1965, 133). One can feel "down" or oppressed, be elated or superficial, soft or hard, tightening up or widening out—these are still spatial in a certain sense and "make room," but in an affective, not necessarily physical, sense, although they can also manifest or be expressed physically (133). Even these affective expressions and experiences require muscles and other physical substructures. If the physical is throttled, the emotional dimension is often also cut off (134). The human requires a body (*Leib*) in order to feel affect; "mere soul" is impossible (135).[20] Through these biological, physical, chemical, and evolutionary substructures, the human self emerges and manifests in individualized fashion, that is, as a self (*Ursprungsselbst*). The self is thus shaped by its genetic make-up, its racial, ethnic, gender, and other determinations, which permit it to live in its own particularized fashion (1960, 30). She refuses a purely causal account of genetic determination or materialist conceptions, but she also rejects a simplistic theological account of traducian or creationist versions of the soul (1960, 30–42).[21]

The spirit, as intellect, understanding, reasoning, etc., can elevate itself above this, thus transcend its bodily and affective being, albeit without leaving them behind (Conrad-Martius 1965, 138). The being of spirit is always a kind of "having" or of being "alongside" rather than full submersion. Unlike animals, we can think about our thinking, understand our understanding, and thus establish a kind of distance from it (in the sense of distinction from or freedom in regard to it). This "existential freedom" should not be absolutized, however, as she thinks occurs in existential philosophy (especially Heidegger and Jaspers), which, she contends, is why they are unable to provide a convincing account of corporeality or embodiment (ibid.). She puts it pithily by insisting that "if one cannot furrow one's brow, one is unable to brood or ponder" (1965, 139). The spirit is completely dependent on the proper functioning of its corporeal substructures. Mental processes like abstraction, synthesis, categorization, imagination, or memory are impossible without the corresponding neuronal activity and relevant brain areas (ibid.). At the same time, she acknowledges that this is a more complex relationship than that of the affect-soul to the lived body. And obviously the spirit is also firmly connected to the affective soul and not only to the lived body (1965, 140). This exemplifies a "deep interwovenness" (*tiefe Verflochtenheit*) between these various dimensions (i.e., "Leiblichem, Leibseelischem, affektiv Seelischem und Geistigem"), such that it is one and the same self that experiences them (ibid.). My body is not an "it" that a soul and a spirit directs, but I am one whole: *I* decide, think, sense, act, move as an embodied, ensouled, affected, "spirited" self. The capacity for these abilities ("das Vermögen zu all diesen Vermögen") lies within the self as its source (1965, 141). This *Ursprungsselbst* makes a body a specific lived body of not just any human, but of this particular person, here and now (ibid.). In hermeneutic terms, one might say that it provides the horizon or ground for our concretely and variously embodied condition.

Thus, although Conrad-Martius speaks of an "inner space" for the soul (*Seelenraum*), she is clear that this is not a literal physical space that one could locate in surgery, but that the psyche reaches through the entire body and "feels" its affect throughout the body (1960, 69). Similarly, although she describes the function of spirit primarily in its ability to rise up from and maintain a relation with the body, it does have a physical substructure in the brain and cannot exist without it, at least in humans (1960, 70). It is neither reducible to the brain (she is quite clear that *Geist* is not simply mind) nor separable from it (except possibly in death). If the brain is harmed in an illness or accident, impairment of thinking and feeling results (1960, 71). Birth, development, growth, and so forth all require the physical, chemical, and molecular processes without which no being can exist.[22] This is not a mere physiological-psychological development, but an actualization of the four material grounds/foundations of potency explored earlier in progressive fashion: both the twofold self-detaching into the external and the twofold self-attaching into the interior ("der nach aussen hin zweifachen selbstlosen [Ausgestaltungsbereiche], der nach innen hin zweifachen selbsthaften") (1960, 73). It is a fully embodied development that is always also an affective and psychic one. The human is an integrally embodied being whose "substantiality" requires a "physical-embodied formation" (*physisch-leibliche Ausgestaltung*) (1960, 74). Although "personal life" is most fully expressed in the deepest and innermost life of affect and spirit, it cannot exist or experience without psychosomatic embodiment in all its enfleshed, incarnate, and "excarnate" aspects. Thus, our ontology, even in a phenomenological sense, cannot be thought without biology, morphology, genetics, and other insights from the natural sciences, even if phenomenology is able to explore more fundamental questions about these issues (such as their *Wesen* or nature) than those considered by the natural sciences themselves (1965, 381–384).

Although Conrad-Martius' phenomenological explication is obviously deeply informed by the biological and physiological insights of her day and thus presumably requires at least some updating, this close attention to the natural sciences is also one of the strengths of her account. Her analysis of human embodiment collapses neither into a Cartesian dualism nor into phenomenological poeticizing without relation to other forms of scientific knowledge, as one sometimes has the impression in Heidegger or other "continental" treatments. In this regard, her phenomenological account can make a contribution to Kearney's emphasis on our sensory existence and provide a substantive phenomenological grounding for it. At the same time Kearney's more hermeneutic and ethical "angle" might allow us to extend her phenomenological insights beyond her more explicitly "ontological" interests. Her account of the intimate links between *Leib*, *Seele*, and *Geist* can provide a fuller account for how the "knowing" of the body, to which Kearney points repeatedly, actually operates, thus showing how hermeneutics does, in fact, "go all the way down." Maybe this "down" could be explicated in terms of her description of the affect-soul as sinking into the body or lowering itself into it, permeating it entirely into its outermost tips, but also creating a space within it from which it can be directed and moved to action. Carnal hermeneutics may go all the way in, all the way down, but also all the way up, because we can only know as complexly and completely embodied creatures whose embodiment is simultaneously mediated through its relation to its bodily being through affect, thought, creativity, and so forth. Are tact, savvy, flair, insight, or resonance purely bodily processes? They are ways in which our affect and spirit are embodied, in which affect lives and moves its body, spirit directs and interacts with its body, while also being themselves sustained and enabled by it.

In Conrad-Martius, the accounts of human embodiment and that of all living beings are closely connected. The consideration of animals or plants or the environment as a whole is not a different topic we consider in some context or discipline separate from our attempts to know who we are. We always are with and besides other creatures, dwelling on the same earth that sustains similar bodily and affective processes and ways of being, in each case subtly adapted to the particular kind and make-up of each being. Although she does not extend this into an ethical account of ecological companionship or a consciously hermeneutic treatment of embodiment, the potential is there. Conversely, while the phenomenological and ontological structures of embodiment are not yet as fully developed by Kearney, the ethical and the hermeneutic dimensions are always closely connected: carnal hermeneutics leads to carnal hospitality; carnal hospitality requires carnal hermeneutics. This similarly holds promise for a fuller discussion of ecological hospitality and carnal discernment. Kearney's accounts of tact thus can show more fully how the embodiment Conrad-Martius describes works hermeneutically and epistemologically—and how it might be extended ethically. Bringing the philosophical insights of both thinkers together can help us think more fully and deeply about the being and wellbeing of all embodied creatures on this earth.

Notes

1 Brian Treanor in his contribution is right to criticize the strong hermeneutic emphasis on language and to call for non-textual and non-linguistic understandings of otherness, especially in regard to empathy with non-humans.

2 Or is changed significantly. See Tamsin Jones' timely reflections (in the present volume) on the spectacle presented to the technological gaze, especially for instances of trauma.

3 This is worked out most fully in her *Metaphysische Gespräche* (Conrad-Martius 1921, 3–25). See also the essays collected in *Schriften zur Philosophie III*, especially "Seele und Leib" (1965, 107–124) and "Die menschliche Seele" (1965, 125–143). Although Conrad-Martius thinks of the line between animal and human as absolute in her earlier work, she is more tentative about transitions between species in her later work—freely admitting that her earlier statements went too far and do not square with biological and evolutionary insights—and in this respect her account has potential for thinking of the human as fully part of the natural order in an ecological sense. In this regard, it might also be able to contribute to Treanor's and Fitzgerald's attempts to explore the possibility of empathy or sympathy with animals and the natural world in their respective contributions to the present volume.

4 The dialogue partners in these conversations are very clear that these are phenomenological thought experiments to get at questions of nature or kind (*Wesen*), not claims about actual empirical existence of such beings. (She does, however, in this context provide an interesting discussion of "depth"—distinguishing between *Tiefe* and *Untiefe*—that might be of relevance to Dan Bradley's exploration of this theme in Kearney's narrative work. Her account of the demonic might also be able to provide some relevant phenomenological categories for Brian Gregor's analysis in the present volume.)

5 For a discussion that complicates the traditional accounts of distinctions between soul and body, see Murray Littlejohn's contribution to this volume.

6 One might be able to simplify her terminology by referring to them as *Leib, Seele, Gemüt, Geist,* and *Selbst,* although that would ontologize her more relational categories. Conrad-Martius herself does not use the term *Gemüt* in this context, but sometimes identifies the *Gefühlsseele* with the heart (1949, 135). (On the heart, see also brief comments in 1921, 240–241; 1949, 135; 1960, 75–76; 1965, 419.) This might also provide interesting possibilities for Neal DeRoo's attempt (in this volume) to negotiate carnality and materiality phenomenologically beyond the distinction between *Leib* and *Körper* for an account of personhood.

7 In fact, "selbstlos" might be better translated as "self-loosening" or "self-detaching," because "selbsthaft" means something like "self-adhering" or "self-attaching" (Conrad-Martius 1960, 73).

8 See her review of *Being and Time* and various other essays (1963, 185–193, 194–227; 1965, 403–420). She frequently makes this comment as an aside also in other contexts (e.g. 1963, 421–423; 1965, 371–373, 393). Her own writings

on "being" (1957) and "time" (1954), both preceding Heidegger's work but published later, are also relevant. Her *Realontologie* (1924) was published as a Festschrift for Husserl's 60th birthday as Vol. VI of the *Jahrbuch für Philosophie und phänomenologische Forschung. Sein und Zeit* appeared as Vol. VIII of the same series.

9 In several essays, she interacts with the claims of evolutionary biology regarding whether it is the species that shapes its environment or the environment that shapes the development of the species. Early 20th-century biology for the most part defended the latter, but Conrad-Martius wants them to consider the former—and draws on biological research to make her point.

10 The chapter included in *Radical Hospitality* (2021, 49–57) focuses exclusively on the handshake; the earlier version that combines linguistic and carnal hospitality is slightly broader.

11 He briefly summarizes in an appendix Richard Louv's discussion of a kind of mutual attunement between some humans and animals, but this is still primarily about the implications for human therapy/healing (Kearney 2021, 110–111). See Treanor's and Fitzpatrick's contributions in the present volume for a fuller account.

12 Better art or "ana-technology" does not seem a sufficient solution to this (cf. Kearney 2021, 130–131, 137–139).

13 This raises the question of whether such an ethics of hospitality must always be reciprocal (albeit not necessarily symmetrical), as Kearney suggests. He argues that "the carnal gesture of hospitality does not entail a reduction of guest to host, nor a surrender of guest to host—but a sharing across differences" and that "true hospitality" is an exchange "between similar and similar" (Kearney and Fitzpatrick 2021, 56). Are the differences between human and non-human beings or the risk involved in extending hospitality too great to allow for ethical hospitality in Kearney's sense? (Treanor raises this question more trenchantly and more fully.)

14 Kearney also points out that it is important to know "when *not* to speak or when *not* to touch." Carnal hermeneutics "invigilates the limits of the sayable and tangible" (2019, 86). In fact, touch is handled quite differently in different cultures. Therefore, "we need a 'pedagogy of tact' regarding modalities of contact" (ibid.).

15 He suggests that his reading in *Touch* (2021) is "phenomenological" (34), but explicates it primarily in hermeneutic ways (39). He goes on to focus again on ethical ramifications (44–45), before returning briefly to a summary of Husserl's and Merleau-Ponty's phenomenology (46–49) and to Irigaray's and Kristeva's psychoanalysis (50–51), culminating in a "reading" of the body (52). For a much fuller account of Kearney's notions of touch and embodiment, see James Taylor's contribution to the present volume. For a more detailed discussion of the hermeneutic dimension and the need for bodily attunement, see the contribution by Christopher Yates.

16 See DeRoo's contribution to the present volume for one attempt to do so.

17 Interestingly, she claims that it might be more correct to say that the animal "is" soul—rather than "having" a soul—because animals are not able to separate themselves from their soul but are fully immersed in it; they have no experiential standpoint that allows them to stand over against it in the way in which the human does, just as plants have no experiential standpoint vis-à-vis their bodies in the way in which all animals, including the human, do. Plants in some sense "are" bodies rather than "having" them as animals do via their souls (Conrad-Martius 1963, 418).

18 Conrad-Martius does entertain the possibility that a self might "leave" its body in pathology, religiously ecstatic experience, schizophrenia, or ultimately in death. This might suggest—although she obviously does not explore this in the early 20th century—that our current virtual existence (what Kearney calls "excarnation") promotes a form of body-separated or at least body-poor pathology. (On this issue, see Jones' contribution to the present volume.) In this case, the personal self would become unable to guide or govern its body; spirit and body would become separated and attempt to act independently of each other (1949, 135).

19 She speaks of them as "felted" together (*verpfilzt*), a process in which no seams remain, but the two materials become completely one and create a much sturdier material (Conrad-Martius 1965, 131).

20 She does sometimes envision that such a body might not be purely material but that one could think an "ethereal body," which might explain paranormal experiences like telepathy or other forms of "seeing" without mediation of the senses (Conrad-Martius 1921, 135). She is quite clear, however, that although there can be spirits (*Geister*) without bodies, there is no such thing as a disembodied soul; the soul cannot exist without a body. She does also in some contexts consider divine embodiment. God exists "leibhaftig" (1921, 67). Here *Leibhaftigkeit* means *Wirklichkeit*: "zum leibhaften Wesen gehört jedoch an und für sich seine Offenbarungsmöglichkeit" (1921, 69).

21 She insists that any theologically interested account must square with the biological realities, just as any biological account must do justice to our lived experience as unique individuals.

22 For a far more detailed account of this, see her lectures series "Der Mensch in der heutigen Naturwissenschaft und Philosophie" (Conrad-Martius 1963, 363–426).

References

Conrad-Martius, Hedwig. 1921. *Metaphysische Gespräche*. Halle: Verlag Max Niemeyer.

Conrad-Martius, Hedwig. 1924. *Realontologie*. Halle: Verlag Max Niemeyer.

Conrad-Martius, Hedwig. 1938. *Ursprung und Aufbau des lebendigen Kosmos*. Salzburg: O. Müller.

Conrad-Martius, Hedwig. 1949. *Bios und Psyche*. Hamburg: Claassen & Coverts.

Conrad-Martius, Hedwig. 1954. *Die Zeit*. Munich: Kösel Verlag.

Conrad-Martius, Hedwig. 1957. *Das Sein*. Munich: Kösel Verlag.

Conrad-Martius, Hedwig. 1960. *Die Geistseele des Menschen*. Munich: Kösel Verlag.

Conrad-Martius, Hedwig. 1961. *Der Selbstaufbau der Natur*. 2nd edition. Munich: Kösel Verlag.

Conrad-Martius, Hedwig. 1963. *Schriften zur Philosophie*, vol. I. Munich: Kösel Verlag.

Conrad-Martius, Hedwig. 1964. *Schriften zur Philosophie*, vol. II. Munich: Kösel Verlag.

Conrad-Martius, Hedwig. 1965. *Schriften zur Philosophie*, vol. III. Munich: Kösel Verlag.

Kearney, Richard. 1999. "Narrative and the Ethics of Remembrance." In *Questioning Ethics: Contemporary Debates in Philosophy*, edited by Richard Kearney and Mark Dooley, 18–32. London: Routledge.

Kearney, Richard. 2008. "Narrating Pain: The Ethics of Catharsis." In *Difficulties of Ethical Life*, edited by Shannon Sullivan and Dennis Schmidt, 181–194. New York: Fordham University Press.

Kearney, Richard. 2010. "Imagining the Sacred Stranger: Hostility or Hospitality?" In *Politics and the Religious Imagination*, edited by John H.A. Dyck, Paul S. Rowe, and Jens Zimmermann, 15–30. London: Routledge.

Kearney, Richard. 2011. "What Is Diacritical Hermeneutics?" *Journal of Applied Hermeneutics* vol. 1 (December): 1–14.

Kearney, Richard. 2012. "Diacritical Hermeneutics." In *Hermeneutic Rationality*, edited by Maria Luisa Protocarrero, Luis Antonio Umbelino, and Andrzej Wiercinski, 177–196. Berlin: Lit Verlag.

Kearney, Richard. 2015. "The Wager of Carnal Hermeneutics." In *Carnal Hermeneutics*, edited by Richard Kearney and Brian Treanor, 15–56. New York: Fordham University Press.

Kearney, Richard. 2019. "Double Hospitality: Between Word and Touch." *Journal for Continental Philosophy of Religion* vol. 1, no. 1: 71–89.

Kearney, Richard. 2021. *Touch: Recovering Our Most Vital Sense*. New York: Columbia University Press.

Kearney, Richard and Melissa Fitzpatrick. 2021. *Radical Hospitality: From Thought to Action*. New York: Fordham University Press.

Part II

Touching the Sacred

Carnal Sacrality: Phenomenology, the Sacred, and Material Bodies in Richard Kearney

Neal DeRoo

The main thesis of this chapter is that Richard Kearney's work on touch grows out of problematics that Kearney has been wrestling with for decades, and its full significance for our engagement with the world emerges more clearly if we can situate it vis-à-vis some of those larger issues. More specifically, *Touch: Recovering Our Most Vital Sense* (2021) hinges on a certain presumed understanding of the material make-up of our world that Kearney never fully thematizes, but which is the background for his work on both religion and the carnal. It is this presumed understanding—which I will call "carnal sacrality"—that I want to bring to light, showing its continuity with Kearney's work as a whole.

Overall, I take Kearney's work to be characterized by two related impulses: first, the movement of the "ana" (returning to X after X has been critiqued, deconstructed, or problematized within a particular tradition); second, this movement's being carried out in service of healing (being better able to navigate our world in ethical, other- and self-honoring ways).[1] In light of this, one might wonder about the carnality that is being returned to in "anacarnation": how is carnality being "returned to" (from where to where), and how is this meant to help us live in healthy ways in the world? I will endeavor to answer this via a kind of ana-retrieval of the bond or relation between carnality[2] and sacrality within the realm of Kearney's thought itself,[3] though certainly not for the benefit of Kearney's thought alone. Once the dualistic dichotomy between the sacred and the carnal is problematized, a "new" notion of the relation between sacrality and carnality can be recovered—what I will call "carnal sacrality"—that maintains the possibility of properly honoring both the (ethical and religious) Other and the self.

This notion of "carnal sacrality" is not itself the explicit focus of any of Kearney's work to date, but rather functions as the philosophical background of his work. It emerges out of (and helps us contextualize) several important moments in Kearney's oeuvre. The first of these is the self-described "phenomenological" distinction between *persona* and the (empirical) person, which we will see is primarily a methodological

DOI: 10.4324/9781003285649-7

(rather than an ontological or ethical) distinction (Section I). The two are mutually coordinated as asymmetrical elements of our phenomenal experience, thereby clarifying the expressive nature of this distinction as a phenomenological distinction (Section II). This, in turn, enables us to clarify Kearney's use of the "fourth reduction" as a methodological principle (Section III), a principle that can then be applied beyond the *persona*-person distinction to the sacrality-carnality distinction more broadly: carnal hermeneutics is therefore shown as a mere prolegomenon to "carnal sacrality" (Section IV). From this, the implications of "carnal sacrality" for a healthier religious living can be laid out: rather than simply being asked to "acknowledge" the sacred or "perform" the sacred, religious living is revealed to be an expressive endeavor in which we are (poietically, and not simply cognitively) attuned to the sacred in and through our everyday interactions with the world (Section V).

The Persona and the Person

We begin, then, with the distinction Kearney makes between the *persona* and the person. The former refers to "the otherness of the other," that "eschatological aura of 'possibility' that eludes but informs a person's actual presence here and now" (Littlejohn 2020, 171), while the latter refers to "my fellow insofar as he/she is the same or similar to me (empirically, biologically, psychologically, etc.)" (171).[4] This distinction is necessary and crucial for Kearney: the *persona* safeguards "the inimitable and unique singularity" of the other (171) and so preserves the possibility of an ethical relation with the other. Yet if we overvalue the *persona* and fail to adequately account for the empirical nature of the other qua person, we threaten to idolize or divinize them, and thereby lose their concrete singularity: we value the Other, but not *this* particular other (person) currently before me. As Kearney sums up the tension: "we disregard others not just by ignoring their *transcendence* but equally by ignoring their *flesh-and-blood thereness*" (172), and this is why he insists on the necessity of both the *persona* and the person.[5]

But it is not always easy to pinpoint precisely how we are to understand the relation between the *persona* and the person. On the one hand, the *persona* seems to define me in my "thisness," my haecceity (174–175). But on it is own, this would leave us with a strange result: what makes me *me*, what defines me as *this* person rather than *that* person (or simply as (a) person), seems to have nothing to do with any of the empirical, biological, or psychological particulars of my life. While this is plausible in one sense, insofar as the *persona* stands in for the alterity of the other itself, and hence cannot be defined by any one particular character trait of any one particular other, in another sense it seems counter-intuitive to say that what makes me me, my utmost "thisness," is simply that I am "other."

But rather than absolutizing our thisness, perhaps we are to understand the *persona*-person relationship as a kind of "this-ifying" of alterity, an inscription of alterity always already within particular conditions such that alterity is not absolute, but always conditioned. In this other way of making sense of the *persona*-person relation, then, we encounter a profound rethinking of the relationship between "transcendent" conditions (like Alterity, Otherness, etc.) and what they condition (like empirical, flesh-and-blood people). Here, the *persona* is neither identical with our person-ness (for then the distinction between *persona* and person would not be necessary) nor entirely separable from our person-ness, either.

Kearney struggles, at times, to find the right language with which to articulate this unique nature of the *persona*-person relationship (which, as we will see, stands already for an entire category of fundamental relations: sacrality-carnality, eschatological possibility-everyday actuality, divinity-mundanity, etc.). Often this relation is circumscribed negatively: the *persona* is *not* some ontological character of the person (like a soul), distinct from the "empirical" nature of the person's body; it is *not* itself an individuated entity, unconscious illusion, or idealized "Same-One" (Littlejohn 2020, 176); it is *not* a for-itself-in-itself (177). The positive characterizations of this relation tend to be allusive rather than straightforwardly defined: vis-à-vis the person, the *persona* is "both there and not there, transcendent and immanent, visible and invisible" (177), "an *achronic* figure," a "difference that differentiates itself *ad infinitum*" (178), simultaneously "*no*-one" and "*this* one and no one but this one" (179).

Perhaps the strongest articulation of this relation we get is when, building on Merleau-Ponty, he describes the *persona* as always inscribed in the body as "a singular style and manner of existing that is unique to each person" (Littlejohn 2020, 175). In this sense, the *persona* "can never really exist on its own (*atomon*) but emerges in ethical relation to others" (180), that is, emerges within the person's life as lived. The *persona* is the person *as the unique person they are*, in relation to others, themselves, and the world. The *persona* is not a distinct individual in relation to other individuals or to the person, but precisely, the relating itself at work in the relation: the *persona* is how I live as me in relation to others. The *persona* is therefore not a distinct thing or phenomenon, but a way of looking at phenomena that is not merely a subjective attitude—an "idea," "thought," or intellectual "category"—but a transformative force that differentiates (e.g., *my* life from the life of another) without reifying itself as an ontologically distinct thing or substance. That is to say, the *persona* is simply the person, looked at or considered as absolutely unique, as *this* person (and therefore as other than *that* person).

Persona and/as Expression

Understanding and appreciating the *persona* and its relation to the person therefore emerges as the result of a certain kind of (phenomenological) reduction, and the *persona* is a phenomenological claim whose ethical and religious implications remain to be fully articulated and appreciated. But before we move on to examine the precisely phenomenological nature of the *persona*-person relationship and its implications, it may help us to take a brief detour into expression as a fundamental phenomenological principle. This will ultimately enable us to both better understand the relationship between the *persona* and the person and to articulate the religious implications of that relationship.

Expression is, perhaps, under-appreciated as a fundamental phenomenological principle, but it is fundamental nonetheless.[6] It is significant for our analysis of carnal sacrality in Kearney that the one phenomenological thinker who does more than any other to acknowledge and describe the centrality of expression is the same thinker (Merleau-Ponty) that Kearney invokes in attempting to articulate the relation between the *persona* and the person as described earlier, and whom he describes as "the most important of these [phenomenological] thinkers" when it comes to thinking about touch (Kearney 2021, 48). Indeed, as we will see, clarifying the phenomenological account of expression will help us clarify more precisely how the *persona*-person distinction operates, why it requires a unique kind of "reduction," and how this opens us on to the carnal background of touch.

In brief, expression is the constitution of a "phenomenal unity" (cf. Husserl 2000, 188) between asymmetrical elements (such that I "live through" one so as to "live in" the other; Husserl 2000, 193; see also Husserl, 1989, 248) that are mutually coordinated such that a change in one element necessarily enacts a change in the other. As such, expression functions as a kind of auto-poietic unfolding[7] in which an expression necessarily alters both the expressed and the expressing of it such that a new expression is required to continue to express the expressed, which in turn alters again the expressed and the expressing, leading to another "new" expression, and so on, *ad infinitum*. These alterations are small—infinitesimal[8]—and for the most part pass unnoticed, though occasionally they lead to large and noticeable changes.[9] Regardless, this necessarily ongoing alteration is the engine or force that drives generativity, that is, the unfolding of "new" things and conditions out of actually existing conditions.

Perhaps a quick example will clarify some of the above. The most easily recognizable instance of expression is linguistic expression. As you read this article (for example), the lines on the page *express* to you a particular sense or meaning. You do not pay attention to the lines qua perceptual elements, but rather you "live through" the perceptual elements so as to "live in" the meaning contained therein: your eyes pass over the lines, but what you "see" is the meaning of the words, and that is what you pay attention to. The perceptual elements (e.g., the lines on the page) and the epistemological elements (e.g., the meaning of the words) are presented to you in your experience as a unity—you do not need a second act to say "these lines must mean that," but you simply perceive the meaning in and as the lines; yet, this unity can easily, upon later reflection, be distinguished into its constitutive parts (printer ink on carbon paper, graphemes, meaning, etc.). It is not a unity of identity or of ontology, but simply of experience: a phenomenal unity.

In reading for meaning, you necessarily draw upon all your previous instances of reading words similar to these, and the meanings those words have. This is, partly, what enables you to read them as meaningful so easily and quickly. But in reading the words this time, you add new instances to the background or horizon of meaningful language use that you will draw on the next time you read. This affects both what the words mean and the "expressive" nature of the relationship itself: in reading, you are not merely learning some new insights that are "expressed" in the words, but you are also recasting your sense of the English language (as the horizon in which you make "sense" of these—and other—words). The Saussurian distinction between *langue* and *parole* is instructive here: every present use of language necessarily draws on *langue*, the "system" or "structure" of rules, guidelines, etc. that provide the framework in which any particular use of language (*parole*) can find its meaning. Yet that *langue* is itself determined by previous uses of language (*parole*): the system of *langue* has no other originating source than previous uses of language. The two are mutually coordinated such that a change in one necessarily alters the other, which in turn alters the former, leading yet again to changes in the latter, etc.: you read this article according to the "rules" of language you operate within [*langue*], and this enables you to understand the article as saying something meaningful (a "successful" instance of *parole*). Yet, your reading of the article also, perhaps infinitesimally, alters the "rules" of language you operate within, giving new connotations (and perhaps denotations) to certain terms, altering the possibilities of word combinations, etc. in a way that both requires those "rules" in order to make sense and alters those rules insofar as it *makes* (new) sense.

This mutual coordination is matter of touching and being touched by each other. Hence, when Kearney draws our attention to the way in which our "sense" of touch (as sensation, meaning, and orientation; Kearney 2021, 9) is both shaped by our empirical conditions (e.g., how our current digital age gives us a reduced sense of the importance of touch; Kearney 2021, 2) and itself shapes the transcendental engagements of the world known as visibility (via insight; Kearney 2021, 24–27), smell (via flair; 21–24), taste (via savvy; 17–21), and aurality (via resonance; 27–31), he is making a phenomenological point about both touch (as a distinct sense) and about the expressive nature of our experience as a whole (which is, like touch, always touching and touched-by, always expressively coordinated). This is why experiencing well is a question of "tact," of a "common touch" (Kearney 2021, 10) that is "reciprocal" (11) insofar as it is a "two-way sensation" (12) that "stays in contact" with the world "so we can be touched by [it] in return" (13).

Expression, therefore, operates via a force of unfolding that necessarily draws on certain conditions (like *langue*) that are not simply empirical (*langue* is not a particular use of language, but the rules or guidelines that make possible particular uses of language), even as they are not entirely separable from the empirical, either (*langue* requires *parole* for its sense). Merleau-Ponty uses the notion of *Stiftung* (institution or tradition) to help make sense of this: each of us operates via *Stiftungen* that have historical and empirical provenances, even as they exceed that strictly empirical provenance by offering the conditions or guidelines within which we make sense of the world. The "lifeworld" names the most basic of phenomenological *Stiftung*, the "universal horizon" (Husserl 1970/ 1954, 147) or "horizon of all horizons"[10] that is, nevertheless, necessarily conditioned as this or that lifeworld. The "Greek" or the "Biblical" function, in *Touch*, as two distinct (but overlapping) *Stiftungen* that help form the horizon within which we think (and touch) today.

Empirical facticity, therefore, can be said to express its transcendental conditions, even as those transcendental conditions can also be said to express (if we look at it slightly differently) that empirical facticity: *langue* expresses *parole* when we are "living in" our awareness of *langue* (e.g., when we are doing linguistic analysis), and *parole* expresses *langue* when we are "living in" our awareness of *parole* (e.g., in most "everyday" uses of language).

My claim is that expression also marks the best way for us to understand the relationship between *persona* and person: every person expresses its *persona* as the "singular style and manner of existing that is unique to each person" (Littlejohn 2020, 175), and every *persona* expresses a person as a Person (that is, an Other with an infinite depth, uniqueness, perhaps even a "sacrality" of its own). Hence, *persona* and person are necessarily mutually coordinated to each other, and so mutually affect each other in the ongoing dance that is a person's life (cf. Kearney 2021, 11),[11] and our infinite value, therefore, cannot be divorced from the details of our factical existence because it is necessarily expressed through it. And by "expressed" here, as should be clear, we do not mean simply "made manifest" or "appearing." The *persona* does not simply show up in the person but is constituted or instituted therein: one's depth or ethical worth is not *because of* the things they've done, but it is not *distinct* from those things, either. Rather, the *persona* is touched by the empirical particularities of the person such that our infinite value is what it is because of who we are. The "thisness" that makes us Person (with transcendent value) cannot be distinguished from the "thisness" of our particular empirical details, including the details of our particular, concrete body. Who I am—my haecceity—is not simply the product of my life circumstances (such that anyone who lived through exactly those circumstances would be or become me), nor is it distinct from my life circumstances (such that I would still be who I am if I had undergone different circumstances); rather, who I am—my haecceity—is the value of having lived through those circumstances as a Person who is, necessarily, the expressive coordination of *persona* and person.[12]

The Reduction(s)

Because of that expressive coordination, a Person should be immediately recognized as Person. However, because our phenomenal experience is a series of overlapping expressions, each of which is always (infinitesimally) self-altering, it is not always as simple as that. The theoretical tools which we develop to try to make better sense of our experience inevitably end up shaping or changing that experience (cf. Kearney 2021, 33–34). If our theoretical tools over-emphasize the factical, we may lose sight of the *persona*, and so fail to register the person as Person. Conversely, if our theoretical tools over-emphasize the *Transcendence or Alterity* of the other (as Other, that is, as abstract "transcendence"), we may lose sight of the person, and so fail to register the person before me as Person. This is the tension in the two different ways we can disregard others that we mentioned earlier.

Kearney's emphasis on the *persona*-person distinction is meant to reawaken us to the particular nature of the relationship between those things so that we can again perceive (and not merely theorize) the person before us as Person. To do this, though, Kearney's work must make us aware of the expressive relationship between *persona* and person by helping us see that the two are simultaneously distinct and mutually coordinated in a way that we experience directly, without need of a secondary act of judgment to actualize the coordination: a tactful person is always already "in touch" (Kearney 2021, 14) with the humanity of their interlocutor, "open and vulnerable" (16) to their deep worth and significance through the medium [*metaxu*] of their flesh (37–40).

Recall that, phenomenologically, the experienced unity of mutually coordinated asymmetrical elements is the hallmark of "phenomenal unity." And we have already said that this phenomenal unity is a unity of experience alone: it is not a logical or ontological unity, since its constituent elements can be distinguished via further reflection. The type of reflection that enables us to distinguish these constituent elements of our experience (s) is known, in phenomenology, as the reduction. Via a reduction, the constituent elements of our experience are pried apart (as elements of experience) such that we are lead back to (re-*ducere*) one or another of those elements. Kearney's call for a "fourth" (micro-eschatological) reduction (after the three reductions laid out by Marion[13]), therefore, cannot be separated from his calling us to pay attention to the *persona*-person distinction. The *persona*-person distinction is here revealed to be a uniquely phenomenological distinction: it refers to two different ways of looking at or understanding the Person and not to two different (ontological, ethical, religious, etc.) dimensions of the person. The *persona* and the person are "parallel" categories, having no distinction in content between them, but simply a distinction in phenomenological approach. That is to say, in either case, I approach the whole of the person, in all the particularity of their life: I do not approach, say, their ethical worth or religious value in one category (*persona*) and their factical, "everyday" or quotidian existence in another (person); rather, I see that the two "categories" are experienced, in the moment, simply as the Person, and both refer, ultimately, to the whole of that Person. The only difference between a Person's "everyday" life and their "ethical worth" or "religious value" is a difference in attention that I pay to them: I can apprehend them in a way that puts more weight on one or the other of those things (I can be more "touched" by their deep value and distinct uniqueness in one moment and by the banality of their overwhelming similarities to me as parent, friend, worker, etc., in the next moment), but that is a matter of my apprehension (as a matter of later reflection and judgment) and not a matter of a difference within the Person themselves or my initial experience of them. I do not add any of those things to the Person with my attention (I do not make them have ethical worth or religious value if I choose to apprehend them that way), nor do I subtract any of those things from the Person with my inattention (I do not make their everyday life trivial if I do not pay attention to it). In fact, those things can be distinguished only as features of (my) experience: they are phenomenological elements of an experience of the Person, and not ontological, ethical, or religious elements of the Person itself. Kearney's "phenomenology of the *persona*" is therefore distinctly not a philosophical or theological anthropology of the person.

In calling for a "fourth reduction," Kearney is attempting to help us see the need to re-articulate the expressive relation between *persona* and person as phenomenological elements of our experience. It is an attempt, that is, to have us see in other people "an Other whose very transcendence traverses and invests its immanence here and now" (Littlejohn 2020, 186). The task of the "fourth reduction," then, is not to add something new to the situation, but to see differently what was always already there though perhaps not acknowledged or consciously brought to attention: "there is nothing at all new about the [*persona*] itself. All that is new is our way of *seeing* and *hearing* [and being touched by] it. But it was always already there, summoning us, from the start" (187).

The fourth reduction therefore "leads us back (*re-ducere*) to the *eschaton* curled at the heart of quotidian existence" (Littlejohn 2020, 184). This *eschaton*, in turn, is defined as a "space that makes each reduction possible" because it is itself the "*possibilizing* of essence, being and gift" (187). That is to say, the fourth reduction returns us to the fact that all phenomenological transcendentals (including essence, being and givenness, the points of emphasis of the first three reductions) necessarily emerge, as transcendentals, within historical and empirical circumstances: every *langue* emerges out of *parole*, even as it constitutes that *parole* and therefore remains a (phenomenological) transcendental. That is to say, every transcendental is incarnate through and through, not simply "manifesting" itself in some particular carnal instance, but expressing that carnality in and through its very self. As such, the fourth reduction leads us "back to the everyday" (185), not in the sense of engaging us with the everyday world (for what else could we be engaging with, even when we are performing the reductions?), but in the sense of highlighting the transcendental significance of the everyday, the empirical and concrete, in and for experience itself. So, again, qua reduction, the fourth reduction does not somehow create some "new" significance for the everyday but reveals to us that the everyday has always already been transcendentally significant: transcendental possibilities are always actualized in and out of concrete, particular, historical—that is to say, *carnal*—conditions. "Eschatological possibilizing" is always itself situated in some particular historically carnate community.

This is why Kearney claims that the fourth reduction leads phenomenology back to hermeneutics (Littlejohn 2020, 189). For showing the transcendental necessity that every (transcendental) condition necessarily emerges out of empirical (and therefore carnal) conditions, the fourth reduction makes clear that every phenomenological concept—no matter how universal or transcendental—necessarily emerges within some *Stiftung* or other, and hence can only properly be understood by paying attention to the *Stiftung* in which it emerges. And, qua expressive, the concept does not simply "show up" in a *Stiftung*, but expresses, and thereby (infinitesimally) alters, that *Stiftung*. In doing phenomenological description, then, we are not simply describing our experience but, in describing it as (an) expression, we are necessarily causing it to unfold differently. And because we are inevitably shaping and changing the *Stiftung* and our experience within it in and through our (phenomenological) descriptions of them, the fourth reduction also "signals a return to poetics" (191).

Phenomenology and Sacrality

We see, then, how the *persona*-person distinction has been elaborated as a phenomenological distinction that can only be properly accessed by way of a unique phenomenological reduction. In calling this "fourth" reduction the (micro-) eschatological reduction, Kearney obviously opens the reduction on to a religious register. The "eschatological" space of "possibilizing" that is opened at the heart of all experience—what we in the last section described as the necessity of all experience being transcendentally rooted in empirical carnate circumstances—is here cast explicitly and purposefully in religious terms: the "fourth reduction leads us back ... to a sacred space at the heart of things" (Littlejohn 2020, 190). This is a purposeful hermeneutic move by Kearney. It is intended to help us rethink both religion (in more ethical and carnally situated ways) and experience (in ways that are not restricted to the "physical" but retain a sense at least of the possibility of non-physical meanings or values), as should be clear from Kearney's own attempts to cast this in terms of a "phenomenology of religion" (181).

This double re-thinking is not simply doubled but is itself coordinated: the rethinking of religion is coordinated to the rethinking of experience. We see this in the notion of a "sacred space at the heart of things." Kearney is adamant in distinguishing this "sacred space" from any one particular theological understanding of it (Littlejohn 2020, 192): he is not interested in articulating a Christianized space at the heart of things, or a Buddhist space, but a space that rediscovers "*posse* in *esse*" (193), an "infinite capacity for being" (194).

This "infinite" possibilizing—which is to say, this capacity for things to be other than they are—is ethically and religiously significant: it is a necessary presupposition of any distinction between that which is and that which ought to be, between the good (and bad) that we encounter and live through, and the Good that calls us to something better. It is this that Kearney seems to mean by the sacred. And by showing such sacrality to be "at the heart of things," at the very basis of banal, everyday, quotidian experience, Kearney does with experience what he earlier did with the Person; and shows that our experience of it is not simple, but necessarily requires an expressive coordination of (at least) two mutually asymmetrical elements. Whereas the Person is the name for the expressive coordination of *persona* and person, experience is the expressive coordination of sacrality and materiality. Indeed, this double is, perhaps, not even distinct from the *persona*-person distinction: the *persona* is the sacrality of the Person, necessarily intertwined and coordinated with the "materiality" of the person. But now we see that this "materiality" is itself not strictly physical stuff, nor historical-social meaning: it is the expressive intertwining of both of those, an intertwining that occurs, not simply in *Geist* (in human "mental" or "spiritual" performance) but in carnality itself.

The invocation of carnality is significant, in relation to "flesh." Flesh, of course, is the term Merleau-Ponty uses to refer to the "same stuff" of which both the body and the world are made.[14] Flesh functions, not simply as a transcendental concept, but perhaps an ultra-transcendental concept,[15] depicting the non-empirical conditions that condition transcendental conditions like visibility, tactility, etc. as various "sensings," and condition "the body" as an individualized locus of such sensings. So, while flesh is central to Merleau-Ponty's account of embodiment, qua ultra-transcendental it neglects the actual physical substances that we experience: flesh, as a phenomenological concept, is not the same as the "flesh and blood" of the person here before me.[16] Of course, it is not entirely different from that either: flesh precedes the distinction between living body [*Leib*] and corporeal body [*Körper*], and hence is expressed in each.

Carnality also operates as a kind of phenomenological transcendental. It can be equated with neither *Leib* nor *Körper*, since those refer specifically to (individualized) bodies, while carnality is a broader (phenomenological) principle. Carnality is akin to materiality, but with a stronger focus on the, well, *carnal* nature of materiality: it is materiality experienced in, by, and as bodies. It is, therefore, a particular expression of flesh in concrete circumstances.

Calling carnality a transcendental here is not to divorce it from the empirical, since "the rigid dichotomy between 'transcendental' and 'empirical' is ruinous" (Littlejohn 2020, 99). Rather, if we take it in light of the fourth reduction, we see that, qua transcendental, carnality remains essentially tied to the empirical, "an embodied manner of being in the world" (Kearney 2021, 16). Hence, the project of "carnal hermeneutics" is to make clear that carnality itself—not just individual bodies, but carnality as the "field" out of which bodies are generated—is always already infused with sense, in its full three-fold connotation of sensation, meaning, and direction (9). Bodily or carnal sensation—pre-eminently touch (33)—is never "mere sensation" as the early empiricists might have us believe. Instead, the "simplest sensations are already shot through with all kinds of values and desires, withholdings and givings" (Littlejohn 2020, 110), and sensation is already sensible, sensitive, savvy/savory (96): it is inherently caught up in the realms and movements of sense, and therefore caught up inexorably in the ongoing unfolding of experience.[17]

Part of that unfolding of experience, we have seen, is the "possibilizing" that ensures that things can be different, and so simultaneously pushes for "new" unfoldings and ensures that experience is always already ethically opened to the new. Therefore, by showing that carnality is inherently "hermeneutic," Kearney is also, in light of the fourth reduction, showing that carnality is inherently intertwined with sacrality, that infinite possibilizing that always comes to us within some *Stiftung* or other. Hence, the project of "carnal hermeneutics"—to show that carnality is itself hermeneutically interesting because it is always already meaningful—but is a prolegomenon to a "carnal sacrality," which shows that that "meaningfulness" is not simply epistemological, but eschatological: it does not merely give us a "meaning," but also a "direction" that affects even our "sensation," and hence puts us into a world that is full of possibilities (even as it also, in its necessary rooting in *this* or *that* particular *Stiftung*, makes some possibilities more likely than others). Carnality, therefore, is inherently a matter of tact, of touching and being touched in a mutually reinforcing way.

The (Religious) Implications of Carnal Sacrality

A lot of work remains to be done to flesh out this notion of carnal sacrality. My task here has been to show how that notion grows out of earlier moments in Kearney's thought, and how it provides a kind of phenomenological background for the analyses carried out in *Touch*. To end, I'd like to speak to the "healing" facet of Kearney's work (as exemplified by chapters 3–5 in *Touch*) by briefly examining the religious implications of characterizing the relationship between carnality and sacrality at work in "carnal sacrality" as one of expression. We can appreciate the implications of this claim if we compare it to other alternatives: insofar as the sacred is expressed in the carnal, the sacred does not simply *appear* in the carnal nor is it *constituted* by the carnal nor does it *constitute* the carnal; rather, it is mutually (and asymmetrically) coordinated with it.

The significance of this for religious living comes in the answer it gives to the response we are supposed to have to the sacred: is the religious task to *acknowledge* the presence of the sacred in the carnal, or is it to *perform* the sacred? That is, are we merely pointing to the presence of the sacred in the carnal, indicating and perhaps rejoicing in that presence—or are we in fact enacting the sacred in the carnality in and through our religious acts? There are ontological and theological claims concerning transcendence caught up in this question, of course, but that is not our primary interest. Rather, we are interested in understanding, philosophically, religion and the role it plays in our experience of the world: what, precisely, are we doing when we are "doing" religion?

At stake in the question about whether we acknowledge or perform the sacred is our relationship to the sacred and the sacred's relationship to carnality. It corresponds, then to the issue of whether the sacred appears in the carnal, whether it constitutes the carnal, or whether it is expressed in the carnal. If the sacred were simply to appear in the carnal, this would suggest that the sacred and the carnal are distinct realms such that the latter provides a "stage" or a "place" for the former to manifest itself and make itself known. The religious task would then be to learn how to see or decipher the sacred in its carnal appearances or epiphanies and recognize and acknowledge it as sacred. Here, the most that must be said about the relationship between the carnal and the sacred is that it must be possible that the latter can appear in the former; there is no suggestion that this appearing has any profound effect on either the carnal or the sacred.

A second possibility is that a causal or constitutive relation holds between sacrality and carnality. This can have two forms: either the sacred constitutes the carnal, or the carnal constitutes the sacred. If we begin with the latter, the sacred is understood as emerging in some significant causal fashion from the carnal: carnality gives rise to sacrality as another mode of carnal existence. The religious task would then be to structure material conditions in such a way that they are more likely to give rise to the sacred (or to the sacred in some particular form): we do not merely acknowledge the presence of the sacred, but we are called on to *perform* it, to help bring it into being. Here, the conditions of carnality ultimately come to determine the conditions of sacrality, which is nothing other than a particular modality of carnality.

Of course, we could also understand the sacred as constituting the carnal. In such a case, the carnal would emerge in some significant causal fashion from the sacred: the sacred gives rise to carnality as another mode of sacred existence (or, perhaps, as the material existence of the sacred, the sacred in material form). The religious task would then be to appreciate the sacred nature of carnality itself: we do not simply acknowledge one or other carnal manifestation as an appearance of the sacred, but we live in the sacrality of carnality itself. Here the conditions of sacrality ultimately come to determine the conditions of carnality itself, which is nothing other than a particular modality of sacrality.

Finally, we could understand the sacred as being expressed in the carnal. In such a case, the sacred and the carnal would be ontologically and logically distinct, such that the conditions of one can never be wholly reduced to the conditions of the other. At the same time, that distinction is not experienced as distinct, but rather as a mutual and asymmetrical coordination: we "live through" one so as to "live in" the other in a way that necessarily affects both. The religious task is then to be attuned to this expressive coordination, such that one *acknowledges* the distinction between the sacred and the carnal while simultaneously *appreciating* their phenomenal intertwining: one does not simply perform the sacred, though sacrality is continually generated out of carnal conditions and vice versa. Here, every acknowledgment of the sacred necessarily has performative or poeitic force (theopoesis)—thereby granting significance to the acknowledgment of the sacred—without this wholly conflating the sacred with human (or carnal) activity.

There are times when Kearney's work seems to come close to adopting the first strategy of religious acknowledgment. His notion of "epiphanies of the everyday" can be read in this regard. Similarly, there are times when he seems to hue closer to the third strategy of religious appreciation; some of his work on micro-eschatology can perhaps be read as a sacralizing of all of carnality. Even the second strategy of religious performance, while more evocative of Caputo and the "event-al" religious approach, can seem to come close to Kearney's own work on the enacting of the sacred.[18]

However, I believe the fourth approach of religious attunement is the one that best applies to Kearney's carnal sacrality. This only emerges clearly, I would argue, with the work on carnal hermeneutics and touch, which enables us to pay closer attention to the phenomenological register of Kearney's earlier work on religion. It is the uniquely expressive nature of the relationship between the carnal and the sacred that lets us distinguish Kearney's theopoetics from a more simple conflation of sacrality with human or carnal activity, without overemphasizing the distinction between them, as the religious acknowledgment approach does.

The claim that I am making, then, is that Kearney sees the task of religion as attuning ourselves to the intertwining of sacrality and carnality. This attuning is not primarily a cognitive or mental activity, but an embodied, phronetic one: our attunement is revealed primarily in our day to day incarnate existence, in the way we "touch" and are "touched by" the world in every action we undertake and every passion we undergo. Every such minute, micro-eschatological interaction with the world is a further act of attunement, insofar as it not only performs the sense (in its three-fold focus of sensation, meaning, and direction) we have of the world, but also re-entrenches it within ourselves and communicates it (implicitly or explicitly) to others. This is the poeitic nature of our activity, which Kearney has highlighted from his earliest work on imagination and which, I am claiming, has never left his thought. His earlier emphasis on the "narrative" nature of this poeisis can be situated, within the context of carnal sacrality, as not simply a linguistic telling of our stories, but as the very "incarnate phronesis" (Littlejohn 2020, 92) of our everyday lives. Telling the story shapes how we live the story—but the point is how we live it, not just how we tell it. Similarly, how we acknowledge the sacred shapes how we live out (of) the sacred, how we attune ourselves to it—but the point is very much how we live it out.

This is what, ultimately, distinguishes Kearney's theopoetics from a strictly process-based account of religion or theology. In Kearney's view, our theopoetics are not equivalent to the sacred (or to God), but are part of "a double act where humanity and divinity collaborate in the coming of the Kingdom" (Littlejohn 2020, 199). For Kearney, we are always responding to the call of a sacred that necessarily exceeds us,[19] even as it also (partially) constitutes us from within. Hence, we can never be equivalent with the sacred, even as we are not entirely distinct from it (and its call on us), either. We see this as early as the *persona*-person distinction, but it remains fundamental to the whole notion of a carnal sacrality and the expressive relation it holds so dear. The sacred (*persona*) does not attach itself to us as something entirely distinct from our empirical, carnal existence (person). Nor is the sacred simply equivalent to our empirical, carnal existence. Rather, our empirical, carnal existence is always living attuned to a sacrality that is expressed in each and every action or engagement we have with the world, and every one of those actions and engagements in turn generates new sacral conditions (Kearney would probably prefer to say possibilities) that in turn generate new carnal conditions, further generating new sacral conditions, and so on, in the ongoing carnal sacral generation that is human living.

Notes

1 For more on this as a "reading" of Kearney's work, cf. DeRoo's essay "Richard Kearney's Relevance to Psychology" (2020a).
2 And not simply of materiality; cf. Kearney's discussion with Falque about the non-carnal nature of "flesh" and the need to recover a more carnal notion of materiality in Falque and Kearney (2018) and van Troostwijk and Clemente (2018, 88–109).
3 To emphasize the historical nature of Kearney's thought as an oeuvre, whenever possible I will be citing from the recent collection of Kearney's writing: *Imagination Now: A Richard Kearney Reader* (Littlejohn 2020).
4 This distinction is discussed at length in *The God Who May Be: A Hermeneutics of Religion* (Kearney 2001).
5 This is not simply a theoretical or phenomenological problem, but one that pertains directly to "healthy" living in the world: the tensions between "a positivist science of facts and a postmodern culture of fantasies" and "in the religious world, between the seeming extremes of fundamentalism and New Ageism" (we might say now: between fundamentalist religion and the spiritual-but-not-religious) both emerge from the failure to adequately keep this tension between the *persona* and the person intact (Littlejohn 2020). But so, too, do megalomania, co-dependence, and various other psychological and psycho-analytical issues.
6 It is not, therefore, accidental that the distinction between expression and indication is the first of the "essential distinctions" with which Husserl kicks off his *Logical Investigations* (2000). For more on the significance of expression for Husserlian phenomenology, cf. DeRoo (2020b); for its significance to phenomenology as a whole, cf. DeRoo (2022).
7 Cf., for example, Ferrari (2018) and DeRoo (2022), chapter 3.
8 Leibniz's development of the infinitesimal calculus is an essential element in Deleuze's account of the genetic operation of expression; cf. Deleuze (1992), Deleuze (1993), and Smith (2006).
9 Cf. Deleuze's distinction between "ordinary" and "singular" points. Dan Smith discusses the significance of this distinction for Deleuze's thought in "The Conditions of the New" (Smith 2012, 235–255).

10 *Phenomenology of Perception* (Merleau-Ponty 1974).
11 See also Olthuis (1999).
12 Henceforth, Person (with a capital P) will designate the mutual coordination of *persona* and person: the person as we "should" see them, according to Kearney.
13 Cf. Marion (1998), Marion (2002), and Manoussakis (2006).
14 Merleau-Ponty (1964, especially p. 163).
15 Cf. Derrida (2011, 13).
16 Cf. Kearney's discussion with Falque on this topic *Richard Kearney's Anatheistic Wager* (Troostwijk and Clemente 2018, especially 104–108).
17 A point made already in Husserl's account of sensings [*Empfindnisse*]; cf. Husserl (1989).
18 Cf., for example, Kearney's evocatively titled "God Making: Theopoetics and Anatheism" (Kearney 2017, 3–28).
19 This affirmation of "excess" seems to relate to some account of "transcendence." If that is true, we must still situate what type of transcendence it affirms (Marion's work on excess in relation to God would, of course, prove crucial here), and how that may or may not relate the transcendence of the sacred to traditional notions of God, divinity, etc. Situating Kearney's work vis-à-vis traditional notions of God requires strict adherence to the distinction between phenomenology and hermeneutics. For the broad, structural outline we are providing here is very much a phenomenological understanding, speaking of structures of experience, etc. But we have already made clear that, for Kearney, these structures are, as a matter of phenomenological transcendental necessity, rooted in some concrete hermeneutic (that is to say, empirical, historical, social, material—carnal) situation or other. The phenomenological structure outlined here, qua phenomenological, brackets the details of any one particular hermeneutic situation. Hence, it neither confirms nor denies those details, though it does itself grow out of some particular *Stiftungen*, as Kearney always attests. As growing out of Christian and Western notions of religions, then, the ontological (and, for that matter, ethical) transcendence at work in Kearney's thought is a matter of methodological (or hermeneutic) presupposition, and not a matter for philosophical or phenomenological argumentation.

References

Deleuze, Gilles. 1992. *Expressionism in Philosophy: Spinoza, Difference and Repetition*. Translated by Martin Joughin. New York: Zone Books.
Deleuze, Gilles. 1993. *The Fold: Leibniz and the Baroque*. Translated by Tom Conley. Minneapolis: University of Minnesota Press.
DeRoo, Neil. 2020a. "Richard Kearney's Relevance to Psychology." *Journal for Phenomenological Psychology* vol. 51, no. 2 (November): 207–225.
DeRoo, Neil. 2020b. "Spiritual Expression and the Promise of Phenomenology." In *The Subject(s) of Phenomenology: New Approaches to Husserl*, edited by I. Apostelescu, 245–269. Cham: Springer.
DeRoo, Neil. 2022. *The Political Logic of Experience: Expression in Phenomenology*. New York: Fordham University Press.
Derrida, Jacques. 2011. *Voice and Phenomenon: Introduction to the Problem of the Sign in Husserl's Phenomenology*. Translated by Leonard Lawlor. Evanston: Northwestern University Press.

Falque, Emmanuel and Richard Kearney. 2018. "An Anatheist Exchange: Returning to the Body after Flesh." In *Richard Kearney's Anatheistic Wager*, edited by Chris Doude van Troostwijk and Matthew Clemente, 88–109. Bloomington: Indiana University Press.

Ferrari, Martina. 2018. "Poietic Transpatiality: Merleau-Ponty and the Sense of Nature." *Chiasmi International* vol. 20: 385–401.

Husserl, Edmund. 1970. *The Crisis of European Sciences and Transcendental Phenomenology*. Translated by David Carr. Evanston: Northwestern University Press. (Original work published 1954).

Husserl, Edmund. 1989. *Ideas Pertaining to a Pure Phenomenology and to a Phenomenological Philosophy. Book 2: Studies in the Phenomenology of Constitution*. Translated by Richard Rojcewicz and Andre Schuwer. Dordrecht: Kluwer Academic. (Original work published 1952).

Husserl, Edmund. 2000. *Logical Investigations*. Translated by John N. Findlay. London: Routledge.

Kearney, Richard. 2001. *The God Who May Be: A Hermeneutics of Religion*. Bloomington: Indiana University Press.

Kearney, Richard. 2017. "God Making: Theopoetics and Anatheism." In *The Art of Anatheism*, edited by Richard Kearney and Matthew Clemente, 3–28. Lanham: Rowman & Littlefield.

Kearney, Richard. 2021. *Touch: Recovering Our Most Vital Sense*. New York: Columbia University Press.

Littlejohn, Murray E., ed. 2020. *Imagination Now: A Richard Kearney Reader*. Lanham: Rowman and Littlefield.

Manoussakis, John Panteleimon. 2006. "Toward a Fourth Reduction?" In *After God: Richard Kearney and the Religious Turn in Contemporary Philosophy*, 21–37. New York: Fordham University Press.

Marion, Jean-Luc. 1998. *Reduction and Givenness: Investigations of Husserl, Heidegger, and Phenomenology*. Translated by Thomas A. Carlson. Evanston: Northwestern University Press.

Marion, Jean-Luc. 2002. *Being Given: Toward a Phenomenology of Givenness*. Translated by Jeffrey L. Kosky. Stanford: Stanford University Press.

Merleau-Ponty, Maurice. 1964. "Eye and Mind." In *The Primacy of Perception*, edited by James E. Edie, translated by Carleton Dallery, 159–190. Evanston: Northwestern University Press.

Merleau-Ponty, Maurice. 1974. *Phenomenology of Perception*. Translated by Colin Smith. London: Routledge & Kegan Paul.

Olthuis, James H. 1999. "Dancing Together in the Wild Spaces of Love: Postmodernism, Psychotherapy, and the Spirit of God." *Journal of Psychology and Christianity* vol. 18: 140–152.

Smith, Daniel W. 2006. "Deleuze on Leibniz: Difference, Continuity and the Calculus." In *Current Continental Theory and Modern Philosophy*, edited by Stephen Daniel, 127–147. Evanston: Northwestern University Press.

Smith, Daniel W. 2012. "The Conditions of the New." In *Essays on Deleuze*, 235–255. Edinburgh: Edinburgh University Press.

van Troostwijk, Chris Doude and Matthew Clemente, eds. 2018. *Richard Kearney's Anatheistic Wager*. Bloomington: Indiana University Press.

Chapter 5

Deep Calls to Deep

Daniel O'Dea Bradley

Introduction

This chapter investigates the metaphor of "depth" as a source for philosophical thinking and, in particular, for the thought of Richard Kearney. The theme provides a unifying thread that links Kearney's current interest in the carnal and the sacred back to his early focus on the moral imagination and forward toward suggestive new avenues for his "Theopoetics of Creation." I hope this is of value for Kearney scholars and, indeed, for anyone drawn to "the watery depths." But it also addresses the theme of "touch" in a more than merely "tangential" (L. *tangere*) way, for reflections on tactility tend to emphasize the horizontal and reciprocal aspects of reality. Thus, the vertical and asymmetrical features of depth provide an important balance that helps safeguard a more holistic understanding of reality and Kearney's engagement with it, while opening space for reflection on less obvious but highly evocative experiences of touch not marked by symmetry and reciprocity.[1]

Using this theme as a hermeneutic key, we can discern three movements in Kearney's oeuvre, each marked by the adoption of a specific role for depth: (1) Moral Imagination (depth ethics), (2) Carnal Hermeneutics (depth ontology), and (3) Theopoetics of Creation (depth metaphysics). The first begins with Frederic Jameson's critique of the post-modern collapse of all things into a "depthless present." As an alternative, Kearney calls on us to cultivate moral imagination as the basis for an ethics of discernment that is both transcendent and transformative. This culminates in *Strangers, Gods, and Monsters* with the choice between "God or *Khora*," in which Kearney argues that despite all we can learn from contemporary philosophies that highlight the indifference of the abyss, they do not give us a fundamental account of reality. This is because they ignore the even deeper possibilities of moral transformation for which we longingly appeal to a source of goodness beyond our own power: "the void within us crying out to the unfathomable deep of God" (Kearney 2003, 210). From this work, we gain an insight into the

DOI: 10.4324/9781003285649-8

transcendence of the good that will be important to retain in light of the later examination of the carnal.

The second movement is rooted in a new use of depth adopted from Merleau-Ponty's reflections on Gestalt psychology and the reversibility of touch. This work highlights the intertwining of the material and the intelligible and is marked by the turn from ethics to ontology. It gives rise to Kearney's exposition of the "sacramental imagination" at work in Joyce, Proust, and Woolf as well as other depictions of the sacredness of the material world in which the most mundane of daily realities come to be recognized as marked with the overflowing depth of the sacred. The vertical elements of depth, however, exceed this interpretive strategy, particularly in the work of Woolf, and Kearney's search for the depths leads him toward another methodological transition in which metaphysical questions come to the fore.

This third movement, "Theopoetics of Creation," is less distinct than the two previous, for it calls on both. It is also the most ambitious, most recent, and least developed of the three. But already we can say that it is a response to two important limitations in Merleau-Ponty's early phenomenology. The first is due to the way depth had been re-oriented as a horizontal relation based on the reciprocity of touch and the gestalt nature of our field of vision. This is an extremely productive line of thought, but it tends to obscure the vertical dimensions that make depth such an existentially powerful trope and that link it to the rich poetic reflections on "the watery depths" and the "highest heavens" that mark Hebraic and other Near-Eastern traditions. Second, as with all philosophies that make an important place for tactility, Merleau-Ponty's project is irreducibly marked by gaps and therefore remains ambiguous. This ambiguity is not a defect, but rather an intrinsic part of all properly human philosophy. It does, however, leave carnal hermeneutics open to a deconstructive reading that reinscribes goodness and beauty within the realm of *human* productive activity *alone*. This, again, forces the question, "God or *Khora*?" But now it arises not at the level of queries about the origins of ethics, but at the level of an ontology of nature.[2] In response, and inspired by John Scotus Eriugena, Kearney has proposed a theopoetics of material creation that makes a place for divine creative activity, more primordial than the human, as again the deeper response to this question. This allows us to integrate a primarily horizontal understanding of depth (the sensible and the intelligible) into a more vertical one (Word and Flesh).

Historical Prelude

In the aftermath of Nietzsche, philosophy has been made acutely aware of the metaphorical origin of its language. In that vein, it is interesting to note that our experience of "depth" has not contributed much to our technical philosophical vocabulary. In this, it is unlike other evocative experiences (such as "seeing," "growth," or "wealth") that have provided the central concepts for our discipline.[3] But depth occupies a middle position, for it is also unlike other significant experiences (such as bleeding) which tend to be ignored or repressed by philosophy altogether.[4] In fact, although not a source of its technical terminology, "depth" has been closely associated with the discipline since its inception. The connection is so close that philosophy is often satirized as the hubristic, impractical, or merely silly desire to think "deep thoughts." This is manifest in the recurring charges of *obscurantism* made against thinkers like Hegel, Heidegger, and Derrida—and even in pop-cultural forms such as the ridiculous musings of the Saturday Night Live character Jack Handy. Already in the 3rd century, Porphyry tells the student-reader of his textbook, *On Aristotle's Categories*, that the ontological status of universals will not be covered, because the subject is too "deep [*bathus*] and ... beyond the level of comprehension of a beginning student to know" (72.25).

While the attribution of "depth" is first of all a reference to epistemological difficulties, it also opens easily onto more ontological considerations. The first of these has to do with an ontology of the person. The depth of personhood, which is related to the difficulty of self-knowledge but not reducible to it, is quite familiar to us (as for example in Augustine's "inner-man" and Teresa of Avila's "Interior Castle"). There are scattered precursors for this early in the Greek tradition in the lyric poets and pre-Socratic philosophers—but evidently not as early as Homer.[5] Famously, Heraclitus writes, "You will not find the boundaries of soul by travelling in any direction, so deep [*bathos*] is the measure of it" (fr. 45).

This metaphor remains relatively undeveloped, however, until it comes into contact with the Hebraic tradition, where "the depths" play two important and inter-related roles. As with other Near-Eastern Semitic peoples, Hebraic cosmology understands the materiality of primordial, undifferentiated reality explicitly in terms of dark, watery depths. This tradition traces its origins back to the Sumerian-Akkadian *Tiamat*, primeval goddess of watery creation, and it clearly marks the opening of the Hebrew Scriptures: "In the beginning when God created the heavens and the earth, the earth was a formless void and darkness covered the face of the deep [*tehom*], while a wind from God swept over the face of the waters." *Tehom*[6] occurs throughout the Psalms where it calls on these ancient cosmological traditions but also becomes a powerful tool for examining the depths of the interior life, particularly the moral anguish of our inability to achieve the kind of goodness we desire. In this way, *depth* becomes intimately linked to the *heart*[7] in the Hebraic imagination and the traditions that derive from it. "I sink in the miry depths, where there is no foothold. I have come into the deep waters; the floods engulf me" (Psalm 69:2). In particular, Augustine will give great importance to Psalm

129: "*De profundis clamavi ad te, Domine*" [Out of the depths I have cried to thee, O Lord].

The ways that the early Hebraic tradition interweaves existential desires and the tribulations of the impassioned soul with a meditation on the fundamental nature of the cosmos—in the single metaphor of "deep waters"—proves to be a fertile catalyst for later Abrahamic philosophers. Alternatively, the dominate metaphors for thinking about primordial materiality in Greek philosophy are more closely related to extension and limit (*khora* and the *apeiron*). Thus, while never developing into a fully-fledged philosophical concept, "depth" is already a semi-technical term for early Christian thinkers, one that moves beyond reflections on the status of knowledge toward ontological considerations about the nature of the person and its place in the cosmos, as well as the interrelations between the sensible and the intelligible, the finite and the infinite, and (most importantly of all) the ethical and cosmological. From the later Middle Ages and into the Modern period, these reflections on Genesis and the Psalms tended to be purged from philosophy and, with notable exceptions such as Leibniz, the notion of depth lost its privileged place for thinking about ontology.

In the 20th century, there arose a renewed interest in asking what philosophy might learn from Christianity's claims about the nature of finitude. Under the influence of Kierkegaard and the early (Lutheran) Heidegger, these efforts focused on the doctrine of *creatio ex nihilo,* and they resonated most intimately with the tradition of voluntarism that emphasizes the gratuity and contingency of being. The dominant metaphor in this tradition is the *abyss,* which is a metaphor so close and yet also so far from the watery depths of the goddess Tiamat.[8] In recent years, this privileging of the abyss over the watery depths is waning as philosophy learns to embrace liturgical theology and all the variants of the new materialism. What I offer here is not a comparative assessment of the way Kearney's use of depth relates to thinkers such as Catherine Pickstock, Catherine Keller, Emmanuel Falque, David Abram, and others.[9] I show only some of the ways it has worked in the internal development of his own thought, with a particular emphasis on situating a philosophy of touch in his wider philosophical project, but hopefully resonances with the broader 21st-century retrieval of materiality will be heard throughout.

Moral Imagination—Depth Ethics

From the Depthless Present to Eschatological Hope

Kearney's first English-language monograph, *The Wake of Imagination,* was a celebration of our human capacity to use imagination in ontologically and epistemologically interwoven ways to both enrich reality and our understanding of it. An important part of this project was polemical and recuperative, as he sought to creatively retrieve a place for the imagination in our contemporary world. In this polemical stance, Kearney calls on "depth" in its privative mode as a critique of the "depthlessness" of postmodernism, a critique that he adopts from Frederic Jameson. This critique becomes a major theme in the early Kearney and one that dominates the final pages of *Wake*. Toward the end of the book, he writes,

> the allegories of anti-art present us with an experience of *depthlessness* which accurately reflects the commodified nature of contemporary culture. But in thus reducing art to a random collection of empty objects, does anti-art not run the risk of augmenting the very cult of *superficiality* which it is ostensibly exposing? (Kearney 1998, 337)

Particularly troubling to Kearney is the lack of historical and moral depth by which experiences of the present could be integrated into a meaningful and coherent ethico-temporal narrative.

> To abandon the imaginative quest for historical depth would be to surrender to the prevailing positivism which declares that things are the way they are and cannot be otherwise. And this would be tantamount to embracing the postmodern cult of 'euphoric surfaces' which dissolves the critical notions of authenticity, alienation, and anxiety in a dazzling rain of 'discontinuous orgasmic instants.' The gravest error of anti-historical postmodernism is to neglect the hermeneutic task of imaginative recollection and anticipation, to dismiss such a task as no more than a 'pathological itch to scratch surfaces for concealed depth.' (Kearney 1998, 393)

The positive side of this critique is the attempt to creatively retrieve a cultivation of the imagination, and in particular that of the moral imagination. Significantly, it is just at this crucial moment that the appeal to depth comes to the fore.

> This call of the other to be heard, and to be respected in his or her otherness, is irreducible to the parodic play of empty imitations. It breaks through the horizontal surface of mirror-images and, outfacing the void, reintroduces a dimension of depth. (Kearney 1998, 361)

This trajectory, which begins specifically with Jameson's critique of the "depthless present" in postmodernity and moves toward the depth-dimension manifest in a hermeneutical ethics of discernment and hospitality, will provide a structure that allows rich development over the next two decades. This can be seen, for example, in *Poetics of Modernity* (1995), "Narrative and Ethics" (1996), "Crisis of Narrative" (1997), *On Stories* (2002), *On Paul Ricoeur* (2004), and "On the Hermeneutics of Evil" (2006). Thus, throughout an almost 20-year period (1988–2006), we see Kearney continue to develop this theme to significant effect as he defends ethical discernment and responsibility in his ongoing dialogue with Derrida, Caputo, and others.

Strangers, Gods, and Monsters does not cite Jameson or use the term "depthless present," but the book, and in particular the chapter "God or *Khora*," is the culmination and completion of this line of thinking. Kearney begins the work by explaining that "strangers, gods, and monsters" are experiences of extremity that make appeals we cannot ignore, for a philosophy of hospitality requires us to be open to that which exceeds our capacities for full comprehension and control. And yet, as he has now long argued: "some hermeneutic stitching and weaving needs to be sustained if we are to keep alive the practice of responsible judgment and justice," a wisdom that would differentiate between "(a) those aliens and strangers that need our care and hospitality, no matter how monstrous they might first appear, and (b) those others that really do seek to destroy and exterminate" (Kearney 2003, 10). The intervening years have largely shown Kearney's claim to be correct.

Of course, the deconstructionists have always claimed that they are not proposing practical ethics or politics, but merely describing the ground (or groundless ground) that makes any normativity possible in the first place. Thus, what is in question is the nature of reality, prior to its being shaped by human beings. In particular, the monstrous and the sublime point to the question of what reality is like before our human/humane categories of understanding come into play. If this is a perennial question, the fact that it has become an obsession following the victory of Kantian transcendental philosophy is quite understandable. Kearney's critique of the depthless present (flattened into the abstractions of positivism and the nominalist historicism of postmodernity) had always been that it fails to see the historical depths in which ethical discernment and moral responsibility become possible. But why would we think that ethical claims truly do reach into the depths? Why are they not rather the useful creations of human society, a thin veneer over something very different? This is just what the monstrous puts into question. Should we say that good and evil are merely humane and humanizing ways of looking at things, while the pre-human reality remains *fundamentally* beyond these categories?

A decision to ignore the "pathological itch" (Deleuze) would allow this question to be forever deferred. Kearney's explicit commitment to following the desire for depth as a guiding philosophical principle,[10] however, makes facing the question inevitable. The issue finally comes to a head in the debate about *khora*. What Kearney disputes is Caputo's claim that this primordial reality is axiologically indifferent, that it is "neither good nor generous nor giving" (2003, 201). Thus, it is not that Kearney wants to ignore our suffering of abandonment, nausea, and emptiness. Quite to the contrary, he treats these experiences with great care and respect. Rather, the problem is that

> as one reads Caputo, one cannot help surmising that for him *khora*—at bottom and when all metaphysical illusions are stripped away—is the way things are. It is a better, *deeper* way of viewing things than its theological or ontological rivals. (203)

Against this view, Kearney argues that there is something more fundamental than *khora*, namely a source of goodness that pre-exists our efforts and to which we call out in recognition of our inability to provide the ground for the goodness that we desire to exist in ourselves. Earlier, Kearney had noted that "while nature and subject were reconciled under the category of beauty, they are radically opposed under the category of the sublime" (2003, 92). In the defining move of Modernity, we are forbidden from finding goodness and purpose outside the human being in the transcendence of nature—that which pre-exists us ontologically. In this phase of his career, Kearney remains agnostic about this prohibition, and it will remain for his investigations of carnality and touch to lead him toward a more definitive stand. But already he is adamant that there is an *ethical* goodness that does transcend human acts of willing and making. This "good" is not a clear and distinct idea. It is not the conclusion of a rational argument or the culmination of a conceptual structure. Rather, it remains an existential wager, but with a substantive content. Negatively formulated, it is the wager that our darkest hours do not point to a cold and indifferent—amoral—reality, out of which a humanizing response to the plight of the other may (or may not) bring meaning. Positively, this wager maintains that our experiences of powerlessness can point toward the help of goodness that lies beyond the human altogether, and indeed pre-exists it. As such, its elucidation is to be found only at the margins and limits of our philosophical systems. In fact, the formulation from which I take the title of my chapter is not found in the body of "God or *Khora*" at all, but in an appendix—and in barely legible 9-point font. But if it appears only with difficulty and only at the extremities of systematic philosophy, it is because it points to something deeper than human transcendental seeing:

> Despite numerous cross-cuttings, there is a radical difference, in the final analysis, between Derrida and Silesius. Silesius sees our experience of the place of play [the primordial] as 'one abyss calling to the other' (echoing Psalm 41)—the void within us crying out to the unfathomable

deep of God ... By contrast, Derrida construes this place as the 'indestructible *Khora,* the very spacing of de-construction' ... Where Silesius' God promises peace and healing, Derrida's *Khora* is 'gulf and chaos.' (Kearney 2003, 210)

Kearney's view is not to be collapsed into some form of naivete; it is neither the psychological defect of pollyannaishness, the political fallacy of utopianism, nor the religious heresy of apokatastasis.[11] We have no reason to believe that humans will necessarily act for peace and goodness (either individually or collectively, in any particular instance or finally). However, when they do, it is Kearney's contention that they are acting in accord with the deepest nature of reality, and the source of that goodness does not lie in them alone. This goodness remains primarily ethical and does not yet give a central place to materiality. However, when the turn to tactility and carnality does occur, it will be of vital importance to re-member the transcendence of the good developed here (transcendent in the sense of irreducible to a human origin alone).

Carnal Hermeneutics—Depth Ontology

The Horizontal Interweaving of the Sensible and the Intelligible

After 2006, the references to a "depthless present" become scarce or absent. Cultivating a place for ethical discernment remains an important part of Kearney's project, but as the pre-eminence of postmodernism wanes his philosophy develops in other directions. In particular, Kearney's polemical focus shifts away from the shallowness of the postmodern preoccupation with captivating but unintelligible sensuous experiences—shards of splintered glass—and toward the perennial dangers of a philosophical/scientific idealism that sees truth in pure intelligibility—the shiny but shadowless platonic heaven. The metaphor of "depth" continues to play a central function in this new context, but under the influence of Merleau-Ponty it takes on a new role. The fruits of this adoption include important new insights into the sacramentality and sacredness of the sensuous world. Kearney programmatically announces this new approach and its promise at the beginning of his essay, "Between the Prophetic and the Sacramental":

My suggestion in what follows is that a specific phenomenology of flesh ... may help us to foster and appreciate a sacramental account of the sensible universe. My concern here, and elsewhere, is not just to restore an ontology of actual incarnation to an eschatology of possibility, but also to consider the option of restoring a post-confessional sense of the sacred to the profane world of ordinary experience. (2009a, 142)

This project is developed in a burst of creative output over a four-year period (2009–2012) that included a number of articles on the topic[12] and the highly influential book, *Anatheism.*

In this body of work, it becomes clear that attention to the intertwining of the sensible and the intelligible involves a methodological shift toward phenomenology.[13] This renewal of philosophy begins with the work of first- and second-generation phenomenologists including Husserl, Scheler, Stein, Heidegger, Ingarden, and others. As Kearney argues, however,

> It is really only with Merleau-Ponty that we witness a fully-fledged phenomenology of flesh. Here at last, the body is no longer treated as a mere project, cipher or icon, but as flesh itself in all its ontological *depth.* The ghost of metaphysical idealism is finally laid to rest. We return to the body in all its *unfathomable* thisness. (2009c, 58)

It is well understood that Merleau-Ponty takes this notion of "depth" from figure-ground theories in Gestalt psychology and puts it to use at the heart of his phenomenology. Under this influence, depth shifts from a way of thinking about interiority (the interior castle) or the contingency of being (the abyssal nature of finitude), to become a way of thinking about the chiasmic interweaving of matter and form. Recognizing this shift, Kearney even applies the label "depth phenomenology" to the method he adopts from Merleau-Ponty (2009a, 149).

This approach gives Kearney a new way of revealing the limitations of post-structuralism and deconstruction (and their Modernist roots),[14] and as an alternative it provides him the creative tools for a renewed reading of fiction that adds an emphasis on the sacramental to the hermeneutics of narrative temporality and narrative ethics that he had learned early in his career from Ricoeur. In the book, *Anatheism,* and the larger project that bears this name, Kearney continues to utilize the best of the legacy of Levinas and Derrida (Kearney 2011, 63). However, along with the ongoing reproach that deconstruction's emphasis on absolute alterity forecloses the possibility of ethical discernment (critically judging the difference between strangers, gods, and monsters), Kearney now adds this new criticism:

> Faith in messianicity, for Derrida, seems at times to mean a radical absence of any historical instantiation of the divine—no epiphanies, songs, testimonies, no sacred embodiments or liturgies … Such messianic universality is only guaranteed, it seems, at the cost of particularity; it forfeits the flesh-and-blood singularity of everyday epiphanies. (2011, 64)

Kearney goes on to include Bonhoeffer with Derrida in this wider critique, and his diagnosis of their loss of the sacred serves as a pivot to the central section of the book where Kearney turns to Merleau-Ponty for the methodological tools to solve this lacuna and to his sacramental reading of Joyce, Proust, and Woolf for examples of its substantive elaboration.

This work has become quite influential and has already generated a large body of scholarship. For my purposes, I want to make two related points about the project. First, while the sacred nature of the material world is certainly revealed by these novelists, all three have an abiding preoccupation with *human* artistry. As we will see, this highlights the need to address the ambiguity inherent in a phenomenology of "gaps." Second, the language of "depth" is far more important to Woolf than either of the others. It is to her work that Kearney turns last, and his engagement with her helps to reveal the limits of the merely horizontal understanding of depth that he had adopted from Merleau-Ponty and that naturally comes to the fore in a phenomenology of touch. Both of these factors create tensions that prepare for Kearney's turn toward the third role for depth in his Theopoetics of Creation.

Kearney is clear that anatheism is motivated by a desire to recover a sensitivity toward the sacredness of the material world that had been lost in Cartesian-Lockean-Kantian Modernity. He explains in the early pages of *Anatheism* that the prefix *ana-* and all its variations "designate a process of retrieving the divine in a world ostensibly estranged from God, recovering the sacred in a time of disenchantment" (2007, 11). Significantly, however, he is not very interested in wilderness in this work. Instead, he writes about human artistry, and not romantic primitivism, but art in its most virtuosic forms. Imagine the different emphasis that would emerge from turning to comparable contemporary novelists working with similar genres but very different thematic interests (e.g., Yates instead of Joyce, Tolkien instead of Proust, Willa Cather, or Zora Neal Hurston instead of Woolf). Kearney's paradigmatic examples allow for an important, but very particular, connection to sacramental theology—one that highlights human activity. As Kearney notes, Joyce self-consciously "invokes the idioms of transubstantiation to describe the writing process" (2009b, 249). This is particularly evident in the character of Stephen Dedalus, who "describes himself as a 'priest of the eternal imagination,' transmuting the 'bread of daily experience' in the 'womb' of art" (249).

This emphasis on the priestly role of human creativity is extremely fruitful, but it gives a rather one-sided inflection to Kearney's work on the sacred that favors the interpretive pole of the intentionality/givenness correlation. Thus, in the following years, a more hermeneutically dominant method and greater horizontal emphasis naturally return to the fore in Kearney's work. The emergence of the horizontal as a result of a focus on tactility is particularly evident in the important book, *Carnal Hermeneutics,* and the centrality it gives to Aristotle's understanding of touch. Here we see a line from *De Anima* that becomes a guiding aphorism for the project: "Flesh is a medium, not an organ." As Kearney elaborates:

> Unlike Plato, who denigrated touch and taste as unmediated senses, helpless before the flux of things, and contrary to the materialists who claimed touch brings us into immediate contact with material stuff, Aristotle insists on the mediating character of tactility. To be tactile is to be exposed to otherness across gaps. (2015, 19)

There is a great deal of truth in this insight, and it provides a rich ground for a research project. It does, however, reveal a tension in Kearney's philosophy. This can be formulated as a question in light of two methodological decisions: if (1) we are to emphasize the crossing of gaps in a carnal hermeneutics and, in particular, the priestly role of human creativity in transforming the profane into the sacred; and (2) if depth is to be understood as a horizontal relation exemplified by figure-ground psychology, why would we not think that Kant's noumenal-phenomenal dualism provides the best metaphysical frame for understanding this interpretive activity?

Kearney suggests that the central insight of Proust's *In Search of Lost Time* occurs when "Marcel is ready, at last, after many thousands of pages questing for the perfect work of art, to renounce his elite romantic pretensions and acknowledge that real art is an art of flesh—a literary transubstantiation of those contingent, fragile, carnal, and seemingly inconsequential moments that our conscious will is wont to consign to oblivion" (Kearney 2009b, 260). Kearney calls this a "sacramental aesthetic" (2011, 113). But why not interpret this as analogous to Kant's "transcendental aesthetic," such that sacredness becomes a category bestowed upon things by the transcendental function of human creativity? This parallels the question at the heart of Kearney's disagreement with Caputo and Derrida over the nature of *khora*. In that context, Kearney forced the question, "Does the *ethical goodness* of the *moral world* pre-exist human generativity?" And he answered in the affirmative. Now we must ask, "Does the *sacred goodness* of the *material world* also pre-exist human generativity?" This remains unanswerable at the level of a carnal hermeneutics, alone. Thus, we may have been tempted toward a deferral of the question. Woolf's reintroduction of a vertical element to the theme of depth, however, both forces a confrontation with the issue and begins to offer a way out of the dilemma it poses.

The language of depth occurs frequently in Woolf's fiction as well as her private writings, and Kearney cites many of them. For her, this trope consistently serves to draw the human mind outside of itself. As Kearney notes, in Woolf's *To the Lighthouse* it is the language of "unfathomable depth" which shows us that Mrs. Ramsey's soul is not a solipsistic prison, but "is somehow porously interconnected with the scattered souls of those around her" (2009b, 272). Kearney also points to Woolf's diary which reveals that "she used this narrative voice as a 'tunnelling process' deep into the minds of all her characters … [to] reach a point where they could all connect, have similar thoughts and all move to the same deep 'rhythm'" (272).

Most importantly, this desire for depth serves as more than just a revelation of human intersubjectivity (or trans-subjectivity), for it appears in richly carnal ways that point to our situatedness in the material world. Regard for other people is manifest in, and interwoven with, the development of embodied skills and careful attention to materiality that accompanies the practices of cooking, painting, sailing, and long walks in the natural world. These activities are not simply instrumental or merely a manipulation of the surfaces of things; rather, they are a participation in the deepest nature of reality, and even when they draw us beyond the temporal flow of finite human life altogether toward a transcendent goodness, this remains tied to the carnal. As Kearney notes, at the peak of her "Eucharistic meal," Mrs. Ramsey pauses in the recognition that "there is a coherence in things, a stability; something, she meant, is immune from change, and shines out … in the face of the flowing, the fleeing, the spectral, like a ruby" (2009b, 273). Even more significantly, if this is revealed in art (the priestly role of transubstantiation), Woolf is adamant that it only occurs in art that recognizes its own responsiveness to that which it cannot make, that which precedes it. Woolf's painter in the novel, Lily Briscoe, expresses this in her desire to encounter "that very jar on the nerves, the thing itself before it has been made anything" (2009b, 276). Kearney quite rightly interprets this in light of Woolf's other claims to mean that

> the 'pattern,' the 'real thing' [that which endures] is not *made* but *given*.[15] It is not the product of creators—human or divine—but an intimation of some anonymous unfathomable love which connects all beings behind and *beneath* the appearances of agency and artifice. (276)

This all indicates that human activity responds to, and participates in, some kind of goodness that precedes it. As we have seen above, in Kearney's early work on narrative ethics this is an *ethical goodness* that lies deeper than the indifference of *khora*. Here, in the context of the interweaving of the sensible and the intelligible, it is an *ontological goodness* that exists in "Creation" prior to any act of human creation. Kearney is not explicit about this in *Anatheism*, but the more he engages with Woolf's use of depth, the more he seems ineluctably pulled in this direction. For example, he recognizes of Mrs. Ramsey that "her own 'unfathomable deep' blends with the depths of the ocean" (274), and he notes her attraction "to inanimate things; trees, streams, flowers" (275). Yet, this never becomes thematic. It cannot be otherwise, for Kearney's method is still inspired predominantly by Merleau-Ponty's horizontal use of depth[16] and the reversibility that structures tactility.

As we would expect, this horizontality also dominates the book, *Touch,* where under the guidance of a tactile hermeneutic, reversibility becomes the prominent feature of experience. For example, in this work, Kearney challenges Marion's famous reading of the Byzantine Icon, a reading which had focused on the inaccessibility and withdrawal of the pupils as they provide nothing to be seen (empty black holes). In contrast, Kearney claims that "the tangibility of vision reveals a reversibility at work in the believer's experience of the icon ... [Such that] the eyes touch us in an act of double sensation" (Kearney 2021, 73). In light of this interpretive strategy, even "nature" comes to be seen as a collection of subjects *with which we are in reciprocal relation.* The paradigmatic example is Cezanne, who experiences the trees and mountains that he paints as looking back at him, in turn (24). Thus, it is unsurprising if nature is described not as *physis,* ground, home, or ecosystem—but as an egalitarian relationship (like a proper modern romantic liaison): "If touch is something we do to the world, it is also something the world does to us" (40). This strategy provides a treasure trove of insights. It remains, however, fundamentally marked by gaps, and thus must necessarily be understood as a carnal hermeneutics, a method that remains finally ambiguous about the extent to which we are reading meanings *from* the material world or are reading meanings *into* the material world. Therefore, as rich as this work is, the vertical element of depth continues to reassert itself in ways that cannot be contained,[17] thus prompting us, often against our inclination, to a third way of thinking depth that is highly suggestive but not fully developed.

Theopoetics of Creation—Depth Metaphysics

From Horizontal Depth (Sensible and Intelligible) to Vertical Depth (Word and Flesh)

Theopoiesis is a term used by early Greek Christians as a supplement to the term *theosis* for describing the way humanity is transformed as it comes to share in the divine life. As Athanasius famously summarizes the theme in *De Incarnatione* (quoted in Kearney 2019a, 31): "God became human so that the human could become divine." By giving such an exalted role to the human being, it could be thought to produce a worldview in which theocentrism and anthropocentrism become scarcely distinguishable. As such, it would support the tendency to privilege (human) eschatology over (non-human) ontology and Soteriology over theologies of Creation. In this vein thinkers such as Caputo have tied theopoetics to mid-twentieth century philosophies of the event. Kearney's search for depth, however, opens us beyond this narrowed view, for once we accept a commitment to the "unfathomable depths," they become an irrevocable opening onto the "non-humanity of the world ... before it has been made anything [by us]" (Kearney 2019a, 279).

The language of depth was used in a similar way to describe the influence of the first modern geological discoveries in the mid-18th century (as it is again by Meillassoux and others). In his prominent book on the topic, Stephen J. Gould begins his first chapter, "The Discovery of Deep Time," with an appeal to a now famous metaphor: "Consider the Earth's history as the old measure of the English yard, the distance from the King's nose to the tip of his outstretched hand. One stroke of a nail file on his middle finger erases human history" (1987, 3). The role of "depth" in connecting an epistemic realism about the vast reaches of (pre-human) geological time and an axiological humility about the value of (non-human) nature is made even more explicit by E-an Zen, former president of the Geological Society of America. Describing his project in "What Is Deep Time and Why Should Anyone Care?" Zen writes:

> Early naturalists realized that the earth has a multi-million-year history ... Being observation based, deep time is readily taught to students using local features, and its validity follows simply from the premise that natural phenomena contain real information. Appreciation of deep time helps us to define the limits to human consumption of Earth resources, as well as to provide a framework for debates among those who hold different views on the domains of validity for science and religion and on the meaning of scientific inferences. (2001, 5)

It is not a coincidence that the geologists call on "depth" to describe the *truths* of the earth that existed long *before* our existence, while the "deep" ecologists use it to describe the *values* of the earth that exist *apart from* our existence.[18]

It is in the context of this insistence on depth, this drive to respond (both epistemically and axiologically) to a world that pre-exists us and would exist without us,[19] that Kearney develops his thinking on poiesis. In doing so, he aligns himself with a more scientific understanding of truth as well as a more traditional understanding of poiesis than Caputo and others. For, if it might seem at first glance that *deification* would lead to some version of gnostic dualism or other anthropocentrism (in which material nature is devalued), the opposite was traditionally the case. Poiesis was generally tied to an Incarnational soteriology which understands salvation as rooted in God becoming flesh, and indeed it was brought to its most complete development by Athanasius as a way of combatting Arianism. Further, Patristic thinkers highlighted the claim that the Word of the Incarnation is one with the Word of Creation. For this reason, classical versions of theopoiesis were allied with the inclination to see divinity in nature, and (unlike Modern Philosophy) the scholarship it generated was methodologically oriented toward integration: the integration of ethics and ontology, eschatology and hierophany, theologies of salvation history and theologies of Creation, etc.

While responding to more contemporary concerns, Kearney shares much with this Patristic sensibility. He claims, for example, that the significance of theopoetics for our own time is revealed by the answer to the question: "Why is creation a matter of *making* as well as *revealing*?" His answer: "poetics is the first bridge between word and flesh" (2019a, 41). This formulation remains couched in the unstable language of gaps, but already we see a shift. Namely, flesh, here, is not a relation but a relatum. No longer defined only as a mediation between sensibility and understanding, flesh is now understood to be itself mediated by poesis. Further, the relation in which flesh participates can no longer be interpreted primarily in terms of reciprocity. This does not mean that philosophies of tactility, as developed for example in *Carnal Hermeneutics* and *Touch,* are in any way misguided. But it does mean that the theme of reciprocity, which tends to be emphasized by our experience of touch, does not have the last word. For Kearney's theopoetic investigations reveal responsiveness and mutuality, but also important asymmetries. As Kearney puts it, theopoetics means that "first creation calls for second creation," and this second creation is specifically a "re-creation or creation again (*ana*)" (2019a, 31). It is not human activity that first brings meaningful things into being, for our activity is always a response to (and a participation in) a meaning-making that precedes it—the making that gave rise to all the beautiful and bewildering diversity of flowers, trees, animals, rivers, mountains, galaxies, sub-atomic particles, dark matter, and everything else we haven't yet encountered but that populates our cosmos. Thus, it is true that "certain expressions of artistic imagination offer ways of responding to the call of creation which *precede and exceed* the abstract systems of philosophy and theology" (Kearney 2019a, 32), precisely because the divine poiesis precedes and exceeds human poiesis.

This brings to the fore difficult and complicated metaphysical questions that have traditionally been bracketed by phenomenology. But already we have some scouting expeditions into this new territory in some of Kearney's recent work, particularly in his reading of the 9th-century Irish philosopher, John Scotus Eriugena. Above, we noted Kearney's agnosticism about the ways that the ascendency of the sublime has ruptured the integration of "nature and subject." He now seems to find in Eriugena a way to decide for their reconciliation. This is due to the fact that Eriugena "makes no opposition between being and consciousness or consciousness and nature" (2019b, 236). Further, Kearney notes that Eriugena is a part of a broader Celtic tradition marked by a "deep love of the earth," a perspective from which we can see that "nature and the sensuous world are *sacramental*; that is, [we can recognize] things, beings, and events as *theophanies,* manifestations of the divine" (237, Kearney's emphasis).

Many of the details of this "depth-poesis" still remain to be elaborated, but it is already clear that in its dialogue with "religion," this kind of philosophy will need to turn from an exclusive emphasis on salvation history toward a reflection on Creation, from an exclusive reading of the Prophets, Parables, and Pauline letters toward Genesis, Song of Songs, and the Psalms, and from the written word alone toward ritual and liturgy. The work on *Touch* is a part of this transition and has helped motivate the turn to the carnal, but it also calls to be completed by a reflection on Creation. This, indeed, is what is happening. Kearney has been among the first contemporary continental philosophers to return to that infamous Patristic form: an erudite, allegorical "Commentary on Genesis." In doing so, he points out the significance of the Hebrew word "aleph-tav," which functions as a case-marker to indicate a direct object. In this light he reads the opening line of Genesis:

> 'In the beginning God created *aleph-tav'* where *aleph-tav* is a merism for the alphabet and a synecdoche for language. The *aleph-tav* appears twice (because there are two noun-objects). In the second instance, it mediates (with the conjunction) 'the heavens' and the 'the earth.' *Language* [before humans evolved from our primate ancestors] graphically *'holds/pulls together'* the merism of *heaven and earth.* (2019a, 147, 148)

Thus, this new emphasis on Creation integrates both the horizontal and the vertical and the lines of descent and ascent within the vertical itself.[20] In doing so, it sets "Abrahamic" spirituality free from the Modern demands for autochthonous religious purity. With Celtic spirituality as a third, we are no longer Jewgreek, alone, forced to choose between Greek "rationality" and Semitic "faith." This is also of course true of Congolese or Mexican or Persian spirituality (and on and on), and it opens the place for a more fluid metaphysics, one that makes room for faith and reason, but also myth and liturgy, and that allows for dialogue with indigenous spiritual traditions from around the world, but also neglected areas of the Greek and Hebraic traditions themselves.

****

This all means that Kearney's reading of Merleau-Ponty stands, and the central role of touch in opening reversible relations must be recognized. But they must also be situated within their proper place. Because flesh—as lived—is a medium and not an organ, there remains in embodied experience an irreducible gap between sensibility and intelligibility. Even if this relation is reversible, and chiasmatically crossed, it remains ambiguous, such that the choice between a Derridean "khoratic" reading of the locus of meaning and the "sacramental" reading of Kearney and Merleau-Ponty both remain plausible. In other words, Kant is right to retreat from the desire to find a human faculty that would be the transcendental root that seamlessly (gap-free) unites sensibility and understanding. However, in response to the demand that we tunnel down toward the depths of that which precedes human making, Kearney has reached a new level of discourse: the Theopoetics of Creation. This acceptance of the Woolfian depth challenge breaks with all "correlationist" interpretations of phenomenology by arguing that poiesis precedes human beings. The common root of understanding and intelligibility is a creative activity, but it is not a merely human faculty. Rather, it is a pre-existent source of creation *in which* human imagination participates, but *for which* it does not provide the ground. This means that in an ontologico-epistemic register, Kearney is correct to say that poetics *bridges* word and flesh. But his depth-poetics also points to the claim that, metaphysically, it is more complete to say that poetics is the common *root* of intelligibility and sensibility. Thus the work on touch is extremely fruitful, but if we are to seek answers to our deepest questions or to work toward a more holistic and systematic philosophy (and these desires cannot be suppressed for long) the truths of a tactile hermeneutics must acquiesce to taking a place within a broader theopoetics, as Kearney's other work shows. When open in this way, a philosophy of touch is not at all antagonistic toward the attempt at a more synoptic approach; indeed, it is the intertwining character of materiality as both opaque and responsive (as revealed through touch) that is perhaps the best hope for keeping a theopoetic metaphysics of Creation from collapsing into a productionist metaphysics of Instrumentality, a tendency critiqued so powerfully by Heidegger. Nonetheless, reality is a matter of revealing *and* making. And despite Heidegger, making is the deeper of the two.

Notes

1 An example with a strongly vertical component is feeling the water surround you and grow colder against your skin as you dive down into the depths of a lake or an ocean and conversely to feel it grow warmer and lighter as you return upward to the surface. A related experience is feeling the air grow warmer and more humid (accompanied by the pungent smells of organic life) as you descend from a high mountain in late spring.

2 While Merleau-Ponty's later thinking on nature has resources for addressing this question, when Kearney calls on his work it tends to be in reference to the reciprocity of touch.

3 For example, from "seeing": wisdom, theory, speculative philosophy, species, idea, *eidos*. From "growth": metaphysics and being. From "wealth": reality (*res*) and ontology (*ontos*). From *standing* (as opposed to laying in sleep or in death): existence, substance, subsistence, epistemology.

4 It is very strange that despite its extremely evocative nature and central importance for early Greek and Hebraic religions, and, indeed, for Christianity, "blood" has had such little impact on philosophy. "Sanguinity" is hardly a central concept for psychology let alone philosophy—and its ties to "blood" have been mostly sanitized anyway.

5 See Snell (2011, 17–18).

6 *Tehom* and *Tiamat* are etymologically related to a common root, the Proto-Semitic *tihām: sea.

7 The "Heart" has played an important and enduring role in Kearney's thought. This is evident in his early work on the Hebraic imagination (Kearney 1998). Significantly, it also reappears in his engagement with non-Christian Wisdom traditions, including Islam, Hinduism, and Buddhism and provides an important bridge toward the recovery of an emphasis on embodiment in the Christian tradition that occurred at precisely this time in Kearney's development (Kearney and Rizo-Patron 2010).

8 Interestingly, in the Septuagint, *tehom* has two different translations. In most places, including Genesis 1, it is given as *abussos* (abyss) and only rarely as *bathos* (the deep). Yet *abussos* is derived from *bathos,* and the Greek ear would have heard resonances between the two words, helping the reader understand "the abyss" in its resonances with "watery depths." In the transition from the Septuagint to the Vulgate, however, *abussos* is generally translated as *abyssus*, and *bathos* as (the unrelated) *profundis*. Thus, the connection becomes much harder to hear, perhaps leading the later Scholastic and Modern philosophers toward an interpretation of the material realm emerging out of the abyss in a voluntaristic act of pure dependency on God's will, rather than in a more processual way out of the possibilities held within the material world itself. This choice of the Latin *abyssus* to render *tehom* cannot be the whole story, however, for when Genesis is translated into the vernacular, it is true that *tehom* is given in Spanish as *abismo* (not *las honduras* or *las profundidades*) and in Fenech as *l'abîme* (not *la profondeur*), but it is translated into English (as far back as Wycliff) as *depth* (not abyss) and into German (as far back as Luther) as *Tiefe* [deep].

9 See, for example, *After Writing* (Pickstock 1997); *Faces of the Deep: A Theology of Becoming* (Keller 2003); *Becoming Animal: An Earthly Cosmology* (Abram 2011); and *Wedding Feast of the Lamb* (Falque 2016).

10 "The postmodern cult of the timeless, depthless space appears *to jeopardize the vocation of philosophy itself,* i.e., as an investigation into the hidden or undiscovered dimension of things" (Kearney 1998, 31).

11 I understand hope for universal salvation to be an orthodox position (and in fact the most faithful). The problem with apokatastasis, at least as it is often understood, is to posit the universal return to God in quasi-mechanical terms and as *guaranteed,* thus precluding any role at all for hope, freedom of choice, and the gratuity of the divine gift. These elements have often been exaggerated in the soteriologies of the Latin West (and Soteriology itself has often outshadowed theologies of Creation), but even when returned to a more balanced way of thinking, they have a role to play.

12 See "Reference" page.

13 As Kearney writes, "some might say, indeed, that phenomenology thus reo-
   pened the possibility of a kind of incarnational ontology not seen since
   Thomas wrote of quiditas or Duns Scotus of haecceitas" (2009a, 143).
14 Thus, this methodological shift is a movement forward from Descartes and
   Kant toward the new phenomenology, but it is also a movement (chron-
   ologically) backward from an exclusive emphasis on hermeneutics and deconstruction toward a renewed phenomenology.
15 It remains to show that what Kearney calls "given" here is the making I call
   "Creation" below, and that what he calls 'making' here is what I call "instrumental" (2009b).
16 Toward the end of his life, Merleau-Ponty is, himself, drawn to the language
   of "verticality." Significantly, he appeals to this concept in his critique of
   Sartre's notion of the abyss. However, it appears only in "Working Notes,"
   the least developed part of what gets published as *The Visible and the Invisible*
   (234–236, 272), and its full implications remain to be worked out.
17 See, for example, the last pages of *Touch*, chapter 2 (p. 53ff).
18 Epistemic humility does not automatically yield axiological humility, however. In fact, the critique of "anthropomorphism" often results in "anthropocentrism." See Latour (2017); and my own Bradley (2020). For the
   pathological role the desire for depth can play in this anthropocentrism, see
   Baker (2003).
19 It is ontological rather than temporal priority that is the crucial issue, but the
   latter helps to reveal the former.
20 For most creatures on Earth, a horizontal orientation tends to be directionally
   undifferentiated such that no direction is fundamentally different than any
   other, but our gravitational field means that this is not true of the vertical, in
   which up and down remain very different in constant ways. In philosophy and
   theology, we are most familiar with the theme of "verticality" as the upward
   orientation of "height." This is particularly true when verticality arises as a
   corrective to an overly "flat" ontology of horizontality and in its related
   function as an appeal to ethical responsibility toward the other. This is
   manifest in the prophetic call uttered by Isaiah on behalf of God: "As the
   heavens are higher than the earth, so are my ways higher than your ways and
   my thoughts than your thoughts" (Isaiah 55:9 and Psalm 103:11). In contemporary philosophy, this "desert sky" has become a touchstone for Levinas
   and Derrida. On the other hand, a philosophy deeply attuned to the creative
   potential of materiality, such as Keller's, will tend to focus on verticality in the
   line of descent. An integrative approach such as Kearney's, which sees desire
   ascending and descending, must find ways to include both. In other work, I
   call on the water cycle, particularly in the thought of Teresa of Avila, as a
   moving and poetic image that integrates the horizontal (rivers and irrigation
   channels) and the vertical (evaporation, precipitation, and percolation) and
   that includes a harmonious integration of height and depth within the vertical
   itself.

References

Abram, David. 2011. *Becoming Animal: An Earthly Cosmology*. New York:
   Vintage Books.
Baker, Lynne Rudder. 2003. "Belief Ascription and the Illusion of Depth." *Facta
   Philosophica* vol. 5, no. 2: 183–201.

Bradley, Daniel O'Dea. 2020. "The Fruit of the Vine ... and the Work of Human Hands: Latour's 'Catholic' Environmental Philosophy." *Satya Nilayam: Chennai Journal of Intercultural Philosophy* vol. 38 (October): 65–87.

Falque, Emmanuel. 2016. *Wedding Feast of the Lamb*. New York: Fordham University Press.

Gould, Stephen J. 1987. *Time's Arrow, Time's Cycle: Myth and Metaphor in the Discovery of Geological Time*. Cambridge: Harvard University Press.

Heraclitus. 1920. *Fragments*. In *Early Greek Philosophy*, translated by John Burnet. https://en.wikisource.org/wiki/Fragments_of_Heraclitus

Kearney, Richard. 1998. *Wake of the Imagination*. London: Routledge.

Kearney, Richard. 2003. *Strangers, Gods, and Monsters*. London: Routledge.

Kearney, Richard. 2009a. "Between the Prophetic and the Sacramental." In *Gazing Through a Prism Darkly: Reflections on Merold Westphal's Hermeneutical Epistemology*. Edited by B. Keith Putt. New York: Fordham University Press.

Kearney, Richard. 2009b. "Sacramental Imagination: Eucharists of the Ordinary Universe." *Analecta Hermeneutica* vol. 1: 240–288.

Kearney, Richard. 2009c. "Sacramental Imagination and Eschatology." In *Phenomenology and Eschatology: Not Yet in the Now*. Edited by John Panteleimon Manoussakis and Neal DeRoo, 55–67. London: Routledge.

Kearney, Richard. 2010. "Merleau-Ponty and the Sacramentality of the Flesh." In *Merleau-Ponty at the Limits of Art, Religion, and Perception*. Edited by Kascha Semonovitch and Neal DeRoo, 147–166. New York: Continuum.

Kearney, Richard. 2011. *Anatheism: Returning to God After God*. New York: Columbia University Press.

Kearney, Richard. 2012. "Eucharistic Imagination in Merleau-Ponty and James Joyce." In *Human Destinies: Philosophical Essays in Memory of Gerald Hanratty*. Edited by Fran O'Rourke, 415–433. Notre Dame: Notre Dame Press.

Kearney, Richard. 2019a. "God Making: An Essay in Theopoetic Imagination." In *The New Yearbook for Phenomenology and Phenomenological Philosophy*, vol. 17, 145–160. London: Routledge.

Kearney, Richard. 2019b. "My Way to Theopoetics through Eriugena." *Literature and Theology* vol. 33, no. 3: 233–240.

Kearney, Richard. 2021. *Touch: Recovering Our Most Vital Sense*. New York: Columbia University Press.

Kearney, Richard and Eileen Rizo-Patron, eds. 2010. *Traversing the Heart: Journeys of the Inter-Religious Imagination*. Leiden: Brill Press.

Kearney, Richard and Brian Treanor, eds. 2015. *Carnal Hermeneutics*. New York: Fordham University Press.

Keller, Catherine. 2003. *Faces of the Deep: A Theology of Becoming*. London: Routledge.

Latour, Bruno. 2017. *Facing Gaia: Eight Lectures on the New Climatic Regime*. Translated by Catherine Porter. Cambridge: Polity Press.

Merleau-Ponty, Maurice. 1968. *Visible and Invisible*. Edited by Claude Lefort, translated by Alphonso Lingis. Evanston: Northwestern University Press.

Pickstock, Catherine. 1997. *After Writing: On the Liturgical Cosummation of Philosophy*. Oxford: Blackwell Publishers.

Porphyry. 2014. *On Aristotle's Categories.* Translated by Steven K. Strange. New York: Bloomsbury.

Snell, Bruno. 2011. *Discovery of the Mind: In Greek Philosophy and Literature.* New York: Dover Books.

Zen, E-an. 2001. "What Is Deep Time and Why Should Anyone Care?" *Journal of Geoscience Education* vol. 49, no. 1: 5–9.

Chapter 6

Strangers, Gods, and Demons: Toward a Carnal Hermeneutics of the Demonic

Brian Gregor

Carnal hermeneutics is a vital development in Richard Kearney's contribution to the phenomenological and hermeneutical tradition. This hermeneutics is "carnal" insofar as it attends to "the surplus of meaning arising from our carnal embodiment, its role in our experience and understanding, and its engagement with the wider world" (Kearney and Treanor 2015, 1). Too often hermeneutics has prioritized language and texts in a way that loses touch with the embodied, corporeal basis of our being in the world. Thus Kearney, along with Brian Treanor and a distinguished group of collaborators, has sought to reorient hermeneutics to the lived body (*Leib*) as a locus of understanding and interpretation. This move takes hermeneutics back to the school of phenomenology and its rich tradition of describing the lived body, from Husserl to Merleau-Ponty, Sartre, Levinas, and Ricoeur. Our bodies are hermeneutical sites—texts that give meaning and call for interpretation—and it is precisely as lived, corporeal bodies that we understand and interpret. Kearney's newest book *Touch: Recovering Our Most Vital Sense* continues this project of interpreting the incarnate nature of our being in the world by attending to tactility—what he calls "the touchstone of carnal hermeneutics" (2021, 38).

Kearney's reorientation of hermeneutics invites new exploration in every region of Continental philosophy, not the least in the philosophy of religion. The lived body has figured more prominently in current phenomenology of religion, including discussions of religious phenomenality, the possibilities of revelation, the experience of the divine in the sacraments, as well as suffering and trauma. All excellent topics. Another area that deserves the carnal treatment is the question of evil. What would it look like to give a carnal reorientation to the hermeneutics of evil? Such a question is no doubt too big to answer in one essay, so I will focus on one specific aspect of evil: the *demonic*. How might the interpretive lens of carnality sharpen our understanding of the diabolical and demonic?

The demonic is an uncomfortable topic for the philosophy of religion. Most philosophers—whether modern or postmodern—hardly touch it.

DOI: 10.4324/9781003285649-9

To his credit, Kearney does. When I first read Kearney's trilogy comprising *On Stories, Strangers, Gods, and Monsters* (2003), and *The God Who May Be* (2001), one of the things that most impressed me was his hermeneutics of evil, specifically in his examination of depictions of the demonic other. The demon is a figure of threatening otherness, which is why we identify certain kinds of rhetoric as *demonization,* insofar as they depict the other as fundamentally evil. Kearney shows this in vivid detail in *On Stories*, where he cites some startling examples of the practice of depicting those beyond our borders as inhuman monsters (2002, 70–76). He explores this in even greater depth in *Strangers, Gods, and Monsters* (2003), where his stated aim is to make the foreign more familiar and the familiar more foreign. This task requires the crucial work of hermeneutical discernment: the discernment to recognize and resist the false demonization of the other, as well as the discernment to recognize the truly monstrous and demonic.

In honor of Kearney, then, I would like to sketch a carnal hermeneutics of the demonic. I will not pretend to offer a comprehensive theory of the demonic, but an interpretation of the demonic as it pertains to the carnal, corporeal aspects of being. This will entail a dark variation on hermeneutics à la Kearney and Ricoeur, who attend to the way texts disclose new possibilities of being and refigure our world. The demonic is a kind of imaginative *dis*figuration of being. Here I take a cue from Simone Weil. In *Gravity and Grace* (1952, 48) she makes this rather startling claim:

> Man has to perform an act of incarnation, for he is disembodied (*désincarné*) by his imagination. What comes to us from Satan is our imagination.

I take this claim not as a denunciation of imagination *per se* as Satanic, but as an insight into the disincarnating effects of the specifically diabolical or demonic imagination.[1] Rather than refiguring being so as to draw out new possibilities of goodness, the demonic imagination disfigures—*dys*figures—being. The demonic revolts against the goodness of incarnate existence. It enacts a disincarnation—in Kearney's terms, "excarnation."[2] It revolts against the goodness pronounced in the book of Genesis, as God beholds the material creation: *it is good*. The demonic also enacts a *dys*incarnation, insofar as it distorts and disfigures our relation to our embodied being, both of self and of others.

In order to deepen our understanding of demonic imagination and its effects of disincarnation and dysincarnation, I will offer a hermeneutical detour through a series of literary figures of the demonic. The case studies in the first part reveal a recurring theme of the demonic as an intensification of incurvature, a withdrawing into the self in opposition to the goodness of material creation—both our own carnality, and the carnality of others. The second part offers a carnal interpretation to the New Testament idea of principalities and powers, such as institutions, technology, ideology, and images that distort the concrete, corporeal reality of human beings and our relations with each other. Where the imagination disincarnates, one important work of opposition is, as Weil puts it, to "perform an act of incarnation" by recovering contact with others in their concrete corporeality.

The One Principle of Hell

In *The Sickness Unto Death*, Kierkegaard describes the demonic as a heightened condition of despair. Despair is the condition of misrelation to oneself and to God, and in demonic despair the self defies God by refusing the possibility of repentance and reconciliation. This defiant, demonic despair is, in Kierkegaard's words, "inclosing reserve," or better still "inwardness with a jammed lock" (Kierkegaard 1980, 72). Inwardness is a good thing, since it constitutes our existence as spirit, but demonic despair disfigures it. "Rebelling against all existence," the self posits its existence as an act of spite, a protest against the goodness of God and his creation (73, 74). With my first set of texts, I will focus on the demonic as defiance of the goodness of corporeal being.

Paradise Lost

The classic literary depiction of demonic defiance has to be John Milton's *Paradise Lost*. Milton's celebrated figure of Satan is a perfect picture of the spiteful refusal of the goodness of God and creation. Milton describes a creation in which all things exist to glorify God: the celestial hierarchy, the splendors of the heavens, the created world and its inhabitants. Satan rejects this order. Instead of transcending himself in worship, he turns in on himself. Satan resents the divine appointment of Christ as Lord over all creation, thinking that role should be his. Satan becomes all wounded pride and envy, and "from sense of injured merit" (Milton 2000, I: 98) he sets out on his path of revenge.

Many find Milton's Satan a sympathetic, even heroic, figure. Yet on closer reading, what stands out is the smallness of Satan's motives. Everywhere he turns, he sees the wonder and beauty of creation, yet all he can feel is resentment (2000, III: 552–554). He hates the sun's rays (IV: 37), and beholding the new creatures in the Garden, "the fiend/ Saw undelighted all delight" (4.285-86). Satan cannot abide creation's goodness: "all good to me becomes/ Bane" (IX: 122)—and he sets out to tear down the humans: "others to make such/ as I, though thereby worse to me redound:/ For only in destroying I find ease/ To my relentless thoughts … ” (IX: 128–130). Torn between the goodness of creation and his infernal pride, refusing to repent, Satan tries to resolve his inner conflict by going all-in on the path of destruction.

When Satan sees the humans, he is struck by the corporeal manifestation of God's image: “Creatures of other mold, earth-born perhaps/ not spirits, yet to heavenly spirits bright/ Little inferior … ” Satan wonders at these creatures—“so lovely shines/ In them divine resemblance”—and admits that under different circumstances he could have loved them (IV: 360–364). This wonder lasts only a moment, though, because Satan is intent on revenge (IV: 391–392). He sets his sights on the humans, since an attack on them is the closest he can strike at the heart of God.

Satan is especially disturbed by sex. Just as humans bear the divine image in corporeal form, so they experience spiritual communion in their carnal embrace. “Aside the devil turned/ For envy, yet with jealous leer malign/ Eyed them askance, and to himself thus plained:/ ‘Sight hateful, sight tormenting! Thus these two/ Imparadised within one another's arms/ The happier Eden, shall enjoy their fill/ Of bliss on bliss, while to hell am thrust … ” (IV: 502–506). Satan hates how this carnal knowledge unifies self and other. Their union arises from the essential reversibility of touch: in touching the other, the self is also touched (Kearney 2021, 11, 40–42). As Kearney shows, touch is inescapably exposed to the other, while vision without touch enables the illusion of the isolated spectator, an untouched subject observing the world. Thus Satan: he sees Adam and Eve, touching and being touched, but all he can do is look. An envious voyeur, Satan has lost all tact—Kearney's term for the “carnal wisdom of tactility” (Kearney 2021, 10). He does not know the embodied practical wisdom that comes with touching well.

Adam and Eve do not stay in this state. The fall undoes their harmonious union, replacing it with a desire to possess (IX: 1011–1015, 1110–1130). The carnality of the other diminishes into an opportunity to please the self; what remains is carnality without the other, and thus a carnality without union.

Satan's resentment of sex is the root of a long campaign of disinformation claiming that he has a more positive view of sex than God does. On this account, Satan represents freedom and happiness against the arbitrary commands of a tyrannical God. Better to reign in hell than serve in heaven … .

Why does Milton's Satan have all the best lines? Maybe because Sophists often do. What is surprising is that people are so quick to take Satan at his word; evidently it hasn't occurred to them that the devil might be lying. It's true that the most interesting, dramatic details in *Paradise Lost* revolve around Satan and his demons. They should, since that is what the poem is about. But is Satan really all that attractive? Consider the difference between Satan and Adam: Satan adds excitement to the plot, while Adam seems a bit dull. But who would you actually want to spend time with?[3] Adam is attuned to the vast wonders of creation. In his speeches he talks about

> God, the Forbidden Tree, sleep, the difference between beast and man, his plans for the morrow, the stars, and the angels. He discusses dreams and clouds, the sun, the moon, and the planets, the winds, and the birds. He relates his own creation and celebrates the beauty and majesty of Eve. (Lewis 1942, 101–102)

If philosophy begins in wonder, then Adam is well on his philosophical way. He is interested in everything. Satan, on the other hand, is only interested in one thing: himself. Surrounded by wonders, "he could think of nothing to think of more interesting than his own prestige" (Lewis 1942, 96, 102).[4] Whatever he sees, he can only think of it in terms of how it affects him and his position. From afar he appears a dashing rogue, but how long would you want to spend time with someone like that?

According to Milton's theology, Satan's incurvature is the condition of Hell. Hell is not primarily a place, but a state of mind. Thus, Satan: "Which way I fly is hell; myself am hell … " (IV: 75). In the words of the great fantasist, George MacDonald:

> For the one principle of hell is—'I am my own. I am my own king and my own subject. I am the centre from which go out my thoughts; I am the object and end of my thoughts; back upon me as the alpha and omega of life, my thoughts return.' (MacDonald 1889)

Hell is not other people. It is the self, cut off from all others.

Descent into Hell

This conception of hell as the incurvature of the self is also a central theme in Charles Williams' 1937 novel *Descent into Hell*. This descent does not take place in a grand epic or mythic setting, but in ordinary, everyday situations through unremarkable deeds (Howard 1991, 249). Salvation and damnation often go unobserved, because the mundane has cosmic significance. Here we think of Kearney's notion of "epiphanies of the everyday," his term for the way we come "face-to-face with the infinite in the infinitesimal, and "touch the sacred enfolded in the seeds of ordinary things" (Kearney 2006, 3). Is it also possible that epiphanies of the demonic might also manifest amidst the small business of our everyday lives? Williams' novel suggests so.

The novel is set in a small region north of London called Battle Hill, the residents of which are preparing to stage a play by the celebrated poet

Peter Stanhope. The demonic figure is a fairly minor character, a witchy woman named Lily Sammile—*Lily* as in Lilith, the legendary night hag and first wife of Adam, and *Sammile* as in Samael, the Talmudic figure of Satan. Lily moves at the edges of the plot, but when she shows up it is to offer her therapeutic services to the main characters. She offers the consolation of wishful thinking, the imagination that damns by offering the comfort and solace of stories. False stories. This is a disincarnating imagination. Lily offers "tales that would shut everything but yourself out" (Williams 1937, 109). Her *therapeia* is an escape from reality into the unreality of the incurved self. As we will see, this escape into incurvature is ultimately loss of contact with the embodied other.

The character who follows this path of escape is Lawrence Wentworth, an academic historian and historical advisor to the play. Wentworth is an ambitious scholar, and has an ongoing (and largely unrequited) rivalry with another historian called Aston Moffat. He also has a rival in love. Wentworth has taken a fancy to the actress Adela Hunt, who enjoys talking with him, but has her heart set on the younger and more exciting Hugh Prescott. Wentworth's envy—and incipient hatred—of his two rivals is what sets him on his course of damnation.

Wentworth's problem is that he will not accept a reality that conflicts with his own private, preferred vision of things. As a scholar, he loves the schematic clarity of diagrams, but he has begun to bend historical evidence to fit his diagrams. This unwillingness to accept truth also distorts Wentworth's attitude as a would-be lover. He will not accept that Adela prefers Hugh to him—and that is how he begins his descent into hell. This is damnation as a conscious refusal of what *is*. Wentworth chooses illusion over reality (Howard 1991, 274, 275).

The novel depicts Wentworth's descent with a recurring dream. He is climbing on a rope that is illuminated by moonlight, and which appears to lead endlessly both up and down. There are knots in the rope, and each knot represents a further choice. The choices, however, are small and in themselves appear relatively insignificant. Damnation does not come in a grand cry of defiance, but through small refusals. There is "no shouting or heroic leaps into the abyss" (Howard 1991, 266). Just one small choice after another.

When Wentworth realizes that Adela has ditched him for an evening with Hugh, he is angry. He wants Adela, and he cannot accept that she has chosen someone else over him. Instead of accepting her absence, he demands her presence (Williams 1937, 78), even if that presence is a false image. He opens himself to a demonic imagining, conjuring up a succubus who bears the likeness of Adela. Like an incubus, the succubus is a demonic parody of incarnation—a figure of dysincarnation. The succubus also offers a false, demonic parody of carnal union. Far better than the flesh and blood Adela, the succubus is entirely responsive to Wentworth's imagination and will; she arrives and departs on his schedule, performing his every command and satisfying every wish.

Wentworth's union with the succubus makes for unsettling reading. In a chapter entitled "Return to Eden," Wentworth finds himself in an Eden that overlaps with the garden outside his home. But this is an inversion of Eden. He hears a pronouncement, "It's good for man to be alone" (Williams 1937, 86). The succubus is a simulacrum of otherness. It is "the she that was he" (89). Thus instead of the two becoming one flesh, the succubus allows one flesh to become two (143). As in Milton, this is a carnality without an other, and thus carnality without union.

Wentworth's succubus gradually leads him down into a world of his own imagining, and he loses touch with the human world. He not only prefers the succubus to the real Adela; he even comes to dislike the real Adela (Williams 1937, 131, 132). At the dress rehearsal of the play, he finds the sensation of real flesh and blood others to be physically jarring, almost intolerable. Their voices are piercing. He cannot recognize the people, and can barely respond to them. Eventually, even the succubus ceases to satisfy, since even she is finally too other than himself (199).

At the novel's end, Wentworth takes the train into London to attend a banquet in honor of his rival, Aston Moffat. What follows is a horrifying vision of the loss of all carnal-hermeneutical contact with the world. A fog is gathering around Wentworth, blocking off his senses and preventing him from grasping the sense of anything. Words cease to mean. Speech sounds like sheer gibberish. His senses cease to have sense. Earlier in the novel Lily Sammile tells of her ability to enhance the senses: "If you come with me, I can fill you, fill your body with any sense you choose. I can make you feel whatever you'd choose to be" (Williams 1937, 109). He has lost all contact with anything other than himself. A closed circuit of self touching only itself. As Wentworth discovers, the fulfillment of this promise is not bliss but oblivion.

The Exorcist

In the popular imaginary, surely the most formative text on the demonic is William Peter Blatty's *The Exorcist*. William Friedkin, who directed the film version, once commented that Blatty's novel "invented exorcism and possession for the modern world" (Crucchiola 2018). The novel and its film adaptation are an onslaught, a horrific and very literal spectacle of the demonic in its carnal manifestations. Whether this is a good thing is debatable. It's probably not helpful that there is an assumption that the "classical symptoms" of possession are spinning heads and levitation. Nevertheless, amidst the shock and scares, there is profound insight into the demonic as an attack on the goodness of material creation.

We demonize that which is other, that which we perceive as a threat to our selves. The other in question might be an alien or foreigner, an opponent or an enemy. As Kearney observes, in psychoanalytic terms monsters and demons are often the return of the repressed—i.e., those aspects of the self that the self does not want to confront and therefore projects as a demonic other. "The irrepressible return of the monstrous has reasons that Reason may not always understand" (Kearney 2003, 34). Thus Kearney argues that what we need, "when confronted with extreme tendencies to demonize or deify monsters, is to look into our own psyches and examine our consciences in the mirror of our gods and monsters" (42–43).

In *The Exorcist,* the repressed returns with a vengeance. Eleven-year-old Regan MacNeil is trapped in herself, under the assault of a demon called Pazuzu, which she knows as Captain Howdy. Her strange, shocking behavior has her mother at a loss. What could explain it? The audience knows what the characters are slow to recognize: modern Reason is wholly incapable of diagnosing or treating what is clearly a case of demonic possession. The psychiatrists, with their clinics and EEGs, are not up to the task. Nor is the modern, liberal Catholicism of the Jesuit priest Fr. Karras. In Charles Taylor's terms, the doctors and priests assume we are buffered selves living in a disenchanted world. There is no place for gods or demons. Yet the case of Regan O'Neill is a reminder that the self is more porous than we would like to think.

The Exorcist also confronts the return of the repressed body. It expresses an abject horror of the flesh. The body at once me, myself, and mine, yet also strange, foreign, and unfamiliar. This strangeness can manifest as the demonic. One interpretation of *The Exorcist* finds in it the threat of contamination by contact with the strangeness of feminine sexuality. Regan is about to enter puberty, when the body becomes strangely other. There is some merit to this reading, but in *The Exorcist* it is not only sexuality that threatens to contaminate. It is materiality itself (Yost 2014; Mäyrä 1999, 143–168). The demon—Pazuzu—debases the body and reduces it to the bestial. Regan makes animal sounds, and the demon even refers to her as such: "The sow is mine!" As Kearney notes, images of devils and demons are often half-human, half-bestial (Kearney 2003, 28, 29). His point is that such depictions degrade others and thereby justify their exclusion, persecution, and scapegoating. *The Exorcist* excavates another layer of meaning: while the sad history of demonizing others is all too common among human beings, demons too render the human image in demonized, bestial form. The novel and film are most shocking when we see the demon distorting Regan's humanity—in voice and visage—as half-bestial. It is an assault on the embodied image of God.

This point becomes clear in a conversation between the two priests, the younger Fr. Karras and the older, more experienced Fr. Merrin. Fr. Karras asks why the demon would possess this young girl. Fr. Merrin responds:

Who can really hope to know? And yet I think the demon's target is not the possessed; it is us ... the observers ... I think the point is to make us despair; to reject our own humanity, Damien: to see ourselves as ultimately bestial, vile, and putrescent; without dignity; ugly; unworthy. And there lies the heart of it, perhaps: in unworthiness. For I think belief in God is not a matter of reason at all; I think it finally is a matter of love: of accepting the possibility that God could ever love us. ... Long ago I despaired of ever loving my neighbor. Certain people ... repelled me. And so how could I love them? I thought. It tormented me, Damien; it led me to despair of myself and from, very soon, to despair of my God. My faith was shattered. (Blatty 2011, 345)

The demonic imagines our embodied being with disgust, turning its otherness into a threat that will close us in on ourselves. Fr. Karras must confront young Regan in her offensive carnality, overcoming his revulsion with love.

Recall Weil's point is that the demonic imagination is a disincarnating imagination. It seeks to cut ties with the body and be free of the material. Commenting on Weil, Alan Jacobs writes that the created (and the converted) imagination grounds us in the body, and in the world (Jacobs 2018, 76). It responds to the other in love. Yet loving the concrete, carnal other is precisely what Fr. Karras struggles with. It is no accident that his name is Damien, for his namesake, St. Damien of Molokai, spent over a decade ministering in a leper colony in Hawaii, eventually succumbing to the disease himself (Yost 2014).

By contrast, Fr. Damien Karras struggles with the body. He undertakes a dual *askēsis* to liberate himself from the body, training as a boxer to perfect the body and as a psychiatrist to treat the soul. But he cannot avoid that which he wants to repress. Early in the novel, he encounters an old, drunk derelict while waiting for the subway. The old man is repulsive: lying in a puddle of urine, wearing remnants of vomit. Karras doesn't want the old man to call him. He tries to look away. This is a horrifying call to hospitality: "He could not bear to search for Christ again in stench and hollow eyes; for the Christ of pus and bleeding excrement, the Christ who could not be" (Blatty 2011, 49). Likewise, he struggles to love his mother in her dingy apartment:

Dark complexion. Stubby, gnarled legs. He sat in the kitchen and listened to her talk, the dingy walls and soiled floor seeping into his bones. The apartment was a hovel. ... He went to the bathroom. Yellowing newspaper spread on the tile. Stains of rust in the tub and in the sink. On the floor, an old corset. These the seeds of vocation. (Blatty 2011, 51)

Fr. Karras's vocation would lead him to love others in their unpleasant carnal, material conditions—like Fr. Damien of Molokai, and like Christ. He fears he has lost this vocation, and indeed his faith, precisely because of this disgust at the material. Even his daily routine disgusts him: "*The need to rend food with the teeth and then defecate.*" For Fr. Karras, this disgust belongs to his existential struggle with evil. He sees no sign of hope for a redemption of the corporeal. "The raising of Lazarus was dim in the distant past" (Blatty 2011, 52).

The Exorcist dives head-first into this horror of the body. Yet rather than surrendering to this horror, the novel actually challenges us to overcome it by revealing it as a failure of charity—a failure to love others in their living, breathing flesh (Yost 2014). The self is locked within itself, unable to connect to others. Likewise, we see Regan trapped in herself, struggling to reach her mother and the priests. On her abdomen we see letters start to take shape in her own handwriting, "a bas-relief script rising up in clear letters of raised and blood-red skin. Two words: help me" (Blatty 2011, 307). This horrific text is inscribed in her flesh, in her own handwriting, crying out of isolation. Like Fr. Karras, she is in desperate need of contact with the incarnate—and Incarnate—other.

***

Descartes saw retreat into the self as a retreat into certainty. Faced with the possibility that an evil demon might be deceiving him about everything he believes, Descartes seeks a foundation that promises to withstand all doubt: *Cogito, ergo sum.* Even if Descartes is deceived about everything else, this judgment is necessarily true the moment he utters it.

How much of modern society has been shaped by this fateful argument? The cogito promises to be the indubitable truth from which the self can regain contact with God and the world. What if the cogito is not a refuge of certainty, but instead the demon's most clever ploy, isolating us from the world of our embodied relations with others? "To vanquish the devil is hard; for it involves renouncing our dearest illusion – the illusion of the self and its sovereignty" (Scruton 1994, 481). The illusion—the one principle of hell—that I am my own.

Principalities and Powers

So far we have seen how the demonic distorts and disfigures embodied relations between self and the other. A carnal hermeneutics of the demonic must also contend with the influence of the demonic on a larger, social level, in what the New Testament describes as principalities and powers. In the Epistle to the Ephesians we read the following:

> For we wrestle not against flesh and blood, but against principalities, against powers, against the rulers of the darkness of this world, against spiritual wickedness in high places. (Eph. 6:12)

This notion of the principalities and powers is an important expansion to any carnal hermeneutics of the demonic. What are they, and what is the carnal significance of these spiritual powers? What would be a carnal interpretation of the claim that we wrestle not against flesh and blood?

Theologically, the principalities and powers are realities created by God to order creation, for the organization and flourishing of human beings in their life together. They include the symbols, systems, and institutions that form our social imaginaries. These spiritual dominions become demonic when they turn and revolt against God, positing what René Girard calls a kind of false transcendence (Girard 2001, 17, 96). This is not merely a figurative way to characterize the influence of "dehumanizing institutions and social systems." This figurative language names "the *actual inner spirit of these suprahuman entities*" (Wink 1986, 42). They have rejected their divine vocations, which exist to order the world so that human beings can live together and flourish.

For example, institutions play a necessary role in the well-being of society: unions, universities, churches, charities, courts, departments, and agencies all exist to serve persons. And yet as William Stringfellow observes, too often persons are sacrificed to the preservation of the institution, in such a way that individuals experience a kind of bondage to the institution (Stringfellow 2006, 56–57).

Technology is another such principality. It has the power to promote human flourishing, yet can turn against this vocation and disfigure created being. Neil Gaiman's novel *American Gods* offers a perceptive take on this point. The story novel centers on the conflict between the old gods that came to America with generations of immigrants, but who were slowly fading away with the forgetfulness of their devotees. One might expect the twilight of these gods was a consequence of materialistic disenchantment, but America has new gods feeding on new beliefs and devotion: "gods of credit-card and freeway, of internet and telephone, of radio and hospital and television, gods of plastic and of beeper and of neon" (Gaiman 2011, 176).

At one point the novel's protagonist, Shadow, meets the god of TV herself, speaking out of the television:

> "I'm the all-seeing eye and the world of the cathode ray. I'm the boob tube. I'm the little shrine the family gathers to adore."

> "You're the television? Or someone in the television?"

> "The TV's the altar. I'm what people are sacrificing to."

"What do they sacrifice?" asked Shadow.

"Their time, mostly ... Sometimes each other." (Gaiman 2011, 221)

This is an entertaining conceit for a fantasy novel, but it is also a genuine theological insight. The power of television may not be personified in this way, but it is nevertheless a principality with the power to turn demonic.

The same might be true of other technologies. They demand our allegiance, form us with their own liturgies, and tempt us to sacrifice ourselves and our embodied being. Kearney discusses this point at length in chapter 5 of *Touch*, where he considers the need to "reclaim touch in an age of excarnation." The possibilities of digital technology tempt us with disincarnation, to seek a kind of gnostic salvation from the flesh as we transcend into the virtual. Technology also tempts us with a kind of *dys*incarnation, a disfiguring of flesh, which we no longer see as a good gift of creation and giver of intrinsic meaning, but as raw material to transform by the powers of imagination and will.

Here we recall Weil's point regarding the demonic imagination as a power of disincarnation. Image and imagination are by nature good, but they pose temptations of their own. This is true of the images we have of ourselves. Every person has an image that focuses their sense of who they are and who they might become (Stringfellow 2006, 54–57). This good power turns bad when the image takes on a life of its own and exerts its power over the person. The image can control them, take possession of them, and even destroy them. The image becomes larger than life—an icon, an idol with an attendant cult of personality. Historically, this has been the privilege of the few, mostly kings and emperors. Mass communication made a new kind of celebrity possible. Now with the digital technologies of social media, any person can experience this bondage to their image. Thanks to digital devices, we can all be like Dorian Gray, envious of the image that mere flesh cannot match.

Another aspect of the powers is ideology, in the many -*isms* that claim to disclose the hidden truths and promise liberation and salvation: "Each principality claims a man's loyalty, service, and worship; each makes essentially the same demands that a man regard it as his god, as the one in the idolatry of which a man's life will gain moral significance" (Stringfellow 2006, 57–60). When these powers exalt themselves as gods demanding this kind of worship, they become demonic and have the power to possess.

Dostoyevsky's novel *Demons* is a masterful diagnosis of such ideological possession. The reader never encounters these demons directly, because they are ideologies like rationalism, empiricism, idealism, utilitarianism, materialism, positivism, socialism, nationalism, nihilism, and atheism (Pevear 1994, xvii). These *isms* take some truth about the human person—freedom, rationality, truth, equality, fraternity, justice—and distort it so that ideals become ideologies. This is what possesses the radical intelligentsia in *Demons*. We tend to think of ideas as something *we* have, but Dostoyevsky describes what happens when ideas have us. Or as one character says to another, "it was not you who ate the idea, but the idea that ate you" (Dostoyevsky 1994, 558, cf. 616). The outcome of this ideological possession is violence, including a series of horrific murders and suicide.

In the modern era, the power of ideology is heightened through mass society, culture, and communication. Kierkegaard was especially sensitive to the ways these powers can dehumanize and even demonize people. Kierkegaard identifies the pointedly modern form of possession. In one of his journal entries he writes:

> In contrast to what was said about possession in the Middle Ages and times like that, that there were individuals who sold themselves to the devil, I have an urge to write a book:
>
> ### *Possession and Obsession in Modern Times*
>
> and show how people *en masse* abandon themselves to it, how it is now carried on *en masse*. This is why people run together in flocks—so that natural and animal rage will grip a person, so that he feels stimulated, inflamed, and *ausser sich*. The scenes on Bloksberg are utterly pedantic compared to this demonic lust, a lust to lose oneself in order to evaporate in a potentiation, so that a person is outside of himself, does not really know what he is doing or what he is saying or who it is or what it is speaking through him, while the blood rushes faster, the eyes glitter and stare fixedly, the passions boil, lusts seethe. (Kierkegaard 1975, 167)[5]

Kierkegaard's description of the carnal manifestation of this possession are striking. The self is lost, depersonalized, dehumanized in this ecstatic state. Something else is speaking through the self as ideas, slogans, and phrases take possession and turn destructive. This condition manifests in the body: rushing blood; fixed, flashing eyes; boiling passions, and seething lusts. How does this kind of unclean spirit overtake a crowd? How do people become possessed and obsessed *en masse*? And how are they delivered from it?

Unfortunately, Kierkegaard never wrote this book, but there are other works of fiction that can help us understand the way these powers possess. Dostoyevsky's *Demons* is the preeminent example. More recently, the film *Jojo Rabbit* has explored similar territory—albeit not in the milieu of the Russian intelligentsia, but in the *Hitlerjugend* of 1940s Germany. It's an unlikely and off-putting premise for a comedic film, but it gives genuine insight into the struggle between the human and the demonic.

Jojo Rabbit

Jojo Betzler is a young boy in WWII Germany. His father is away (fighting for Germany, Jojo believes) and his sister has recently died, so he lives alone with his mother Rosie. Jojo is an avid booster of the Nazis and an enthusiastic member of the Hitler Youth. It is no exaggeration to say he is possessed by Nazi ideology.

Jojo is not the only one. The opening credits of the film make the audacious move of setting archival footage of Nazi rallies to a German version of The Beatles' "I Wanna Hold Your Hand." What seems like flagrantly bad taste is actually quite perceptive regarding the power of mass hysteria in a crowd. Beatlemania and Nazi rallies are different things, but this pairing of image and music tells us something about the power of the image to possess *en masse*. Hitler's fans did not think they were being overtaken by an unclean spirit; they saw him as the next big thing in world history.

Similar to the way Regan O'Neill befriended Captain Howdy through her Ouija board in *The Exorcist*, Jojo has his own personal relationship with Hitler. Rather than scares, though, this movie plays the relation for laughs. Jojo is a Hitler superfan. He has posters in his room. But he also imagines Hitler as a kind of imaginary friend. Hitler is his advisor and confidante, and is about as silly as a cartoon devil sitting on his shoulder.

Jojo's mother, who is secretly involved in the anti-Nazi resistance, confesses her distress over her son's enthusiasm. "He's a fanatic … I know he's in there somewhere. The little boy who loves to play and runs to you because he's scared of thunder. Thinks you invented chocolate cake." That is the tension in Jojo: he is a sensitive young boy, yet he fancies himself a fierce Nazi. On a camping trip with his troop of Hitler Youth, he is too afraid to kill a rabbit, yet he boasts that he is ready to kill Jews for Hitler.

On the same campout, the troop receives a lesson on how to identify Jews. The lesson is a case study for Kearney's discussion of the demonized other in *Strangers, Gods, and Monsters*. On the chalkboard is a ridiculous sketch of "*der Jude*" as a devil, complete with scales, fangs, and serpent's tongue. That night in their tent, Jojo's friend Yorki confesses:

"Jews sound scary, huh?"

"Not to me. If I met one, I'd kill it like that." (Jojo snaps his finger).

"But how would you know if you saw one? They could look just like us."

"I'd feel its head for horns."

Imagine Jojo's surprise when he meets an actual Jew. One day while he is home alone, he hears a noise in his sister's room. Scratches on the floor point to a hidden door, which opens to a secret compartment in the wall. Inside JoJo finds a teenage girl. "Are you a ghost?" he asks. She replies, "I'm something much worse. I think you know what I am." Not a ghost, but the very devil Jojo had been waiting for: a Jew.

There is, however, a problem. This girl, Elsa, is his mother's guest. She was friends with Jojo's sister, and Jojo's mother Rosie has been hiding her from the Nazis. Jojo can't report her to the Gestapo without implicating his mother, so he finds himself implicated, without his consent, in a criminal act of hospitality. Jojo is, to borrow a phrase from Kearney, "hosting the stranger." His home is contaminated. His clear opposition of self and other is under threat. To recall Kearney's point, the other we demonize is not so wholly other. Prior to any choice or consent of his own, this demonic other is already there, in his home. Jojo is hosting the very devil he fears.

Since he cannot report Elsa's presence, Jojo decides to interview her. He has been working on a book about how to identify Jews, under the working title *Yoohoo Jew*. He starts talking to Elsa. At times she toys with him, telling him outrageous stories about how Jews originally lived in caves before they moved into towns, they cast magic spells, they can read minds, and they hang from the ceiling like bats. Other times she is more frank: Jews are like Jojo, "but human." And this is what Jojo gradually starts to see. Jojo's conversations with Elsa, the real flesh and blood person, reveals her humanity. She ceases to be the demonic other. And as Elsa shows her humanity to Jojo, so Jojo's own humanity starts to return. As Elsa becomes less demonic, Jojo becomes less possessed by his own demon—namely, Hitler.

The most daring thing about *Jojo Rabbit* is not that it humanizes Elsa, but that it humanizes Jojo. As an aspiring Nazi, it would be easy to demonize him. Instead, the film surprises us by giving a profound expression of the biblical idea that we wrestle not against flesh and blood. The incarnate other is not our enemy. Rosie and Elsa are not wrestling against Jojo, but the principalities and powers that have captured his mind: namely, the mystique of Hitler and the ideology of Nazism.

Jojo's deliverance is gradual, but there are two decisive moments. The first comes after his mother is executed for treason. Jojo finds her hanging in the town square. He is alone. Elsa is the only one left in his home, and she makes the ideal scapegoat. He walks up to her, angry and scared, and feebly plunges his knife into her shoulder. The wound isn't serious, but it reveals a new level of Elsa's humanity to Jojo, manifest in her vulnerable flesh and blood. Against his earlier boasting about killing Jews with a snap of his fingers, Jojo finds he can't kill Elsa. This is a deep insight into carnal ethics, as actual contact with Elsa ultimately disarms Jojo.

This moment of recognition leads to the other decisive moment in Jojo's deliverance. It's an exorcism of sorts, though the rite is decidedly more profane than sacred. Hitler is desperate, since he knows his time is up. He insults Elsa. He barks orders at Jojo. Finally, he pleads pitifully to stay, until Jojo kicks him straight out the window with a resolute "Fuck off, Hitler." Like the climax of *The Exorcist*, Hitler is expelled through the bedroom window. Not quite "the power of Christ compels you," but an exorcism nonetheless.

Jojo struggles against a grotesque, demonic image of Jews. This demonization is the work of a disincarnating imagination, which sees only abstract categories rather than the surplus of carnal humanity. Jojo's deliverance from this possession comes through the encounter with the incarnate human being—better known as *Elsa*. In Elsa, Jojo meets a surplus of humanity that exceeds and ultimately drowns the demonic abstraction that had possessed him.

Dostoyevsky points to a similar deliverance in describing his own ideological possession as a young man. During the 1840s he was involved with the Petrashevsky Circle, a literary group whose politics led to charges of conspiracy and even a death sentence. Dostoyevsky narrowly avoided execution but spent four years in prison, an experience that transformed him dramatically. He recounts his mindset as he stood on the scaffold and heard his death sentence. There was no repentance of "those ideas and notions which possessed our spirits." Instead, the death sentence promised to purify them as martyrs: "nothing broke us, and our convictions only supported our spirits by the awareness of a duty fulfilled" (Dostoyevsky 1993b, 288, 289).

What ultimately freed Dostoyevsky and his comrades from their ideological possession was neither arguments nor ideas, but something else: "direct contact with the People, the brotherly union with them in common misfortune, the awareness that we ourselves had become as they, equal to them, and even placed on the very lowest of their levels" (Dostoyevsky 1993b, 289). Note that phrase: "direct contact." It is another way of describing what Kearney calls "tactile proximity" (Kearney 2021, 7). It was the real encounter with incarnate, flesh and blood people rather than abstractions. This happened gradually as Dostoyevsky and others returned "to the root of the people, to discover the Russian soul, to recognize the People's spirit," which Dostoyevsky knew from his upbringing.

Of course, this talk of "the People" with a capital P is also susceptible to falling into socio-political abstraction—another work of the disincarnating imagination. Dostoyevsky recognized this danger, and was keenly aware of the gap between the concrete existing human being and intellectual categories. In the words of Mikhail Bakhtin, "An individual cannot be completely incarnated into the flesh of existing socio-historical categories ... There always remains an unrealized surplus of humanness" (Morson 2009, 274). This truth bears repeating in our current moment, when our relations with each other are increasingly mediated by identity markers, which are in turn mediated by technological devices. It is too easy to hate the other when we see them on a screen as the virtual icon of all that we oppose and all that threatens us. *They* are the problem. An incarnating imagination can help us to see the surplus of humanity that exceeds our group identities.

Conclusion

Let me close with two points of caution. First, I do not want to propose a facile, sentimental model of dialogue. The problem with sentimentalism is that it subsists on abstractions. It fails to see others in their flawed humanity. It's easy to conjure up a sentimental love for an abstract humanity. Much harder is loving our neighbor (or uninvited guest) concretely. As Ivan Karamazov confesses: "In order to love a person it is necessary for him to be concealed from view; the moment he shows his face—love disappears" (Dostoyevsky 1993a, 272). If the encounter with the embodied other is often necessary to overcome ideological possession, it is not always sufficient. It might also provoke greater distaste or even hostility.

Flannery O'Connor writes that sentimentality is an "excess," "an overemphasis on innocence" that distorts because it does not reckon with the fallenness of human beings. Redemption requires more than tender sentiments; it requires participation in the cross of Christ. This participation is a long, slow process, but sentimentality wants to jump ahead to "a mock state of innocence" (O'Connor 1969, 147, 148). Out of these sentimental visions of innocence, "we govern by tenderness … When tenderness is detached from the source of tenderness, its logical outcome is terror. It ends in forced-labor camps and in the fumes of the gas chamber" (O'Connor 1969, 227). This might seem like a big leap, but O'Connor's point is that sentimentalism sorts people into abstract categories: innocent victims who need no redemption, and guilty villains who are incapable of redemption. Both fail to see the surplus of humanity in our neighbor.

My second point of caution: a full carnal hermeneutics of the demonic cannot avoid theology. When O'Connor notes that tenderness is "wrapped in theory," she attributes this to being "cut off from the person of Christ." A fully theological response to the demonic would need to consider not only the ontological surplus of the carnal human person but also the ontological ground of personhood in Christ. The enemy is not ultimately flesh and blood persons, but principalities and powers. These are not overcome by force of flesh, but by spirit. In the words of Paul the apostle, "the weapons of our warfare are not carnal, but mighty through God to the pulling down of strong holds; casting down imaginations, and every high thing that exalts itself against the knowledge of God, and bringing into captivity every thought to the obedience of Christ …". (2 Cor. 10: 3–5)

Yet if the weapons of our warfare are not carnal, it is precisely the carnality of Christ—the Incarnation and bodily resurrection—that establishes his dominion over the demonic and reclaims the material creation.

Notes

1 Commenting on this passage from Weil, Alan Jacobs writes: "To imagine rightly is to be truly embodied; to be truly embodied is to imagine rightly. It is just this proper grounding in the world that the demons wish to deny us ... " (Jacobs, 2018, 77).
2 See Kearney (2021, 2): " ... if incarnation is the image becoming flesh, excarnation is flesh becoming image. Incarnation invests flesh; excarnation divests it."
3 I am borrowing this question and the contrast that follows from Lewis (1942, 101, 102).
4 Satan is not a world of wonder, but "a world of lies and propaganda, of wishful thinking, of incessant autobiography" (Lewis, 1942, 102).
5 Cf. Wink (1986, 50).

References

Blatty, William Peter. 2011. *The Exorcist*. 40th Anniversary Edition. New York: HarperCollins.
Crucchiola, Jordan. 2018. "The Exorcist's William Friedkin on Filming an Actual Exorcism." *Vulture*, April 20, 2018. https://www.vulture.com/2018/04/william-friedkin-on-the-terror-of-filming-an-actual-exorcism-in-the-devil-and-father-amorth.html
Dostoyevsky, Fyodor. 1993a. *The Brothers Karamazov*. Translated by David McDuff. London: Penguin Books.
Dostoyevsky, Fyodor. 1993b. *A Writer's Diary*, vol. 1. Translated by Kenneth Lantz, 1873–1876. Evanston: Northwestern University Press.
Dostoyevsky, Fyodor. 1994. *Demons*. Translated by Richard Pevear and Larissa Volokhonsky. New York: Random House.
Frank, Joseph. 2010a. *Between Religion and Rationality: Essays in Russian Literature and Culture*. Princeton: Princeton University Press.
Frank, Joseph. 2010b. *Dostoyevsky: A Writer in His Time*. Princeton: Princeton University Press.
Gaiman, Neil. 2011. *American Gods*. Tenth Anniversary Edition. New York: William Morrow.
Girard, René. 2001. *I See Satan Fall Like Lightning*. Translated by James G. Williams. Maryknoll: Orbis Books.
Howard, Thomas. 1991. *The Novels of Charles Williams*. San Francisco: Ignatius Press.
Jacobs, Alan. 2018. *The Year of Our Lord 1943: Christian Humanism in an Age of Crisis*. New York: Oxford University Press.
Jojo Rabbit. 2019. Directed and screenplay by Taika Waititi. Distributed by Fox Searchlight Pictures (Century City, California). *Release date (USA)*. October 18, 2019.

Kearney, Richard. 2001. *The God Who May Be: A Hermeneutics of Religion.* London: Routledge.

Kearney, Richard. 2002. *On Stories.* London: Routledge.

Kearney, Richard. 2003. *Strangers, Gods, and Monsters: Interpreting Otherness.* London: Routledge.

Kearney, Richard. 2006. "Epiphanies of the Everyday: Toward a Micro-Eschatology." In *After God: Richard Kearney and the Religious Turn in Contemporary Philosophy*, edited by John Panteleimon Manoussakis, 21–37. New York: Fordham University Press.

Kearney, Richard. 2021. *Touch: Recovering Our Most Vital Sense.* New York: Columbia University Press.

Kearney, Richard and Brian Treanor. 2015. "Introduction: Carnal Hermeneutics from Head to Foot." In *Carnal Hermeneutics*, edited by Richard Kearney and Brian Treanor, 1–12. New York: Fordham University Press.

Kierkegaard, Søren. 1975. *Søren Kierkegaard's Journals and Papers*, Volume 4, S-Z. Edited and translated by Howard V. Hong and Edna H. Hong. Bloomington: Indiana University Press.

Kierkegaard, Søren. 1980. *The Sickness Unto Death: A Christian Psychological Exposition for Upbuilding and* Awakening. Edited and translated by Howard V. Hong and Edna H. Hong. Princeton: Princeton University Press.

Lewis, C.S. 1942. *Preface to Paradise Lost.* New York: Oxford University Press.

MacDonald, George. 1889. "Kingship." *Unspoken Sermons.* Series III. Retrieved from Project Gutenberg. https://www.gutenberg.org/cache/epub/9057/pg9057.html

Mäyrä, Frans Illka. 1999. *Demonic Texts and Textual Demons: The Demonic Tradition, the Self, and Popular Fiction.* Tampere: Tampere University Press.

Milton, John. 2000. *Paradise Lost.* London: Penguin Books.

Morson, Gary Saul. 2009. "The Intelligentsia and Its Critics." In *A Companion to Russian History*, edited by A. Gleason. New Jersey: Wiley-Blackwell.

O'Connor, Flannery. 1969. *Mystery and Manners: Occasional Prose.* Edited by Sally and Robert Fitzgerald. New York: Farrar, Straus and Giroux.

Pevear, Richard. 1994. "Foreword." In *Demons*, by Fyodor Dostoyevsky. Edited by Richard Pevear and Larissa Volokhonsky, vii–xxiii. New York: Vintage Books.

Scruton, Roger. 1994. *Modern Philosophy: An Introduction and Survey.* London: Penguin Books.

Stringfellow, William. 2006. *Free in Obedience.* Eugene: Wipf & Stock Publishers.

Weil, Simone. 1952. *Gravity and Grace.* Translated by Emma Craufurd. London: Routledge and Kegan Paul.

Williams, Charles. 1937. *Descent into Hell.* Grand Rapids: Eerdmans.

Wink, Walter. 1986. *Unmasking the Powers: The Invisible Forces That Determine Human Existence.* Minneapolis: Fortress Press.

Yost, Julia. 2014. "Fear of Children: What the Exorcist Makes Us Confront." *First Things.* October 31, 2014. https://www.firstthings.com/web-exclusives/2014/10/fear-of-children

Part III

Touching Imagination

Chapter 7

Earth Creatures: Anacarnation in an Excarnate Age

M. E. Littlejohn

Richard Kearney's latest book, *Touch: Recovering Our Most Vital Sense* (2021), brings to the fore a theme that runs throughout his work: the deep human tendency toward various manifestations of "excarnation."[1] As Kearney observes on a transit ride into Boston, today we are "in touch" like never before, and yet out of touch with touch—like transit riders, devices in hand dissociated from the changing cityscape, as the train runs its course, and people get on and off. We are present, yet not present at all, so uncomfortable are we in our own skin. The spectacles on "touch" screens hold us captive to that which is outside, intangible, ethereal, yet more real than real, till the battery runs out and the ordinary returns, but now seeming anemic, dull, and pale after our excarnate excursions. We return to ourselves suddenly, but it is as though we are self-vacant, and can no longer be ourselves except as we extend ourselves outside ourselves and into the great ethereal expanse of cyberspace. While much of the world awakens to the incarnate reality of hunger pangs in their bellies and the feel of the meager handful of rice that must sustain their bodies till the next day, for many in "developed" societies their first action on waking is to reach for devices to reengage the digital world. This absorption in the virtual continues throughout the day, while sipping lattes at coffee shops, in transit on the bus, at work, and again at home.

Kearney is no Luddite, and openly acknowledges the value of digital technology. Yet he also recognizes the danger of losing ourselves in excarnation; we touch our screens but the "double sensation" of carnal, communal contact becomes merely "one-way voyeurism" (Kearney 2020, 326). But this is not a new trend, only a novel manifestation of an old malady, an ongoing temptation that appears in various guises at different times. Philosophy is not an innocent bystander, often generating and perpetuating these frameworks. As an antidote to our current predicament, where our digital tools and devices are working on us, shaping our self-understanding, and reinforcing excarnation, Kearney bids us to get back in touch with each other and with the world, returning to and restoring our tactile and dialogical mutuality in "anacarnation."

DOI: 10.4324/9781003285649-11

In *Touch*, Kearney's path leads through a conceptual, linguistic, herme-neutic, and dialogical retrieval (2021, 6). He demonstrates how the incarnate wisdom of "Tact," "Savvy," "Flair," "Insight," and "Sound" efface any clear line between body and mind, and explores myths and philosophies that have been formative in shaping our current understanding of carnality (9–31). Kearney suggests that it was Platonism, if not the subtle philoso-phical dialectics of Plato himself that served as a major source for ex-carnation. The Platonic tradition perpetuated "a system governed by the soul's eye," a metaphysical extension of the sense of sight (2021, 33–34). In it, human beings are identified as *anthropos*, "upward gazers," and detached seers (*theoria*) surveying the theatre of the universe as speculative, dis-embodied theorizers of life. In response to this excarnate tendency of the Hellenic tradition, Kearney provides several paths of anacarnational re-covery. He first proposes a return to the philosophy of Aristotle, which gives primacy to touch over sight (34–45). By exploring the concept of incarnate wounded healers, he also provides a hermeneutic retrieval of the Judaic and Christian tradition, which is too often skewed when viewed through the prism of an eroded Platonism (73–83). Yet, there is still more philosophical territory to explore in the return to incarnate living, and Kearney, a dialo-gical thinker par excellence, invites us to join in the project of diagnosis, hermeneutic retrieval, and ongoing recovery.

This chapter traverses a parallel path to the one Kearney takes through the Hellenic and Judaic traditions, culminating with the great transitional figure of St. Augustine, who did his thinking at the intersection of these two great traditions. First we will explore how a myth of soul-body du-alism entered philosophy and exerted its power over the philosophical imagination. Next, close reading of the profoundly incarnate texts of the Judaic imagination will serve as, a counterweight to this anthropological dualism. We will then clarify how an appropriately "carnal" hermeneutics can avoid the temptation of "excarnate" hermeneutics, which often governs our contemporary readings of the past. Finally, all these ideas will be put to work through the example of St. Augustine, who has been accused of transmitting dualism to Western thought. But if we read his *Confessions* with a similar hermeneutic nuance to the one Augustine himself employs as he reads and retrieves the Hellenic and Judaic tradi-tions, we discover that his narrative journey of the restless heart is not one of excarnate dualism but a path to anacarnation.

The Hellenic Imagination and the Myth of Dualism

The view of human beings as a composite of soul and body, or mind and body, has had a remarkable resilience across time. Perhaps this is because it is rooted in human life, in the reverie of thought and dreams, and ultimately in our fear of death. It is with respect to "last things" that our abstract thought and existential questions are forced to meet, for we are possessed with immortal longings and are deeply concerned as to whether these longings are founded or in vain. These questions reached an early climax in the *Phaedo,* when Socrates' friends gathered in his cell to discuss the fate of human beings and hear the sage's thoughts as his end drew near. At least on the standard text-book reading (which, while questionable, has had enormous influence on the philosophical tradition), Plato here embraces a thoroughly excarnate account of human nature.

Fearful that the soul ceases to exist at death, "scattering like a breath or smoke" (Plato 1966, 70a), Socrates' friend Cebes requests a reasoned explanation of the ancient belief that the soul is immortal. According to the *Cratylus,* it was the religious cult of the Orphics who named soul ψυχή (*psyche*) and imposed the name σῶμα (*soma*) on the body, a contrast that lends each part the status of an entity (400c).[2] *Soma*'s etymological link to σῆμα (*sema*), "prison" or "tomb," indicates that the body is the place of the soul's rehabilitation and expiation for a prior fault. The path to salvation lies in detachment, purification, and eventual liberation from the body. The *Phaedo* considers the position that the human being is composed of two different persisting *things,* neither dependent on the other for its existence: souls can exist without a body, and, in the same way, a body can continue to exist without a soul. The soul, responsible for intelligence and thought, has no parts or components (78b–c). It is in some ways changeless, abstract, eternal, and invisible to sight, and while it is said to be a "prisoner in the body" (78d–79e), it is not made of matter, and it does not require any material thing in order to exist.

This anthropological dualism is wed to a dualistic epistemology, where the body is a hindrance to the attainment of wisdom: understanding the true essence of each thing is not possible by "dragging in" the lowly senses but rather only through the exercise of immaterial "pure absolute reason." The soul thinks best "when alone by itself, and takes leave of the body." Therefore, "the soul of the philosopher greatly despises the body and avoids it and strives to be alone by itself" (Plato 1966, 64b–c). The philosopher who prepares to understand the pure absolute essence of each thing "removes himself ... from eyes and ears, and ... from his whole body, because he feels that its companionship disturbs the soul and hinders it from attaining truth and wisdom" (65e–66b). Therein lies the powerful mutually reinforcing co-dependence of dualism and rationalism, where rationalism is a consequence of dualism, and dualism is a consequence of rationalism. The primacy that Socrates gives to the care of the soul in the *Apology* is now interpreted as the primacy of care of the soul over the body. Hence the "true philosophers" who "pursue philosophy aright study nothing but dying and being dead," that is, detaching the soul as much as possible from the body in the pursuit of truth, anticipating the soul's liberation at death.

Plato's appeal to Orphic myth gave this ancient conceptual picture the full weight of philosophical authority, bequeathing soul/body dualism to Western thought. In the 3rd c. A.D., Plotinus further systematized soul-body dualism, rationalism, and cosmology at the reestablished Platonic school in Athens. Each of the *Enneads* contains the glimpse of a unified vision of the architecture of the universe. Knowledge attained in each region of inquiry is dependent on the soul's immaterial nature, which allows it to traverse the lowest regions of the sensible material and the highest levels of Divinity (Porphyry 1966, 4.11; 5.5).

For Plotinus, the body does not belong to our true nature. The immaterial human soul emanates from the absolute abundance of the One, through Nous, and Universal Soul. But in a moment of self-assertive audacity, τόλμα (*tolma*), the soul leaves its highest activities to plunge into the body, where it now suffers alienation and imprisonment for the duration of earthy life (Plotinus 1966–88, IV: 8.4, 360). The embodied soul may choose to fall even farther, becoming slave to material pleasures, submitting itself to that to which it is by nature superior (IV: 8.5, 361–362). To become what it is in truth, the soul must remember its true nature, exercising its proper rule over the body, rather than being ruled by it (I: 2.3, 32–33). Philosophy helps guide the soul beyond sense perception and beyond discursive thought to union with the *Nous* and finally with the One (IV: 7.20, 578). This journey beyond the body is characterized as an ascent "from the alone to the Alone" (VI: 9.11, 625; translation modified).

The dualist myth of the Orphics was not the only strain of Hellenistic thought—again, Kearney recognizes Aristotle as the most obvious counter-example. And while it would be wise to question the veracity of the "standard reading" of the Platonic tradition, the fact remains that it has been a deeply influential one. This philosophical myth carried in the texts of Plato and the Neo-Platonists passed through Augustine and eventually to Descartes, whose new formulation made the immaterial cogito the first principle of philosophy. Whether or not these thinkers themselves actually adhered to dualism, this conceptual picture has informed readers' understanding of these texts and profoundly marked their philosophical imaginations. So remarkably resilient is dualism that even contemporaries who reject traditional body-soul dualism accept it under a new form: the materialist brain-body dualism tailor-made for consumption in our age of scientism. The brain is a computational machine, the mind software, and the body a "laboratory vat" within which rests the brain, that organ which is the true "essence" of human beings. "The brain sees," "the brain speaks," "the brain choses" (Bennett and Hacker 2022, 79–93; 123–125)[3]—however much one would like to dismiss such language as "figures of speech," this excarnate mereological fallacy pervades the discourse of cognitivism. Brains, of course, do not decide to go on picnics or feel the grass under foot, worry about children getting into a good school and having good luck when there, ponder the past and the shrinking days before it, feel a lover's caress and return a kiss. Whole persons do. Our current brain-body dualism is no more coherent than its ancient counterparts and yet it continues to exert an enormous hold on our imaginations.[4]

The Earth-Creature: An Incarnate Myth

Another stream of ancient myth, by contrast, provides a rich vein of corporeal imagination: the Hebraic tradition. The two creation myths that open the Book of Genesis were brought together between the 7th and 5th century BC, as the Torah or Pentateuch took the form that we know today. The redactor placed the more recent and urban creation account of the "P" or Priestly tradition first, followed by the older and more rural account of the "J" or Yahwist tradition.

The "P" account, the more abstract and structured of the two myths, depicts God, אֱלֹהִים (Elohim), creating and arranging the universe. The opening verses compound negative words, "formless void," תֹהוּ וָבֹהוּ (thohu vavohu) "darkness," חֹשֶׁךְ (hoshekh) over the "face of the deep," תְהוֹם (thehom) to depict the abstract concept of nothingness as well as imagery can. The spirit of God hovers over the waters in preparation for the creative act. It is through the power of the efficacious word alone that the cosmos is created and ordered around the weekly cycle of temple life in a logical, liturgical and poetic structure where all things are pronounced "good." The sixth day culminates in the "very good" creation of human beings: "And God said, 'Let us make mankind, אָדָם (adam), in our image, after our likeness'" (Gen 1:26), whose embodied character is clear through the gloss, "male, זָכָר (zakhar), and female, וּנְקֵבָה (uneqevah), he created them" (Gen 1:27). God then rested on the seventh day, making of it the hallowed day, the Sabbath.

The "Yahwist" or "J" account, beginning in Genesis 2:4b, is older and originates in a rural agricultural setting. Nothingness for a farming culture is depicted as absolute aridity where nothing could grow and survive, and the first creative act is making the rivers flow so the garden can flourish. God is intimate with creation, walking in the Garden. More intimate still is the way the human being is shaped by the "touch" of the Divine Artisan out of the moistened, fertile earth of the garden. While often translated "man," the word for this human, אָדָם (adam), does not mean "male," but a non-gendered creature made of "earth," אֲדָמָה ('adamah) (Gen 2:7)—much like the Latin play of homo (human) and humus (ground, soil). The "hands-on" creation is not complete until God breathes into the not-yet-living earth-creature's nostrils, and with this breath it becomes a living being (נֶפֶשׁ nefesh) (Gen. 2:7). The Hebrew word nefesh is often rendered "soul," but *nefesh* is not the Orphics' *psyche*, a spiritual entity within a body. Rather the linguistic root of *nefesh* relates to the neck, the passageway so vulnerable to attack yet simultaneously so receptive to the divine breath of life, the channel of breath, of food, of drink, and the flow of blood.

The human is a relational creature, first and foremost to God but also to the garden which God gives the creature to enjoy and cultivate. But the human being is still a work in progress, for something is lacking. Unlike the Plotinian souls in eternal contemplation of the One, the creature is lonely. Although it shares intimacy with God, the human creature needs another: "It is not good for the earth-creature to be alone. I will make him/her a helper fit for him/her" (Gen 2:18). God creates from the earth animals and birds, and while the human creature greets them and names them, still there is something lacking, a truly "suitable helper." God's care for the creature's need leads to a second creative act, where the Divine Artisan becomes the Divine Surgeon, putting the earth-creature, הָאָדָם (*ha'adam*) into a deep sleep. The common translation has God removing a diminutive rib from an originally male creature, but the word צֵלָע (*tsela*) also means "side," which leads us to a more compelling interpretation of this text: God divides the solitary earth-creature in half, making the singular being into two. God then refashions the body, closing up the wound of division, and for the first time there is man (*ish*) and woman (*ishah*). This provokes a joyous cry of recognition that breaks the loneliness:

> This at last is bone of my bones
> and flesh, וּבָשָׂר (*ubasar*) of my flesh, מִבְּשָׂרִי (*mibbesari*);
> she shall be called Woman, אִשָּׁה (*ishah*)
> because she was taken out of Man, אִישׁ (*ish*).
> (Gen. 2:23)

This differentiation and recognition is an embodied, sexual one, as the "flesh," בָּשָׂר *(basar)* can also be a euphemism for male genitalia. Thus, when God heals the earth-creature's two halves by "closing up the flesh," he is also creating a way for them to join back together again. This etiological story provides an explanation of why a man, very useful in an agricultural society, must leave his family to begin a new household with another (Gen 2:24). Yet we can see here a deeper meaning, that the union in the dialogical community of two, most incarnate in sexual union, is more profound than the unicity of the one.[5]

The Adamic Myth does not end with conjugal bliss. When God first brought the human creature into the Garden, he issues a command to not eat the fruit of the tree of the knowledge of good and evil, "for the day that you eat of it you shall surely die" (Gen 2:16–17). The command is placed "upon,"־עַל ('al) the earth-creature, like a sower would place a seed "upon,"(*al*) the earth and wait for it to be accepted, to spread deep roots, and in time come to fruition. The relationship of the earth-creature with the Maker is thus also like the relation between gardener and earth, echoing the human task of tending in care the fertile garden.[6] The most prominent symbol of this soil in which the seed of God's Law is accepted is the heart. We might call it a symbol of "interiority" or depth, as the place of conscientious deliberation, pondering, understanding, discernment, and much more (Kearney 1998; 67, 73–74). The heart of flesh, shaped from the fertile earth of Eden, can become a listening heart, לֵב שֹׁמֵעַ (lev shomea'), deeply receptive to the Law which bears fruit in hospitality and care for the orphan, the widow, the stranger. Or it can become arid, dry and hardened into stone, making the Law into a superficial weapon of ideology and judgment. Again and again in the Judaic Scriptures, the divine promise is to change our hearts of stone into hearts of flesh, reincarnating our full humanity and inscribing the Law there once again as life-giving for those who cultivate it (e.g., Ez. 11:19, 36:26; Jer. 31:33; cf. Heb. 8:10).

Will God's command to the earth-creature be kept, like a seed nourished in fertile soil? The story can go in one of two directions. Being made in the image and likeness of God, human beings are gifted with both freedom and imagination. As Kearney discusses in *Wake of the Imagination* (1998), it was through the Divine imagination, יֵצֶר (*yetzer*) that the God created. The Divine *yetzer* is always good, yet human beings in their freedom can employ imagination in both a good inclination, the *yetzer ha-tov*, or in an evil inclination, the *yetzer ha-ra* (Kearney 1998, 65–66).[7] It is through the *Yetzer hara* that human beings fall. God has provided for every need of the human creature including mutual companionship. The snake, however, the original advertiser, is able to play on the human imagination to create a "lack" where none exists. Eve is stronger and needs to be seduced directly, while Adam folds immediately. This "lack" succeeds in captivating the evil imagination, suggesting God is withholding something more, something better, something Godlike. In the dizzying conversation, the Creator-God is cast as adversary and the snake as advocate. In the journey from fallibility to fault, the couple do acquire the knowledge of good and evil, for prior to their act, they only knew the good. The "fall," the deviation, occurs through a carnal act, eating fruit, but it was not the creatures' embodiment that was the cause of error. As Kearney explains, the *yetzer* is neither limited to "higher" or immaterial things or "lower" or material things but always mediates between the two (1998, 49, 65–66, 68). That is, the deviation is not about being too far into our bodies, but a rejection of the limitations of the life that God has given: the earth-creature is lured into a desire for a greater, higher, universal grasp of knowledge that soars above the ground and forgets the patient task of tending the garden, living in relation to each other, and bringing God's word to fruition.

Thus, the Genesis myth marks a strong contrast to the Orphic myth that views the body as a prison. Where the dualist myth separates soul and body as independent substances, in Genesis the human being is created from the earth and the divine breath, both essential to existence. Where the dualist myth identifies the essential being within the single locus of "soul," the Hebraic myth refuses reduction to a single human essence, instead preferring a multiplicity of corporeal symbols: we mentioned the vulnerable passage of the neck, the breath or spirit, and the depths of the heart, but might add as well the lips used for a kiss or for giving one's word, the hand that forms, grasps, and reaches out with the strength of the arm. The Orphic world is a place filled with temptation and carnal distraction, and the path to salvation from the world lies in detachment and liberation of the soul from the body, from the alone to the Alone. In the Hebraic myths, by contrast, the world is affirmed as good, an inviting fertile garden, a place where humans belong and belong to each other, affirming Kearney's words, "We are betrothed to the earth. And one of our most basic needs is to love and feel beloved on this earth" (Kearney in this volume, p. 235). The fall is not into the world, but the rejection of it, rupturing reciprocity with suspicion and mistrust, desiring to seize the power to transcend our limited embodied situation once and for all. The way back to salvation from this perspective thus requires an embrace of our reality as earth-creatures, an acceptance of finitude and community, our relation to the earth and the environment, and our interdependence on God and on each other. In short, the radically non-dualist, profoundly relational Genesis myth offers a salutary contrast to the ancient myth of material body against immaterial soul and its privileging of the latter. The Judaic perspective is non-reductive and communal, placing priority on the whole, incarnate person, living, loving, rejoicing, hoping, yearning and suffering in community with each other, with the whole of the created earth, and with the Creator who cares for them all.

Excarnate and Carnal Hermeneutics

Some philosophers are in the habit of opposing text to body, and so perhaps they wonder if Kearney's recent focus on flesh is a departure from his teacher and friend, the exemplary hermeneut Paul Ricoeur, who seemed so text-centric. Yet Kearney's achievement here is *not* one of mediating separate realms. No one can deny, of course, that Kearney can play the role of Hermes better than anyone. The problem is that assuming a chasm between text and body misses the most important point: Kearney's philosophy has from the beginning been about the whole person, and his recent work brings to the fore what was always there. Indeed, Kearney suggests, "all hermeneutics is carnal hermeneutics ...

Our truest ideas – no matter how abstract – are indebted to our tangible body. We think well when we think with our senses, tactilely, reciprocally, dialogically, diacritically" (Kearney in this volume, p. 236).[8] This exchange is always a back and forth, always the double move of the "ana-."

If there is a *carnal* hermeneutics, I suggest there is also an *excarnate* one. More than just a philosophical error, "excarnate hermeneutics" may be founded on a desire of the evil imagination, the *yetzer hara*. For like the temptation of the garden, it seeks to take flight from embodied finitude to secure a godlike knowledge, leaving the "prison" of particular words for the pure and universal mastery of theory.[9] The epistemology born from dualist anthropology leads to just such excarnate readings. Disconnected from the life and the world of their authors, it flies high above the tensions within texts struggling to capture the complexity of human experience. The result is that it blinds us to any true dialogical opening to the other, confirming only the same ideas we already have decided upon in our theoretical solipsism. Such readings can be disarming because they powerfully channel some of our deepest tendencies and temptations. This is often where dominant "textbook" interpretations are born, employing conceptual pictures to trap us in the same frames which we trace over and over. The force of these readings allows them to excarnate even thoroughly incarnate texts like the Genesis myth, reducing Eve to a rib, whitewashing the Semitic soil from the garden-tending earth-creature in order to justify all forms of human domination: men against women, humans against animals, profiteers against environment.

Against this temptation, we must reclaim the *yetzer hatov,* the liberating power of the good imagination, to accept our embodied finitude and find new possibilities precisely there. The recognition of ourselves as finite, earthy, communal beings presents an alternative to theoretical rationalism. This in turn presents a new way of reading and approaching the texts of the past: one imbued with carnal hermeneutics.

We are faced, in other words, with a double possibility of excarnation: the excarnation of myths and philosophies, on the one hand, that seek flight from the body. This can then be filtered through a further excarnation in the reading of it, which takes flight from the actual texts it is extracted from. The result is a redoubled and exacerbated alienation from our incarnate life. Similarly, just as we seek to return to the earthy reality of the body, it is also imperative to return to the rich earth of the texts. Thus, in his *ana-* explorations, Kearney invites us to reread and retrieve, as he does in his own conversations between Aristotle and Merleau-Ponty, Dostoyevsky, and Virginia Woolf. If we do as he suggests, and allow texts to unfold with more grounded hermeneutic tact, we will see a counter-tension of incarnation that plays against the excarnate readings of our history. Even major "dualist" thinkers of the tradition turn out to be more complicated than the textbook "excarnate hermeneutics" would have them.

For example, bloodless readings of Plato have long extracted arguments, theories, and ideas as the substance of his texts. If we make room for a carnal hermeneutics and pay closer attention to the characters, dramatic setting, actions, and mythical references, we will find cracks in the dualist "textbook Plato" everywhere. Even in the *Phaedo*, the dialogue most credited as perpetuating Orphic dualism, Socrates directly counters the vision of the Orphic-Pythagorean sage as he cracks jokes, caresses the distraught Phaedo's hair, and ultimately keeps his feet on the ground until the very end—literally as well as philosophically. This is hardly a man detaching himself from the body but rather one living up to death in fully incarnate dialogical engagement. Descartes, meanwhile, is well-known to every student of philosophy as *the* dualist par excellence. Yet, under the scrutiny of contemporary philosopher Jean-Luc Marion, this "textbook Descartes" is itself shown to be a myth, perpetuated by a well-entrenched excarnate reading first propagated by some of his lesser interpreters (Marion 2018). Even the Orphic myth itself can be retrieved and reread sympathetically, as Ricoeur does in the *Symbolism of Evil*.

Perhaps the most interesting here is the case of St. Augustine. While he is often accused of perpetuating the Neo-Platonic reframing of the Orphic myth, we might better see him as performing an anacarnate hermeneutics which retrieves this heritage alongside the biblical Genesis myth. And instead of seeking flight from the body, Augustine's keen understanding of the mechanics of materialism can help us better understand excarnation in our own day.

Confessional Anacarnation

Philosophical readings of Augustine's *Confessions*, like the standard reception of Plato, have tended to isolate the "philosophical" passages, bracketing out the rest as rhetorical flourishes or hallmarks of religious writing of the era. This hermeneutics of extraction, combined with the tendency to reduce Augustine to his Neo-Platonic sources, impose on his work a definitively dualist slant.[10] Such excarnate readings are difficult to maintain when one attends to the whole work, allowing it to show from itself. Can there be a more poignant cry than that of Augustine the Bishop, evoking the Genesis myth as he recalls years later his forced separation from his life partner and the mother of his son?: "She with whom I had lived so long was torn from my side ... My heart which had held her very dear was broken and wounded and shed blood" (Augustine 2006, VI: 15.25). It is true that Augustine's sharp philosophical insights make him one of the great names of the tradition, as his thoughts on time have directly inspired phenomenology (Kearney in this volume, p. 237).[11] Yet his questions are always deeply rooted in the flesh and blood and soil of his life, leading him to transform abstract inquiries about human nature into the deeply existential quest for his own self-understanding which calls for narrative response. His *Confessions* is not the story of an imprisoned soul but the drama of a "restless heart." Even if hardened through disorientation and rebellion, it is the listening heart (*lebh shomea*), not abstract thinking, that discerns the weight of desire and the way of responding to its call.[12] In all of this, whether his conversion to philosophy, the grief at the death of a friend, the visceral struggle of will in the Garden in Milan, the events described are thoroughly incarnate. Guided by Kearney's terminology, we might say that the *Confessions* is a vital story of anacarnation, recovering the carnal after excarnation had plunged Augustine into isolation and closure.

The *Confessions* climaxes in Book 10 in what is perhaps the most famous passage Augustine ever penned, where we can read his life encapsulated (Augustine 2006, X: 27.38):

> Late have I loved you, Beauty so ancient and so new, late have I loved you!
> Lo, you were within,
> but I outside, seeking there for you,
> and upon the shapely things you have made
> I rushed headlong – I, misshapen.
> You were with me, but I was not with you.
> They held me back far from you,
> those things which would have no being,
> were they not in you.

One may hear echoes of the myth of the fallen soul channeled through Plotinus, reading it as a rejection of the body in favor of the higher, spiritual world. However, if we unfold this text carefully in context, it is not the cry of a soul trapped within a material prison, but rather of a person caught outside himself, alienated from his own human carnality. Excarnation is not merely taking flight from flesh but plunging ourselves into it in a way that leaves us dispersed and scattered, unable to engage, and thus alienated from ourselves and the other. Augustine in his way of relating to the world is experiencing something similar to the people on the transit train, unable to put down their screens, unable to stop their fingers from scrolling to the next tweet, unable to be attentive to each other, and unable to be with themselves. Far from being opposed, the dispersion into the virtual and dispersion into the sensational result in the same excarnation, the same inability to arrive at reciprocity or connection, expressed eloquently by Leonard Cohen in his confessional song "Hallelujah": "I couldn't feel, so I tried to touch."

This forgetfulness of self and its dispersal in sensation becomes especially insidious, Augustine observes, for in prioritizing the corporeal, we begin to regard that which is "without bodily phantasm as nothing."[13] Sensuous excarnation thus quickly pairs up with crude empirical reductionism.[14] While the senses allowed Augustine's immersion in bodies, the ignorance of the interiority of his soul and its active role in sensation led him to see himself as just another body among bodies. Despite terms like "soul" and "body," or "interior" and "exterior," it is not dualism he is describing here, for his goal is not to detach a higher spiritual entity from a lower material body. We can reframe his concerns in phenomenological language: the capacities unique to his *Leib* are being employed to reduce himself to a mere *Körper*.[15] The result is that by plunging into sensation, Augustine becomes so estranged from his own embodied life that he is trapped outside himself, caught in the grip of a materialistic worldview that indiscriminately labels all things and persons—including himself—as mere objects.

This rush to the outside, this obsession with the possession of external objects, produces a chronic forgetfulness, an ongoing "turning away," and ongoing fall. Yet, Augustine understands this "fall" not as in Plotinus but as in Genesis, as a rejection of human limitations as a corporeal, finite being, a desire for autonomy, a refusal to accept responsibility for or dependence on the earth, the other, or God (St. Augustine 1963; X: 5.7, 301). Thinking that God's way is marked by "lack," and preferring the solipsism of his own carnal pleasure, Augustine breaks away from all of the reciprocal relations which would bring him life and instead plunges himself into a life of unrelieved indigence, seeking satisfaction in ways that prohibit him from ever being satisfied. Thinking he is becoming more and more, he is in fact becoming less and less—estranged, dissipated, dispersed (ibid).[16]

To recover from the fall into excarnation, Augustine explains, it is necessary to "re-collect" or "re-cognize" one's proper relationship to material things and embodied life. But how to return after being so thoroughly lost? It is not as if a pure act of will can float unencumbered above one's situation—another excarnate fantasy. It is the other who must break through the solipsism of excarnate alienation, reopening the channels of a dialogical and reciprocal carnality. Augustine first needed the texts of Platonism to remind him of the interior and the transcendental. This allowed him to escape from empirical reductionism and recover the meaning of his life, his touch, his actions, and his words, but it did not yet free him from the intellectual elitism that made him turn up his nose at biblical texts which lacked Hellenic rhetorical flourish. These final barriers against reciprocity were at last broken down in his conversion, which allowed him to retrieve the deep wisdom from the earthy biblical texts. Far from any possible dualism, the second half of the famous passage in Book X, describing the encounter with the living God, is thoroughly imbued with sensuality, touching on each of the five senses:

You *called*, shouted, broke through my deafness;
you *flared*, blazed, banished my blindness;
you lavished your *fragrance*, I gasped; and now I pant for you;
I *tasted* you, and now I hunger and thirst;
you *touched* me, and I burned for your peace.
                    (Augustine 2006; X: 27.38, emphasis mine)

Here touch is not the last and least of the senses but the culmination of a carnal journey that began with the call in the opening of the work. The solipsism of excarnate dissipation, the rebellion from earthy inter-dependence had trapped Augustine in the echo chamber of ego, and in his isolation he quickly downgraded himself into a mere object, unable to re-cognize the reciprocity with the world outside of himself. By contrast, the post-conversion, post-excarnate Augustine who penned the *Confessions* has become a profoundly dialogical thinker. Even while telling his own story at length, the book is other-oriented to its very core. It begins as an explicit address to the Other—to God—and then recognizes this address as re-sponding to a call that has already been made. Augustine does not dominate the stage with his individual rhetorical genius but employs all his linguistic craft to allow the ancient biblical language of praise to shine as it speaks through him. The texts of Genesis which inform the structure of the work are especially present in Books XI–XIII, in a new carnality that opens his eyes to see in the world around him the traces of the hands of the Creator God, opens his ears to hear the symphony of creation, and frees his voice to join in the same communal hymn. His very existence, like all of creation, rests on nothing other than this call and response, to become who he is in his freedom and uniqueness in this dialogue. There is no self-possession, no self-substantiating and self-preservation apart from this confessional and communal conversation. Finally, where Augustine had failed to achieve a Neoplatonic ascent of the soul from the "alone to the Alone," he is lifted up in a moment of mystical ascent with his mother. Thus, in recovering from his "fall" into excarnation, Augustine does not thereby abandon the body; as his evocatively carnal language attests, he remains thoroughly in touch with our shared embodied life and our shared cosmic community of creation. We can easily imagine Augustine affirming with Wittgenstein that it is not "my abstract mind" which needs saving, but "my soul, with its passions ... with its flesh & blood" (Wittgenstein 1998, p. 38)—although following the or-ientation of the *Confessions* we might add, "my whole incarnate history, in all the complexity of its relationships with the Other and others"—but to unpack the richness of his narrative response to temporality would require a fuller investigation than the present space allows.

   This too-brief foray into Augustine's *Confessions* nevertheless attests that excarnation is not only a problem of escape from materiality, but a flight from the vulnerability, mutuality, and limitation of our true condition.

Today, too, we can find ourselves lost not only within screens but within narcissistic sensationalism, in a paradoxical alienation where, as Kearney writes, we "obsess about the body in ever more disembodied ways" (2021, 2). In either case, excarnation is marked by a "one-way *illusion* of presence" which replaces authentic "*double* sensation," effacing mutuality and closing off the community essential to the anacarnational resonance of flesh (2021, 119).

Conclusion

"There is no escape from our tactile sensible incarnation in this world," Kearney observes, and while we are not thereby bound to acknowledge it, "[t]hose who renounce the flesh pay an existential price" (this volume, p. 235) For, as Stanley Cavell writes, we come "to grief not in denying what we all know to be true, but in our effort to escape those human forms of life which alone provide the coherence of our expression." The solution is not to circumvent this limitation but to accept it, lest we be "chafed by our own skin, by a sense of powerlessness to penetrate beyond the human conditions of knowledge" (Cavell 2002, 57) which are not barriers to be escaped but the only path of self-knowledge, self-betterment, and transcendence.

Embracing carnal reality is an urgent task, yet it cannot be accomplished in one fell swoop. This, too, would be an excarnate desire, which is why we must pair a "hermeneutics of affirmation" with a healthy "hermeneutics of suspicion" (Kearney in this volume, p. 242). Even the thinkers who have been labeled dualist—like Plato, Descartes, or Augustine—are far more nuanced than we realize. Even those who seem to have escaped dualism must battle its temptations, as in Genesis, which some have interpreted as justification to abandon care for the earth, or Husserl, whose phenomenological validations of embodied experience are immediately jeopardized by his dream of a universal science of the disembodied transcendental ego.[17] Excarnation thus proves to be an ongoing temptation, and in every age we must find ways to resist it with the wisdom of the ana-, to return, back, up, again. Time and time again, Kearney has bid us to resist our tendencies to seek easy transcendental passage and urged us to return to the ground of our relational carnality rather than succumb to the craving to quit the earth for the frictionless sky.

Notes

1 As Kearney notes, the term "excarnation" was first coined by Charles Taylor (Kearney 2021).
2 See also Paul Ricoeur (1986, 283).
3 See also Bennett et al. (2007).
4 On how tacitly assumed, primitive pre-philosophical conceptual pictures hold thinkers captive and inform complex philosophy, see Wittgenstein's *Philosophical*

Investigations: "A picture held us captive. And we couldn't get outside it, for it lay in our language, and language seemed only to repeat it to us inexorably." We think we are seeing deeper and deeper, making progress, "tracing an outline of a thing's nature over and over again, and one is merely tracing round the frame through which we look at it" (2009, PI §115).

5 Contrast this to the myth told by Alcibiades in the *Symposium,* where the original human is divided into halves. While that myth is inclusive of greater possibilities of gender and sexual orientation, it is imbued with Greek pessimism, for this separation is a punishment of the gods, trapping one in the near hopeless task of seeking one's exact other half.

6 Cf. Isaiah 55:10,11, Luke 8:11, Mark 4:14, James 1:21,1 Peter 1:23.

7 Rabbi Hayyim of Volozhyn's *Nefesh Hahayyim* and the Midrash (*Genesis Rabba,* 12) quoted in Kearney (1998).

8 See also *Carnal Hermeneutics* (Kearney and Treanor 2015, 1–3).

9 See Brian Gregor's chapter in this volume: "Strangers, Gods, and Demons: Toward a Carnal Hermeneutics of the Demonic" pp. 107–125 which also addresses this theme.

10 Shortly after his conversion Augustine outlined his two-fold path to wisdom by way of faith and understanding: he uses the reasoning of the Platonists insofar as they assist in understanding and do not contradict Sacred Scripture, but full authority is given to Christ. See, *Answer to Skeptics*, Ch. 20, 43, p. 220. Augustine's guiding hermeneutic principle was succinctly characterized by Aquinas' judgement that "Whenever Augustine, who was imbued with the doctrines of the Platonists, found in their teaching anything consistent with faith, he adopted it; and those things which he found contrary to faith he amended." See, St. Thomas Aquinas, Summa Theologica, Vol. I, Pt. I, qu. 84, art. 5, p. 477.

11 For more on this point as well as the theme of evil, see also "Time, Evil and Narrative: Ricoeur on Augustine" (Kearney 2005).

12 "Give your servant *lebh shomea* [a listening heart] so as to be able to discern" (1 Kings 3:9).

13 This phrase is taken from *Trinity* (1963, X: 7.10, 304), but it echoes Augustine's commentary on his chronic materialism in the *Confessions*, (2006; VII: 1.2, 158).

14 As Kearney warns, "a crass and eliminative materialism" may deny "our lived carnality as much as our spirituality" (2020, 235).

15 See Kearney's essay in this volume, p. 242.

16 Cf. *Confessions* (Augustine 2006, X: 6.10, 253).

17 See Filiz and Romano (2021, 185–185).

References

Aquinas, Thomas. 1947. *Summa Theologica*, Vol. I. Trans. Fathers of the English Dominican Province. New York: Benziger Brothers, Inc.

Augustine. 2006. *Confessions*. 2nd edition. Translated by F.J. Sheed. Indianapolis: Hackett.

Augustine, *Answer to Skeptics*, Trans. Denis J. Kavanagh, O S A, S.T.M., in *The Fathers of the Church: A New Translation*, Vol. 5, ed. Ludwig Schopp (New York, The Catholic University of America Press Inc., 1948).

Bennett, Maxwell R., Daniel Dennett, Peter Hacker, and John Searle. 2007. *Neuroscience & Philosophy: Brain, Mind, and Language*. New York: Columbia University Press.

Bennett, M.R. and P.M.S. Hacker. 2022. *The Philosophical Foundations of Neuroscience*. 2nd edition. Oxford: Wiley Blackwell.

Cavell, Stanley. 2002. *Must We Mean What We Say? A Book of Essays*. Cambridge: Cambridge University Press.

Filiz, Kadir and Claude Romano. 2021. "Phenomenology with Big-Hearted Reason. Conversation with Claude Romano." Translated by Christina M. Gschwandtner. *Philosophy Today* vol. 65, no. 1 (Winter): 183–200.

Kearney, Richard. 1998. *Wake of the Imagination: Toward a Postmodern Culture*. London: Routledge.

Kearney, Richard. 2005. "Time, Evil and Narrative: Ricoeur on Augustine." In *Augustine and Postmodernism: Confession and Cirucmfession*, edited by John D. Caputo and Michael J. Scanlon, 144–158. Bloomington: Indiana University Press.

Kearney, Richard. 2020. "In Conversation with Richard Kearney." In *Imagination Now: A Richard Kearney Reader*, edited by M.E. Littlejohn, 313–333. London: Rowman and Littlefield.

Kearney, Richard. 2021. *Touch: Recovering Our Most Vital Sense*. New York: Columbia University Press.

Kearney, Richard and Brian Treanor, eds. 2015. *Carnal Hermeneutics*. New York: Fordham University Press.

Marion, Jean-Luc. 2018. *On Descartes' Passive Thought: The Myth of Cartesian Dualism*. Translated by Christina M. Gschwandtner. Chicago: University of Chicago Press.

Plato. 1966. *Euthyphro. Apology. Crito. Phaedo*. Plato in Twelve Volumes: Volume 1. Translated by Harold North Fowler. Cambridge: Harvard University Press.

Plotinus. 1966–1988. *Ennead*. 7 volumes. Translated by A.H. Armstrong. Cambridge: Harvard University Press.

Porphyry. 1966. *The Life of Plotinus and the Order of His Books*. Translated by A.H. Armstrong. Cambridge: Harvard University Press.

Ricoeur, Paul. 1986. *The Symbolism of Evil*. Boston: Beacon Press.

St. Augustine. 1963. *The Trinity*. The Fathers of the Church series, volume XLV. Translated by Stephen McKenna. Washington: Catholic University of America Press.

Wittgenstein, Ludwig. 1998. *Culture and Value*. Revised 2nd edition. Translated by Peter Winch. Oxford: Blackwell Publishers.

Wittgenstein, Ludwig. 2009. *Philosophical Investigations*. Revised 4th edition. Translated by G.E.M. Anscombe, P.M.S. Hacker, and Joachim Schulte. Oxford: Wiley-Blackwell.

Chapter 8

Richard Kearney, Terrence Malick, and the Hidden Life of Sense

Christopher Yates

While Richard Kearney produced his remarkable early wave of scholarship with works like *The Wake of Imagination* (1988), *Poetics of Imagining: Modern to Post-Modern* (1991), and *On Stories* (2001), Terrence Malick had stunned the film world with his directorial work in *Badlands* (1973), *Days of Heaven* (1978), and *The Thin Red Line* (1998). Kearney's focus lay with the rich possibilities of imagination and narrative in the operations of understanding and social existence. Malick trained his camera on the wonder lodged inside moments of lives unfolding across exilic journeys. Kearney bracketed the pretensions to objectivity in scientific and trans-cendental epistemes in order to focus on the surpluses of sense at work in the folds of lived experience. Malick moved cinematic point of view away from the abstractions of traditional establishing shots and formulaic plot, and into the expansive visual field of his characters' finite attentiveness. Where Kearney summoned the *poiesis* of "imagining otherwise" than vapid post-modern simulacra, Malick seemed to provide the *aisthēsis* for doing just that. Both took their bearings from Heidegger.

Separate mediums notwithstanding, with the recent release of Kearney's *Touch: Recovering our Most Vital Sense* (2021) not long after Malick's film, *A Hidden Life* (2019), we have today a welcome opportunity to formally consider the question of the two auteur's intertextual coordination. Doing so, I believe we find a mutually enriching alignment of phenomenological orientations and provocations. In what follows I consider their exchange in two related ways: (1) how Kearney's philosophy helps us appreciate the real fullness of the film's hermeneutic work, and (2) how the film helps us in-tegrate two driving foci in Kearney's itinerary—*hermeneutic imagination* and *carnal hermeneutics*.

Since I will give most of my attention to the second matter, let me briefly justify its need. Though *Touch* must be regarded foremost as an elaboration of Kearney's discourse on carnality, there is a moment in the text in which he finds "the tactile calling for the poetic" (2021, 39). Sense incarnate, I take him to mean, calls for the sense of storied form. Of course, it would be a capacitating sort of call, for flesh and narrative are

DOI: 10.4324/9781003285649-12

co-primal partners at the wellsprings of all hermeneutic mediation. Suppose we put the question to Kearney's own itinerary: Could we say that carnal hermeneutics still "calls for" the hermeneutic imagination? One could be forgiven for thinking a *Kehre* has occurred in his thought as the carnality discourse has taken center stage. But if we explore how Malick's film can be regarded as an enactment of the *narrative imagination* that at the same time discloses and substantiates the primacy of *touch*, we find an aesthetic way to integrate these two sides of Kearney's hermeneutic phenomenology. If, further, we stay alert to the issues of socio-ethical concern that stand on the front edge of the imagination and carnality projects alike, we will also appreciate how *A Hidden Life* exemplifies the "*ana*"-enacted outcome Kearney intends through "imagining otherwise" than the cultural degradations of sense.

The Task and Tact of Carnal Hermeneutics

A consistent feature of Kearney's scholarship that is easy to take for granted is the way in which concrete cultural predicaments motivate the technical analyses. Be the issue imagination, carnality, religion, politics, hospitality, and so on, he will identify contemporary social and epistemic norms that tend to corrode the integrity of *sense-making*, then undertake a deep intervention that animates the promise abiding inside the perils. There is a spirit of urgency to this work, a dogged persistence to map the horizons converging around us, and a resolve to engage them with care. So it is that *Touch* (2021) addresses "an age of simulation informed by digital technology and an expanding culture of virtual experience" (2) in which "more and more of our existence is being lived at a distance" (4) and the "human exceptionalism" of the Anthropocene leaves us abandoned to a state of "touch hunger" (7). To such a troubled milieu of *excarnation* Kearney offers "a new *commons of the flesh*" (7) that would overcome the devastating "eclipse of the tactile" (125) and the deadlocked paradox of "[h]yperconnectivity and hyperisolation" (122). The advance toward a healthier Symbiocene could begin with small but significant footholds, such as asking whether "certain forms of digital pedagogy" (129) could begin to redirect the problematic course from within.

   If that is something of what carnal hermeneutics might do when put to work in the predicaments of our social imaginaries, what are its own interior workings? For the sake of a basic synopsis, we may hear the phrase in two ways. *Adjectivally*, "carnal" signifies a shift Kearney brings to the existential trajectory running from Husserl to Heidegger, and onward to Gadamer, Ricoeur, and Vattimo (among others), with Aristotle as an abiding touchstone. The movement's agenda was to depose the naively iron-fisted subject-object model of thinking truth and the objectivist model of conceiving personhood and things, replacing these with a focus on intentionality and prereflective experience in the operations of consciousness, the "as"-structure of Dasein's broader involvement in the world of things and projects (including itself), and the textual operations of human understanding and agency. Kearney (2015) affirms these pathways into the immanent and "prior." But "carnal" declares the need to venture still further into the phenomena of our bodily involvement with the world. He wants to *ana*-mize hermeneutics by "carnalizing" it. Where this first signification identifies matters of orientation and method, the second addresses its phenomenological locus – how we *are* carnally-hermeneutic entities: "We are not, in the first instance, cerebral sovereign egos but perceiving incarnate bodies" (Kearney 2015, 111). There is a *humus* to all human understanding, for "[b]ody and mind are like the inside and outside of our skin—two sides of one sleeve" (Kearney 2021, 47). "Carnality" as hermeneutic focus thus entails a phenomenological reduction to touch, to flesh, to a bodied being-toward-sense—a reduction that brackets egoism, conceptualism, and excarnation … any species of a "natural" epistemic or cultural attitude that tends toward the virtualized and presumptuous dominion of self and thought over the things themselves of objects, experiences, and ideas. The primacy of the carnal, then, is disclosed through phenomenological maneuvers. And the operations of the carnal there arise as hermeneutic.

What is the nature of these operations? A field of generative mediation "that makes all sensible congress between outer and inner worlds possible" through touch, "the most holistic and synesthetic of the senses" (2021, 43–44). That superlative designation does not mean the mediating work is a matter of finality and closure, nor something reducible to a cause-and-effect relation between what the body feels and the mind in turn knows. The physicality of touch always already moves along a hermeneutic path. What Kearney calls "tactility" is a matter of somatic attunement as touch occurs across the synesthetic "relations between the five senses" and generates "our underlying carnal intelligences," such as "savvy, flair, insight, and resonance" (16). Sensation—*in* the doing—already bears the marks of sensibility. Kearney (2015) explains how the Latin *sensus* connotes physical sensation, meaning, and direction—which together "signify how we make sense of our lives in the flesh" (5). It is helpful to bear in mind, on this point, Tamsin Jones' reminder in this volume that the term "sense" in carnal hermeneutics includes, importantly, "action" that is "directed or oriented intentionally" (Jones, "No Longer a Spectator Only," p. 223). To characterize this action, Kearney (2015) resources Aristotle's provocation in *De Anima* that "sensing" is not a "*sensing through distance*" but a "*sensing through mediation*" (108), where *sarx* (flesh)f mediates touch, carrying the motion forward in the tactile genesis of "wisdom" (*sapientia*) (Kearney 2021, 36). Thus, somatic mediation and sense orientation are interlaced. *Hermeneuin* is always at root a matter of embodied tact, and interpretation never sheds its somatic skin.

Kearney is careful to point out qualities of *vulnerability and risk* in this matrix. The mediating operations happen in the context of, and in many ways for the sake of, our relations with "other embodied beings" (2015, 103). On one hand, our tact affords possibilities for empathy and moral evaluation. At the same time, the "membrane" of touch is "the first place of pain, suffering, and pathos" (107). Kearney explains:

> For tactility is the ability to experience and negotiate the passion of existence, understood etymologically as *pathos/paschein*—suffering, receiving, or undergoing exposure to others who come to us as this or that ... Flesh is open-hearted; it is where we experience our greatest vulnerability. (105)

This feature accompanies the movement toward sensibility in our pursuit of the *sapientia* noted above. We must likewise come to terms with how hermeneutic tact has no assured refuge in a paradigmatically visual "dominion over external persons and things" (2021, 110) or, indeed, ideas. Our bodies and judgments are ever inserted "into the flesh of the world" (110). Sight is crucial but touch is the more "intimate mediation" (2017, 82).

This issue of vulnerability and risk in the life of touch is the context in which Kearney speaks of the "tactile" calling for the "poetic." Several clues from *Touch* and elsewhere suggest that he is working out a connection between the Aristotle of *De Anima*, for whom touch is first in the order of discernment, and the Aristotle of the *Poetics*, for whom the affective dimensions of *pathos* and *phobos* converge inside the cathartic operations of *muthos-mimesis*. In *Touch* Kearney (2021) describes tactful sensation as "already a reading of the world" (36)–*sensus* in the mode of the significatory. Drawing on Ricoeur's schematic of narrative identity, he holds that "we are constantly prefiguring, refiguring, and configuring our experience" (39). He intimated much the same in a 2017 interview: "touch itself is already proto-linguistic, sensing is already sensibility" (781). Touch, suffice it to say, has a narrative inclination. The *sarx* complex of discernment in *De Anima* and the *pathos/phobos* complex of transformation in *The Poetics* intersect. If there is an operational link between carnal intelligence and narrative experience, then can we surmise there is a larger reciprocity between the Kearney of carnality and the Kearney of the hermeneutic imagination (where the focus on "narrative" first emerged)? At one point he does link them in reverse order by stating that

> the carnal emphasis was actually there from the beginning though it may not have been entirely explicit ... But it was implicit because imagination as I understand it ... is an indispensable bridge between the sensible (the body) and the intelligible (the mind). (2017, 779)

The statement tells us that carnal hermeneutics was implied in his counter-dualist account of the imagination. But it does not tell us where or whether imagination fits into the focus on carnality. This matter should concern us today for two reasons: First, because one wants to know whether the hermeneutic figurations we compose through narrative poetics and aesthetic creation can assist and advance the nascent intelligence and wisdom of our vulnerable tactility. Second, because the resistance to excarnation (virtualization/digitalization) that Kearney envisions not only targets the offspring of what the hermeneutic imagination was deployed against (post-modern simulacra; cult of the image) but also because the resistance would seem to require works of narrative/aesthetic sense-making. The current *ana*-mization front needs the former's power to "imagine otherwise," does it not?

Hermeneutic Imagination and the Art of the Possible

Though the phrase "hermeneutic imagination" does not encompass all the facets of Kearney's early projects, it coordinates the driving concerns stretching from *Poétique du possible* (1984) to *On Stories* (2001). He uses the phrase in a 2004 interview (Kearney 2004, 672), relating it to the category of *poetics*, a term which "covers my attempt to explore the role of creativity ... in life as much as in art" (670). Some three decades prior to *Touch*, he sought to mobilize the resources of the hermeneutic imagination against what was in many ways the progenitor of the excarnation problem described above. In *The Wake of Imagination* Kearney (1988) lamented a mounting consumeristic postmodern culture of the *image* that paradoxically threatened "the very notion of a creative human imagination" (3). Embracing the spirit of Emily Dickinson's admonition that the "slow fuse" of possibility "is lit by the imagination," he proposed an ethico-poetic way forward by which we might "begin to *imagine* that the world as it is could be *otherwise*" (370–71). A central facet of this path would be to animate afresh the idea of "*narrative identity*" (17) in the creative work of *poiesis* (366), thereby clearing the fog of deconstructive undecidability by enacting "a *poetics of the possible*" (32).

In *Poetics of Imagining* (1998) Kearney drew rigorously on prominent strands of 20th-century phenomenology in order to address "the vexed character of the post-modern imaginary" (219) in which the "irreference of simulation" (225) and "impersonal information" were levied against "the transmission of commonly shared experience" and "historical memory" (241). He envisioned a "critical redeployment of imagination" (223) that would offer renewed "hermeneutic discernment" (225) and "phronetic understanding" (242) through telling "the betrayed stories of history" (223). The way through the crisis would not be a retreat back into the modern "empire of reason" (9), but a commitment to "the poetic activity of imagining otherwise" through the alternative visions found in art and story (233). "Art," he reflected in 2004, "opens up possible worlds in which we may imaginatively dwell" (675). Where sense-making suffers its constraints and mis-directions, "the artistic or poetic imagination" enjoys a native freedom to recreate the world "in light of a secondary reference to the realm of fictional possibility" (675). He is not calling for an escapist embrace of the romantic. The point is to artistically recover and reenchant the creative force of the real by turning us toward the singular power of artworks to be, quoting Joyce, the "bringing of plurabilities" (672) in the poetic and phronetic life of sense.

The distinct work of artworks, so understood, has a widening bearing on questions about imagination in relation to truth (epistemology), to being (ontology), and to the other (ethics). For Kearney, these areas coalesce most poignantly in the quest for "a rehabilitation of the narrative imagination" (1998, 241). Akin to how he later credits touch with the superlative status of "the intersensorial milieu that makes all sensible congress between outer and inner worlds possible" (2021, 43), here Kearney deems poetic imagining "our most redemptive power of mind" (1998, 234). Of particular interest for my purposes are the three "ethical" powers of imagination that he inscribes in its poetic promise: the *utopian*, *testimonial*, and *empathic*. The *utopian* feature of the narrative imagination comes down to the ability to "unrealize repressive realities in favour of emancipatory possibilities" (1998, 228). The task involves redressing the ways in which present identities for selves and communities have been drawn on the basis of differences. Bracketing alike the post-modern tendency toward "irreference and indifference" (226) and the historical tendencies toward totalitarian ideology, *u-topos* signifies a socio-ethical objective of unity-in-difference and difference-in-unity (227). But this undertaking in futural possibilities needs the *testimonial* imagination, "the power to bear witness to "exemplary" narratives legacied by our cultural memories and traditions" (228). It is not just the subjects of these narratives that matter, but the "bearing witness" itself which trains up in us a "hermeneutic readiness" to imagine morally through "recalling what has been silenced and projecting what has not yet been spoken" (229). The act of "recalling the forgotten victims of history," in particular, is about identifying with past people and circumstances that inspire a resistance to evil (230–31). The imagination's *empathic* element centers the utopian and testimonial actions in the site of our receptivity to, and responsibility for, the other. Enter the power of historical and/or fictional literature, where narratives themselves "are a basic agency of moral empathy" (245) that can spur the same in ourselves. Narrative, Kearney explains, is a form of representative thinking that frees the self from its egoism and returns it to itself in the mode of "answerability" (249). (The effect is not limited to strictly literary forms (248).) Taken together, the utopian, testimonial, and empathic elements of narrative imagination hold disclosive capacities suited to engender in us a "phronetic understanding" (242) that can contend with injustices past, present, and future. This ultimate possibility will be important to bear in mind as we soon turn to *A Hidden Life*.

***

My purpose in offering these brief expositions of the two focal areas in Kearney's work has been to highlight their distinct concerns, indicate some overlap in terms of the critical-diagnostic framing he brings to each, and begin to position points of their integration. To summarize: Distilled through the phenomenon of *touch*, carnal hermeneutics pits the primacy of embodied sense against the excarnational drift of a digitalized and virtualized world. Carnal exposure and tact afford intelligence its beginnings, discerning bodies read the world, and our *sensus* develops our sensibility. We risk far more than touch risks if we retreat to the castellated towers of optocentrism. Distilled through the poetics of *narrative*, the hermeneutic imagination pits aesthetic figuration and possibility against the post-modern cult of simulation without referent, surface without depth, and identity without grounded moral responsibility. Beneath the self-deceptive entropy of our social imaginaries abides a redemptive aesthetic capacity to "imagine otherwise" through the utopian, testimonial, and empathic features of the imagination. This art of the possible may lack the alleged security found in the empire of reason, but it can help us avoid and redress the totalizing dogmatisms there propitiated.

Now we ask: How might these two sides of Kearney's work help us appreciate Malick's own inquiry in *A Hidden Life*? And, in turn, how might the revelatory aesthetics of the film suggest that Kearneyan carnality (the *as-sensed*) and imagination (the *as-if*) might radiate from a common center into the lived horizon of sense and possibility? Though my discussion of Kearney's philosophy began with the matter of carnality before moving on to the hermeneutic imagination, my application of these matters to the film will reverse the order.

Malick's Poetics of Possibility

A Hidden Life presents the true story of Franz Jägerstätter (played by August Diehl), an Austrian farmer and family man whose refusal to swear an oath of unconditional allegiance to Adolph Hitler in 1943 led to his imprisonment and execution. He was beatified by the Vatican in 2007. Franz and his wife, Franziska ("Fani," played by Valerie Pachner), were natives of Sankte Radegund, a village nestled in a valley of the northern Alps. His story was lost to history until sociologist Gordon Zahn published a biography in the 1960s. In 2007 a friend of the Jägerstätter's, Erna Putz, compiled *Franz Jägerstätter: Letters and Writings from Prison*. Malick sources the letters for voiceover material, a technique that helps advance the memorializing function of the story through subjectivizing means. Viewers will recognize the film's context: Hitler's 1938 *Anschluss* of Austria and the mounting fascist dream of a German Reich that fueled the machinery of the Wehrmacht, conscripting the lives and imaginations of its people along the way. But Malick's storytelling presents all this from the inside out, focusing on the dramatic four-year pivot that carried Franz from the joys and security of his modest rural dwelling to the tragic consequences of his conscientious objection. It is important to recognize that the interior dimension amasses its thematic weight through a conflict of oaths. There is in Franz and Fani the implicit pledge of fidelity to place, marriage, and family, then the "Holy Oath" asked of Franz to forsake all for Hitler, and finally the oath Franz feels he must, in his Christian faith, maintain to a God who will not countenance complicity with evil regimes. The injustice of the middle oath sets the pairing of the other two at impossible odds. Malick's narrative imagination brings the life of this hidden struggle to light.

I will examine the specific operations of the hermeneutic imagination in the film by considering it on two fronts. The first is the special narrative focus that *Malick* employs.[1] The second operation is the hermeneutic undertaking evident in *Franz* himself as he undergoes the evolving conflict of oaths and suffers his deadly exile.

A Testimonial Hermeneutic Wager

Those familiar with Malick's oeuvre will have noticed that his decision to opt for an emplotted narrative in *A Hidden Life* stands in contrast to his other films of the last decade. We misdescribe this shift, however, if we take it as a matter of directorial whim. It suggests, rather, that questions of hermeneutic security and narrative possibility have been for him a deliberate preoccupation. He produced three features leading up to this one: *To the Wonder* (2013), *Knight of Cups* (2016), and *Song to Song* (2017). The projects were studied reductions into the layered moments of sense intuition and the lonesome pre-conceptual struggles of characters bereft of metaphysical anchors or coherent self-identities. They were laments of lives hemmed in by the allure and fatigue of what Kierkegaard termed the "aesthetic stage" on life's way. And they were difficult to endure. But they were designed to give audiences an experience of the coarse realities at the heart of our post-modern wagers with simulation, undecidability, virtualization, and digitization. Malick's hermeneutic imagination was, in this sense, bent on figuring the corrosive net yield of what amounts to the same social imaginaries motivating both phases of

Kearney's critical-diagnostic work. Though visually entropic and narratively non-cathartic, the films issued a pointed diagnosis of the denarrated self in a disenchanted world. The return to narrative in *A Hidden Life*, then, is a poetic imagining of the hermeneutic hope that we had forgotten we lost until he made us feel its lack. That is not to say the film is strictly plot-rendered. Malick's choice of a historical, "testimonial" and phronetic focus affords the dramatic sequence of events a certain progression, yes, but the viewer must work with the constitution of the story more from within a tableaux of deep presents than any categorical "acts."

The first indication of this task comes with the realization that the protagonist does not fit the normal Hollywood template. Typically, a filmmaker will style his or her story to follow the hero's arduous pursuit of an accomplished identity. Called to a reluctant adventure, the protagonist resolves to bootstrap their agency and actualize their potential by overcoming a steepening slope of obstacles. In Franz, however, Malick has chosen a figure whose journey *begins* from a place of accomplished identity. There is no haunting lack in him that needs the drama of conscientious objection in order to realize his authentic self. The conflict that moves the story consists rather in Franz having everything stripped away *but* the storied identity and meaning that his faith, conscience, memory, love, and (we will see) touch bring. The question is not exactly whether the hero will survive and triumph but whether the original components of his being will persist as true despite being turned on one another through the crisis of oaths. Between Franz's initial flourishing and his later captivity, the object of the "as-if" imagination is, for Malick, the tenability of a hermeneutic fidelity that could in the first context be taken as grounded and life-giving, and in the second context becomes absurd and threatening in the eyes of *das Man*. The *ana* that Malick is seeking through the narrative, then, is the very thing that Franz will embody spiritually, physically, and, in the anguished shadows of both, the faith that the nihilistic need not undo the poetic; darkness need not overcome the light, even though it comes close. And the way Malick conducts his mimesis of this life and this faith is such that we must *empathize* (a focus of the imagination and carnality projects alike) with the figure of Franz in order to share in the lesson. In his opening voiceover Franz reflects, "I thought we could build our nest high up in the trees ... Fly away like birds to the mountains." And Fani recalls, "It seemed like no trouble could reach our valley ... We lived above the clouds." German warplanes then signal the coming assault on these visions, but that does not mean they are naïve or false. The issue is whether the sanctity signified by nest and valley can be refigured anew through each stage of its undoing. How does this "passion of existence" and imagination unfold? Not by the eagerness of an aspiring martyr nor the epistemic assurance of *theoria*. Instead, through the repetition of Franz' *ana* amid a descending slope of vulnerability and risk.

Franz' Projecting of the Otherwise

Franz' objection to Hitler arises on the basis of an affirmation that has over time become intuitive to him, if hitherto implicit: one's allegiance to God supersedes the authority of state interests and ideology. He will not consent to the "Holy Oath" because the actions of the *Wehrmacht* are, simply put, unjust and evil. The position amounts to a basic imperative in which are blended the deontological and divine command principles. But suppose, Malick asks, we were to indeed *live by* the truth of basic imperatives, full stop? The refigurations required of us in life would be a matter of integrity—of re-integrations—as opposed to renegotiations based in pragmatic self-preservation. Orthodoxy and orthopraxy are of a decided piece. The admirable feature of Franz' witness-bearing (the focus of Malick's own) is that it is kenotic, wrought in the service of a story that is his to steward, not his to strategize. Even if one disagrees with the substance of his confessional faith, the sheer integrity of his refusal to see narrative promise kneel before narrative propaganda remains a radical instance of what Kearney called "answerability"—in this case positioning within the story what the film itself, as testimonial narrative, intends to do.

Franz' protest is rendered dramatic only because its stubborn clarity stands in sharp contrast to the distorted reasoning of those around him, be they fellow townsfolk or state and church officials. Early on he refuses to donate funds to the war effort, raising the eyebrows of village gossips. Later, a uniformed passerby greets him with the customary "*Heil* Hitler," to which he, disgusted, he replies, "*Pfui* Hitler!" As tensions escalate locally and the same neighbors with whom the Jagerstatter's work the fields now shun them as pariahs, Franz dutifully seeks counsel from church ministers, asking a bishop, for example: "If God gives us free will, we're responsible for what we do or what we fail to do, aren't we?" And, "If our leaders, if they're evil, what does one do?" Notice that he is trying to reason through the ethical narrative of his faith in relation to the obstacles placed before his narrative identity. The bishop answers that, regardless, one owes allegiance to the Fatherland. The practical efficacy of Franz' protest is also questioned. A priest avers that refusing the oath "would benefit no one." Military officers declaim, "Do you think anyone outside of this room will hear your protest?" Fani's mother and sister ask: "Who are you? ... Even the cardinal orders us to pray for Hitler, to ring the church bells on his birthday." The village Mayor calls him a coward. And so on. Franz is not unmindful of the consequences his stand will bring, and he anguishes particularly over the predicament his imprisonment and possible death foists upon his wife and children. But the more the crooked sense-making narrative of the world around him shows itself, the clearer and firmer the sense-making of his own conscience becomes.

He responds to the threats of a prison captain: "A man worth anything has only one thing to consider: whether he is acting rightly or wrongly." The comment does not reflect a point he has, so to speak, "come to"; it is an iteration of a principle already cemented in him but thrown into explicit relief under the weight of circumstance. In a letter to Fani he asks her forgiveness for the ordeal he is putting her through and reflects:

> You know, dear wife, that I do not engage in this struggle in order to make my life wonderful. As long as I don't lose my faith, nothing can be unfortunate. Our sadness will be changed to joy. All this, in relation to eternity, is less than half a second.

When the judge at Charlottenberg tries one final time to persuade Franz to relent or else face death, he replies simply: "I have that feeling inside me, that I can't do what I believe is wrong." In other words, the "as-if" of his fidelities holds sway in the "as-such" of his reality. The judge, like Pontius Pilate before Jesus, declares that it is not he who condemns but Franz who condemns himself.

Thus far I have highlighted the special way in which *Malick* embraces the work of narrative imagination in coming to this story, and in turn the way in which his *protagonist* does the same as he takes the measure of sense through the identity of his convictions. The doubling puts the poetics of the possible to the test. Transfiguring the past, *Malick* answers Ricoeur's charge, so important for Kearney, that "remembering is a *moral duty*" (1995, 290). Transfiguring his own present by way of his past and future worlds, *Franz* plots his agency within a larger narrative of moral obligation and spiritual freedom. Kearney's three features of the ethics-oriented side of the narrative imagination—the utopian, testimonial, and empathic—interlace the two hermeneutic horizons.

The Aesthetics of Carnality in Cinematic Sense

Still, the question presents itself: What "sense" arena, specifically, stations us in a place of empathic potential for the work that such storied thematics accomplish? The answer is Kearneyan carnality. The work of touch in the film "calls" for the poetics of the narrative imagination to assure the durability of the redemptive amid the tragic. Remember, it is a capacitating call; the carnal milieu of *sensus* both gives the narrative dimensions their tacit reality and at the same time calls for their *poiesis* of possibility. As with the focus above on narrative dimensions, here again we need a two-tiered approach, in this case examining the carnal aspects of the filmmaking and, in turn, those inside the world on screen. I will demonstrate how the directorial and photographic style Malick employs in the film simultaneously (i) attunes the viewer to the particulars of

Franz's corporeal being as it stands between worlds and (ii) presents the carnal horizon of his experience in heightening relation to the narrative domain of his self-understanding.

Envisioning the Tactile

How does the film direct the viewer to the plane of carnality as the hermeneutic imagination composes its narrative quality? To answer this we need to first make a friendly amendment to Kearney's work: the *aisthēsis* in touch can extend to the relationships between camera and subject *in* the artwork, screen, and viewer *through* the artwork. Film production and viewing are obviously vision-centric. But sometimes the cinematic event draws the visual and tactile so close together that the risks of optocentrism fall to the side. Especially in the case of Malick, sight is less a matter of *theoria* and more a mode of "directional" *sensus*, sensing and searching "through mediation." His cinematography closes the distance between viewer-world and storied-world; camerawork and lighting become a sort of *sarx* between viewers and subjects. By making the visual tactile, as it were, Malick places the interiority of characters and world before us.

So what do we see in the film and how do we see it? One remarkable feature of Malick's aesthetic and narrative choices is that he presents the storyline less by way of an "explanatory" cinematic point of view, and more by way of close-up particularization of the singular, finely grained details of Franz and Fani's involvement with one another and their immediate world. More than mere matters of context, the specificity of objects, gestures, expressions, farm chores … all the subtleties of moments and spaces both routine and charged, invite the viewer into his characters' at-handed existence.

Kearney says that touch is never immediate, "but rather mediation through the flesh" (2021, 103). One of the primary ways that Malick presents such mediation is through *motion*, placing his direction in the service of the "directional" movement of *sensus*. In the early portions of the film especially there is very little traditional blocking for the characters. Instead of rigidly stationing themselves before the photographic grid, they, so to speak, dance. "I remember we were never standing still," says August Diehl (who plays Franz) (O'Falt 2020, 5).

> At the beginning, I was thinking, why should I move the whole time, when I don't even know where to go and why? … But then, after a while, you realize it's a dance. There's a musical flow to everything. (Ebiri 2020, 3)

Valerie Pachner (who plays Fani) likewise recalls, "You keep moving, never stop. That was the rule" (O'Falt 2020, 5). Says cinematographer

Jörg Widmer, "If you watch it carefully, you'll see that there's almost no still frame in the whole movie" (Ebiri 2020, 3). Shooting in such a way must have been challenging, but the dance actually presented the camera with a liberating sort of constraint. Widmer and his crew opted for wide lenses (mostly 12 mm) on digital cameras in order to press close to the actions over the long durations that the shooting required so as to leave ample space for spontaneity. The discipline proved fruitful. "We got closer to the actors because of the focal length," says Widmer. He continues:

> When actors move their hands and touch each other, you can follow the hand, and then you come back to a close-up, so if it's all in the movement it looks so natural. It's like the flow of water. It's really a very immediate way of telling a story. (O'Falt 2020, 6)

Water is an apt analogy because so often the field of motion happens at the perimeter crossings of character-to-character and characters-to-world relations. Franz, Fani, and their daughters play a game of blind man's bluff on their grassy slope. Husband and wife harvest the fields of wheat alongside each other, and playfully wrestle as they plant potatoes in the black soil. Tender affections of the flesh happen in concert with tending the *humus* of their world. We see the carnal genesis of living sense in the smallest, truest of details. The same is also true for built spaces. One would seldom find a doorway interesting, for example, but Malick loves to capture the passage of a character from room or hallway to world. The editing will often cut from a threshold in one scene to the spreading space of another. When the motion does ease a bit the focus falls on the objects and faces and discrete touches that constitute the dance. As critic Justin Chang (2019) observes,

> Malick finds a transporting loveliness in images and exchanges that another filmmaker might have dismissed as banal: in the baking of bread and the milking of cows, in the steady flow of a babbling brook and the way a toddler's legs dangle after she's fallen asleep in her father's arms. (5)

Even the auditory becomes singular at times, passing us through a split-edit transition from one scene to another. In one instance, for example, we hear the percussive sound of Fani's heels on the kitchen floor before Malick cuts to her on camera beside her pensive husband at the table. The technique, an almost imperceptible device known as a J-cut, has the effect of insinuating underneath the visual composition a particularized movement of human presence. All told, nothing is unremarkable. Touch, says Kearney (2021), "is not confined to touch alone but is potentially everywhere" (16) and "[t]actful sensation makes us human by responding to singularities here and now" (31). Malick also relays as much by shooting from multiple angles, and he will even "cubize" some scenes by running the same one in different locations (Ebiri 2020, 2), in order to catch the birth of carnal intelligence in the trans-immanent act. It is the visual cousin to Gerard Manley Hopkins' "sprung rhythm" in the acoustics of prosody. Malick especially values the unscripted accidental moments of touch underway, leaving space for them through a practice he calls "Quail Hunting." It could be the sudden emergence of a "perfect light," says production designer Sebastian Krawinkel, or a "shy moment" such as when "the actor is lying in the shadow under a tree and there's a fly on his nose" (Ebiri 2020, 2).

Scenes drawn from moments such as these relate to what Roland Barthes (1977) called an "elliptic emphasis" (57), a rift in the usual signifier-signified relationship of cinematic language that allows a "third" (64) mode of meaning to jut out from the default semantics of narrative representation. An expression, a gesture, or a slight intrusion in the space of the frame can disclose some aspect of a "life" that is extant to the normal logic of reference. Barthes terms this effect the "filmic" element (64). I think Kearney would identify in its poetic play the dappled threads of sensibility and possibility. The result is a further instance of how, at the heart of *A Hidden Life*'s hermeneutic tact, there lies a focus on the mosaic details of our sense-involvement with people and things that are far more than subjects and objects.

Along the way, another technique allows the visual medium to serve the tactile by bridling its own ocular control: *lighting*. To be sure, Malick cherishes light cataphatically and often uses it to signify goodness, transcendence, and wonder. But light in this manner is never had without shadow, as though to convey how the onset of blessing or truth is a gesture of apophatic faith more than certainty. During production, he in fact made the use of light as difficult as possible. Eschewing all artificial sources, the effect is not just a more natural compositional tableau but a self-discipline in the filmmaking that honors (however modestly) Franz's own discipline to hold to the light of conscience. Malick tasked his actors with placing themselves in the right light at the right time—particularly as it fell upon their faces in indoor scenes. He would direct them to "Search the light," recalls Pachner (O'Falt 2020, 9), and "Vermeer yourself" (Ebiri 2020, 2). The camera does this too; doorframes and windows—frames within frames—become apertures through which the viewer's imagination seeks the light. The search becomes harder, and camera motion becomes slower, as the walls close in around Franz. Overall, then, direction, for Malick, is a mode of discovery and disclosure, a search to present the irreducible features of life through which the larger sense of existence comes to be and comes to terms.

Incarcerating the Carnal and Imagining Otherwise

The mechanisms of sense mediation in particularization, motion, elliptic emphasis, and lighting on the side of cinematic style are also the points of reference through which Malick unfolds the storied sense of Franz' tragic fate. Here we come to the matter of a possible integration of the "as-sensed" and "as-if" in his physical and poetic states, with special implications for Kearney's combined work. Over time we see Franz exiled from his first order of carnal mediation. He is physically stilled, confined, beaten, altogether abstracted from his *humus*, and we feel the weight of phronetic answerability for history's injustices. Thresholds and windows narrow in the distance as he is forced to "search the light" from a prison cell and courtyard and entrust the movement of his faith with a mediative capacity sufficient to defy this incarceration of his carnate freedom. Malick's ability to affect this special convergence of body and story in the film entails holding in balance two modes of our evolving relationship with Franz. I am thinking of Neal DeRoo's treatment in this volume of Kearney's distinction between *persona* and *person*. Where *persona* refers to one's special singularity—their "transcendence" and "haecceity"—*person* designates one's concrete material being. DeRoo cautions that "if we overvalue the *persona* and fail to adequately account for the empirical nature of the other qua person, we threaten to idolize or divinize them, and thereby lose their concrete singularity" (see DeRoo, "Carnal Sacrality: Phenomenology, the Sacred and Material Bodies in Richard Kearney," p. 70). Applied to the case of Franz, privileging his righteous conviction would mean diminishing his carnality. But Malick honors *persona* and *person* by showing how Franz' narrative faith and moral determination have their unique being *in* his carnal horizon, not above it. Following Franz from Radenburg to Charlottenberg, we witness his adherence to imagination's possibility-function in the context of his finitude's materiality and affiliate wisdom. Malick's success on this score pays a formative dividend in his overall *aisthēsis*. The viewer is able to face with Franz the interrogative challenge emerging at the site in which Kearney's two projects meet: can an art of the possible contend with, as it were, the incarcerating forces of excarnation? We feel the effect of Franz's arrest so powerfully because his otherwise free and natural movement has been, literally, *arrested*. His tactile agency is narrowed into the confines of austere offices, trains, prisons, and finally the dark closure of the executioner's chamber. By first revealing Franz's life by way of its captivating motion and particulars, Malick had attuned us to the full tragedy of its capture and hiddenness. Now the tactile calls urgently for the poetic.

Two scenes will suffice to help us grasp what this integration of carnality and imagination involves. Both lament the crippling of sense within the banality of evil, and both magnify the urgency that calls for a *muthos* that would restore it. Early in the story, Franz comes upon an old painter at work on scaffoldings in the vaulted nave of an empty (as though spiritually muted) Catholic church. He is restoring images of prophets and saints, but reluctantly so, for the aesthetic end assigned to him amounts to a requisite betrayal of Christ and art alike. He speaks in scene and through voiceovers that span the breadth of a day with Franz—reflections seasoned by time and toil and now confessed plainly to his visitor and himself. "Christ's life is a demand," the painter reflects. And of the congregation: "I paint their comfortable Christ, with a halo over his head … Someday I'll paint the true Christ." What does it mean "to paint" in this context? To do a work of the hands in the service of religious imagination and story. Though the mood is embittered, *Someday I'll paint …* still conveys what Kearney would call an *ana*-theistic aspiration—a "utopian" determination even—to live by a spiritual hermeneutic. The artist's desire is to transmit the moral authority of Christ's teachings and passion into the aesthetic field, thereby interrupting the decadent social imaginary of the congregants. But his touch is constrained, bound, cut off from the real narrative of his subject—an incarnate God who touched and healed as he taught and suffered. Suffice it to say that the artist's situation mirrors that of Franz, who is trying to concretize the true Christ in his own more tragic circumstances. The painter will, so to speak, pass the brush to Malick to complete the revelation of Christ's passion as figured in one of his pilgrims. The tragic weight of this passion culminates later when Fani and their village priest visit Franz in Berlin when he is on the brink of execution. The priest pleads with him to make the oath: "God doesn't care what you say. Only what's in your heart." An impossible distinction for Franz. They are surrounded in a small room by state officials and guards. Franz and Fani tremble in the urgency to embrace one another. Guards brace them apart. They are thus unable to touch each other and regain the sense of their prior world. But there is a cataphatically tactile light in the room and the words of Franz' letter, his *ana* of the otherwise, still sound—"Our sadness will be changed to joy." Fani assures him she is "with him always."

I do not think it stretches things too much to identify—extrapolating from Barthes—elements of the Kearneyan *ana* underway in the filmic composition of these scenes. In each one the "third" meaning softly irrupts out from the narrative's surface—the synoptic sense of a martyrdom unfolding—and, so doing, replaces viewer distance with sensory empathy and possibility. In Franz' exchange with the painter the filmic is conveyed through Franz' reflective gaze, which is searching for the absent but intended image of Christ (he never looks at the artworks). Moreover, Franz' lingering at the church in effect presents *him* as a third meaning to the world around him. A signifier without a fully-realized signified, the unanticipated permutation in the story's narrative field also passes an "elliptic emphasis" through the screen such that the viewer is asked, as it were: "How would *you* respond to the true Christ, the incarnate third

between church and state?" In the intense drama of the prison room, the filmic element arises emotively between the referential power of procedural discourse and the raw emotions of love and anguish. The narrative authority in the moment belongs to the force of *anthropos*. Yet against that background is foregrounded, through carnal desperation, the authority of longing and life-giving oaths to marriage and God. The fullness of such "signs" can only be a matter of anticipatory faith, but there is "wisdom" in the couple's touch. While Malick leaves the question of an *ana*-theistic catharsis itself in an elliptic state, his portrayal of the loss felt by Franz and Fani does not prove the lie of faith and fidelity, nor snuff out the fuse of possible ascendence over all existential incarceration and separation.

***

By accounting for the formative elements of Kearney's work on the hermeneutic imagination and on carnality, and by reading *A Hidden Life* through the frameworks, we have seen how the life of sense entails a collaboration between the tactile and the poetic. Their co-constitution has, I believe, been implicit in Kearney's work all along. And by tracing their overlapping functions in the narrative and style of the film we have been able to appreciate Malick's presentation of the "as-if" and "as-sensed" dimensions of a life that is not our own but is of the same hard freedoms. The film, to borrow from both phases of Kearney's work, presents an aesthetics of possibility (2004, 675) that helps us "reinhabit our world" (2021, 129–30). It should be said, finally, that neither the art nor the theory is meant to leave us in a state of undecidability when it comes to our hermeneutic bearings. They together recognize the unfinalizable life of sense, but still make us answerable to the praxis of stewarding that life. The poetic answers the call of the tactile in a praxis of *phronesis*. Today our excarnate captivity hides in plain sight and incarcerates diffusely, whereas Franz' asserted itself directly and brutally. But the singular intensity of his predicament might be one severely taut instance of our own (*pathos* and *phobos* have their reasons, after all). Kearney once said, in understated terms, that "the hermeneutic detour through art usually leaves some mark on our everyday manner of being-in-the-world" (2004, 675). When Malick selected as his epigraph George Eliot's appeal to "the growing good of the world" he may well have intimated the living sense of what embracing that mark might entail.

Note

1 By "Malick" I mean his authorship in writing and directing the work, as well as the larger apparatus of the filmmaking including the production design and actors, camerawork, editing, score, etc.

References

Barthes, Roland. 1977. *Image-Music-Text*. Translated by Stephen Heath. New York: Hill and Wang.

Chang, Justin. 2019. "Review: 'A Hidden Life' Is Terrence Malick's Strongest Film in Nearly a Decade." *The Los Angeles Times*, December 12, 2019. https://www.latimes.com/entertainment-arts/movies/story/2019-12-12/hidden-life-review-terrence-malick

Ebiri, Bilge. 2020. "Quail Hunting Down Rabbit Holes: How Terrence Malick Blended Improv, Dance, and History to Create the Expansive *A Hidden Life.*" *Vulture*, January 23, 2020. https://www.vulture.com/2020/01/behind-the-scenes-of-terrence-malicks-a-hidden-life.html

Kearney, Richard. 1988. *The Wake of Imagination: Toward a Postmodern Culture*. London: Routledge.

Kearney, Richard. 1998. *Poetics of Imagining: Modern to Post-Modern*. New York: Fordham University Press.

Kearney, Richard. 2004. "A Conversation with Richard Kearney." Interview with Felix Ó. Murchadha. *Symposium: Canadian Journal of Continental Philosophy* vol. 8, no. 3, 667–683.

Kearney, Richard. 2015. "What Is Carnal Hermeneutics?" *New Literary History* vol. 46, no 1 (Winter): 99–124.

Kearney, Richard. 2017. "Narrative and Recognition in the Flesh: An Interview with Richard Kearney." Interview with Gonçalo Marcelo. *Philosophy and Social Criticism* vol. 43, no. 8: 7 77–792.

Kearney, Richard. 2021. *Touch: Recovering Our Most Vital Sense*. New York: Columbia University Press.

Malick, Terrence, director. 2019. *A Hidden Life*. Fox Searchlight Pictures. 2h, 54min. Released in the United States on December 13, 2019. https://www.imdb.com/title/tt5827916/

O'Falt, Chris. 2020. "Working with Malick: Inside the Dance Between Camera, Actor, and Light in 'A Hidden Life.'" *IndieWire*. January 6, 2020. https://www.indiewire.com/2020/01/a-hidden-life-terrence-malick-process-cinematographer-jorg-widmer-valerie-pachner-august-diehl-interview-1202200111/

Ricoeur, Paul. 1995. "The Memory of Suffering." In *Figuring the Sacred: Religion, Narrative, and Imagination*, edited by Mark I. Wallace. Translated by David Pellauer. 289–292. Minneapolis: Fortress Press.

Chapter 9

Kearney's Journey between Imagination, and Touch—in Dialogue with Ricœur

Eileen Brennan

The journey from imagination to touch is central to Richard Kearney's work. It starts with an apprenticeship with Paul Ricœur on narrative and empathic imagination and then develops into a dialogue that continues right through to Kearney's most recent work on touch. Ricœur turned his attention to the phenomenology of imagination and the related topic of a critique of ideology and utopia when lecturing at the University of Chicago in the mid-1970s. It was only a short time later that Kearney started his apprenticeship with him. The fact that the imagination was a topic that was still relatively new to Ricœur when Kearney undertook doctoral studies at the University of Paris may explain why Kearney has never simply deferred to Ricœur's expertise in that area but has always engaged Ricœur in robust dialogue, whether face-to-face or as a reader of one of his texts. However, Ricœur is not the only traveling companion whose company Kearney has appreciated on an intellectual itinerary that comprises several major stages, just two of which I will be able to discuss here: (1) his early work re-imagining imagination, and (2) his most recent work on touch. Those other influences include: Derrida, Levinas, and Heidegger, although I shall only be able to mention two of them in the story I want to tell about the development of Kearney's thought over a 30-year period, the relationship of his thought to Ricœur's, and the significance of some of his recent contributions both to phenomenology and to ethical thought.

Re-imagining Imagination

Kearney describes himself as "a hermeneut" who has a foot in two camps: deconstruction and phenomenology (Littlejohn 2020, 321). He suggests that the bond between hermeneutics and phenomenology can be understood in three stages: (1) proto-hermeneutic experience; (2) phenomenological bracketing; and (3) hermeneutical retrieval. Proto-hermeneutic experience, the first stage, is not quite at the level of understanding. Following Heidegger, Kearney uses the term, "pre-understanding (*Vorverständnis*)" to indicate how

DOI: 10.4324/9781003285649-13

we initially grasp things. Although it is only pre-understanding and not understanding proper, proto-hermeneutic experience always involves interpretation. That is to say, in "our natural condition" we always see things in
terms of an "as-structure" and "fore-structure" (Littlejohn 2020, 321).
Phenomenological bracketing, the second stage, involves the use of a methodological technique that was developed by Edmund Husserl and which is
more commonly termed the *epochē*. As Kearney explains, the assumption
behind phenomenological bracketing is that we all impose our own prejudices, presuppositions, and projects onto the things we perceive, thereby
blocking them from manifesting themselves to us. Phenomenological
bracketing allows us to suspend all that we impose on what we see, clearing
the way for us to "enter a space where we can have a fresh experience of the
pure 'thisness' and 'thereness' of things" (Littlejohn 2020, 320).

As already mentioned, the third and final stage in understanding the
bond between phenomenology and hermeneutics is hermeneutical retrieval. Hermeneutical retrieval is where hermeneutics is "grafted" back
onto phenomenology, a process that evinces Kearney's debt to Ricœur
(Littlejohn 2020, 321). It was in *The Conflict of Interpretations* that
Ricœur famously likened phenomenology to a young plant and "the
hermeneutic problem" to a slip taken from a much older one (Ricœur
2007, 6). He said that it was his intention "to explore the paths opened to
contemporary philosophy by what could be called the graft of the *hermeneutic problem* onto the *phenomenological method*" (2007, 3). Echoing
much of what Ricœur says in the opening chapter of that book, Kearney
clarifies that the point of hermeneutical retrieval, by which he means
revisiting the "as-structure" of our pre-philosophical understanding, is to
"recognize from the beginning, [that] all our experience is deeply mediated by our desires, our dreams, our heritages, our legacies—our imaginings!" (Littlejohn 2020, 321).

Kearney's early work on the imagination can be shown to proceed
methodically through the above-mentioned three stages. "Imagination
Now: The Civilization of the Image" is a case in point. There the young
Kearney comments on the "as-structure" and "fore-structure" in terms of
which his generation tends to see things. He observes that "the contemporary eye is no longer innocent. What we see is almost invariably
informed by prefabricated images" (Kearney 2020, 4). It does not matter
whether we are gazing at some natural landscape or whether it is a case of
our most private thoughts, how we see things is something that has been
colonized by the image industry (Kearney 2020, 3). In making that observation, Kearney is positioning himself close to the postmodern writers,
artists, and filmmakers of his generation. Underscoring the connection,
he notes that there is a growing awareness at the level of contemporary
artistic culture, "that images have now replaced the 'original' realities
they were traditionally meant to reflect" (Kearney 2020, 4).

But Kearney's postmodern sensibility is atypical. He admits to being troubled by postmodernism's "suspension of subjective inwardness, referential depth, historical time, and coherent human expression" (Kearney 2020, 7). He also makes it plain that he rejects postmodern theory "from Lacan and Lévi-Strauss to Barthes and Derrida" because it poses a threat to the very notion of a creative human imagination (14–15). Even at this early stage, he is emerging as a thinker who, though drawn to postmodernism in certain respects, is still capable of maintaining a critical distance from it.

The example of phenomenological bracketing that we find in "Imagination Now: The Civilization of the Image" is really very sophisticated. It also points to an abiding interest that Kearney has in stories of evolution and development. The following statement signals the move from the proto-hermeneutic stage of Kearney's reflection to the phenomenological bracketing stage: "The story of imagination needs to be told. Like all species under threat of extinction, the imagination requires to be recorded in terms of its genealogy: its conceptual genesis and mutations" (Kearney 2020, 8). We might have expected, given his account of the goal of phenomenological bracketing—gaining access to "a space where we can have a fresh experience of the pure 'thisness' and 'thereness' of things" (Littlejohn 2020, 320)—that the "thing" that Kearney would want to reprise is some kind of imagined object or perhaps even the imagination as object. However, the young Kearney's interests lie elsewhere. He wants to contemplate the evolutionary development of the concept of imagination. There is a form of phenomenology—genetic phenomenology—which is perfectly suited to identifying the origins of a concept, mapping its mutations, and so on, and that is precisely the form of phenomenology that Kearney uses when he sets out to re-imagine imagination.

The inspiration behind Kearney's use of genetic phenomenology is almost certainly Martin Heidegger's *Being and Time*. Heidegger, whose position might be encapsulated by his resonant thought from §7 of *Being and Time*: "Higher than actuality stands possibility" (Heidegger 1962, 63), certainly indicated a way forward for the young hermeneut with an interest in deconstruction. Heidegger showed that, for all its wrong turns and dead ends, the history of ontology still retained "positive possibilities" for correctly formulating the question of the meaning of being (1962, 44), and that provided Kearney with the template he needed for telling the story of imagination and giving it a new ending. But what could that new ending to be? Toward the close of the chapter, Kearney offers a first glimpse of what he has in mind: "I propose the possibility of a postmodern imagination capable of preserving, through reinterpretation, the functions of narrative identity and creativity—or what we call a poetics of the possible" (Kearney 2020, 18). That he should categorize the form of imagination he envisages as postmodern should come as no surprise. As I noted when commenting on Kearney's early proto-hermeneutic experience, he describes his own sensibility as postmodern, albeit in a qualified sense. Just like the experimental artists, writers, and filmmakers of his generation, he has a strong sense of his gaze having been colonized by the image industry. It is inevitable, then, that any new form of imagination to emerge from his work would be marked by that same postmodern sensibility.

If we are looking for an example of hermeneutical retrieval in "Imagination Now: The Civilization of the Image," we need to look no further than the list of things that Kearney's possible postmodern imagination will be required to do. As he explains, the purpose of a postmodern imagination is to "disclose how things might be" (Kearney 2020, 18). It is therefore required to do the following: (1) "follow in the wake of imagination"; (2) strive to "open us to the concrete needs of the other in the postmodern here and now"; and (3) endeavor to "explore how we might effectively engage in the transformation of our social existence" (Kearney 2020, 18). He then goes on to describe what he envisages as "a practice of imagination" (2020, 19) that "repudiates any cognitive model that dismisses morality, and by extension human rights and needs, as an ideological leftover from bygone days" (2020, 18). He notes that this new practice will be "capable of responding to the postmodern call of the other reaching toward us from the mediatized image" (2020, 19). But what is it about that list of requirements that allows it to function as an example of hermeneutical retrieval? Simply put, it casts light on the sort of things that mediate Kearney's own experience in a postmodern world, which he cannot fully escape. As already noted, Kearney thinks that the point of hermeneutical retrieval is to "recognize from the beginning, [that] all our experience is deeply mediated by our desires, our dreams, our heritages, our legacies—our imaginings!" (Littlejohn 2020, 321).

Re-imaging Imagination in Dialogue with Ricœur

There is no denying Kearney's debt to Heidegger in his earliest attempts to re-imagine imagination, but the project has also been shaped by a critical engagement with Ricœur's work on imagination. In *From Text to Action*, Ricœur identifies four basic meanings of the imagination, and observes that they are all marked by a "radical equivocalness," which cannot be clarified at the level of theory (Ricœur 2007, 166). Kearney's "Imagination Now: The Civilization of the Image" identifies those same four meanings as the four main uses of the term "imagination," adding a textual acknowledgment of Ricœur's *From Text to Action* as one of the sources for them. However, Kearney rejects the claim of *radical* equivocalness and looks instead for a middle ground: equivocalness combined with "certain common features." Without explicitly mentioning Ricœur, he accepts that the concept of imagination is "equivocal," open to multiple interpretations, but he insists this does not mean that the various interpretations have nothing in common. He maintains that the "pluralist notion of 'family resemblance' enables us to appreciate the equivocal nature of the concept of imagination while also acknowledging certain common features in its different versions and contexts" (Kearney 2020, 8). Then, drawing on ancient Greek and Medieval philosophy, he declares that "imagination lays claim to a certain analogical relation of unity through resemblance" (2020, 8). His next step is to conduct the already mentioned analysis of the conceptual genesis of imagination and its mutations. He is particularly interested in the way the concept of the imagination mutates over time, and he wants to show that there is now the possibility of a new mutation: the postmodern imagination, something I have already commented upon above.

Another thing that Ricœur's *From Text to Action* does is draw attention to the problematic nature of certain "imaginative practices" and the urgency of subjecting them to critique. Here is Ricœur on the topic:

> The truth of our condition is that the analogical tie that makes every man my brother is accessible to us only through a certain number of *imaginative practices*, among them *ideology* and *Utopia*. These imaginative practices possess the general characteristics of defining themselves as mutually antagonistic and of being destined, each in its turn, for a specific type of pathology rendering its positive function unrecognizable: this positive function is its contribution to the analogical tie between myself and others like me. It results from this that the productive imagination ... can be restored to itself only through a *critique* of the antagonistic and semipathological figure of the social imaginary. (Ricœur 2007, 177)

Toward the close of the essay, Ricœur describes the named imaginative practices—ideology and utopia—as "two figures of false consciousness," underscoring the point that it is "only in a critical relation with them" that "[w]e take possession of the creative power of imagination" (2007, 183).

I have already noted that there is also a reference to "a practice of imagination" in "Imagination Now: The Civilization of the Image." Kearney's "practice of imagination" is meant to help the postmodern subject respond to the other *through* the mediatized image, and to always see that other as the bearer of human rights and as someone with basic human needs. Kearney's postmodern subject is a possible subject that can be made real only through a "postmodern deconstruction of the humanist subject and its pretensions to mastery" (Kearney 2020, 19), a critique inspired by Heidegger, Foucault, and of course Derrida. The thought seems to be that for a form of imagination to qualify as ethical-poetical—Kearney describes his possible postmodern imagination in those terms—it cannot involve pretensions to mastery over others. Indeed, Kearney talks about the need for his possible imagination to be "schooled in the postmodern truth that the self cannot be 'centered' on itself" (Kearney 2020, 19). Kearney's proposal for a critique of the imagination clearly differs from the type of critical work that Ricœur has outlined in *From Text to Action*. And that is to be expected. His possible postmodern imagination was never designed to meet the needs of a sociopolitical project like Ricœur's. The issue was not whether the deconstructed humanist subject could see the analogical tie between itself and others, but whether it could learn *not* to make its interaction with others an occasion for claiming that it had control or superiority over them. Putting differences aside, there is no doubt that dialoguing with Ricœur was useful to Kearney as he set about developing the critical apparatus for his early work re-imaging imagination.

The "Double Sensation" of Touch

Kearney's most recent work, *Touch: Recovering Our Most Vital Sense*, is "concerned with the crisis of touch in our time—an age of simulation informed by digital technology and an expanding culture of virtual experience" (2021, 2). His key question is: Are we losing touch with our senses as our experience becomes ever more mediated? He also wonders whether ours might not be "an era of 'excarnation,' where we obsess about the body in ever more disembodied ways"? (2021, 2) Kearney explains that it was Charles Taylor who introduced him to the term "excarnation." Taylor used that term to express the idea of "flesh becoming image." Its inverse, "incarnation," then came to mean "the image becoming flesh." However, it would be a mistake to assume that because Kearney makes use of Taylor's idea of excarnation, he also readily adopts Taylor's definition of "incarnation." When Kearney talks about incarnation, he is actually referring to an experience that Ricoeur had commented upon in *Freedom and Nature*: the experience of the sensed body. Ricoeur distinguished "incarnation" in that sense from "incarnation" in the sense of the experience of the body in action. Later, I shall say something about Kearney's refusal to follow Ricœur in confining ethical considerations to the practical field, thus opening up a philosophical discussion on ethical considerations to do with the sensed body. But for now, I want to concentrate on the way Kearney's most recent work develops some of the themes, but also some of the methodologies, that I have already identified in his early work on the imagination.

As already demonstrated, Kearney's early work on the imagination proceeded methodically through the same three stages that he would identify many years later when he set about explaining the bond between hermeneutics and phenomenology. Its point of departure was proto-hermeneutic experience from where it proceeded first to phenomenological bracketing and then to a hermeneutical retrieval of that earlier experience. For the young Kearney, the difference between his initial proto-hermeneutic experience and subsequent hermeneutical retrieval was that the latter recognizes that our experiences are mediated by our legacies, heritages, dreams and imaginings, while the former does not. Kearney would have known even at that early stage that his mentor and friend Paul Ricoeur liked to describe those first and final stages of hermeneutical phenomenological inquiry as a "first" and "second naivete" but those were not descriptions that he felt able to adopt. Indeed, he observed that the perspective he shared with his contemporaries was "no longer innocent" (Kearney 2020, 4), which is another way of saying "no longer naive." But as we shall see, by the time Kearney comes to write his monograph *Touch*, the gap between his and Ricoeur's ways of describing the first and final stages of hermeneutical phenomenological inquiry has narrowed considerably.

There is no explicit reference to proto-hermeneutic experience in *Touch*, although Kearney does refer to something that looks and sounds rather like it: "the inaugural act of what I call carnal hermeneutics" (2021, 18). That inaugural act is said to occur, not at the stage of young adulthood, the stage commented upon in "Imagination Now: The Civilization of the Image" but rather in infancy. The focus of Kearney's attention is the way infants *touch and taste* the world:

> From the moment of birth, the child uses the mouth not just as an organ of ingestion (*bucca*) but as a means of communication (*ora*). The infant's mutation from buccal cavity to oral mouth is one of the most formative moments of natality. It marks the inaugural act of what I call carnal hermeneutics, where the initial contact of touch and taste is informed by the infantile fantasy of the 'good and bad breast.' We first taste the world through our tongues and only later translate these infinitesimal sensory tastings into words and thoughts. (2021, 18)

As I have already noted, in his early work on the imagination Kearney moved from a proto-hermeneutic stage of reflection to a phenomenological bracketing stage, which allowed him to focus on a genealogy or developmental story: "the story of imagination." Something similar happens in *Touch*. Without suggesting that there is any urgency when it comes to the development of carnal hermeneutics, Kearney draws attention to a possible pattern in human development:

> One speaks of a dialectical development from a first naivete, where the child perceives the interconnectedness of things, through a flattening of sight as one-dimensional perception, to a second naivete of renewed holistic insight: a doubled vision where we see once again with the 'eyes of the heart'. (2021, 24–25)

In highlighting that possible development from a first naivete to a second, Kearney is echoing something that Gabriel Marcel wrote about and Ricœur then referenced in *Freedom and Nature*. I shall say more about that connection later. One example Kearney offers for the flattening of sight into one-dimensional perception, at least in the 21st Century, is an increased reliance on cyber technologies. As he remarks, "Our putatively materialistic world is becoming more immaterialized by the day, with multitouch screens serving as exits from touch itself" (Kearney 2021, 4).

The key question for Kearney is, as already mentioned: Are we losing touch with our senses as our experience becomes ever more mediated? To clarify what he means by "senses," he turns to ordinary speech. He notes that in colloquial speech "the term sense has three distinct meanings: as sensation (our five senses), as meaning (in what sense do you mean that?), and as orientation (as in sense of direction in Romance languages)" (2021, 9). A claim that is central to one of the arguments he makes is that all five sensations—sight, hearing, taste, touch, and smell—are capable of *reciprocal experience* thanks to the "double sensibility" of touch (2021, 15). He acknowledges that only one sensation is properly termed "touch," but he makes the case that touch is present in all the other senses as well. It was the Husserl of *Ideas II* who first identified the phenomenon of "double sensation" that is the feeling of both touching and being touched at the same time. Husserl observed that "double sensation" is part of touch, but it is not part of vision (*Ideas II*, §37, p. 155; IV 147).[1] He was exploring the phenomenon with a view to explaining how sensations give rise to the concept of space and the experience of spatiality. Differentiating his own position from that of Husserl, Kearney writes: "We are talking about touch in a more inclusive way, as an embodied manner of being in the world, an existential approach to things that is open and vulnerable, as when skin touches and is touched" (2021, 15). With that broader conception of touch comes a new interpretation of "double sensation." It becomes "an interplay of far and near, knowing how to be subjects *of* our actions while being subject *to* others' actions—being touched even as we touch" (2021, 11). There is an unmistakable moral tenor to that statement, but there are others that harken back to the Greek conception of ethics. Kearney talks about a reciprocity, born of "double sensibility," that is "the golden rule" (2021, 10) when it comes to distinguishing "between good and bad taste, sight, scent and sound" (16–17). He has a name for what it is that good sensations embody. He calls it "the carnal wisdom of tactility" or "*tact*" (9).

Thinking About Incarnation in Dialogue with Ricœur

The first thing that Ricœur does when he starts to think about incarnation is check to see what Marcel has to say on the subject. The inspiration for *Freedom and Nature* may come from Husserl, and the methodology used may be recognizably phenomenological, but Ricœur is unequivocal when it comes to naming the underlying support or foundation for all the analyses in the book. The basis for those analyses is, he says, a meditation on Gabriel Marcel's work (Ricœur 1966, 15). Ricœur takes seriously Marcel's word of warning: if thought holds clear and distinct ideas *at a distance from itself*, it will lose the ability to experience incarnation (1966, 15). However, Ricœur worries that an outright ban on the use of "abstractions" in philosophy will lead to a loss of methodological rigour (1998, 24). So, in *Freedom and Nature*, he tries to strike a balance between a short-term, somewhat anxious engagement with Husserl and a long-term commitment to Marcel and his philosophy of incarnation. Ricœur almost certainly drew strength from Marcel's assurance that it is always possible to *rediscover* or *regain* the experience of incarnation. He also took Marcel's assurance to mean that all humans have had some experience of incarnation at some point in their lives. He comments that childhood offers "glimpses of the mystery of the unity of body and mind" (1966, 439 [trans. modified]). He also suggests that we may well have had experiences of incarnation in the womb.

One of the things that Kearney does when he starts to think about incarnation is engage in dialogue with Ricœur. On the issue of Marcel's warning that thought loses the ability to experience incarnation whenever it holds clear and distinct ideas *at a distance from itself*, Kearney clearly agrees with Ricœur that one must proceed with caution. But where Ricœur's idea of proceeding cautiously means spending as little time as possible engaged in a Husserlian-type eidetic abstraction (Ricœur 1966, 37), Kearney's idea of proceeding cautiously means avoiding only those forms of philosophy that take their inspiration from Platonism. He accepts that there are ingrained prejudices in the philosophical tradition that go all the way back to 5th century BCE, but he argues that the propensity for abstraction has its roots in Platonism, not in any other type of philosophy and certainly not in Aristotelianism. As is well known, Plato spoke about abstract, perfect, unchanging ideals, denigrating the body. But Aristotle was different. Kearney maintains that "A first philosophy of touch was sketched by Aristotle at the outset of Greek thought. He deemed tactility to be the most pervasive and intelligent of the senses. But his claim was largely sidelined for two thousand years" (Kearney 2021, 33). It was not until contemporary phenomenology made "a revolutionary effort to redeem Aristotle's inaugural insight," that Platonism's optocentric paradigm was challenged and touch restored to its rightful place (2021, 34). Viewed from the point of view of Kearney's own development, this aligning of his recent work on touch with that of Aristotle—the father of realism—is effectively a declaration that his thought is now shifting from a relatively narrow interest in the *possible*—possible postmodern imagination, possible postmodern subject—to a broader interest in the possible and the *real*.

Like Ricœur, and indeed Marcel before him, Kearney is energized by the prospect of *regaining* or *rediscovering* incarnation. The evidence is there for all to see in the full title of his book: *Touch: Recovering Our Most Vital Sense*. And he too considers childhood and the prenatal development stage to be times when humans experience incarnation. I have already commented upon the passage where Kearney talks about child development following the pattern of a first naivete, a levelling of perception, and then, but only if all goes well, a "second naivete." It emerges from other discussions in the book, that both forms of naivete involve "a synesthetic communion" with others (Kearney 2021, 24). Kearney would consider that to be the optimal condition for humans. He finds it remarkable that, even at the prenatal stage of human development, our sense of touch and sound are connected:

> they are the first senses to develop fully in utero and the last to leave us at death. The foetus's early learning often occurs around rhythmic hand-mouth coordination, and its discrimination of sound is linked to an early apprehension of space. (2021, 28)

Kearney thinks about prenatal development in much the same way that most of us do. It is a question to be answered by medical science, using medical technology such as an ultrasonography machine. Medical science has certainly provided insights into human gestation that were simply unimaginable when Ricœur wrote *Freedom and Nature*. When Ricœur thinks about life in the womb, he focuses on an "infant consciousness" (1966, 440) that can never be accessed directly. He comments that "our infant-consciousness" will stay with us all our lives, prolonged in the form of the "un-knowledge of our unconsciousness." From time to time, "in our dreams and in our attitudes as waking men," we will express a desire to return to the womb (1966, 440). Ricœur explains that it was Freud who first identified the relevant oneiric icons and slips of the tongue. But what does it mean to want to return to the womb? Ricœur claims that it is only a "decipherer of dreams" that can help the waking man understand. He goes a step further when he observes that the "un-knowledge of our unconsciousness" represents "a valuable testimony for the philosopher seeking roots and ways of approach" to incarnation (Ricœur 1966, 440). And again, he thinks that the philosopher will not be able to decipher the meaning of that testimony unaided. He has not yet formulated the idea of the need for a "hermeneutics of suspicion" in philosophical inquiry, but he already envisages a situation where the philosophy of incarnation will need the assistance of psychoanalysis.

That is clearly not the route that Kearney wants to take. Although he shares Ricœur's view that what happens at the prenatal stage, and then in early childhood, provides valuable examples of the experience of incarnation for a philosophical inquiry into that subject, he does not appear to see any role for a specialized form of interpretation like psychoanalysis. Rather, he puts all his trust in a form of hermeneutics—carnal hermeneutics—that operates below the level of cognition. Of course, that could leave him open to the charge that his most recent work lacks a critical apparatus. One way to respond to that criticism would be to draw attention to the way *Touch* focuses on *discernment*, and to claim that the book deliberately eschews critique. The key concept in that regard is "tactility" or "tact." As Kearney explains, "Tactful perception—across all the senses—ensures a proper relation of mutuality between perceiver and perceived. Its presence or absence is what distinguishes between good and bad taste, sight, scent and sound" (Kearney 2021, 16–17). As I have already noted, he also describes tact as a "carnal wisdom" (2021, 9), a phrase that invites comparison with the ancient Greek notion of *phronesis* or practical wisdom. If there is indeed a family resemblance between carnal hermeneutics and virtue ethics, it would make little sense to complain that Kearney's carnal hermeneutics lacks a critical apparatus. To do so, would be to misunderstand the type of philosophy it is.

"Voluntary Incarnation" and/or "Involuntary Incarnation"?

Ricœur, who translated Husserl's *Ideen I* into French, was always on the lookout for comments or asides in Husserl's texts that could be read as invitations or encouragement to do something new in phenomenology. To take a first example, Ricœur discovered in *Ideas I* what he took to be an open invitation for researchers to transpose the method of intentional analysis from the field of representational consciousness to "the field of practice" (1998, 26). Ricœur soon took up that invitation and followed Husserl in positioning forms of consciousness like sensing, perceiving, imagining, and judging in the field of representational consciousness, and others like wishing, commanding, and willing in the field of practical consciousness. He then began to analyze willing using the method of intentional analysis.

Throughout his long career, Ricœur continued to think of phenomenological research as something that was divided along representational/non-representational lines, and to see his own work in phenomenology as something that belonged to the field of practice. Even when, in the mid-1970s, he turned his attention to the phenomenology of imagination, he did so with a view to determining the role that imagination plays in social and political contexts, the problems it can give rise to in those contexts, and what remedies might be available. I have already compared Kearney's work on imaginative practices with Ricœur's, noting discontinuities but also continuities. However, in his recent work on touch, Kearney is no longer simply following Ricœur into the practical field, looking to carve out a space for the possibility of a new, postmodern imagination with a distinctive ethical purpose. By turning his attention to the hermeneutic phenomenology of *sensation*, and analyzing the ethical as well as the unethical functioning of all five sensations, Kearney is broadening the scope of ethics beyond anything seen in Ricoeur's practical philosophy. And as he does so, he is demonstrating that hermeneutic phenomenology has the resources to respond to the needs of a new generation, whose ethical concerns are not confined to principles of conduct but extend to ethical norms of perception.

Ricœur's decision to include consciousness's "own relation to the body" (1966, 19)" in his intentional analysis of the will is yet another example of taking up a suggestion that he found in one of Husserl's texts, in this instance a late work that addresses the question of the *Lebenswelt*. There are, Ricœur suggests, just two broad options when it comes to the way consciousness relates to the body: either (1) it relates to the body as "organ-body, the moved organ" or (2) it relates to the body as "a sensed, imagined, represented body" (1966, 215). He explains that his phenomenology of the will concerns "the organ-body, the moved organ ... my body-moved-by-me" (1966, 215). And he emphasizes the point that the will does not relate to the sensed, imagined, represented body. Focusing now on the cogito or subject side of consciousness, Ricœur observes that the cogito has a different meaning depending on how it relates to the body. He notes that if it relates to "the moved organ ... my body-moved-by-me," "cogito" means "voluntary incarnation." If it relates to "a sensed, imagined, represented body," it means involuntary incarnation. Ricœur offers two examples of involuntary or "passive" incarnation: (1) suffering (here incarnation just "happens to me"); and perception (here incarnation is "implicitly felt"). Ricœur does not waver on the active/passive distinction. As far as he is concerned, volitional consciousness involves active incarnation whilst representational consciousness involves passive incarnation. However, the research that Kearney has conducted for *Touch* appears to overturn that thinking. If Kearney is right and the experiences of seeing, hearing, touching, tasting, and smelling are all cases of *touching and being touched at the same time*, then the meaning of the cogito must change to reflect that. No longer to be understood, following Ricœur, as being either an active or a passive incarnation, the cogito must be seen as a form of incarnation that is *both active and passive.*

Kearney's relationship with Ricœur is certainly complex. He willingly acknowledges that Ricœur, along with several other phenomenologists, contributed deep contemporary insights into our embodied being. But he has been openly critical of Ricœur in other forums, observing that Ricœur began to neglect the body as soon as his philosophy underwent a linguistic turn.[2] He thinks it is a great pity that Ricœur, who did such important work in the 1940s and 1950s on the role that the body plays in the act of willing, did not build on what he had achieved in the decades that followed. When I first read *Touch*, I read it as a work that more or less banked the deep insights into our embodied being that *Freedom and Nature* offers, and then continued Ricœur's legacy in new and exciting ways. I was not entirely mistaken, but I failed to appreciate the pressure that Kearney's argument for the "double sensibility" of the five senses brings to bear on Ricœur's suggestion that a given cogito can have only one of two possible opposed meanings: voluntary incarnation or passive incarnation. A case can doubtless be made for reading *Touch* as a work that does what Ricœur failed to do from the 1960s onwards, that is to build on what he had achieved in terms of an understanding of our embodied being. But it is important, I think, not to forget Kearney's challenge to suggestions made in Ricœur's work of the 1940s and 1950s about the mutually exclusive character of active and passive forms of incarnation. That disagreement with Ricœur is significant and it merits further and very careful consideration.

Notes

1 See Moran (2009).
2 Kearney made the point at a seminar hosted by The School of Philosophy, University College Dublin, on the 8th April 2021.

References

Heidegger, Martin. 1962. *Being and Time*. Translated by John Macquarrie and Edward Robinson. Oxford: Basil Blackwell.

Kearney, Richard. 2020. "Imagination Now: The Civilization of the Image (1988)." In *Imagination Now: A Richard Kearney Reader*, edited by M.E. Littlejohn, 3–22. London: Rowman and Littlefield.

Kearney, Richard. 2021. *Touch: Recovering Our Most Vital Sense*. New York: Colombia University Press.

Littlejohn, M.E., ed. 2020. *Imagination Now: A Richard Kearney Reader*. London: Rowman and Littlefield.

Moran, Dermot. 2009. "Husserl, Merleau-Ponty and the 'Double Sensation.'" Lecture, CFS, University of Copenhagen. 10 November, 2009. https://cfs.ku. dk/calendar-main/calendar2009/dermot/

Ricœur, Paul. 1966. *Freedom and Nature: The Voluntary and the Involuntary.* Translated by Erazim Kohák. Evanston: Northwestern University Press.

Ricœur, Paul. 1998. *Critique and Conviction.* Translated by Kathleen Blamey. Cambridge: Polity Press.

Ricœur, Paul. 2007. *The Conflict of Interpretations.* Evanston: Northwestern University Press.

Part IV

Touching Flesh

Chapter 10

Anaskesis: Retrieving Flesh in an Age of Excarnation

James L. Taylor

With his recent work on *Carnal Hermeneutics* (Kearney and Treanor 2015), *Radical Hospitality* (Kearney and Fitzpatrick 2021), and *Touch* (Kearney 2021), Richard Kearney reminds us that to be fully alive as a human being is to exist as a carnal body exposed to the world and others through our living senses. Human life is lived on the ground—"at sea level"—immersed in the plenum of sensation that tirelessly envelops us, solicits us, and to which we always respond, even when we try not to. We translate with our bodies and through our senses all that intersects with us, from sense to symbol and back again. In *Touch* (2021) especially, Kearney makes a strong case that we are first flesh and second mind, which is always an abstraction from the bodied and open-hearted self that first feels and senses its way through the world and its relationships with others. If we want to be fully alive, Kearney intimates, we should retrieve and re-enter this primal and visceral experience of ourselves, by and large forgotten by philosophy and concealed by technology.

Retrieving this experience, however, is not a straightforward task. Vital though our senses are to our sense of self, we live now in what Kearney terms a state of "excarnation." It is not that our senses have been denied but that they have been captured and reconfigured by our digital media platforms—our phones, televisions, and computers—all of which shield us from physical contact and mediate our senses to us. Virtuality is so effective because it provides surreptitious sensual satisfaction—through video games, artificial environments, and titillating programs—by engrossing us fully, simulating that we are fully alive, not only by thinking our thoughts for us but by sensing our senses through us as well. This virtually sensing life moreover is thereby shielded from the risk of exposure to the world and from the potential for transformative encounters with others.

Kearney describes our current predicament but he also provides us with the tools for retrieving our flesh. Before I turn to Kearney's program for retrieving flesh, however, I want to add a layer to the story of excarnation by attending to the way that we have been formed by power

DOI: 10.4324/9781003285649-15

relations. By drawing from the work of Michel Foucault, I will show that we can only gain a full picture of our current relationship with virtual culture through attending to the ways we have been formed by power into docile and desensitized bodies. I will show moreover, that because power constrains experience and produces us from the ground up, it presents us with a unique challenge: how do we retrieve flesh from a power that is invested in keeping it docile?

After clarifying the role of power in producing docile bodies, and with the link between docility and excarnation established, I will turn to Kearney's proposal for getting us back "in touch" with ourselves. Kearney recommends that we retrieve our flesh not by going back in time but by repeating forward, by drawing out what has become concealed and sedimented in order to engender new possibilities for sensate living. I will examine Kearney's art of movement, paying particular attention to the way his figure of "ana" serves as the bedrock for an "art of living" capable of resisting the coercive effects of power and of reinvesting an experience of flesh. I will argue that by bringing Kearney into direct conversation with Foucault and with the question of power, we can see more clearly that Kearney's project is not an *anamnesis*—designed to recall our primordial condition—but an *anaskesis* designed to enliven our senses and transform our capacity for carnal living with and for others.

The Eclipse of Flesh

Much of Kearney's recent work is devoted to reminding us that we exist carnally, through the flesh (*sarx*). I am not first a mind and second a body. I first live, act, sense, and engage the world and everything in it—my neighbors, the strangers I meet, the institutions in which I work, the earth that sustains my life—through my flesh. As flesh, my body is neither a vehicle for my mind to instruct nor a collection of blind physiological processes, but rather the specific "thisness" (*haecceites*) of me. As the locus of myself and all my powers, my flesh is an "I can" through which I move around, express myself, love and hate, dream and build, through which I accomplish all that I do in this world.

With his emphasis on the flesh, Kearney is part of a recent philosophical turn to a consideration of our material life and embodied condition. To this more general return to the body, however, Kearney adds a distinctively hermeneutic dimension. Especially by foregrounding the role of the senses and of touch in particular, he points out that this "I can" is not simply a capacity to exist but an interpretive enterprise. Flesh is a medium (*metaxu*) for touch, Kearney insists, which is sensitive to all the differences that make up its environment. This primary sensitivity is there at the beginning insofar as a baby's "first touch is not neutral but already a reading between the lines—of skin and bone, of soft and hard, of hot and cold, of far and near." With flesh as its medium, touch is not a brute mechanism for transferring information, but a "responsive membrane" that is always already filtering, accepting, rejecting, and modulating. Through "a highly sensitive *Befindlichkeit* which evaluates and discriminates in the most concrete of situations," (Kearney and Treanor 2015, 21) discerning "choices" are constantly being made throughout the body, on the surface of its skin as it touches the air, the earth, and other living bodies. This carnal body, therefore, is not merely an object used by a thinking mind but is itself an active and interpreting agent in the world.

Flesh is not only active but is also deeply receptive. That flesh operates as a medium for our senses means that it serves as both a passage for reaching out to the world and as an opening for the world to reach in. As characterized by a two-way "double sensibility," flesh touches and is touched simultaneously. This bi-directional quality applies to all the senses, moreover, insofar as touch operates through them. "Touch is the heart and soul of the senses, the intersensorial link and milieu which makes all sensible mediation between the outer and inner world possible in the first place" (Kearney and Treanor 2015, 23). This reciprocity of the senses is significant insofar as "[to] touch and be touched simultaneously is to be connected with others in a way that prizes us open. Flesh is openhearted," Kearney tells us, "where we are most exposed, skin on skin" (Kearney 2021, 41). As a medium that opens outward and inward and that therefore allows us to make and receive sense, flesh is the primary way we exist as human beings, and the primary way we relate to others and to our environment.

But flesh is now relegated, Kearney bemoans, to a tertiary condition. We live away from our bodies, alienated from our flesh through our virtual entanglements. Kearney warns that "more and more of our existence is being lived at a distance—through social media and digital communications, e-gaming, e-mailing, e-banking, e-schooling, e-dating," etc., (2021, 4). These days we come to dwell easily and frequently in virtual environments that exacerbate our alienated condition. Although we may long for contact through human touch, we settle instead for the convenience of a digital liaison, whether at the bank or at the restaurant, or now through the phone app which will arrange to have dinner brought to and dropped at our doors, so we never have to suffer the awkwardness or summon the energy for personal interaction. Kearney marshals other relevant examples like "internet sex via chat rooms, Instagram, and advanced simulation technologies" (2021, 113) that are dangerous insofar as they provide a surrogate connection and simulated intimacy, but increase distance instead. To these, I can add the especially dystopian example—which Kearney also mentions in his contribution to this volume—of the "un-tact society" being developed in South Korea. Ostensibly to manage the pandemic, multiple billions of dollars are being spent to invest in high-tech robotics and other technologies that will minimize the need to interact in person for commerce, health services, entertainment, etc. Kearney notes that most residents are appreciative of this program, with "80% ... who have engaged in such 'non-face-to-face activities' [saying] they are happy with the experience". South Korea of course is not alone. All of the western world and most of the rest is eagerly embracing this shift from tangible to virtual ways of being-with one-another.

Why have we chosen alienation over intimacy and embraced excarnation so enthusiastically? Kearney proposes that one central reason we live in excarnate ways is that to be carnate is to be exposed and vulnerable. "To live fully is to be constantly exposed to the elements, to being, to life, to others; it is to be forever attentive and attended, from head to foot, to pain and pleasure, to happiness and grief, to good and ill." Kearney writes that flesh is "for these very reasons, the first place of pain and pathos" (Kearney and Treanor 2015, 24). Faced with the risk of suffering, we choose security over vulnerability.

Our virtual culture, Kearney explains, is perfectly designed to shelter us from the exposure of flesh. He surmises that one reason that we are drawn to our screens is that they provide this form of unidirectional experience which occupies and entertains us without asking anything in return. Since "[being] in touch with flesh means being at risk" (Kearney and Treanor 2015, 24), we take refuge instead in the comforts of virtual culture, which shelters us by simulating one-way rather than two-way experiences. When we play our video games, shop online, or interact through virtual personae, for example, we see others without suffering the risk of being seen ourselves. More sophisticated virtual technologies, in fact, simulate not only sight but the other senses as well, creating a surrogate world in which all the senses are "working" without ever exposing us to flesh and blood others through that bi-directional touching that makes all sensing possible in the first place.

I think Kearney is right that virtual culture provides an escape, but before I turn to Kearney's solution, I want to explore the role of power in excarnation and to understand more fully why we escape into virtual interactions. I will show that there is an important link between the docile body and our virtual culture and that any retrieval of flesh must intervene not only at the level of ideas but at the level where this power produces us as docile.

Divested Flesh and the Disciplined Body

This intervention at the level of power relations is complicated because power doesn't want to let the body go, and in fact is invested in keeping it docile. Power, in fact, uses certain weapons to keep us divested of our agency, most prominently the fact that it hides its operations. It is not ostentatious and loud, as one might expect, but rather operates secretly and through back channels by inciting and influencing behavior rather than forcing it outright. This means that we will have to catch power in the act by attending not to what it says about itself but to what it does from below to form us—not to repress us, per se, but to produce us into beings that act, think, feel and *sense* in ways that are useful for the administration of living.

Foucault first discovered this power that doesn't repress but produces bodies through his examination of prisons, hospitals, and army barracks. But his point wasn't to understand prisons, for example, but to grasp how this power works so that he could determine how it was being used across many of our everyday institutions to train, surveil and organize bodies so that they become useful and obedient. He points out that this disciplinary power operates through regimenting a subject's actions so that it experiences its body in a new way, no longer as active flesh (*Leib*) but as an available object (*Korper*). This operation in turn, would make the body more susceptible to being integrated into "normal" and manageable societies. Along with biopower, disciplinary power operates from the ground up rather than top-down, transferring its influence in a capillary way from one specific operation to another and forming docile bodies in the process.

By docile body, Foucault doesn't mean a body incapable of action, but a body that has been programmed to react to its environment and others around it in ways that increase efficiency. This body is manipulable insofar it is trained through discipline to obey managerial prerogatives. The docile body was born in the eighteenth century through the application of what Foucault calls the "arts of time and space," which disassembled the body so as to divest it of its agency and built it up again as manipulable and useful. To provide maximum control of variables, disciplinary power initially worked through enclosed spaces to subject the body to

> a collective and obligatory rhythm, imposed from the outside ... A sort of anatomy-chronological schema of behavior is defined. The act is broken down into its elements; the position of the body, limbs, articulations is defined; to each movement are assigned a direction, an aptitude, a duration; their order of succession is prescribed. (Foucault 1995, 152)

Through this human technology in which "[time] penetrates the body and with it all the meticulous controls of power" (152), the experience of the body was transformed so as to make it totally available for knowledge and power as a political project. The regimentation of time was used to "[extract] ... ever more available moments and, from each moment, ever more useful forces" from the body. Through carving up its time, therefore, discipline turned the body itself into a harvested resource, available and ready to be used, "as if [its] time, in its very fragmentation, were inexhaustible or as if ... one could tend toward an ideal point at which one maintained maximum speed and maximum efficiency" of the body (154).

We notice the same logic with regard to the arts of space, where disciplinary power breaks down the body according to its function and builds it up with new and useful capacities. In "the eighteenth century," through a social organization in which, for example, "rank begins to define the great form of distribution of individuals in the educational order," and schools and barracks are designed with "rows or ranks of pupils in the class, corridors in courtyards," discipline begins to isolate and connect bodies according to what features they may provide for the management of society (Foucault 1995, 146). Through an "ensemble of compulsory alignments, each pupil, according to his age, his performance, his behavior, occupies sometimes one rank, sometimes another," according to how his body may benefit or hinder the regulation of living. This technology of bodies operates by "[moving] constantly over a series of compartments, marking a hierarchy of knowledge or ability," eventually achieving "a perpetual movement in which individuals replace one another in a space marked off by aligned intervals" (147). Like resource in Heidegger's "standing reserve," bodies are made to be as interchangeable and replaceable as possible. If one part of the spatially segmented machine breaks down, the whole suffers, and therefore it is necessary to have other bodies available on hand to fulfill the function as efficiently as possible. In these ways, the arts of time and space collaborate to manage bodies so as to produce totally available sources of energy.[1]

Through these disciplinary technologies, power divests flesh by producing a new and docile experience of the body. One reason that this production is so effective is that power hides its operations, convincing its subjects that it is basically neutral, like a tool that one picks up or lays down and that can be used for good or ill. As such, we take our basic experience of ourselves—in this case of our docile bodies—for granted, experiencing our bodies as "natural," essentially untouched by a power that only infringes on our choices and desires when they are criminal, immoral, or unnatural. From the vantage point of these operative power relations, we can see that "through this technique of subjection," "a new object [is being] formed," a "natural body" that is now accessible to science (Foucault 1995, 115).[2] We can grasp that it was only through the application of "specified operations, which have their order, their stages, their internal conditions, their constituent elements" that the body became "natural," which means knowable, predictable, and therefore available to strategies of power (155). This is discernible from the meta, or better sub-level, of power relations, while from the level of first-person, immersed self-experience, this whole operation is concealed: the body is taken to be a natural object, free of the corrupting influence of power relations. This experience of the naturalness of the docile body both contributes to the spread of power and makes it especially difficult to retrieve flesh.

Disciplinary power produces this "natural" experience of the body by causing us to internalize imposed norms of behavior. With carceral technologies, for example, we can discern an operation whereby, through a totalizing surveillance in which we can never be sure when we are being watched and therefore must assume we are always being watched, we take over the responsibility of adhering to imposed behavioral norms for ourselves. Although it was never built, Jeremy Bentham's Panopticon is exemplary of such totalizing surveillance in that its prisoners would have to assume they were always being observed and were therefore constantly in danger of punishment (Foucault 1995, 195). Because they would always be potentially exposed, the prisoners would police themselves, eventually becoming "the principle of [their] own subjection" (1995, 203). This internalizing human technology, Foucault insists, was actually developed in correctional institutions but "became de-institutionalized" (211) and exported in a more diffuse way to every area of our lives, thereby increasing our subjection to power and further divesting our flesh. Through this disciplinary application of power, we adopt values and forms of behavior that are not drawn from our living engagement with the world, through our flesh, but are rather imposed upon us to engender strategic outcomes. As such, we don't question our "natural" experience of our bodies and therefore don't notice that our bodies are not our own, that we don't live in and through our flesh.

Power also hides its operations through what Foucault calls "the repressive hypothesis," a scheme that uses the promise of freedom or health as a lure to more effectively incorporate the body into its operations (Foucault 1990a, Part II). Drawn from psychoanalysis, but applied more generally across a range of emancipatory practices, the "repressive hypothesis" incites the self to speak its "deep truths" so as to free itself from repression. The experience of repression, however, is not a natural given, but an essential element in the operations of power; through this confession, the self is actually being formed "as repressed," brought into being as a temporarily obstructed inner truth and site for free action and thought. Through this seduction, we subject our minds and bodies to those authorized human sciences that tell us who we are and how we should feel and act, what we should desire, so that we may be healthy and normal. Just as with carceral operations, the repressive hypothesis generates an experience of the body as natural or normal—as not generated—while hiding its generative character. Thus, by virtue of a slight of hand, we embrace our docility unthinkingly because we don't recognize it.

This slight of hand is particularly evident when it comes to the senses. We recall that excarnation has reconfigured the senses so that what is supposed to be a two-way, reciprocal experience—of sensing and being sensed—has become a one-way operation: like the wearer of Gyges' ring, one sees, hears, and touches, without being sensed in return. Power also reconfigures sensation but in a different way. Formed by discipline, the docile body is seen without seeing, heard without hearing, and touched without touching. This can be seen most directly through the previous example of panoptical technologies that ensured that one was "totally seen, without ever seeing" (Foucault 1995, 211).[3] This reconfiguration, however, was not confined to sight. Discipline transformed hearing (through psychoanalysis one is heard without hearing), smell (through poverty, madness and physical illness one is smelled without smelling), and taste (through normalizing pressures to ingest proper foods and drinks and use pleasure correctly). In each case, one is touched to the extreme, to the point of coercion, without being aware of this touch, as though the senses were operating freely and without constraint. By transforming space and time into fields for visibility, observation, and knowledge, discipline reversed the direction of sensing so that everything relevant about a person—body and soul—could be known, documented, collated, and calculated. Especially through the deployment of touch, this disciplinary reversal of sensing was essential to the production of the docile body.[4]

It is worth pausing for a moment to consider this extraordinary situation and to ask how this disciplinary reversal of sensing relates to the imbalance that characterizes the excarnate subject. For both docile and excarnate selves the senses are non-reciprocal, which means that they fail to mediate between the self and its others—the environment, world, other selves, etc. But if I am right that we have not simply fallen into this condition but have been placed here by relations of power, then we can also conjecture that the sensory imbalance characteristic of the docile body is related to the sensory imbalance of the excarnate self. I cannot here provide a full analysis of the relation between these two forms of sensory imbalance. But given the steady, if hidden pressure of a disciplinary power that makes every aspect of our lives "constantly visible" (Foucault 1995, 200), it makes sense that we would seek refuge from this pressurized situation in the simulated pleasures of one-way sensibility. We embrace digital technologies, for example, that allow us to live vicariously through avatars and virtual personae because they provide us with a temporary reprieve from the invasive strategies of power.

How might this work in the concrete? I will stay with the example of virtual personae, which features prominently Kearney's *Touch* (2021). This persona that we develop to present a virtual face to the world, Kearney notes, is for many, every bit as significant and real as our flesh and blood persons. We interact with other digital personae and develop virtual relationships that include virtual/social capital, and we live vicariously in this virtual environment for much of our waking life. Sometimes, the virtual relationships take over to the point that a person will suffer greatly or even commit suicide when his or her virtual persona is rejected. But for the most part, we enjoy the freedom; we find refuge in these personae insofar as they allow us to exist as "better" or "more interesting" versions of ourselves, or as someone else altogether. Ultimately, these avatars allow us to see without being seen and to enjoy a sovereign unaccountability that is not available in our daily life. Who among us doesn't recognize the relief experienced when, after a long day, one can snoop around and interact online without consequences, connecting with others, often strangers, in such a way that one is never really exposed but only entertained?

If this figure exemplifies our excarnate condition, it also reflects our docility. It is precisely because we are seen so pervasively—through the pressures of our disciplined world—that we seek refuge in this digital world. But of course, everything we do in this digital world—through which we attempt to escape our "flesh and blood" existence—is also seen, and in fact recorded, so that the quality of our virtual activity is two-sided. The more we attempt to escape our docile visibility, the more we become integrated into the circuits of power that produce it. How much online rage has been generated by the fact that the freedom, connection, and pleasure we seek through virtual technologies instead incorporate us more fully into systems that manage our living? This example helps us to understand how docility and excarnation are linked, like two sides of the same touch-screen, with the self now touched without touching and now touching without being touched. I will return to this example below when I show how Kearney's anaskesis can help us to retrieve flesh.

Retrieving Flesh through Askesis

This analysis of the docile body has shown that we don't simply find ourselves given, as natural, but are formed from the ground up through power relations. That we are formed rather than found as such means that we can't simply remember our way back to a former self but must form a new self; we must repeat our way forward to a new way of being-in-the-world, or as we will see in Kearney's case, to a new way of being-in-the-flesh.

Foucault's analysis of power led him to a similar conclusion, namely that the only way to contend with disciplinary power is by undertaking spiritual practices capable of resisting its effects. Thus, he harkens back to Greek and Roman philosophy—Socrates, the Stoics, Cynics, Skeptics, etc—which cast philosophy as an art of living and through which he could conceive of a non-disciplinary way of relating to self and others (Foucault 2005). Foucault found these ancient forms of philosophical engagement intriguing not because they were free from power, but because they allowed their practitioners to creatively participate in their own ethical and spiritual formation. By engaging in philosophical exercises designed to help subjects get ahold of themselves—to modify their desires, capacities, and emotions so that they are no longer driven by harmful passions and insecurities—ancient philosophers achieved excellence, beatitude, or ataraxia. Foucault believed that this way of doing philosophy could provide an important counter-force to disciplinary and other forms of modern power (Foucault 1990b, Chapter 1).

Foucault's retrieval of ancient arts of living is complicated, however, both because premodern metaphysical and cosmological assumptions—which provided the framework for ancient forms of philosophical practice—are no longer tenable for us, and because—and this is significant—there is no space entirely free of disciplinary influence. This last challenge is particularly fraught because modern power operates—as we have seen—by promising emancipation only to intensify domination. This means that even the arts of living proposed by Foucault may be co-opted by power and used to confine rather than to liberate. Foucault was highly sensitive to the precarious and almost Sisyphean nature of any modern philosophical askeses. Rather than counseling despair, however, he suggested that we become alert to the way self-formative practices can be transformed into coercive practices and that we develop critical diagnostic tools and agile arts of resistance that can be reworked and redeployed so as to counter the constant pull toward the calculative administration of life.

But beyond general remarks as to why ancient askesis would be salutary, Foucault didn't say much about how we might practice these arts of life today. Likely out of desire to avoid any normative and therefore to his mind coercive proposal, he refuses to articulate a pattern or logic for such a project. Kearney on the other hand does provide us with a contemporary, concrete, and relevant program for formative philosophical practice.

At the heart of what I am framing as Kearney's spiritual approach is the figure of "ana." Ana means a movement "back, up, after, again in space and time," (Kearney in this volume, 235) and involves the practice of returning and repeating so as to reopen and transform what has been closed off. Formulated first in Kearney's *Anatheism* (2011), "ana" was conceived as a way to retrieve faith in a living and loving god after the death of the sovereign god. In his recent work and in his contribution to this volume, Kearney has applied the movement of ana to the task of retrieving the living body from the excarnate body. I am pushing further here to show how anacarnation can serve as a philosophical program for retrieving flesh from the reductive operations of power.

What I am calling Kearney's "anaskesis" is composed of three basic moments, each of which serves as a coordinate in an active and formative process rather than as a fixed position. Although Kearney doesn't unpack his "ana" in just this way, we can identify these three basic movements from his use of ana across different topics, like theism, imagination, and now carnal embodiment. I should mention two provisos here: first, I am analyzing these moments as distinct when they should be grasped on a continuum. I am approaching the moments this way to show how they can serve as effective markers for what I am calling Kearney's art of living. Second, we should not think of these moments as moving from incomplete to complete—anaskesis is not sublation—but as indicating a continuing path or way of living.

The first moment affirms our essential connection with others and the world around us. It reminds us that we are relational, that life is good, and that being is gratuitous. Before any critique, the gift of existence is originary and arrives unbidden, beyond our capacity and our control. With this first moment Kearney aligns himself with a phenomenological hermeneutics that does not create from scratch (*ex nihilo*) but always works with what is already given to us. And what we find, even through suffering, is a world filled with meaning and significance.

The second moment is the critical moment of withdrawal from immediacy into mediate forms of engagement like imagination, critique, and ascesis. This moment receives the gift from the first moment but recognizes it also as a task that must be evaluated and reworked in light of coercive ideologies and relations of power. Thus, we distance ourselves from our situation, subject it to critique, and detach ourselves from the harmful elements. This is the working moment in which we voluntarily embrace a critical suffering through which we may choose to withdraw from certain relationships and detach ourselves from oppressive structures, all of which can lead to "instants of deep disorientation, doubt, or dread, when we are no longer sure exactly who we are or where we are going" (Kearney 2011, 5). Through this second moment, Kearney links up with that long tradition of spiritual philosophers that counsel detachment from desire and pleasure. Through what he calls a "creative not-knowing" (2011, 7), Kearney provides the tools to evaluate our situation and the resources to abstain or limit our engagements.

The third moment returns us to a fully affirmative but now deeper engagement with our world. Alive now to the corrupting effects of coercive power, we can see our way through the pitfalls to an authentic and enlivening contact with others. In *Anatheism* (2011), Kearney explained that through this third moment, we may return with new eyes to an experience of the sacred in the mundane elements of our daily living (2011, 8). But here in the context of the retrieval of flesh, he suggests that the third moment allows us to "return to the lived body" and thus to the "interconnectedness of things". Hence, we cease to experience ourselves "as some disembodied consciousness experiencing a mere thing amidst things" and retrieve that primal dimension in which "flesh [experiences] flesh in a fundamentally reciprocal way" (Kearney 2021, 46).

Application

Let's examine how the ana movement works with regard to our current, virtual mode of excarnation, but with attention to its relation to disciplinary power. The first ana moment reminds us that it is good that we exist in relation with others, even when those relations are mediated largely through digital avatars. Where we may be tempted to criticize first, especially when it comes to our digital interactions, Kearney reminds us that critique comes second, only after affirmation has acknowledged that any form of living—even excarnation—is better than none. Kearney notes for example, that "The internet allows us to exchange culturally, socially, and commercially with all kinds of people in all parts of the world" (2021, 3), remarking further that even "social media also plays a positive role in our lives—inviting us to empathize 'imaginatively' with people in far-flung corners of the globe" (119). Indeed, our virtual interactions still connect us. Even those virtual personae we inhabit still connect to each other, still establish relationship, which is better than no connection at all.

This affirmation then passes over into critique through which we become aware that we often interact in virtual space and inhabit virtual personae to seek refuge from a total visibility that bears down upon us at all times. That is, through this critical moment, we begin to see that disciplinary power prompts our escape into virtual culture by forming us as docile bodies and therefore as seen without seeing. In this stage, we come to understand that our virtual personae are attempts to generate an artificial sovereignty through which we may reverse our imposed blindness and instead see without being seen. We grasp, moreover that power therefore engenders a cycle which causes us to oscillate between this false sovereignty in virtual space and a docile obedience in our non-virtual interactions. Through the second critical moment, as placed against the first affirmative moment, we will then be able to see that although culture may attempt to convince us that our digital interactions have no effect on our flesh and blood selves (the clandestine operation of power), even our virtual actions are driven by real feelings and desires that have material effects on our real lives. This insight may lead, in turn, to action, as we recognize the need not only to diagnose but to resist the coercive pressures by which the docile body is formed and which motivates our virtual escape. We may choose therefore to engage in certain disciplines of abstinence—like fasting all digital interactions to the degree possible or dedicating time for solitude and contemplation—that can equip us not only with critical insight but with new capacities for engagement.

After having passed through the crucible of criticism and now armed with a better sense of how our self is shaped by unreflective engagement with the virtual space, we will complete the movement of ana by reconnecting to our world. The second moment has provided us with the tools to discern which practices will contribute to our docility and which will increase reciprocity and revitalize our capacity for living-in-the-flesh. Kearney suggests that we might engage through what he calls "ana-technology" by which he means that we would retrieve digital practices for the purpose of authentic connection. He points to "ventures in haptotechnology ... that portend productive possibilities of collusion between virtual and embodied experience—ways in which our real and simulated worlds may cooperate rather than compete ..." (2021, 130). And he provides examples that were especially life-giving at the height of the Covid pandemic in which "multi-sensory events" were held "that enabled spatially separated participants to meet in a common space" (139). But whatever forms of engagement one would choose, the point is that virtual technologies may be retrieved in ways that foster greater sensory connection. That is, through this third moment, we may return to the first moment of engagement, but now at a deeper level and imbued with greater sensitivity and wisdom and greater appreciation for the double-sensation that characterizes our living flesh.

This three-fold approach of ana then allows us to respond effectively to disciplinary strategies by recognizing the life-giving, flesh oriented aspects of our existence, by exerting a counter-pressure to power through the negative, critical moment, and finally by calling us to inhabit our interconnectedness with others through our carnal, sensing bodies.

Kearney's art of living is also useful for resisting the strategies of power insofar as it is flexible and provides us with the tools to navigate a constantly shifting environment. Even those initiatives initially designed for resisting power can become reintegrated into the very dynamics of power, i.e., by narrowing meaning, policing identities, or coercing behavior. For example, a grass-roots green movement that brings industry to heel at one moment becomes used the following week by that industry to increase profits and exploit its workers. We can never—at least on this earth—completely twist free of power, but through anaskesis we can continue to retrieve the experience of flesh right in the middle of the storm of influences attempting to reconfigure it and deploy it for malignant purposes. We will remain on the move therefore, attached not to any one practice or idea, but rather to the movement itself by which such relations of power are navigated. This is why the ana at the heart of anaskesis is better understood as directions for movement or as notes to a song than as fixed positions. The movements of engagement—detachment—reengagement distinctive of ana can allow us, therefore, to discern with a light and agile touch, how and when to connect and when to withdraw, under which conditions and through which circumstances, in order to re-sensitize our bodies so that we may relate carnally and tangibly to one-another in what Kearney calls a "commons of the flesh" (2021, 7).[5]

Kearney's philosophy therefore calls for the self to undergo a transformative process. The ana is a roadmap for a "way of living" that requires us to proceed through the moments and be changed by the movement. By suggesting that Kearney's philosophy is an "anaskesis," I am aligning Kearney with Pierre Hadot, Foucault, and others, who view philosophy not merely as a form of discourse or analysis but as a committed and transformative task that involves the whole person. Like Foucault, Kearney recognizes that we must be transformed, but he adds that this transformation takes place not simply in our souls but at the root of who we are in our very flesh. It is "experienced in our bones—moods, affects, senses, emotions—before [it is] theoretically interrogated by our mind" (Kearney 2011, 5).

Notes

1 For what can be considered Kearney's rejoinder to these disciplinary arts of time and space, see his chapter "Anacarnation: Recovering Embodied Life" in this volume. Kearney suggests that through the practice of what he calls "anachronology" and "anamorphology," we may deconstruct our natural and "surface" way of experiencing ourselves and "[live] more deeply in time and space." Kearney writes that these hermeneutic arts of time and space "[lead] us from our objectified numerical body (Korper) to our recursive lived body (Leib)" (pp. 238).

2 What is "normal" becomes defined within this operation whereby "[behavior is bent] toward a terminal state," an exercise which "makes possible a perpetual characterization of the individual ... [and] thus assures, in the form of continuity and constraint, a growth, an observation, a qualification" (Foucault 1995, 161).

3 "Each individual, in his place, is securely confined to a cell from which he is seen from the front by a supervisor; but the side walls prevent him from coming into contact with his companions. He is seen, but he does not see. He is the object of information, never a subject in communication" (Foucault 1995, 200).

4 With Foucault, Kearney warns us that power creates precarious relationships, but he examines this situation through how it effects our capacity for tact, that ability to act with appropriate sensitivity and care in our contact with others: "Respect requires discernment because touch, as noted, is not always appropriate, especially where power relations are concerned. Being tactful here means being sensitive in our behaviors with others, listening and responding to others in a responsible way. Such two-way sensibility involves a reversibility between oneself and another, striking a balance between distance and proximity, careful not to impose oneself on the other (domination) or to surrender entirely either (submission). Tact is an interplay of far and near, knowing how to be subjects

of our actions while being subject to others' actions—being touched even as we touch" (Kearney 2021, 11). By invoking tact here, in this context of power relations, Kearney alerts us to a question worth our attention: in what way does disciplinary power reconfigure our capacity for tact—our sensitive, reciprocal approach to others—for the production of useful individuals.

5 In this way, anaskesis returns us to a more equitable distribution of sensing, where we not only live through our always interpreting senses, but are also sensed by others and the world around us in return. This receptive dimension of anaskesis signals an important difference from Foucault's askesis, which was oriented, following Nietzsche, primarily toward self-creation. Kearney's askesis does not build a more stalwart self but a more vulnerable flesh, returning the self to its reciprocal sensibility that receives as much as or more than it gives. As Kearney remarks in his contribution to this volume, Anacarnation is "a process of constant refiguring" by one "who acts and suffers in life, who creates and recreates a persona in a world lived with others who configure us as much as we configure them" (pp. xxxxxxxxxxx). That is, conceived as an embodied spiritual practice, anacarnation allows "humans beings to exist by *mutually reconfiguring each other* in time and space" (my emphasis, Karney in this volume, 238). We can suggest then that Kearney's anaskesis is actively creative, that it recognizes, in the spirit of Nietzsche and Foucault, the great dignity of human creative capacities, but that it acknowledges also that everything we create is hermeneutically retrieved and reworked, through our skin and bones, from that which one receives.

References

Foucault, Michel. 1990a. *The History of Sexuality, Vol. 1: An Introduction.* Translated by Robert Hurley. New York: Vintage Books.

Foucault, Michel. 1990b. *The History of Sexuality, Vol. 2: The Use of Pleasure.* Translated by Robert Hurley. New York: Vintage Books.

Foucault, Michel. 1995. *Discipline and Punish: The Birth of the Prison.* Translated by Alan Sheridan. New York: Vintage Books.

Foucault, Michel. 2005. *The Hermeneutics of the Subject: Lectures at the College de France 1981–1982*, edited by Frédéric Gros. Translated by Graham Burchell. New York: Picador.

Kearney, Richard. 2011. *Anatheism: Returning to God after God.* New York: Columbia.

Kearney, Richard. 2021. *Touch: Recovering Our Most Vital Sense.* New York: Columbia University Press.

Kearney, Richard and Melissa Fitzpatrick. 2021. *Radical Hospitality: From Thought to Action.* New York: Fordham University Press.

Kearney, Richard and Brian Treanor, eds. 2015. *Carnal Hermeneutics.* New York: Fordham University Press.

Chapter 11

Female Nakedness in Protest: Tactile Reading

Sarit Larry

Introduction

A woman stands in a city square. The square is full. A protest is going on. She, a protestor like others around her, begins to disrobe. Amongst the men and women, many of whom are strangers, she takes off her clothes. As people notice, they take a few steps back. Minutes pass by and her picture is starting to disseminate through social networks and the media. More people gather to look from a distance, to take a picture, to stare, to stand with or to protect. Police are likely to arrive.

A woman disrobing in the context of a protest creates a focal point. It is an event that attracts immediate attention and rearranges the public space in which it is situated. What does female nakedness as a form of protest do to a protesting arena? What changes? What emerges? What transpires in this moment of radical willful vulnerability? Why do we step back? Is it to observe? Is it to make sure we are not taking part? That we are not vicariously becoming radically vulnerable ourselves?

This chapter applies Richard Kearney's discussion of touch to the dramatic moment of female nakedness as a form of protest. It focuses on two themes in Kearney's discussion of touch. First, the relation between sight and touch, mediation, and immediacy. Touch, unlike any other senses, is reversible: touching necessarily means one is being touched. This aspect of touch was ignored by traditional metaphysics, which relegated touch to lower, non-cognitive sensual levels. Sight was regarded as the highest intellectual sense because of the substantial mediating distance it afforded. However, the inseparable relationship between touch and interpretation at the heart of Kearney's carnal hermeneutics ascribes cognition to touch. This is made possible through a mediation that is not based on distance but transpires through gaps and intervals. The naked female protester makes touch and being touched acutely present. What are the consequences and promises of this tactful possibility?

The second theme addresses the relationship between the excarnate and the carnal. Ours is an excarnate age echoing and intensifying the

DOI: 10.4324/9781003285649-16

traditional metaphysical reverence for sight over touch (Kearney, 2014). Indeed, touch-alienating technology operates significantly and widely in protesting arenas: virtual documentation by police, the media and participants' cameras, official hashtags, and live streaming are common practices. Yet, the protesting arena is not characterized by the quintessential contemporary "opto-centric" experience. Non-virtual protests are centered around and saturated in the carnal. In other words, the protesting arena is an intense intersection of the carnal and excarnate, flesh and image, skin and screen. Concentrating upon the focal point created by female nakedness as a form of protest, this chapter outlines the manifestations of the mediating gaps and intervals, and fleshes out the inseparable relationship between the excarnate and the carnal in the protesting arena. I conclude that female nakedness as a form of protest awakens an awareness of touch and vulnerability and disturbs untactful protest norms.

Touch in Protest

Tact is deeply challenged in a protesting arena. The first stage of planning to go to a protest involves preparation for unwanted and untactful touch. Experienced protesters are well versed in the possibilities of untactful touch in a politically-charged, animated crowd. Novice protesters are likely to be warned, both unofficially and officially. Unofficially, a friend might advise one to come with long trousers rather than shorts, closed shoes rather than flip-flops. Officially, NGOs advise protesters to carry an ID, necessary medication, water (enough to rinse one's eyes), a snack, to attend the protest with someone they know, tell a friend who is not protesting where they are, and so on. They remind one not to carry anything that might be considered a weapon, to charge and to lock one's phone and so on. There are reminders of lawful and unlawful police conduct and advice about how one should act in the case of a police officer approaching, in the case of an arrest, and in the case of police violence (American Friends Service Committee 2020; New Israel Fund n.d.; Strampe and Goode, 2020). These official and unofficial lists, which circle and hover around the preparation for participation in a protest, are an indication of the challenge to tactful touch. One could be hurt intentionally or unintentionally by protesters, bystanders, or the police. One makes the decision to go into a protesting arena with some level of anticipation regarding untactful, unwanted touch.

Tact is the careful and dynamic amalgamation of reciprocity and discernment, the ability to move to-and-fro, "striking a balance between distance and proximity, careful not to impose oneself on the other" (Kearney 2021, 11). "To be tactile is to be exposed to the world across gaps, to negotiate between various embodied beings, to respond to solicitations, to orient oneself in the universe of others" (37). These agile seismograph-like movements—which are seeking to feel, approach, and escape from harm—face an inhospitable environment in the protesting arena. We enter a protesting arena heavily armed with helpful information and objects to answer our justified worry about harm. There need not be any dramatic event. Protesting can be completely civil and tactful. The point is, however, that potentially, and not rarely, it is not. Approaching and being approached tactfully is difficult in a protesting arena. People brush against one another unintentionally. Emotions are high; feelings are vexed. Physical proximity can change quickly and dramatically—not always at will, not always in goodwill.

Describing the corporeal aspect of protest as merely untactful and on the verge of escalation fails to do justice to the role of corporeality in protest. Corporeality is an essential aspect of non-virtual forms of protest which are at issue here. In her *Notes toward a Performative Theory of Assembly,* Butler describes the action of gathering in a square or on a street as a claim on, and at times even a fight over, the public character of the space.

> [Time] and again, mass demonstrations take place on the street, in the square, and though these are very often motivated by different political purposes, something similar nevertheless happens: bodies congregate, they move and speak together, and they lay claim to a certain space as public space.
>
> (Butler 2015, 69)

The mere corporeal gathering in a square is already a claim. If a demonstration moves to a back ally, back yard, a home, Butler suggests, it goes even further to contest the distinction between the public and the private. By protesting in a place that is not an agreed-upon place of protest, attention is brought to the political aspect of the private (71); a question is being raised about the accepted boundaries. Bodies acting in alliance "produce the public through seizing and reconfiguring the matter of material environments;" (70). They pose a challenge "in corporeal terms, which means that when the body "speaks" politically, it is not only in vocal or written language" (83).

Israel's anti-occupation Women-in-Black, for example, protested silently (Sasson-Levy and Rapoport 2003). The protestors, dressed in black, each took a fixed position that repeated itself in weekly demonstrations. This silent and physically expressive protest attracted much verbal violence and social criticism because it challenged the objectification and marginalization of women in the public sphere. It also posed a threat to central Israeli social norms that assign the control over security discourse almost exclusively to men. "[T]he body produces, elaborates, and articulates political ideology. It does not only serve as a medium for change but also realizes it" (400). Before we utter a word, sometimes because we choose not to utter a word, the embodiment of protesting is already posing a challenge, demanding space, articulating a world view, and objecting norms. Corporeality is a language that lays claim as protestors march, dance, sit-in, stand-with, occupy, and chain themselves to significant objects relevant to their protest. Assembled bodies exercise a performative power that "is not only speech, but the demands of bodily action, gesture, movement, congregation, persistence, and exposure to possible violence" (Butler 2015, 75).

Revisiting and drawing on Arendt's distinction between the private and the public, Butler reminds us that all action depends on material support. "[M]ovements have depended on the prior existence of pavement, street, and square, and have often enough gathered in squares such as Tahrir, whose political history is potent" (2015, 71). The material existence of allocated protesting squares—the histories that accompany them as a precedent, inspiration, or cautionary tale—serves as a necessary foundation for collective action. When protesters contest these appointed spaces by moving beyond them, they produce new meanings and boundaries *in reference to* this supporting and limiting material terrain.

While corporeal language in a protesting arena need not be translated into words in order to challenge and re-signify, it should not be viewed as pre-linguistic. Corporeal terms are interpretations manifested corporeally. They emerge from and at the same time challenge tacit and articulated norms and meanings. Butler's discussion of gender identity can serve as a good example of one such structure. Butler argues that gender identity is a product of a social corporeal ritual that we all take part in, creating the illusion of a natural, essential, coherent, and necessary whole. But this social ritual is deeply elaborate. It could and many times does produce new norms that are in conflict with the widely socially acceptable ritual (Butler 1990, 134–141). Protesting bodies, naked or clothed, are both an articulation and productive centers of cultural norms and discourse. In protests, rather than instruments delivering well thought out and succinct verbal messages, protesting bodies are focal points emerging from and at the same time disabling existing norms and orders—challenging power structures while being constituted by and maintaining them.

Female nakedness in protesting arenas is an extreme and especially volatile manifestation of these last observations. Being a part of generally patriarchal-oriented orders that manifest themselves in different manners and levels of intensity in different arenas and eras, female decisions to dress in a certain way or disrobe can create dramatic effects. Here my concern is to consider non-virtual incidents of female disrobing in protesting arenas in which being clothed is the norm. This leaves out quite a lot: virtual naked protest, naked outdoor protests staged in empty or privately-controlled spaces[1], male naked protests, and mixed-gender naked protests. I chose to focus on female nakedness because it inaugurates an extraordinarily vulnerable and volatile moment. This of course must be qualified. First, it might be true that a woman protesting "solo" is generally more vulnerable than a group of men; however, there are gendered, racial, and social status factors to this volatile equation. When members of the Doukhobors demonstrated their dedication to the purity of Christ and objection to Orthodox liturgy by protesting naked in a mixed-gendered group, beating and jailing ensued (Souweine 2005, 526–530). Much in the same way, violently homophobic arenas might be very dangerous for men protesting naked in groups. Second, a preliminary word should be dedicated to virtual spaces. Nakedness as a form of protest is different online, at home, in an empty street, and in a protesting arena. Only in the latter, there is a sharp and tangible sense of the possibility of untactful, unwanted, and possibly harmful touch. My intention, however, is not to suggest that the danger of harm and violence are rare online. The street is not always safer. Alia Magda Elmahdy posed naked in photos online at her home in Egypt. The photos, staged in reference to classical great artworks, came with an online webpage, *A Rebel's Diary* (Elmahdy 2011), evoking art history and female nakedness in order to criticize current norms of female modesty in Egypt and Islam. Both the pictures and the manifesto went viral immediately, unlocking substantial waves of feminist support worldwide. Elmahdy, who subsequently moved to Sweden, received death and rape threats (Elieraas 2014, 40–52). Her family in Egypt is harassed, and she believes that if she returns to Egypt she will be arrested. In Sweden, she protested topless in front of the Egyptian embassy and it seems plausible (but, of course, far from certain) that this corporeal nakedness in the streets of Stockholm was less dangerous than her virtual nakedness while residing in Egypt.

The discussion of touch developed here does not, for the sake of brevity, attend to the racial and social context of naked female protest. However, these aspects are important, and at the heart of an animated debate. SlutWalks are a case in point. SlutWalks' use of partial nakedness as a form of protest turned out to be a method available and safe only for women of class and race privilege. Being naked in public can be a great tension with some cultures, making participation costly or impossible for many. Reclaiming the word "slut" similarly failed to recognize the fact that for many the word is directed not to a style of dress but at skin color. While the movement used partially naked female bodies to help create a key platform for its cause, it also accentuated the embedded power structure in the feminist movement. The assumptions on which SlutWalks were planned emerged from the experience, critics say, of white-identified middle-class women (Hunt 2018) and "illuminated deep divisions within anti-sexual violence and feminist activism, [exposing] the failure of a contemporary movement to integrate analysis of structural inequalities beyond gender" (542). In the same vein, one should be careful not to uncritically take nakedness in protest to be a sign of freedom or veiling as univocally a sign of oppression (Al-Saji 2010, 890). The demand to unveil can be just as oppressive (Al-Saji 2010; Butler 2015, 81–2) and of course religious women can fight for liberties while opting to veil. Nakedness, much in the same way, could be a sign of oppression or freedom, or it can be a manifestation of the relationship between freedom and oppression. The act of reclaiming is exactly reinterpreting and owning what was conventionally forced on one. It is a rebellion that chooses to embrace and reinvent the violent insult, a transformative act that aims to create freedom out of oppression.

To conclude, it is difficult to create a clear-cut scale on which we measure the vulnerability of naked protestors and the attention they might receive. The meaning attached to a naked protest, like all meanings, is prone to slippage and depends on context. In the analysis of touch that follows, there is no claim to universality, or even an exhaustive account of the possible meanings of touch and female nakedness as protest. It is possible and even probable that many different accounts and experiences emerge in otherwise similar contexts in protesting arenas. My hope is that the analysis of female nakedness in the street as part of an overall clothed protest is volatile and pregnant enough with meanings to prove helpful in thinking of other important, risky and inspiring group formations and contexts.

Not-Touching in Kearney's Concept of Touch

Kearney describes our time as an excarnated age. We live, Kearney points out, in a world "offering us enormous freedoms of fantasy and encounter, [yet] digital eros may also be removing us further from the flesh" (Kearney 2014). Technological development, typified by the screen, is a culmination of the Western metaphysical conception of higher intellectual senses, governed by sight, versus lower animal senses epitomized by the alleged undifferentiating blindness of touch (Kearney 2021, 115). Accordingly, the discussion of ex-carnality bifurcates into a discourse centering on the cognition possible through touch on the one hand, and a cultural contemporary analysis of the relationship between technology and touch, on the other. Both aspects are meaningfully present in the protesting arena.

The idea of touch as cognitive shined for a brief moment in the history of Western philosophy when Aristotle at the end of *De Anima*, Book II, insisted that rather than blind immediacy, touch has a medium through which we discern and evaluate: flesh (Kearney 2014; 2015, 102). The reciprocal sensitivity of touch—the fact that one is touched when touching, which constitutes it as ubiquitous, essential, and fundamental—is also the reason it is considered non-cognitive. The Platonic position denied the role of medium to the more carnal senses because of this reversibility. Proximity implied passivity vis-à-vis the world while perceiving things at a distance suggested the ability to discern. Sight was considered the highest sense because it allowed for the most distance. How are we to settle these apparently conflicting qualities? Must touch be either cognitive and far from its cognized objects or immediate and blind?

Adopting Aristotle's rejection of the division of the senses into immediate and mediating through distance (Kearney and Treanor, 2015, 108), Kearney's concept of touch is mediating through and through:

> I may seem to be immediately present to what I touch and immediately touched by what I touch [...] However, there is nonetheless always something mediate in the ostensibly immediate, something "far" in the "near." There is *sensing* in sense, a *making* sense and *receiving* sense from someone or something other than myself.
>
> (103–4, emphasis in the source)

Touch, suggests Kearney, is in constant movement back and forth between self and strangeness. If the platonic view valued sight because it was deemed most distant and hence "most theoretical, holding things at bay, mastering experience from above" (2021, 35), the distance afforded by touch is different. Rather than the detached overview of sight emerging from the greatest mediating distance possible, touch offers us a mediating distance rooted in closeness and vulnerability. It approaches from close by and moves to a rhythm of to-and-fro. These oscillating movements are not linear in their direction, pace, and end. Their pattern is akin to dance; they explore, approach, return, and respond rather than directly inquire. Kearney describes the philosopher's loss for words when accounting for mediation through the flesh. Merleau-Ponty, for example, deployed sacramental and artistic metaphors to account for the amalgamation between sensing and knowing, touching and interpreting (Kearney 2010, 147–166). Kearney's choice of expressions to capture this intricate movement is similarly telling. "Diaphanous spacing" (Kearney and Treanor 2015, 108), "chiasmic tissue and texture," and "multiple carnal reversibilities and doublings" (112) are examples of the need to capture the rhythm, possible repetitiveness, and unpredictability of the intervals and gaps that constitute the mediating aspect of touch. It is an effort to capture and describe the process of discerning through the flesh as a synergy between two necessary aspects: touch and no-touch. Like printed words and the empty spaces around them – touch and no-touch only make sense together.

Of course, contemporary protest is highly complex, involving both corporeal and virtual forms. Some might argue that these forms of protest are at odds—the limited and local scope of physical protest, the disembodied and detached nature of virtual protest. Platonists' glorification of sight as the highest of the senses developed into a schismatic dichotomy between the intellectual and the carnal. This established, says Kearney, Western "anti-carnal doctrines" that culminated in "contemporary culture of digital simulation and spectacle [in which the] eye continues to rule" (2014). However, Kearney argues that we need not live in a world in which virtual and tactile realities compete. Technology can, and already does, open new ways of and spaces for learning, encountering, healing, and experiencing empathy. Kearney names this technological trajectory "ana-technology" (2021, 130)."It is clear," he says, "that to live fully in tomorrow's world we will need both virtual imagination and incarnate action" (132). Applying Arendt's concept of "space of appearance" to the context of protest, Judith Butler echoes a similar approach to Kearney's: if the space of appearance is constituted by plurality then virtual spaces, as well as squares and streets, are spaces of appearance. Butler continues to outline a mutually enhancing relationship between the screen and the street. She does so against the contemporary popular claim that virtual activism, also known as "slacktivism," is diminishing physical spaces of protest. A contemporary version of the public sphere emerges, she explains, from a synergy between street and media. "The media requires those bodies on the street to have an event, even as those bodies on the street require the media to exist in a global arena" (Butler 2015, 94). Indeed, what is the distance between the two in the protesting arena and how does this distance close, open, and inform female naked protest?

Naked Protest: Touch, No-Touch, and Tactful Consideration

Corporeality

Naked protest manifests all the corporal powers discussed in the first part of this chapter. A naked protestor within an ongoing, otherwise clothed protest poses a challenge in corporeal terms and re-signifies the space around her. A naked protestor indicates what she thinks should be permitted, safe, and supported before a word is uttered or read. Protesting naked, can, like other corporeal aspects of protest, also serve as a re-signification of the state apparatus. On July 21st 2020, as part of the anti-corruption demonstrations in Israel, a woman protested sitting half-naked on top of a Menorah statue in front of the Knesset. Both an uproar of condemnations and applause proceeded from her protest. The Knesset speaker went as far as calling for her arrest for a desecrating a state symbol (TOI Staff 2020). In an interview the protestor gave anonymously on the radio a day after the event, she said she did not think a woman's bare body on the monument was despicable, as people suggested. "I think," she added, "[that] a prime minister who is criminally indicted is a very despicable thing" (i24 News 2020). Her protest, standing topless on the menorah, reclaimed the meanings attached to grace and disgrace. The meaning of these symbols, her naked protest claimed first and foremost corporeally, are not to be determined by the state alone.

The corporeal demands of the naked protestor also function as a demonstration within a demonstration. Deciding to protest naked in an otherwise clothed protesting arena re-draws the line in the shifting sands of protest norms. The naked protester is redefining the corporeal protesting language. She is adding a behavior to the accepted and known repertoire. She calls for reflection and conversation about the limits of the protest, the issues it revolves around, and the corporeal language it is willing and unwilling to use. This effect is not limited to naked protesting or touch. One could corporeally test the limits of a protest repertoire by sitting, fully clothed, on top of a police car, for example. As a tactic, though, naked protest—and, specifically, female naked protest—is relatively dramatic. It attracts attention, generates anger, fear, condemnation, and fascination. It has a good chance of becoming a public sensation. This intensity related to female nakedness as protest magnifies the impact of the naked protesting site as a focal point for resignification and challenging norms.

Technology

Demonstrations in the streets are using online platforms as ana-technology. It is a tool to engage distant audiences and to inform them of what takes place in the protesting arena. In today's protests, both police and demonstrators hold cameras. A camera is a protective tool against infringements of one's rights, a way to document violence, a tool for the counter-surveillance of policing forces (Butler 2015, 94), and sometimes simply a means of narrating or offering a counter-narrative to the event. Furthermore, the digital protesting aspect of protests today is often no longer an aggregated, fragmented effort of random tech-savvy participants, but a fully incorporated, user-friendly, planned operation. Having a distinctive hashtag on Twitter, for example, is a common practice in protests. Protesters' leaders might ask people gathering in the square to document or to enter a Facebook streaming link and share it.

As a consequence of omnipresent cameras and digital feeds, every protester deciding to protest naked does it knowing she most probably will become an image on a screen in a manner that is irreversible and uncontrollable. Every person standing next to a naked protestor also knows opto-centric technology is at a hand's reach. Excarnated and ana-

technological considerations arise immediately. These considerations, do not assure a tactful manner. People do take their cameras out and take pictures of naked protestors in a way that is reifying, sexualizing, and many times degrading. However, tactful considerations emerge when naked protest is in progress. One is forced to at least consider what one should do. The naked protestor poses a demand for a pause to consider tactfulness.

Tactful Considerations

Female nakedness as protest can make space for the agility of tactful touch and no-touch. Unlike online nakedness, approaching, standing next to, or standing with a naked protestor brings up considerations of touch. Touching a naked person is being touched by one, and this creates closeness that is unusual for most people with acquaintances and strangers, let alone in a public (virtual and non-virtual) arena. As a consequence, naked protestors, first and foremost, serve as an awareness focal point from which agility can emerge. Questions surface: should I continue to stand close? Walk away? Should I look as if I am watching a screen regardless of the naked person being so close by? Take a picture? Post it? Avoid both? Stand guard to protect? These are tactful considerations. Navigating the possibility of approaching and not approaching as we seek what is right and what is wanted is the definition of tact. Of course, these considerations do not necessarily foster tactful behavior. However, in some sense the pause to consider one's position on the matter is already a tactful approach. The momentary suspension of social norms invites an urgent moment in which we must weigh things. Light on our feet, we need to evaluate, self-reflect and decide (or come to realize) who we are and what it is that we do in the face of radical, courageous vulnerability.

Naked protesting is a choice that commences nonviolently. This means that in the generally untactful, hectic protesting arena, it is a focal point of palpable radical vulnerability that does not emerge from direct violence. Radical vulnerability can and does appear in protesting arenas regardless of nudity. Clothed protestors might find themselves, as we said, in the face of direct and substantial harm. The difference between radical vulnerability that emerges as a result of violence and naked protesting that commences nonviolently is the probability of tactful considerations. A naked protestor allows for some room for thought, consideration, and reflection. There is no immediate need to run away to protect oneself. Female nakedness as protest can offer the protesting arena a gap, an invitation to halt in the midst of the event, to take a step back, and tactfully evaluate as we remember how naked and vulnerable we all are. In a protesting arena such moments are rare.

The woman whom the Internet dubbed "Naked Athena" for her Black Lives Matter protest in Portland is a case in point. She was famously photographed sitting with her legs spread in front of fully geared police officers standing a few meters away. *Unrefined Sophisticates* recorded an interview with her a few days after the events under the name Jen, and she explained that she was shot in the leg with a rubber ball a few minutes before the picture was taken. She sat because it was hard to stand. After sitting for a while, she decided to approach the police officers. Her purpose, as she describes it, was to make them "see what they were shooting at [...] I wanted to say shoot this! You cannot say I have a weapon now" (*Unrefined Sophisticates* 2020). The police officers already saw that she was unarmed. She was naked. Why approach? Jen introduced the volatile possibility of touch by approaching the police officers, something they likely wanted to avoid. She also increased her level of vulnerability. Her nakedness, the wound on her foot, the possibility of touch, all articulated, in corporeal terms, that the police officers needed to decide, *again*, who they were and what they would do in the face of radical vulnerability. She gave them a second chance, another opening for tactful discernment and behavior. She bravely, corporeally, asked them to try again. Jen said she wanted them "to see what they are shooting at." Of course, since they actually managed to wound her, they saw very well what and whom they were shooting at. It seems reasonable to assume that what Jen was aiming at was a morally reflective kind of seeing. She wanted them to realize what they were doing. Indeed, she wanted them to realize that it was wrong. They did not shoot again; they walked away. Female naked protestors can create sensitivity for tactful approach in crowded, mostly insensitive arenas.

In the World Social Forum 2003, a woman standing naked chanting "under our skin we are all equal, we are all human," faced an arrival of mounted police officers (Sutton 2007, 140). However, the crowd around her gathered to protect her.

> With the threat of the police on horses a few meters away, other people started to surround the woman, forming a circle, perhaps to listen, perhaps to look at her body, and perhaps to protect her from the police.
>
> (141)

Here we see the naked protestor attract attention and reorganize the protesting arena. Sutton rightly acknowledges the possibility of an objectifying look. If it was not 2003 it is likely that she would have mentioned cameras. Nakedness as protest does not guarantee kind or tactful behavior. It is, rather, an invitation to *consider* such conduct. And of course, sometimes tactfulness and crudity overlap and blend. We cannot know what a man with a camera pointed at a naked protestor is doing. He might be using ana-technology to protect the protestor. He might be taking pictures to post in a sexually offensive manner. The bystander might not even know exactly which path he is going to take. What is extraordinary and should be fully appreciated is that the naked protestor knows this. The woman on the menorah, Naked Athena, the chanting woman at the World Social Forum—they all know the gamut of potential hostilities they take upon their bodies when they decide to disrobe. It is, I suggest, a moment of awe-inspiring courage and humanity: a rare decision to use one's own body, one's own sense of safety—to call upon others to pay attention and consider tact and care. The moments that these protesters bring about are full of risky possibilities. Tact is not guaranteed. The possibility of touch steps into the protesting arena asking us: *well—now what? Who are you? Who am I in the face of this extreme courage rooted in vulnerability?* They demand and urge that we decide to behave, to stand with, to protect, and to-not-touch.

Note

1 What I refer to here is that one could protest outdoors in a fairly controlled environment. Victoria Bateman, Cambridge Faculty member of the economics department, for example, filmed herself naked outdoors in a monologue protesting Brexit. She wrote on her torso "Brexit leaves Britain naked," stood dressed with a scarf and a handbag in what seems like a public, yet empty, garden (Espinoza 2016).

References

Al-Saji, Alia. 2010. "The Racialization of Muslim Veils: A Philosophical Analysis." *Philosophy & Social Criticism* vol. 36, no. 8: 875–902.

American Friends Service Committee: Quaker Action for a Just World. 2020. "How to Stay Safer at a Protest." September 2, 2020. www.afsc.org/story/how-to-stay-safer-protest

Butler, Judith. 1990. *Gender Trouble: Feminism and the Subversion of Identity.* London: Routledge.

Butler, Judith. 2015. "Bodies in Alliance and the Politics of the Street." In *Notes toward a Performative Theory of Assembly*, 66–98. Cambridge: Harvard University Press.

Eileraas, Karina. 2014. "Sex(t)ing Revolution, Femen-izing the Public Square: Aliaa Magda Elmahdy, Nude protest, and Transnational Feminist Body Politics." *Signs: Journal of Women in Culture and Society* vol. 40, no. 1: 40–52.

Elmahdy, Aliaa Magda. 2011."Nude Art." *A Rebel's Diary* (blog). October 23, 2011. http://arebelsdiary.blogspot.com/2011/10/nude-art_2515.html

Espinoza, Javier. 2016. "'Brexit Leaves Britain Naked': Cambridge Academic Stages Naked Protest against Outcome of EU Referendum." *The Telegraph.*

July 1, 2016. https://www.telegraph.co.uk/education/2016/07/01/naked-don-a-cambridge-academics-protest-against-brexit/

Hunt, Theresa Ann. 2018. "A Movement Divided: SlutWalks, Protest Repertoires and the Privilege of Nudity." *Social Movement Studies* vol. 17, no. 5: 541–557.

i24 News. 2020. "Israel: Topless Protester on Menorah Outside Knesset Stirs Fury." July 22, 2020. https://www.i24news.tv/en/news/israel/society/1595398091-israel-topless-protester-on-menorah-outside-knesset-stirs-fury

Kearney, Richard. 2010. "Merleau-Ponty and the Sacramentality of the Flesh." In *Merleau-ponty at the Limits of Art, Religion, and Perception*, edited by Kascha Semonovitch and Neal DeRoo, 147–166. New York: Bloomsbury Academic.

Kearney, Richard. 2014. "Losing Our Touch." *New York Times.* August 30, 2014. https://opinionator.blogs.nytimes.com/2014/08/30/losing-our-touch/

Kearney, Richard. 2019. "The Recovery of the Flesh in Ricoeur and Merleau-Ponty." In *Somatic desire: Recovering Corporeality in Contemporary Thought*, edited by Sarah Horton, Stephen Mendelsohn, Christine Rojcewicz, and Richard Kearney, 41–55. Maryland: Rawman & Littlefield.

Kearney, Richard. 2021. *Touch: Recovering Our Most Vital Sense.* Kindle Edition. New York: Columbia University Press.

Kearney, Richard, and Brian Treanor. 2015. "What Is Carnal Hermeneutics?" *New Literary History* vol. 46, no. 1 (Winter): 99–124.

New Israel Fund. n.d. "Docorights – Protecting Freedom of Expression and the Right to Protest." https://docorights.org.il/docorights-protecting-freedom-of-expression-and-the-right-to-protest/

Sasson-Levy, Orna, and Tamar Rapoport. 2003. "Body, Gender, and Knowledge In Protest Movements: The Israeli Case." *Gender & Society* vol. 17, no. 3: 379–403.

Souweine, Isaac. 2005. "Naked Protest and the Politics of Personalism." In *Sarai reader 05: Bare Acts*, edited by Monica Narula, Shuddhabrata Sengupta, Jeebesh Bagchi (Sarai), Geert Lovink (Waag), and Lawrence Liang, 526–536. Delhi: The Sarai Programme.

Strampe, Louryn, and Lauren Goode. 2020. "How to Protest Safely: What to Bring, What to Do, and What to Avoid." June 2, 2020. https://www.wired.com/story/how-to-protest-safely-gear-tips

Sutton, Barbara. 2007. "Naked Protest: Memories of Bodies and Resistance at the World Social Forum." *Journal of International Women's Studies* vol. 8, no. 3: 139–148.

TOI Staff. 2020. "34 Held at Anti-PM protest; Anger over Topless Woman Atop Menorah Near Knesset." *The Times of Israel.* July 22, 2020. https://www.timesofisrael.com/fresh-clashes-as-thousands-protest-against-netanyahu-10-arrested/

Unrefined Sophisticates. 2020. "Naked Athena of Portland Interview," podcast, hosted by Kan Jones and Morgan Jones, 1h 56 min. July 2020. https://open.spotify.com/episode/2RLnrwLO4cAMFL9N4PZFBt

Chapter 12

Touch Thyself: Kearney's Anacarnational Return to Plato's Forgotten Wisdom

Matthew Clemente

There is no doubt that we live in "an age of simulation informed by digital technology and an expanding culture of virtual space" (Kearney 2021, 2), that our lives have become increasingly mediated, distanced, disincarnate. We are, as WJT Mitchell rightly pointed out nearly 30 years ago, living at a time when "visual images have replaced words as the dominant mode of expression," (2006, 5) when we use our phones and cameras and even our watches to give voice to who and what we are. But we don't just express ourselves on screen. We find ourselves there, depend upon our technologies to help us understand our place in the world and how we ought to inhabit it. As the aptly titled Netflix series *Black Mirror* suggests, the screen reflects back to us our own likenesses, reveals our fears and longings, our passions and pains, and the recesses of our hearts.[1] At least this is what our devices promise to do: help us to know ourselves. Yet if the screen is a black mirror, perhaps it not only distorts, as every mirror does, but acts more like a black hole, swallowing up both our likeness and the self-knowledge that supposedly comes from seeing it. Perhaps the more we fix our gaze on pixelated imitations of ourselves, the less clearly we see who and what we are.

This, it seems to me, is what is as stake in Richard Kearney's recent work on the sense of touch, particularly when he opposes touch to sight—the sense traditionally used by philosophers to symbolize knowledge. We have, says Kearney, bought into a kind of "optocentrism," a sight-centered way of viewing (*case in point*) ourselves which actually prevents us from seeing (*and again*) ourselves (Kearney 2021, 33–34). For Kearney, we have "lost touch with our primal embodiment" by losing touch with touch (135), have forfeited something essential about ourselves by prioritizing sight over our more carnal ways of knowing the world. Sight, he reminds us, is the sense most amenable to our Gygean desire for power and control (115). That is because vision presupposes distance, the ability to see without being seen, and the power to look and yet remain untouched by the vulnerability of the other.

DOI: 10.4324/9781003285649-17

Nietzsche (1974, 38) has such philosophical *concupiscentia oculorum* in mind when, in the Preface to *The Gay Science*, he quips, "'Is it true that God is present everywhere?' a little girl asked her mother; 'I think that's indecent'—a hint for philosophers!" The indecency of the philosopher (and the Silicon Valley techy who fashions himself the philosopher of today) is the desire to be God, to see that which ought not to be seen and know that which cannot be known—the self most of all. The promise of technology is to fulfill such a desire, to transcend or illimit finite existence toward infinite knowledge, infinite power, a self ever transcending itself. All of which is to say that the promise of technology is to enhance the power of sight exponentially such that one can know life at a distance without ever having to descend into the messiness of the world, without having to touch or be touched by it (see, Kearney 2021, 4).

This link between knowledge, sight, and the lust for power is evident not only in the philosophical tradition—for instance, in Plato's myth of the ring of Gyges—but scripturally as well. Eve *sees* that the fruit on the tree of the *knowledge* is good to eat after the serpent tells her "when you eat of it *your eyes will be opened* and you will be *like gods*, who *know* good and evil" (Genesis, 2:3, emphasis mine). Indeed, the whole Adamic myth can be read as gesturing at the danger of making taste and touch subservient to sight and knowledge. Psychoanalysis too ties together this unholy trinity when Freud connects sight (scopophilia) to mastery (sadism) (Freud 2000, 157) and goes on to tie mastery to man's desire to "become a god himself" (1962, 44). It is technology, Freud tells us—or at least our deployment thereof—that provides us with our "Godlike character" (45). And yet, as Kearney notes, "viewing everything from a distance without actually *touching or being touched* by anything" impoverishes human life, makes it less divine, not more, and leaves us "out of touch with the real" (2021, 115). The real, however, is what we are after when we seek to know ourselves. We do not want the mere images of ourselves. Self-knowledge is not satisfied with appearance which, after all, can deceive. What we want is the truth, the real thing, the mystery at the heart of our existence, a mystery that must be touched in order to be known.[2]

In this essay, I propose to return to the starting point of philosophy, the old Socratic dictum *know thyself*, in order to suggest that, as Kearney has persuasively argued, self-understanding is tied more closely to touching than seeing and that, if we are to know ourselves at all, we must be contented with groping in the dark. This I have argued elsewhere, though perhaps not in the same terms (Clemente 2019, 53–71). Here, however, I would like to begin by returning (*ana*) to two fundamental philosophical principles so often neglected. First, that wisdom is knowing one knows not. And second that, as a consequence of the first, self-knowledge is not something seen and possessed but desired, pursued, aroused into being. Having forgotten or ignored these foundational insights, philosophy has forgotten herself. Yet Kearney brings us back to this wisdom by helping us to recall that "the body is the place where the psyche lives" (2021, 106) and that there is "a special intelligence of the body" which, when cultivated, "spells the recovery of self" (9). Such a recovery is a return (*ana*), a going back to the body in order to understand the self again and anew after passing through an age of "excarnation," a digital age that has traded the body for the all-seeing eye, where "flesh [has] become image" and the self on the screen has been distorted beyond recognition (2).

But whence comes such a recovery? In a sense, Kearney tells us that philosophy, rightly understood, can be the healing muse. He does so, in the first place, by proposing a philosophy of touch, a desire to embody the wisdom of the body. What, after all, does it mean to think about touch if not to recognize that touching and thinking are coterminous, philosophy and feeling fundamentally fused?[3] This longing for the love of wisdom to return to its carnal roots is perhaps nowhere more evident than in Kearney's emphasis on the Asclepian tradition of "accompaniment healing" (2021, 65–71). Asclepius, you will remember, is one of Greek patrons of medicine. Disciple of Chiron, this god of "the art of healing through touch" (65) is the very god to whom Socrates prays at the birthplace of philosophy (Plato 1997, *Phaedo*, 118a). To honor him, thus, is to follow the example of Plato who, in Book III of his *Republic*, praises Asclepius for understanding the subtle art of restorative healing (Plato 1997, *Republic*, 405d-408b). Indeed, throughout the *Republic*, Asclepius is held up as an image of the philosopher who sees his vocation as therapy for the soul. Unlike visual artists, who are chided for creating images of images, Asclepius and his offspring—doctors trained in the art of touch—are praised for healing real bodies instead of manufacturing false ones (599c).

Here, one might say, Kearney diverges from Plato—the former focusing on therapy for the body, the latter concerned with the virtues of the soul. Indeed, Kearney himself pits his work against the Platonic tradition and aligns his ideas with Aristotle who, in *De Anima*, likens the soul to the touching body—more specifically, the hand (1957, III. viii)—and goes on to suggest that it is not sight but touch that is the most philosophical of the senses (see, Clemente 2019, 54-57). As S.H. Rosen argues, for Aristotle, "Knowing is touching" (Rosen 1961, 132). Yet, if we put certain prominent misreadings of Plato to the side and explore the nearness of these thinkers in earnest, we will discover that, like the "subtle sons of Asclepius" (Plato 1997, *Republic*, 408b), Kearney has learned well from his progenitor. Plato, for instance, though often read as denigrating the body, actually shows—albeit in an indirect way—that we are our bodies, whereas the soul is bestowed upon us by the state (Plato 1997, *Crito*, 50d–e). For, while the soul can be shaped and even governed by the influence of education which implants within us the lessons of the educator, the body is by its very nature private and thus one's own (Plato 1997, *Republic*, 464d). It cannot be taken away like one's possessions (cf. Plato 1997, *Laws*, 739c). Nor can it be taught to repress its pains and pleasures and thus deceive itself about what it is and what it wants (Plato 1997, *Republic*, 327a–621d). What is more, unlike the soul which is, in a sense, repeatable and replaceable—think of how social media apps like "_LivesOn" use algorithms to mimic users' posts and syntax thus allowing their "souls" to continue posting long after their bodies have died[4]—one's body cannot be replaced by any other. Your bodily existence is yours and yours alone. Mine belongs only to me. If Heidegger is right that death "is always essentially my own" (2010, §47), that is because my body is my own—it is me—and no one can incarnate (or, as is the case with death, disincarnate) my body but me.

This reading of Plato, provoked as it is by Kearney's reflections on touch, is admittedly at odds with much of the philosophical tradition. By and large, philosophers have tended to view bodies in roughly the same manner as Agatha Christie's famed detective Hercule Poirot who, seeing scantily clad bathers on the beach, is reminded "of the Morgue in Paris" (2011, 6). The detective—whom I have argued elsewhere is the ideal philosopher—sees the body not so much as a prison (Plato 1997, *Phaedo*, 82e), but as a piece of "butcher's meat" (Christie 2011, 6). That such a view is amenable to philosophical inquiry is attested to not only by the long history of philosophers performing autopsies and vivisections but by virtue of the fact that philosophy itself is a kind of autopsy (from the Greek *autos* (self), *opsis* (eye), "seeing for oneself") and "conscience-vivisection" (Nietzsche 1989, 95)—that is, an attempt to see oneself for oneself, to *know thyself*.[5]

Such an approach obviously has its value. In the first place, objective knowledge comes from treating bodies like meat and thus being able to dissect and objectify them. In the second, locating one's identity in one's soul means making oneself articulable and thus understandable. Think of how Kierkegaard's single individual is muted by his individuality; the escape from such seclusion comes by means of making oneself "universal," i.e., likening oneself to everyone else. The way we share knowledge with one another, and even come to understand ourselves, is through the use of common symbols. We "find ourselves" on our devices because we see our souls reflected there. Touch, on the other hand, is (like the body) private. No one can tell me what I feel. It is only by sublimating what I feel into concepts—that is, categories understood by the soul—that I am able to share my feelings with others. The screen represents my soul to me in a language I can understand by depicting such concepts before my eyes and thus showing me a soul like mine, be it a fictional character on TV or the fictional image I create of myself on social media. The rather obvious problem with this is that the soul I see represented on my device is not me. The "self" I come to know when I know myself intellectually, by means of the soul, does not exist. Not really. The denial of the import of the body is the denial of the *principium individuationis*, the refusal to admit that every body is unique.[6] The individual soul is, as Plotinus rightly suggests, subservient to the world-soul, a totalizing oneness that robs each of us of what is most our own. My soul can be likened to every other in that my thoughts and interpretations of life come to me from others. They precede me and are made for me and are thus never really my own.

To know thyself with the knowledge of the soul, then, is not to know thyself at all. It is to know the readymade ideas of a universal world-soul that belong to no soul in particular. But what is one to do? Is self-knowledge even possible? Can philosophy aid in the pursuit of such a noble goal? Or has the ancient love of wisdom deceived us, leading us to identify ourselves with phantoms, perpetuating the flight from the body which is the destruction of self-knowledge itself? When I began writing this essay, I missed the innuendo present in the title (a Freudian slip to be sure). Once I noticed the double entendre, I intended to change it. That's when I remembered a certain passage in the *Gorgias* and it gave me pause. Arguing with Callicles over what constitutes the good life, Socrates points out that Callicles' view—the good life is synonymous with the life of pleasure—implies that the pinnacle of human existence can be found in the life of the "lewd masturbator" (Plato 1997, *Gorgias*, 494e). Callicles balks at the suggestion. But is he right to? Or does not our foregoing argument suggest that Socrates' crass witticism contains a forgotten truth?

This problem bothered me, especially since I have spilt a good amount of ink arguing that such solipsistic attempts at self-affirmation reveal the thanatonic impulse at the heart of our erotic lives. If self-knowledge can only be found in onanistic indulgence, what then becomes of our relations to others? I was pondering this before bed last night and awoke suddenly in the early hours of the morning with a squeezing, wrenching tightness in my chest, a suffocating breathlessness, and the unshakable fear that I was about to die. My heart was racing. The muscles contracted in my shoulders and neck. I felt that I could neither stand nor lie nor sit. I was tension incarnate. The experience is nothing new. I was having a panic attack. (It has only just subsided). I was sitting on the edge of my bed rubbing my neck and doing some slow breathing exercises when my wife awoke and put her hand on my back. She asked if I was all right, gently massaged my shoulders, pressed her forehead against mine. I told her to go back to sleep, went downstairs and let my dog Joey out of his crate, and as I sat on the floor petting him in the dark, my anxiety receded and I felt better (cf. Kearney 2021, 109–111).

Anxiety is a malady of the soul, one that manifests itself in the body. When caught in the clutches of anxiety, it is not a physical reality that fills one with dread but the awareness of the indifference and indeterminacy of the world. It is the overwhelming meaninglessness of everything, the fact that there are too many possibilities and that any of them or none of them might come to fruition that wracks one's body and leaves one breathless. Kierkegaard defines anxiety as "freedom's actuality as the possibility of possibility" (1980, 42). What he means, I think, is that anxiety is my awareness of my freedom, my recognition of the fact that I live as a free being with an infinite number of possibilities before me, so many possibilities that they overwhelm me and I drown in my own freedom. Confronted by this experience, faced with the unbearable weight of indeterminacy—or, as Milan Kundera would have it, the unbearable lightness of being—one's body tightens up. It closes in upon itself and shrinks before that which would crush it. What deliverance can there be?

In one of the most compelling sections of his book on touch, Kearney speaks of an "ethics of tact."[7] He reminds us that not all touch is welcome and not all knowledge beneficial. Touch can be misused and the body abused. Touch can cause harm or, like my early morning attempts at self-soothing, fail to alleviate a harm already done. Nevertheless, touch is the sense that opens us to possibility of being healed by the other. It is that which, making us vulnerable to the other, allows us to be cared for by the other and to care for others in turn. It was only when my wife put her hand on my back and I put my hand on my dog that my symptoms went away. And it was only when my symptoms went away that I was able to sit, organize my thoughts, and finish writing this essay. Touch enabled me to figure out what I wanted to write. It was the wisdom of the body that allowed me to understand myself. But the wisdom came not from my body. It came from the touch of another. To know thyself, then, is to touch and be touched. Self-knowledge cannot be attained alone.

Notes

1 A 2008 commercial for California tourism which features a number of Hollywood movie stars, those icons of the screen, puts it succinctly: "Find yourself here."

2 Even the apparent idealist Plato tacitly acknowledges this point when he has Diotima tell us that the one who sees "true Beauty" is "in touch with no images" "because he is in touch with the true Beauty" itself (Plato 1997, *Symposium* 212a).

3 I am reminded of a beautiful line in Graham Greene's The End of the Affair which captures this sentiment perfectly. "We can love with our minds, but can we love only with our minds? Love extends itself all the time, so that we can even love with our senseless nails: we love even with our clothes, so that a sleeve can feel a sleeve." This, of course, is true of the love of wisdom too. (Greene 2004, 88).

4 Such apps are really no different from books—the present text included—which afford their authors a kind of immortality long after their corpses have been planted in the ground. (Cf. Plato 1997, *Symposium* 209d).

5 This really is the fundamental philosophical task. Every other question stems from it. As Socrates rightly notes, there is no use looking into other matters if one has not looked into oneself. See, "I am still unable, as the Delphic inscription orders, to know myself; and it really seems to me ridiculous to look into other things before I have understood that" (Plato 1997, *Phaedrus* 229e–230a).

6 Indeed, as Poirot insists, it is only by denying the individuality of the body that the detective—and the philosopher—is able to solve the mystery before him. See, "It was on a morning when we were sitting out here that we talked of sun-tanned bodies lying like meat upon a slab, and it was then that I reflected how little difference there was between one body and another. If one looked closely and appraisingly—yes—but to the casual glance? One moderately well-made young woman is very like another. Two brown legs, two brown arms, a little piece of bathing suit in between—just a body lying out in the sun. When a woman walks, when she speaks, laughs, turns her head, moves a hand—then, yes then, there is personality—individuality. But in the sun ritual—no" (Christie 2011, 237).

7 See, "[T]here is touch and touch. And tact knows the difference. Respect requires discernment because touch, as noted, is not always appropriate, especially where power relations are concerned. Being tactful here means being sensitive in our behavior with others, listening and responding to the other in a responsible way. Such two-way sensibility involves a reversibility between oneself and another, striking a balance between distance and proximity, careful not to impose oneself on the other (domination) nor to surrender entirely either (submission). Tact is an inter-play of far and near, knowing how to be subjects *of* our actions while being subject *to* others' actions—being touched even as we touch. This active-passive dialectic is what the phenomenologist, Edmund Husserl, calls 'double sensation.' In the reversibility of touch one has the feeling of both touching and being touched at the same time. And this means being open to how others feel about you as much as how you feel about them. The art of dance, as mutual partnering, offers a model for an ethics of tact" (Kearney 2021, 11).

References

Aristotle. 1957. *On the Soul. Parva Naturalia. On Breath.* Translated by Walter Stanley Hett. Cambridge: Harvard University Press.

Christie, Agatha. 2011. *Evil under the Sun: A Hercule Poirot Mystery.* New York: Harper Collins.

Clemente, Matthew. 2019. *Eros Crucified: Death, Desire, and the Divine in Psychoanalysis and Philosophy of Religion.* London: Routledge.

Freud, Sigmund. 1962. *Civilization and Its Discontents.* Translated by James Strachey. New York: W.W. Norton.

Freud, Sigmund. 2000. *Three Essays on the Theory of Sexuality.* Translated by James Strachey. New York: Basic Books.

Greene, Graham. 2004. *The End of the Affair.* New York: Penguin.

Heidegger, Martin. 2010. *Being and Time*. Translated by Joan Stambaugh. New York: State University of New York Press.

Kearney, Richard. 2021. *Touch: Recovering Our Most Vital Sense*. New York: Columbia University Press.

Kierkegaard, Søren. 1980. *The Concept of Anxiety*. Translated by Reidar Thomte. Princeton: Princeton University Press.

Mitchell, W.J.T. 2006. *What Do Pictures Want?: The Lives and Loves of Images*. Chicago: University of Chicago Press.

Nietzsche, Friedrich. 1974. *The Gay Science*. Translated by Walter Kaufmann. New York: Vintage.

Nietzsche, Friedrich. 1989. *On the Genealogy of Morals and Ecce Homo*. Translated by Walter Kaufmann. New York: Vintage.

Plato. 1997. *Complete Works*. Edited by John M. Cooper. Indianapolis: Hackett.

Rosen, Stanley H. 1961. "Thought and Touch: A Note on Aristotle's *De Anima.*" *Phronesis* vol. 6, no. 2: 127–137.

Chapter 13

No Longer a Spectator Only

Tamsin Jones

Introduction: On the Timeliness of Kearney's Philosophy

The time is right for the philosophy of Richard Kearney. There are many elements from his work we could draw on: for instance, his articulation of the role of hospitality and the decision to welcome (or not) the stranger speaks directly to the ongoing immigration catastrophe at the southern American border, as well as a larger global refugee crisis, fueled by climate disruption and the increasing inhabitability of various regions of the world. However, in our present context of a global pandemic, it is his most recent book, *Touch: Recovering Our Most Vital Sense* (Kearney 2021), that speaks most presciently to our time.

In this recent work, Kearney asks whether we are in danger of losing touch, not only with others but also with ourselves. He contemplates whether one of the most basic crises of our time is "excarnation," the movement from flesh to image. As the proximity and reciprocal responsibility of touch is increasingly replaced with the distance and mediation of digital platforms, a basic human need is threatened: the "double sensation" of the capacity to touch and be touched. Kearney moves from question and critique, through several chapters establishing the foundational necessity of touch to our individual and common selves, to return to an analysis of the "age of excarnation" we find ourselves in at present. Ultimately the book offers a counterproposal to recover the joys of "incarnated" life and subjectivity.

This counterproposal does not eschew digital technology entirely; he does not want to replace the mind-body dualism of old with a re-inserted hierarchy of the actual vs. virtual. Instead, Kearney seeks a balance:

> Let's use GPS and Imaps but also make a point of stopping in the street to ask people directions ... Let's play video games but also attend theaters and street festivals, live shows and concerts. Let's order books on Amazon and consult Wikipedia and Google but also make a

DOI: 10.4324/9781003285649-18

point of browsing material volumes in our local library and bookshop. Let's enjoy simulated fantasy but never forget the real thing. Let's consume e-sports online but also sit in stadiums with hosts of living bodies ... Let's communicate with hundreds of 'friends' on email, Facebook, Twitter and Instagram, but also take time to write a note on paper to someone special in our lives or touch the hand or shoulder of someone present to us in the world. It's not a matter of either/or but of both/and. We need both virtual imagination and real-life action. Both digital touch and actual touch. Both cyber and carnal experience. A commons of the world wide web and a commons of the body.

(Kearney 2021, 100)

The possibility of achieving such a balanced view of embodied existence, however, became much more distant during the past couple of years of a global pandemic and the rolling lockdowns through which we lost access to half of that equation.

As educators we shifted our classes entirely online; students from preschool to graduate school struggled to learn through a screen. For those fortunate enough not to lose their jobs, the work was almost entirely mediated by Zoom or Google Meet. Groceries were ordered online and delivered without contact, dropped on the front steps or in the vestibule. Religious practitioners streamed church, mosque, temple, and synagogue services through Facebook Live. Sports, theatre, and music concerts were canceled. Libraries, cafes, and community centers were closed. Essays were written extolling the health benefits of "riding out quarantine with a Chatbot friend" (Metz 2020). People died alone, their loved ones unable to visit, sit by a bedside, or hold their hand.

Thus, even more than when Kearney wrote the book, we have found ourselves living in the "age of excarnation" in which Plato's "optocentric" philosophy can be seen to culminate in the reigning supremacy of "spectacularity—a digital zone where the eye rules" (Kearney 2021, 85). Such an over-reliance on the reigning sense of vision has worked hand-in-hand with an increasing reliance on the mediation of a screen through which to engage, experience, and understand the world in which we live.[1] How are we to reestablish our enfleshed existence at this moment of critical and enforced excarnation? In this essay, I propose to use Kearney's concepts of diacritical and carnal hermeneutics in order to think critically and constructively about one aspect of this moral crisis: our visual consumption of other people's suffering through the medium of digital images. What does it mean to encounter the pain of another in an age of "spectacularity"? While Kearney's analysis of excarnation develops important insights for our personal experience of the world, for hospitality and welcoming the other, and for the ambiguity of "reciprocal" ethics, I want to bring his thinking to bear on a phenomenon that he has not, as yet, addressed: the ways in which excarnation and the ubiquity of images shape our relationship to the suffering of other persons.

****

Spectral Spectators in an Age of "Spectacularity"—Four Vignettes

I was grading final papers in my office at the University of Victoria when I first heard the news of the bombing at the Boston Marathon in 2013. My husband had called me, and we were both taken back in time to memories of confusion and grief on the streets of Boston on a September day in 2001. We worried about the many friends and colleagues from our time living there, about my father who lives nearby and has run the race before, about my sister who often goes with her rugby friends to watch the runners coming to the end of their race. After briefly scanning the headlines and calling my father, I turned the computer off again and returned to my papers. While I read my students' thoughts on suffering and religion, thoughts of a concrete example of violence percolated and imaginings about the chaos happening three thousand miles away bloomed in my mind. A heightened awareness of my own peaceful, quiet surroundings as I bicycled home was underlined and punctured by pinpoints of a sharp sorrow around the borders of my consciousness.

Eventually, and inevitably, however, I was drawn in through a different lens ... magnetized by the spectacle.

spectacle: 1. "A specially prepared or arranged display of a more or less public nature (esp. one on a large scale), forming an impressive or interesting show or entertainment for those viewing it." (The Compact Oxford English Dictionary 1991, 553)

At the beginning of a *New York Times* slideshow, a warning set up to entice the consumer flashed: CAUTION: THE FOLLOWING IMAGES ARE VERY GRAPHIC IN NATURE AND MAY BE UPSETTING TO THE VIEWER.

The heartbeat increases—anticipation and nervousness about what I will see. The forbidden glimpse of another's anguish. As my children squealed and sang on the trampoline outside, I clicked: photo after photo, bloody image after bloody image. Click: a runner down, three policeman—one with gun drawn—in the immediate reaction to the first blast. Click: two men applying a tourniquet to a woman's bloody thigh. Click: blood and glass covering a sidewalk. Click: a grey-faced young man, eyes wide open, clutching what remains of his leg as he is wheeled in a chair accompanied by a man wearing a cowboy hat. Click ... click ... click.

From the safety of my home, as my children jump in the sun and tulips sway, bright purple, orange, pink, and red, I am drawn into the horror. I am dismayed by the scale of suffering, worried as my mind turns immediately to the political and practical implications, and deeply, deeply saddened by the persistent cruelty of human beings. But I am also hooked. The images have sucked me into their vortex.

Also lurking in the periphery, however, is shame: an awareness that I do not give the same attention and time to images of the carnage caused by bombs dropped on children by American drones. Or images of bodies crushed in the collapse of a dilapidated factory on the other side of the planet, which produced the cheap clothes we happily buy. In her work, *Precarious Life: The Powers of Mourning and Violence*, Judith Butler contrasts the erasure of victims of the American military with the iconic consecration of the fallen who happen to hold citizenship in the right nation, and for that reason alone are considered more grievable. As Butler writes in the preface:

> Some lives are grievable, and others are not; the differential allocation of grievability that decides what kind of subject is and must be grieved, and which kind of subject must not, operates to produce and maintain certain exclusionary conceptions of who is normatively human: what counts as a livable life and a grievable death?
>
> (Butler 2004, xiv–xv)

According to what metric is this specific act of violence and event of collective suffering the one that catches (and holds) my eye?

Yet, there is an even more difficult, yet unavoidable question: in what way is my nervous anticipation at the outset of a *New York Times* slideshow on the Boston Marathon bombing the same as that which a 14-year-old student feels who has been sent an image of the rape of one of his classmates by another classmate? In what precise way does this fascination, this inability to turn away from a scene of massive suffering, differ from other acts of being a spectator to another's suffering? In both, are we not granted the same forbidden access to a gross violation of another?

A decade ago, the newspapers were filled with hand-wringing editorials worrying about the state of our civilization in the context of one specific outcome of having a cellphone with a high-quality camera in your pocket at all times: the *kinds* of images that were being recorded and shared. Specifically, within a couple of years of the introduction of the iPhone on the market, there were a number of cases in which the images of rape and sexual assault of a young person were disseminated on social media and then used to further her suffering: to taunt and ridicule her, to blame and isolate her, and, in too many cases, to goad her to take her own life. We could well ask what is it that enables the significant moral shift from sympathy to attack? What framings are necessary to view the girl, and not her young rapists, as the person responsible and blameworthy—to see the girl, and not her rapists, as morally culpable and sexually transgressive? More to the point, the question I am most interested in here is what framings are necessary to consume these images in such a way that one simultaneously views oneself as an innocent bystander, merely looking at images, and not as significantly implicated in the crime itself?

Let me provide a third example. In the spring of 2011 as I struggled to make a decision about where to take a job—to remain in Boston where we'd been for the last ten years, or to return home to our native British Columbia—my husband joked that, as the Canucks and the Bruins were in the final play-offs, we could let the outcome of the Stanley Cup decide our future. As it was, we made the decision to return to Victoria before the end of the playoffs. We read the news with dismay after the Bruins won and the streets of Vancouver erupted in riots. What was most disturbing, however, more than the individual events of violence and destruction, were the gleefully-detached hundreds of viewers surrounding each burning car, or bleeding man, laughing and cheering as they lifted their hands with their permanently-attached device to record the event in order to revel in the attention their subsequent posting of it would garner. Not participants, they would argue, just spectators.

spectator: 1. "One who sees, or looks on at, some scene or occurrence; a beholder, onlooker, observer" … 2. "One who is present at, and has a view or sight of, anything in the nature of a show or spectacle." (The Compact Oxford English Dictionary 1991, 555)

As with the high school kids at a party where their classmate is forcibly hurt, these riot-recorders are not guilty, they would say, certainly not responsible; instead, they are just spectators enjoying the show. Yet for all involved, actors and spectators alike, the thrill of the violence is not enough on its own; it must be carried forward as spectacle. In the case of sexual assault, it becomes the recorded, posted, and shared exhibition of male power and of the precariousness and worthlessness of young female flesh. As Martha Nussbaum has argued, this is not just a display of objectified flesh, but also the production of guilty flesh (Nussbaum 2010). The mediation of the screen veils the reality of a flesh-and-blood person. It offers distance—a gap between reality and entertainment into which one can deny any responsibility. It is not a *real* girl being hurt, just an image of a girl. Of course, it did not take long at all before we had moved past such regional or localized examples of recording violence and suffering in order to monetize it in the exponentially growing economy of online pornography, which only encouraged the recording and posting at a much greater rate.[2]

spectacle: 2. "A person or thing exhibited to, or set before the public gaze, as an object either (*a*) of curiosity or contempt, or (*b*) of marvel or admiration." (The Compact Oxford English Dictionary 1991, 553).

One final photographic vignette raises the question of the morality of regarding the suffering of others through the mediation of a screen: what are the ethics of recording and publicly sharing the moments of another's death? On YouTube you can watch, not only new life coming into being but collections of hundreds of deaths—people saying their last goodbyes to loved ones and individuals breathing their last breaths. How are we to understand these videos: as bearing witness to our finitude and the bonds of love that surpass our one life, or as sanctioned, voyeuristic snuff films? The eminent essayist and philosopher of photography, culture, and media, Susan Sontag, directs us helpfully on this question.

In her final work, *Regarding the Pain of Others* (2003), Sontag takes up the question she asked in her classic essay *On Photography* (1977) in which she worries that the inundation of "shocking images" would, in their very saturation of our senses, lose their ability to captivate the viewer and to shock us into moral response. Writing during the same year—both in response to 9/11—yet, in a way that nuances Butler's critical analysis of what lives are considered publicly grievable, Sontag raises a different question: whose deaths are sanctioned sights of spectacle and whose are given privacy? She juxtaposes a front-page photographic spread in the *New York Times* of a member of the Taliban in the moments leading up to his death, with the invisibility of American military bodies at the World Trade Center. As Sontag says:

> The exhibition in photographs of cruelties inflicted on those with darker complexions in exotic countries continues this offering, oblivious to the considerations that deter such displays of our own victims of violence; for the other, even when not an enemy, is regarded only as *someone to be seen, not someone (like us) who also sees.* But surely the wounded Taliban soldier begging for his life whose fate was pictured prominently in the *New York Times* also had a wife, children, parents, sisters and brothers, some of whom may one day come across the three color photographs of their husband, father, son, brother being slaughtered. (Sontag 2004, 73)

Sontag reminds us that our awareness of the suffering of others is always a "constructed reality"; that is to say, we are told of some suffering but not of others. Photographic and video images are framed by the recorder, record a certain moment of time and not what comes before or after, and are titled or captioned in ways to prepare the viewer of what they are about to see, indicating how they should interpret what they are about to see. Furthermore, the point of these journalistic "infotainment" slideshows is that we encounter the suffering of others in a way that encourages us to move quickly on from one image to the next. More specifically, certain kinds of suffering are represented as something that happens "over there"; whether depictions of starvation or the evil humans reap upon one another in a civil war, both are things that happen, in our imaginary, to black bodies in Africa or brown bodies in the Middle East, not to white bodies in America. Having herself died in 2004, we do not have the benefit of Sontag's response to the proliferation, in the past ten years, of images and videos of the murder of black and brown men, women, and children at the hands of the police. This brings me to my final example of looking upon the suffering of another, one that will raise its own set of difficult questions.

If I am ashamed of clicking through a slideshow of the aftermath of the Boston Marathon bombing, why am I also ashamed to have *not* watched the final nine minutes of George Floyd's life?

The obvious answer is the shame arises through an awareness that the choice to not watch is a choice afforded through white privilege. However, Sontag's voice continues to echo in my mind: whose bodies are granted the respect and privilege of privacy in death? How are we to parse the difference between the media's passive ignoring of some suffering and the active fetishization of other sufferings? What does a responsible engagement with the suffering of another demand? When the suffering commands our attention, are there ways to look at it without becoming merely a voyeuristic spectator?

I do not know the answers to this. It is not at all clear to me. Does it make a difference to elevate the watching—bringing intentionality, responsibility, and reverence to the horror one visually encounters? How might the meaning of regarding these criminal murders of black people by police shift when one sees them through the framework of James Cone's *The Cross and the Lynching Tree,* in which he explores the interconnection of these two symbols in the African American imagination—the power of persecution and the promise of a liberated life (Cone 2013)? What shift in meaning and experience occurs if I overlay the image of one man calling for his mother as a police officer knelt on his neck with the image of another man nailed to a cross, giving his beloved friend and his mother into the care of another upon his death? Perhaps one's intentionality—for instance, the intention of the young woman who filmed the actions of Derek Chauvin and his fellow police officers and shared her video in order to hold them accountable to their actions—makes all the difference? Or is the difference simply pragmatic, measured by the outcome? In this case, a video of a man's murder becomes the spark to fuel a movement that went out into the streets to demand police accountability and reform.[3]

How does one best bear witness to the life of Floyd and the injustice of his death? Is it by watching the video and not hiding away from the horror it contains? Is it through political activism and protest, or through spiritual lamentation? Or is it by learning of, and imaginatively filling in, the contours of a full, rich, and complex life that touched and was touched by countless other lives? How do we train ourselves to see more than the ghostly outline of another, a mere figure of suffering? How do we stop our own gaze from transforming ourselves into spectral subjects?

spectral: "Having the character of a spectre or phantom; ghostly, unsubstantial, unreal." (The Compact Oxford English Dictionary 1991, 555).

What would it mean to close our eyes, to shutter the recording lens? To instead listen to the sound of moans and cries for help, of the smack of brute force on yielding flesh, as a call for my response? What would it mean to imagine touching the shattered glass and smelling the acrid smoke? What would it mean to contemplate our own breath, to feel air filling our lungs, with the words "I can't breathe" echoing in our consciousness?

Sontag acknowledges our deep fascination with evil and suffering. Yet it is necessary to distinguish whether our desire to look upon suffering is a vicarious curiosity, a voyeurism, or an attempt to be moved into compassion and action. "Narratives can make us understand," writes Sontag. "Photographs do something else: they haunt us" (Sontag, 2004, 89). There is a power in the image, undoubtedly. So, rather than ignoring the image and not looking, what would it take to enflesh or incarnate the image?

In what remains, I will explore the way in which, in order to move beyond "spectacularity," we must also move beyond the practice of excarnation to recover a renewed fullness and complex involvedness to our being-in-the-world. In short, we need to incorporate a diacritical and a carnal hermeneutics, most especially when regarding the suffering of others.

****

Diacritical and Carnal Hermeneutics

Kearney defines hermeneutics as the "art of deciphering multiple meaning" involving a "practice of discerning indirect, tacit or allusive meanings, of sensing another sense beyond or beneath apparent sense" (Kearney 2012, 177). By qualifying hermeneutics as "diacritical," Kearney signals a number of claims regarding the way we decipher meaning, including the following markers: diacritical hermeneutics is (a) critical and diagnostic, uncovering not simply the conditions of the possibility of meaning but also exposing the power structures which shape meaning; (b) criteriological in so far as it acknowledges the need to discern between competing claims of meaning; (c) carnal in its insistence that we are grounded in material, concrete worlds, and (d) relational—we decipher meaning in dialogue. As Kearney writes, diacritical hermeneutics "sounds and resounds across differences between self and other (human, animal or divine). *Dia-legein*—a reading between, through, across (*dia*), an inter-signifying in relation, a welcoming of alterity" (Kearney 2012, 181).

While my reflection on our digital consumption of an other's suffering has, thus far, taken a primarily critical and diagnostic trajectory, for what remains, I propose to focus on the carnality and relationality of Kearney's view of hermeneutics as both are direct correctives to the imbalance of the excarnation and spectacularity in this moment. After discussing these elements of diacritical hermeneutics more generally, I will return to the specific question of how to enflesh the image, or how to see the image in an incarnate way.

Kearney identifies one main goal of diacritical hermeneutics: to trouble our comfortable classifications of the world—to make the foreign more familiar and the familiar more foreign. In other words, this inherently relational endeavor eschews extremes of both the friendly familiar and the frighteningly foreign: "my task is to let the self walk at sea level with its other, avoiding the inhospitable extremities of vertiginous heights and abyssal depths" (Kearney, 2002, 11). Walking along with the other, even at sea level, involves some risk and the likelihood of being altered by the alterity one encounters. The risk of transformation as well as the opportunity for change runs in both directions however; it is taken on by both partners in the dialogue.

In this way, learning from his teacher Paul Ricoeur, Kearney locates his diacritical hermeneutics as a middle way, traversing the gap between the egology of Husserl and the heterology of Levinas: "While the former addressed the movement of sense from me to the other ..., the latter addressed the movement of the other to me" (Kearney, 2015, 55). In other words, Kearney is after defining a way of discerning meaning that moves in both directions and which emerges amidst, and between, self and other. It is not enough to passively receive or consume images of suffering, but nor should we impose our own intentionality and subjective assumptions on the suffering of another. Instead, to bear witness to the suffering of another is also to respond, to ask questions, to share one's own wounds, to allow oneself to be wounded by another's wounds, etc.[4]

Herein lies the wager of a hermeneutical stance which makes meaning in such a way that fragility, vulnerability, and the risk of touching and being touched are a necessary part. Thus, we see that relationality and carnality necessarily go hand in hand.

> To touch and be touched simultaneously is to be *connected* with others in a way that enfolds us. Flesh is open-hearted; it is where we

experience our greatest vulnerability. The site where we are most keenly attentive to wounds and scars, to preconscious memories and traumas ...

(Kearney 2015, 21–22)

As Kearney and Treanor write in their introduction to *Carnal Hermeneutics*, they are proposing a transgressive hermeneutic in so far as it moves beyond the false binary which opposes rational understanding with embodied sensibility and inverts the "prejudicial hierarchy of the senses" in which sight (and to a lesser extent hearing) reigns supreme over taste and touch (Kearney and Treanor 2015, 2).

Further elaborating a carnal hermeneutics, Kearney establishes three significations of the word "sense": sensation, meaning, and orientation. Significantly, this triune structure of sense establishes that carnal hermeneutics is about more than feeling or experience and more than understanding; it also involves action which is directed or oriented intentionally. Carnal hermeneutics, in other words, requires one to do more than passively consume the video of George Floyd's death; it requires that you take your feet to the streets in protest.[5] It is, as the philosopher Kelly Oliver has argued, a form of bearing witness which is responsible; i.e., it requires active response and not simply passive reception (Oliver 2001).

At the same time, the challenge of responsive hermeneutics is not simply to chart a philosophical path between egology and heterology— between the colonial and the subjugated gaze. Diacritical and carnal hermeneutics also has a broadly horizontal scope, which grounds us on this earth and anchors us in this material reality. Amongst a strand of continental philosophers such as Meillassoux, Malabou, and Latour there is, as Brian Treanor remarks, a feeling "that philosophy has lost itself in a linguistic hall of mirrors in which nothing is really real and we are left with only simulacra of simulacra *ad infinitum*. We've strayed too far from experience, from science, from nature, from reality" (Treanor 2015, 60). Thus, by challenging the opposing binaries of word and flesh, language and sensibility, carnal hermeneutics is better able to respond to the criticisms of new realism and new materialism concerning the aridity of the linguistic turn in twentieth-century philosophy. This is especially crucial in an age of a global pandemic.

As the Coronavirus spread across the world in the spring of 2020, and people were sent to work from home, planes were grounded, highways emptied, schools went online, and businesses shuttered their doors, the tight imbrication of our human lives with global structures of trade and the complex interweaving of our material world rose to a stark visibility. We became at once much more reliant on technology, especially digital technology, and more consciously aware of its ubiquity and, simultaneously, painfully aware of the absence of touch and how it could be missed. In order to teach and learn, to work, to order groceries, to have a doctor's visit, to do our banking, to connect with family and friends, we were tethered to a computer from our homes. All these activities took place only through the medium of a screen. A purely deconstructive, or radical, hermeneutics—even in its later ethical orientation—is unable to respond to this crisis.

How are we to read the signs of the times not only for diagnosis and critique, but also for a prophetic imagining of possible ways forward, and a sacramentalized relation to the carnal,[6] in both its human and non-human otherness? Specifically, what does it mean to look upon the suffering of others? How do we shift our gaze upon another's pain from a spectator sport to an incarnational gaze?

The Incarnational Gaze and the Image

Prior to Sontag's meditation on the ethical strengths and dangers of the image, its power has long been recognized, worried about, and fought over. Fear of the image to fixate and stop our gaze, or trepidation lest we give ourselves over too easily to idolatrous veneration of the image, has fueled periodic iconoclasms, notably in the 8th century in Eastern Christianity, and again immediately following the Reformation in the West. In Eastern Christianity, as a result of the Iconoclast controversies, orthodox Christians had to formulate a theological justification for the use of icons. One tireless iconophile, John of Damascus, did this in part through reinforcing a particularly *incarnate* view of material reality—one redeemed through its relation to the Word made flesh (John of Damascus 2003). Another defender of icons, Theodore the Studite, articulated a theory of circumscription, by which the icon is able to circumscribe a hypostatic reality, but in so doing, does not purport to circumscribe the nature, or essence, of it (Theodore the Studite, 2015). The nature remains essentially unknowable, while its existence is perfectly manifest. How do these theological debates about the veneration of the image—the icon—inform different trajectories of the mode of our gaze?

The contrast of inverse perspective in Greek icons with the classical perspective in Western art is germane to the present discussion. In the latter, the vanishing point of sight is central and "behind" the scene or object. On the flat two-dimensional surface of a painting, then, a "real" three-dimensional object is captured and displayed for the regard of the viewer. Thus, "producing a scene that represents nature with close to photographic precision, but also leaves the observer uninvolved and objective in attitude" (Gurtler 1989, 275). The inverse perspective of iconography subverts this approach. The vanishing point in Greek icons is behind the viewer and thus, the viewer is placed within the image depicted and invited to see, as it were, from that perspective. The lack of boundary or separation between the subject of the icon and the one who views it is reinforced by the lack of frame; the person depicted in the inverted icon, figures way out on the edge of the icon, entering the space of the viewer, inviting a communion or, at least, conversation between the two.

There is a fairly obvious polemical tone to such East-West comparisons of religious art, according to which the West frames and freezes an image-made-object, serving it up to the viewer for their consumption and possession. Whereas, the icon of the East dynamically eludes capture, and inverts the intentionality of the gaze, in order to issue forth a summons to which the "viewer" can choose to respond, or can reject, but cannot control. As with any polemical comparison, it is probably too simplistic and reductive. However, it raises the ethical significance of viewing images in a helpfully clear way. Sontag's challenge to the contemporary age arises not merely from the manner of our habituated consumption of images, but the fact that we gorge on them. We devour them so quickly we can, not only no longer see the subject objectified within, but we have lost all ability to distinguish modes of suffering at all.

Jean-Luc Marion, of course, has made good use of this Byzantine understanding of iconography in his own phenomenological reversal of intentionality, which transforms the nominative subject who captures an image with his gaze into the accusative "*me*" who finds himself arrested by the gaze of another (Marion 1991). However, as careful a reader of the Fathers as Marion is, on this point he neglects the way in which the Orthodox understanding of icons is not uni-directional; it too involves a necessary relation between worshipper and venerated. Thus, we have an understanding of looking that not only avoids the voyeurism of spectacularity but also the mastery of the colonial gaze.

Like Kearney's diacritical hermeneutics, one could locate the iconophile defense of the veneration of icons as a mode of looking at images that exist between the extremes of Husserl and Levinas/Marion. We are not simply locking the picture into a framing of our own construction, nor finding ourselves passively questioned, accused, judged, or summoned by the icon regarding us. Rather, there is a relationship between both, a dialogue, and a looking through one another. On this point, Kearney will speak about a "tactful" way of seeing which entails having insight, or "a good eye" (Kearney 2021, 24). A "tactful" seeing entails being "touched" by the image, affectively and ethically. To regard an icon, according to this early Christian theology, requires a vulnerability and the ability to be touched or moved by what one sees. However, at the same time, it is to have some responsibility in the way you respond to it rather than remaining passive.

Diacritical hermeneutics, Kearney argues, is not simply about words; it also involves sensing and touching. As he writes:

> For what kind of language are we talking about? One not only of words and writing, surely, but also of sensing and touching. And what kind of dialogue? One not just between speakers but also between bodies. And what kind of sense and sensibility is at issue here? One not only of intellectual 'understanding' but also of tangible 'orientation'.
>
> (Kearney 2015, 55)

To speak, then, of a transition from the excarnational consumption of suffering to the incarnational gaze, it is necessary to speak of an orientation toward, or relationship between, material bodies. For the same reason, the Byzantine defense of the veneration of icons depends upon an argument that the holy can be made present in and through the material of the icon only as a result of a more fundamental belief that the divine was incarnate in the person of Christ. Central to the Christian belief in the Incarnation is a claim about the redemption of the flesh, and all matter, which, in turn, enables a more en-fleshed, or incarnate, viewing of the icon.

How do we protect from the overwhelming everydayness of radical suffering becoming so common as to be blunted of impact? Sontag writes that "compassion is an unstable emotion. It needs to be translated into action, or it withers" (Sontag 2004). I would add that part of the orientation or action taken in order for compassion to take root, requires an element of sensory imagination. It is not enough to see, two-dimensionally. We must also listen and feel. We must also be able to hear a story about the person whose suffering we encounter. So that when we see an image of another's pain, we feel the full weight of the person so depicted. When we see broken and bloodied flesh, abused and violated bodies, we must be capable, also, of imagining the girl or boy who jumped and played and laughed and sang, who is loved and known by a web of interlocking beings, who once sheltered in a parent's arms, laughed uproariously with a friend, and cuddled with a childhood pet. When we see an officer kneeling on the neck of a human being, the breath in our own lungs catches and freezes before, eventually, it is drawn again.

Conclusion: Reading the Signs of a Pandemic

Developing his understanding of the role of poetics and narrative imagination in an "anatheistic" mode, Kearney identifies three indispensable moments: iconoclasm, prophecy, and sacrament. The first, while propaedeutic, is also never finished; this is the moment of protest and of critique. This is the moment of slaying all false gods and demagogic idols. Next one moves from protest to prophecy, from protest to promise and hope. Still more, however, prophecy must also be translated forward into sacramentalized activity—"the recovery of the sacramental in the lived world of suffering and action" (Kearney 2011, 153). Theory gives way to praxis, the word to flesh, spoken promise to embodied action, "combin[ing] a messianicity of waiting with an engagement with the incarnate stranger standing before us" (Ibid).

Kearney's diacritical and carnal hermeneutics can help us begin to respond to the crises of the current moment: moving from diagnosis and critique, through prophesy, to the sacramental and incarnational.

First, the protest movements that emerged in the wake of George Floyd's murder not only in this country but around the world, bear witness not simply to racial injustice, but also to basic economic inequities which demonstrate whose lives matter and whose are to be sacrificed before the altar of the almighty dollar and the protections of a barely hidden structure of white supremacy. The pandemic has also brought to visibility aspects of our reality too long ignored or avoided: the ways in which the scaffolding of our economic, educational, and judicial systems are riddled with racism; our for-profit health-care system is broken, motivated by greed rather than care; our higher education has become bloated, frivolous, and unaffordable; our belief in the reliability of democratic forms of government has been shown to be fragile and dysfunctional; finally, undergirding all of these diagnoses, the iconoclastic moment of imagining enables a recognition of the dangerous limits of globalized, unfettered capitalism (eg. its contribution to the spread of the pandemic around the globe) and its relation to the present beginnings of a catastrophic climate crisis.

Rather than confront the multiple scenarios of apocalyptic crises in play within our collective consciousness, too often we have sought distractions and diversions with an increasingly delusional refusal to witness the decay and dissolution of our world—culturally, politically, economically, and of course, materially. One of the profound, if painful, gains of the last few years is that it is no longer possible to bury one's head in the sand.

However, in order to accept responsibility, we need a return to our incarnate, fleshly, and responsive/relational selves:

> Flesh is a surface that is always deep. And precisely because it mediates between a self carnally located 'here' and an other located 'there,' it is, at bottom, what allows for empathy. Suffering with, *sym-pathein, Ein-fühlung*. The capacity to feel with others [i.e., other human beings, living beings, and even now, the planet] in and through distance.

(Kearney 2011, 22)

To truly bear witness to the suffering of another is also to bear the burden of responsibility: the ability to respond to the suffering we see affectively, emotionally, pragmatically, politically, and existentially. Responsibility—the ability to respond—requires our willingness to respond to images of suffering not just with our eyes but with our minds and hearts, to respond not just with our minds and hearts but also with our hands and bodies: welcoming the stranger, caring for the sick and hurt, protecting the violated, resisting the oppressor.[7] An incarnational gaze requires our own willingness to be touched and affected, but also offers a possibility of any variety of responses: an action taken to alleviate suffering when possible and to lament it when not. It is an orientation to accept one's own role and complicity in the face of suffering. No longer a spectator only.

Notes

1 See Kearney's comments written before the pandemic shutdown: "Is today's virtual dater not like an updated version of Gyges, who could view everything at a distance yet be touched by nothing? Are we entering an age of excarnation, where we obsess about the body in increasingly disembodied ways? For if incarnation is the image become flesh, excarnation is flesh become image. Incarnation invests flesh; excarnation divests it. In short, are we not inhabiting what Roland Barthes calls a 'Civilization of the Image' where the world is a screen out of touch with what is seen?" (Kearney 2021).
2 For a discussion of the vast proliferation of videos depicting non-consensual and/or underage acts of gendered violence (i.e., sexual assaults and rape) on free viewing sites such as PornHub, see Kristof (2020).
3 On this point, Melissa Fitzpatrick's essay in this volume demonstrates ways in which digital media lends itself to activism and political organization in a way that very necessarily complicates my argument here.
4 On the vulnerability inherent to bearing witness see Felman and Laub (1992).
5 In the context of the general lock-down of the pandemic in the spring of 2020, as people defied their own fear to come together, to march and shout, in order to protest a diseased judicial system, the risk of carnal hermeneutics is even more apparent.
6 See Merleau-Ponty's reflection on the sacramental dimension of perception and the phenomenal body (Merleau-Ponty 2002).
7 This includes, as James Taylor's essay in this volume develops at length, a form of ethical self-formation through practices of discipline, or *askesis*, which open us up to transformation.

References

Butler, Judith. 2004. *Precarious Life: The Powers of Mourning and Violence*. New York: Verso.

Compact Oxford English Dictionary. 1991. *Complete Text Reproduced Micrographically*. Oxford: Clarendon Press.

Cone, James. 2013. *The Cross and the Lynching Tree*. Ossining: Orbis.

Felman, Shoshana and Dori Laub, eds. 1992. *Testimony: Crises of Witnessing in Literature, Psychoanalysis, and History*. London: Routledge.

Gurtler, Gary M. 1989. "Plotinus and Byzantine Aesthetics." *The Modern Schoolman* vol. 66, no. 4: 275–284.

John of Damascus. 2003. *Three Treatises on the Divine Images*. Translated by Andrew Louth. Crestwood: St. Vladimir's Seminary Press.

Kearney, Richard. 2002. *Strangers, Gods and Monsters: Interpreting Otherness*. London: Routledge.

Kearney, Richard. 2011. *Anatheism: Returning to God after God*. New York: Columbia University Press.

Kearney, Richard. 2012. "Diacritical Hermeneutics." In *Hermeneutic Rationality/ La rationalité herméneutique*, edited by Maria Luisa Portocarrero, Luis Antonion Umbelino and Andrzej Wiercinzski, 177–196. Berlin: LIT Verlag.

Kearney, Richard. 2015. "The Wager of Carnal Hermeneutics." In *Carnal Hermeneutics*, edited by Richard Kearney and Brian Treanor, 15–56. New York: Fordham University Press.

Kearney, Richard. 2021. *Touch: Recovering Our Most Vital Sense*. New York: Columbia University Press.

Kristof, Nicholas. 2020. "The Children of PornHub." *The New York Times*, Dec. 4, 2020. https://www.nytimes.com/2020/12/04/opinion/sunday/pornhub-rape-trafficking.html

Marion, Jean-Luc. 1991. *God Without Being*. Translated by Thomas Carlson. Chicago: University of Chicago Press.

Merleau-Ponty, Maurice. 2002. *Phenomenology of Perception*. Translated by Colin Smith. London: Routledge.

Metz, Cade. 2020. "Riding Out Quarantine With a Chatbot Friend: 'I Feel Very Connected'." *The New York Times*, June 16, 2020. https://www.nytimes.com/2020/06/16/technology/chatbots-quarantine-coronavirus.html

Nussbaum, Martha. 2010. "Objectification and Internet Misogyny." In *The Offensive Internet: Speech, Privacy, and Reputation*, edited by Martha Nussbaum and Saul Levmore, 68–90. Cambridge: Harvard University Press.

Oliver, Kelly. 2001. *Witnessing: Beyond Recognition*. Minneapolis: University of Minnesota Press.

Sontag, Susan. 2004. *Regarding the Pain of Others*. New York: Picador.

Theodore the Studite. 2015. *Theodore the Studite: Writings on Iconoclasm*. Ancient Christian Writers 69. Translated by Thomas Cattoi. Mahwah: Paulist Press.

Treanor, Brian. 2015. "Mind the Gap: The Challenge of Matter." In *Carnal Hermeneutics*, edited by Richard Kearney and Brian Treanor, 57–76. New York: Fordham University Press.

Part V

Finishing Touches

Chapter 14

Anacarnation: Recovering Embodied Life

Richard Kearney

Introductory Note: I am grateful to Brian Treanor and James L. Taylor for editing this volume and to all the contributors – former students during my career in University College Dublin and Boston College – who participated, in person or virtually, in the symposium held on Vis island, Croatia (July 4–5, 2021) on the topic of anacarnation. Though I delivered a first improvised version of this paper at that gathering, hosted by the European Center for the Study of War and Peace, the current version was elaborated in the wake of numerous exchanges with the participants. I am indebted to these former students, now mentors, for this continuing conversation on carnal hermeneutics.

The fact that the colloquy on the philosophy of touch occurred in the midst of a pandemic climate is pivotal, given that flourishing life on this planet has rarely been more imperiled. A concern confirmed by the 2021 UNESCO finding that the most pressing global question for young people today is the current ecological emergency. This is why my reflections here lay special emphasis on the eco-phenomenological relationship between human and non-human others. The essay is a plea for a symbiocene *of new interspecies collaboration beyond the Anthropocene of domination that has wreaked so much havoc in our world. It expresses a desire for a more vital enfleshment in our relations with other living beings and concludes with some biographical stories regarding my formative experiences of anacarnation.*

When as a child I sang "I see the sea and the sea sees me," I was bearing witness to the double pulse of anacarnation. I was seeing and being seen, touching and being touched at once. As I approached the ocean over a hill, I felt enfolded in the universe, deeply implicated in the flesh of the world. In short, I was realizing, early on, that sensation is not just something I do to the world but something the world does to me. At such moments, I participated in the carnal universe as a sensing-sensible body, knowing as I looked at the sea that the sea was looking at me. At once host and guest.

DOI: 10.4324/9781003285649-20

The question of embodiment is particularly pertinent at a time when some cyber experts are promoting a culture of excarnation—liberation from the flesh by means of digital simulation. Certain roboticists foresee a virtual utopia of "exes" (ex-humans) where living creatures will be replicated in a post-biological universe. In such a technically engineered world, vital interaction among sentient beings will morph into a network of pure computational data (Challenger 2021, 260; Gray 2021).[1] One futurist thinker pursues body-evasion to the point of envisioning the frontier of space being colonized not by "squishy, frail and short-lived flesh-and-blood humans" but by a new breed of "post-biological mind children" (Challenger 2021, 125).[2] Postmodern enlightenment, by this view, lies in ultimate emancipation from our animal bodies. A final escape from the flesh.

The terminal phase of our Anthropocene displays a marked fear of the animal-animate body, epitomized in the popular horror of monsters from *Jaws* and *Jurassic Park* to the *Alien* and *Vampire Chronicles* series. Strangers have often been demonized as half-animal invaders—from werewolves (*were-*, *wearg*, meaning outsider) to changelings with hoofs and claws—and this anxiety to escape our terrestrial origins may be said to reach its apogee in the contemporary replacement of flesh and blood bodies with virtual replicants. In a major rebrand in 2021, Facebook announced plans to build a "metaverse"—a 3D space where people can work and game in a purely simulated environment. Meta invites users to create avatars of themselves and communicate in Augmented Reality environments. While certain advanced societies pursue the flight from the carnal by investing in technologies which remove physical contact from key aspects of life. The government of South Korea, for example, has launched a program for an "Untact Society" where human interaction is minimalised in health care, entertainment, and commerce (Rashid 2021). The aim is to encourage a "contactless economy" of productivity and security with the deployment of high-tech robotics in "unmanned" business hubs (including "untact phone shops" where clients purchase different models without the need for human contact). Seoul City is planning a virtual zone where one can interact with digital avatars and the welfare of citizens can be monitored on AI "call bots" and multiple government apps. Even K-pop has joined the metaverse where fans can "meet" simulations of their favorite performers. Indeed the government is so committed to the program that it is investing over $7.6bn in an "untact growth fund" in support of 1,200 untact startups by 2025. 80% of residents in the capital who have engaged in such "non-face-to-face activities" say they are happy with the experience, and those that are not are promised a "digital treatment platform for depression" with a fund of $25 m (Rashid 2021).

In the face of such excarnating trends, I propose a philosophy of anacarnation—a reaffirmation of the flesh as our most vital way of being.

What Is Anacarnation?

Let me begin with a definition and move on to some examples.

The prefix "ana" is described in the Oxford English Dictionary as follows: "from the Greek, back, up, after, again in time and space." Add the substantive "carnation" and you have the term ana-carnation.

There is no escaping our tactile incarnation in this world. In spite of post-humanist claims, those who renounce the flesh pay a price. The various attempts of dualists and puritans throughout history to deny carnality always met with a sorry fate. And in spite of efforts by certain Christian Platonists (betraying both Plato and original Christianity) to renounce the flesh, most wisdom traditions attest the fact that spirit exists through nature, that soul lives through the body. Judaism, for example, teaches that if you want to know God you need to wrestle corps-à-corps—like Jacob with the stranger in the night. Christianity proclaims that Christ is first and foremost incarnate: word made flesh. Islam professes the hospitable sharing of food at the Hajj as one of the highest forms of divine-human relations. And for their part, most Eastern religions remind us of the healing power of embodied practices like breathing, yoga, ritual gesture, and pilgrimage. While indigenous spiritualties across the globe celebrate the sacredness of all sentient creatures—animals, trees, rivers, plants—embraced by the elements of earth, sky, water, and fire. American native Lakota, for instance, express this state of radical interbeing with the invocation: "*Mitakuye oyasin* – all our relations." From the beginning of time, eco-hospitality has been an essential dimension of our being.

The return to the lived body signals the interconnectedness of things. As tactile-tangible beings, we co-exist with others in a reciprocal circuit of touching and being touched—from the moment we are born to the moment we die. As even astronauts and the birds of the air remind us: what goes up must come down. What flees returns. We are betrothed to nature. And our most basic desire is to love and feel beloved on this earth.

The Philosophical

So, What Do the Philosophers Say?

Aristotle teaches in the *De Anima*—the first work of human psychology—that our most vital and universal sense is "touch." It is also the most intelligent in making us sensitive to all that is different, new, and other than ourselves. In touching, we are tactile and tangible—active and passive at once. And this "double sensation" of touching and being touched is synesthetically operative throughout all the senses. Even if we presume to see without being seen or to hear without being heard, deep down our eyes and ears are touched by what they see and hear. We only see by being touched by light on the retina and hear by vibrations touching the tympanum. True sound involves speaking and listening. The vital voice resonates. Or as Aristotle says, "voice is sound with meaning," it attends to what is other than itself. It sounds again, re-sounds, echo-sounds, reciprocally, back and forth (*ana*). We are dialogue. And the same goes for sight; while surface sight sees unilaterally—seeing while remaining unseen—deep sight is a being seen by what one sees. Sight becomes insight as bilateral vision. Sages and artists call this "seeing with the heart."

Such ana-sensation is captured by Cézanne when he describes how he felt gazed at by the trees he was painting on the Mont Sainte Victoire in Provence. The forest was seeing itself through him, he noted, making the invisible visible through his painting. But such insight—as mutual vision—is not the sole prerogative of artists. Anyone can experience it. When we see trees the trees see us. We see and are seen simultaneously, recursively. Seeing into the heart of things is ana-sight. And what is true of sound and sight is also true of taste and smell. To really taste is to savor the after-taste, slowly. To attend to what we are eating or drinking. Tasting is not mere ingestion, but a sensibility of the tongue. It involves appreciation of the origin and savor of food. Thankfulness for a gift. Something extra. Just as fragrance involves a "bouquet." Good scent is ana-scent. Carnal discernment. It takes time to know the difference.

Aristotle tells us that our senses "know the difference" (*krinein*) because they are synesthetic. Sight, hearing, taste, and smell are all traversed by the basic sensibility of touch. We sense the world through tactile skin, which brings life to our being on the earth. It is the first sense in the womb and the last to leave us at death. A body without touch is dead. Our living flesh (what the phenomenologists call *Leib*) constantly discerns and differentiates; it filters, mediates, re-cognizes, again and again. That is why, Aristotle insisted "flesh is a medium, not an organ." In short, all hermeneutics is carnal hermeneutics. From head to toe and back again. Our truest ideas—no matter how abstract—are indebted to the tangible body. We think well when we recover our senses, tactilely, reciprocally. When we receive from the other as much as we project onto the other. All genuine thinking—ontological or ethical—is a form of double sensibility. Cognition is re-cognition (*reconnaissance*). Or as Aquinas, interpreting Aristotle's psychology of tactility for the Middle Ages, put it, "*nihil in intellectu quod non prius fuerit in sensu.*" And this basic truth about the primordiality of incarnation is confirmed in the twentieth century by the work of phenomenologists from Husserl and Sartre to Merleau-Ponty and Luce Irigaray, thinkers who remind us that all consciousness operates, primordially, as a body-subject in relation to other body-subjects. Their rigorous existential descriptions amplify Aristotle's basic discovery that we are all spatio-temporal-carnal beings. Knowing is finding ourselves embodied, already in the flesh, again and again.

There is no escaping embodiment. We cannot get enough of incarnate existence. We want more. Savoir vivre as *sur-vivre*, living more by living well. Anacarnation is a way of living deeply in time (anachronology) and space (anamorphology).

*****

Ana-structure of Time and Space

First ana-chronology. Augustine was the first in western philosophy to offer a coherent exposition of the ana-structure of time. This he called the triple-present in the *Confessions* meaning that the now moment is always already differentiated as a repetition of a previous moment and the anticipation of a coming one. No instant is the same as itself. It always differs from itself in prolongation of its former life into its future. Which means every human consciousness is, deep down, a spread consciousness—intended, extended, and distended over time (*distentio animi*).

Husserl develops Augustine's insight into a description of the exploded present as retention-attention-protention in his *Phenomenology of Internal Time Consciousness*; and Heidegger explores this further in his account of the "triple ekstasis" of temporality in *Being and Time*: namely, the extension of our present existence into a constant repetition (*weideholung*) of the past in view of our future possibilities. These works signal a new phenomenology of embodiment in time and space, leading to Sartre's famous description of the self as "the being who is what he is not and is not what he is" (1978, 90). The double "not" in question refers to the structure of no-longer and not-yet that explodes each present instant—making every temporal now a palimpsest of foreing and aftering. This ana-chronology of repetition and differentiation is later elaborated by Ricoeur in his hermeneutic reading of Augustine's "triple mimesis" of time in *Time and Narrative*, where he interprets the ana-structure of life as narrativity—leading ultimately to a "poetic refiguration of time." And, finally, Derrida radicalizes this insight further still in his deconstructive analysis of *différance* through spacing and temporalizing (which inscribes every experience of life). Hence the daring claim that "there is no such thing as perception" (qua fixed presence). All experience is temporalized and spaced—gapped, traced, differentiated, in process, part of an existential *élan vital*.

Now all phenomenologists concede that we don't always see this deep anachronology at work. Why? Because our conventional "natural attitude" induces us to think of time as one discreet moment horizontally succeeding another rather than interconnecting back and forth. So we need to switch to a phenomenological attitude to recognize each moment as a multi-layered flux of anterior-posterior horizons—to see through surface time to deep time (seeing according to receding and succeeding horizons). To see time as "ana" means to see beneath the "meta" (one thing subsequent to another) to the "dia" (one thing through another). Ana-seeing is dia-seeing. Seeing diaphanously. Or as James Joyce puts it in the Proteus chapter of *Ulysses*: "The ineluctable modality of the visible: at least that if nothing more, thought through my eyes. Signatures of all things … *in bodies … limits of the diaphane*" (2000, 45).[3]

So much for the ana-structure of time—but what of space? What applies to time applies equally to our spatial embodiment. The spacing of time is the temporalizing of space. Which means that anachrony is anamorphy—a process of constant refiguring. The French term *figurant* captures this in connoting the self as an "actor" on life's stage—the human person is someone who acts and suffers in life, who creates and recreates a persona in a world lived with others who configure us as much as we configure them. Humans exist by mutually reconfiguring each other in time and space.[4]

Grasping this requires a turn from the conventional to the phenomenological attitude, bracketing our normal prejudices which divide time and space into one-dimensional parcels. The phenomenology of embodiment leads us back from the objectified numerical body (*Körper*) to our recursive lived body (*Leib*). Here we discover that we do not just *have* bodies; we *are* bodies. They are less instruments of mental manipulation than agencies of expressive being. Mind and flesh are inextricably connected. And we experience the earth as ana-carnation when we flip the switch from surface to deep sensibility.

The Poetical

The turn toward deep seeing—what we colloquially call "seeing into the heart of things"—is accentuated by art.

Here we might borrow the term "anamorphosis" used in visual art to signal a mutation from one-way to two-way vision by shifting our mode of attention.[5] Derived from the Greek word to "transform," anamorphosis is used as a technical term in visual arts practice going back to Leonardo da Vinci's notebooks. It refers to a technique of perspective featuring a distorted image in a picture seen from one viewpoint which becomes properly visible when viewed from another (where the distortion disappears). With the shift in perspective—sometimes reflected in a curved mirror or through a peep hole—the image becomes recognizable. The distortion vanishes so that we may truly see. This optical strategy of disfigured-refigured perspective is similar, I believe, to what Husserl calls the "epoché": a suspending of our conditioned vision so that we may see things *again*—more essentially—in the light of freely varying possibilities.

The process of anamorphosis also has parallels with Aristotle's definition of poetic redescription (*muthos-mimesis*) in the *Poetics*. This involves a switch from merely reciting things in a chronicle (one thing subsequent to another) to intuiting things in their essential truth (*eidos*). Such poetic intuition signals a cathartic exercise of refiguration where our primal passions of "pity and fear" are purged into "compassion and serenity." A notion captured in Wordsworth's apt definition of poetry as "emotion recollected in tranquility." Or in Yeats' famous description of art as "gaiety transfiguring all that dread" (Yeats, 1987).[6] This understanding of anamorphosis as an aesthetic description of existence represents a heightened form of anacarnation.

But the depiction of ana-carnation is not the sole privilege of poets and painters. Novelists too have much to say. Dostoyevsky, for example, portrays several of his protagonists making a transition from conventional opinion to wisdom, triggered by some kind of radical experience—that of death, beauty, terror, illness, or intimacy. These trigger moments are what the philosopher Karl Jaspers calls "peak experiences," though they may be found in the most simple of phenomena. Think of the stranger's kiss of the Grand Inquisitor in the *Brothers Karamazov*, when the Cardinal's doctrinal peroration is silenced by the brush of a carnal embrace. Unilateral indoctrination yields to the powerless power of embodied gesture. Or think of Prince Myshkin's fits (epileptic and proleptic) as his body is convulsed by the hidden pain and beauty of the world. Something Dostoyevsky himself experienced in his mock-execution as a youth in Petersburg and in later fits of ecstasy and terror, each one infusing him with a vital new compassion. Joseph Frank terms this a form of "eschatological apprehension," arguing that in such "critical moments" Dostoyevsky realized that what really mattered was what we can do for another person right in front of us right now, "action at every moment, at this very instant, as if time were about to stop and the world come to an end" (Frank 2021, 55).[7] But if these temporal moments of anacarnation—where past and future collide in the instant—are eschatological, they are so in a *micro*-eschatological way. The extraordinary shines through the ordinary. The eternal flashes through finite time lighting up neglected poetic landscapes of the flesh.

There are other examples. Think of the traumatic flashbacks of Septimus at random moments in Virginia Woolf's *Mrs. Dalloway*, illustrating the psychoanalytic discovery that trauma and thanatos are as likely triggers of anacarnal insight as beauty and eros. Freud reminded us of this unsettling truth in his pioneering descriptions of trauma as "aftertime" (*Nachträglichkeit*) and "uncanniness" (*Unheimlichkeit)*—the return of the unconscious past at moments when the foreign infiltrates the familiar (Freud 2003; 2015). Or think of the famous Proustian "epiphanies" in *Remembrance of Times Past*, detailing the sudden anamnesis of the past in the present—in the classic tasting of the madeleine with linden tea, the clink of a spoon on a plate, the stumble on a flagstone in the Piazza San Marco (Proust). Epiphanic instants which Samuel Beckett, writing of "Proust," called "visitations of involuntary memory." In such moments of anacarnation the past, as "melancholic" repetition *backward,* mutates into the therapeutic "mourning" of repetition *forward.*[8]

And speaking of ana-carnation as "epiphany" we might, lastly, recite Joyce's exploration of time as anamnesis in the Proteus chapter of *Ulysses*. Here Stephen Dedalus resolves to become an artist by reading the "signature of things" in the everyday flotsam of a Dublin shore. This requires him to "see through" surface impressions to a world where everything is interwoven (*textum*) and connected. Epiphany as "diaphany." Every phenomenon is revealed as a palimpsest of silted sedimentations, accumulating and unfolding over space and time. Flashback memories revisit Stephen transgenerationally and biographically—unconscious images of his ancestors, relatives, friends, and enemies surging back and forth on the tides of Sandymount Strand. He senses himself sensing the world through touch—"Touch me. Soft eyes. Soft soft soft hand. I am lonely here. O, touch me soon, now" (Joyce 2000, 61)—rediscovering the inner "signature" of phenomena, no matter how mundane or banal, in strand walkers, animals, sea weeds, fungi and fish. Stephen learns to read the writing of flesh as Proteus, god of the shifting sea, is revealed in the everyday transubstantiation of earthly and maritime things—punctuated by the "dringdring" of altar bells. We witness a process of eucharistic anacarnation in which we too, as readers, are invited to participate.

And that is Joyce's point. The transmigration of feeling, from past to present, from generation to generation, is an ongoing process of Protean rememoration: a hidden logos transmitted through the carnal imaginings of Stephen Dedalus to every reader who revisits the unconscious flux of things. From action to text back to action. Where the world of the writer meets the world of the reader. Rereading as a call to reenfleshment. An endless hermeneutics of refiguration.

The Ecological

While phenomenology in the 20th century recognized the bilateral nature of seeing and being seen, based on the carnal act of touching and being touched, there has not been much philosophical analysis of how double sensibility applies to the *other-than-human*.[9] There is a basic anthropocentrism in western thought when it comes to our relations to nonhuman others. In the Anthropocene our understanding of intersubjectivity refers almost exclusively to *human* subjects. It rarely applies to animals, plants or other beings of nature.

My colleague, David Wood—eco-phenomenologist and earth artist—addresses this eclipse of the non-human in an essay entitled "Touched by Touching" (2015). Taking examples of carnal intimacy, artistic paintings of plants, and personal brushes with feral cats, leeches, and snakes, he explores the recursive character of anacarnation as double sensation. Doing so, Wood cites Derrida's description of an encounter with his cat as he steps naked from the shower: "Weren't you asking, even before the beginning, if we could stroke or caress each other with our eyes? And touch the look that touches you?" (Wood 2015 , 173).[10] Wood reminds us that sight is reversible in that it is, like all our senses, synesthetic—namely, crossed by the other senses, but most fundamentally, by the reciprocal sensation of tactility. Sight and hearing for example—no matter how removed from what is seen or heard—are always acts of touching and being touched. When looking at the sun, for instance, the eyes themselves are touched by mutual action at a distance. The very eyes that see the sun are themselves infants of the sun. Without its light, no vision. Without its warmth no life. "Look directly at the sun and your retina will be burned, touched by fire. But are we not already touched, shaped indeed, by what they seem to be looking at?" (Wood 2015, 174).[11]

The ana-structure of seeing is captured here by the phrase "*already touched*"; for every seeing is deep down an always-already seen, a seeing-before-and-after (ana), a looking at what has already looked at us and will continue to look more, enveloping us in its "implicate order" (to cite the quantum physicist David Bohm, 2002). Importantly, this double seeing as already being-seen and always still-to-be-seen extends beyond the human to what is other than human—animal, vegetal, mineral, or divine. It signals the possibility of interspecies perception.

We are ana-carnal beings because we are inter-beings, beings between species, with no rigid divides between us, in spite of the separatist essentialism which informs most western thinking. As Wood observes, "anthropocentrism oversimplifies the *anthropos,* strips us of our layerings and differentiations. Man is a species that is not one" (Wood 2015, 175). Which is not to deny that we humans, qua *homo sapiens*—or more specifically *zoon logon echon* (rational speaking beings)—have a distinct mode of language. But we should never forget that human speech is always founded on a tacit language of gesture and resonance operating before explicit verbal language.

Before language, within language … there is rhythm, pulsation, touch, difference, perhaps even desire of a sort … . Who or what are we that we can be moved by words? A carnal hermeneutics finds new ways of showing how the imagination inhabits our bodies, from the pores of our skin to the way we schematize our dynamic corporeality and our engagements with others. The erotic spawns some of the most telling ways.

(Wood 2015, 175–179)[12]

The mention of eros here is significant, especially if we understand it as a power of ontological embodiment rather than a purely genital function. A power that can experience trauma as well as joy. "The flesh is equally a site of lawless excitation and incitement—pain as well as pleasure, excess, and violence" (Wood 2015, 179). When it comes to ana-carnation the hermeneutics of affirmation needs to be accompanied by a hermeneutics of suspicion. For what comes back through the carnal unconscious is as often thanatos as eros. Uncanny doubles abound, strict borders between categories and species tremble, as ambiguities call for careful hermeneutic discernment. Commenting on a painting by Georgia O'Keeffe, *Two Calla Lilies on Pink*, Wood concludes with these challenging questions:

What if mattering itself had its dark roots in matter? ... If sexuality is something at some level we share with plants, does not that fact make sexuality all the more puzzling? What would it be to understand it better? Is it that whatever else, our sexual being is our incompletely thematizable ground, driving us in ways we cannot wholly explain, and accounting for our existence and the shape of our dwelling in the first place?

(Wood 2015, 177)

It is precisely this perplexing but intriguing experience of border-crossing—between mind and matter, between human and non-human species, between conscious and unconscious drives, between sexual genders and generations, that makes a critical carnal hermeneutics an endless task.

Such carnal hermeneutics goes back to the beginning of time, when the *anthropos* first began to negotiate differences between humans and non-humans—as Lévi-Strauss reminds us in his *Structural Anthropology*—organizing the world into binaries and finding ways of reconciling them. This kind of cross-species imagination is mischievously captured in the 9th-century verse, *Pangur Bán*. The poem describes an exiled Irish scholar playing with a scroll as his cat plays with a mouse. An apt example of human-animal interbeing:

I and Pangur Bán, my cat,
'Tis a like task we are at;
Hunting mice is his delight,
Hunting words I sit all night ...

So in peace our tasks we ply,
Pangur Ban, my cat, and I;
In our arts we find our bliss,
I have mine and he has his.

Practice every day has made
Pangur perfect in his trade;
I get wisdom day and night
Turning darkness into light.

Derrida and his cat would be pleased.

The Biographical

By way of exploring the extension of anacarnation—qua double sensation—to non-human animals, let me conclude with some autobiographical examples.

I grew up in southern Ireland in a family of seven with as many dogs to go around. My parents loved animals—in particular dogs and horses—and each time my mother came home from hospital with a new child my father came home with a new dog for the previously born child (about to be replaced). That way, we each bonded with a dog and lived a happy communal life largely free of sibling rivalry. My dog slept on my bed for the first twelve years of my life before I left home for boarding school. I refused to go at first—as Scamp seemed infinitely better company than a bunch of middle-class boys marooned in a faux-medieval Irish monastery. And so it would have remained had I not fallen madly for a glamorous neighbor who praised Benedictine education to the skies and said it would be a crying shame to prefer a dog to God. I was on the train to boarding school next day leaving my Scamp to my younger siblings. I managed the transition from dogs to gods—and girls—quite well but was inconsolable when I got news of Scamp's demise when I was a student in Montreal in 1977. I suspended my dissertation, midway, to write my first philosophical disquisition—"On the immortality of dogs"—hoping to convince myself it may be my dog looking at me through the eyes of other dogs I passed on the street. (I had forgotten the lesson of Odysseus unable to reciprocate the gaze of his faithful canine, Argos, on his return to Ithaca). My interspecies imaginary is still peopled with dogs to this day, and I am happy to confess that I am working on a book entitled *Gods and Dogs*. I hope to revisit there the whole question of animal anacarnation—or what I might call "anamalcarnation."

I also had a special connection with horses growing up. My younger siblings and I rode bareback in our youth in Cork and had a horse called Billy in our garden by the river. From early on, our mother imparted a deep love of the equine, having spent a happy adolescence riding Connemara ponies with her Daly cousins in Ballinrobe, county Mayo, sheltered from the devastations of the second world war raging on the neighboring island.

The most precious thing by my bedside as a child was, I recall, a rosette horse prize given by a Daly relative placed beside a statue of the Virgin Mary. Flanked in turn, I might add, by a picture of Pat Taaffe riding his gelding Arkle to victory in the Cheltenham Gold Cup in 1964. My favorite films, from the beginning, were about horses—from *Black Beauty* to *Crin Blanc* and *National Velvet* (identifying with Liz Taylor on her beautiful mare was my first childhood experience of transspecies imagination).[13]

And when I succumbed to deep depression in my early thirties I was healed by a mare called Mary. She belonged to my sister-in-law, Olive Murphy, and I rode her daily on Myross Island during the darkest days of my life when she gradually healed me back to wellness. She had been abused by a stable hand and would only allow women and children to ride her. But she allowed me, sensing, I suspect, a psychic wound that engaged her equine empathy. She was my "wounded healer" and whenever I later felt darkness descend I would find a horse and ride it until I felt well again.

My exposure to horse healing was not, however, just personal. When researching my book *Touch* (2021), I was fascinated to discover the extraordinary powers of equine therapy. I learned of this mainly from encounters with horse healers—Petra Belković in Croatia, Nerina Latigan in South Africa—and from my reading of trauma specialists like Bessel Van der Kolk, who documented the benefits of equine therapy for various patients.[14] Here is a testimony from Petra Belković (personal communication):

> In 1993, in the middle of the war in Croatia and Bosnia, Dick and Marj Fischer moved to Croatia with a dream to open a center for therapeutic horseback riding to help those who had bodily and spiritual injuries from the war. The organization was called "Krila," which means, "the Wings." I was 13 when I started to volunteer for the organization. I would prepare a horse and walk beside it watching over our new riders. The task seemed so simple but the benefits were incredible. I learned that the horse's movement allows the rider's muscles to relax and to function even in people who had lost control of their limbs. The riders would report going off all of their medication (for pain and spasms) after a few weeks of this equine therapy. I also loved seeing how blind children learned to communicate with horses, gaining a new sense of control of their environment and their bodies. The horse would lend their eyes to the child, giving it a new sense of freedom and confidence.[15]

Belković's account is borne out by numerous studies regarding the bidirectional healing that occurs when people are near horses. Using a magnetometer to measure the heart's energy field radiating up to 8 to 10 feet around the human body, researchers have shown that the heart has a larger electromagnetic field than the brain; and more tellingly, that the field projected by the horse's heart is five times larger than the human. (Just picture a sphere-shaped field surrounding one). The horse's electromagnetic field is stronger than ours and can directly affect our heart rhythm and blood flow. Horses possess a coherent heart rate pattern (HRV) which can make one feel better when one is around them, inducing positive affective states like calm and joy. A coherent heart pattern writes Michelle Travisnon (quoted in Barbier and Katsamanis 2018):

> is indicative of a system that can recover and adjust to stressful situations very efficiently. Often times, we only need to be in a horse's presence to feel a sense of peace. In fact, research shows that people experience many physiological benefits while interacting with horses, including lowered blood pressure and heart rate, increased levels of beta-endorphins (neurotransmitters that serve as pain suppressors), decreased stress levels, reduced feelings of anger, tension and anxiety, improved social functioning; and increased feelings of empowerment, trust, patience and self-efficacy.

Moreover, as I was composing this essay I received a book written by an old friend, Mark Patrick Hederman, celebrating the therapeutic powers of this extraordinary animal (2021).[16] He notes that horses evolved over sixty million years ago as *Eohippus*, a four-toed, leaf-eating forest dweller with the figure of a middle-sized dog. Today's horse, *Equus Caballus*, has been around for almost 20 million years. Late Paleolithic humans hunted horses for food, deployed them in rituals, and painted them in cave art all over Europe. As herbivores, horses did not prey on other animals but were often the target of predators such as large cats and wolf packs. Horses are thus wont to take flight under stress, but when domesticated for farm work or battle, have been famous for courage and selflessness. If there is belligerence in horses it has been our doing, not theirs. The horse's relation to us is generally one of empathic mirroring. The movement of the horse alters our posture and sensorimotor systems as it responds to the affective state we are in. As herd animals for millennia, horses carry this natural and encoded empathy in their encounters with humans. Which is why to see, touch, or mount a horse is to feel the stirrings of energies inherited from 35,000 years of human-equine contact. The philosopher Martin Buber describes this special interspecies liaison in the following childhood memory (quoted in Hederman 2021, 202):

> When I stroked the mighty mane … and felt the life beneath my
> hand, it was as if the element of vitality itself bordered on my skin,
> something that was not I, was certainly not akin to me, palpably the
> other not just another, really the Other itself; and yet it let me
> approach, confided itself to me, placed itself elementally in the
> relation of Thou and Thou with me.[17]

From the point of view of ecological anacarnation we need to retrieve the
art of double sensation. A symbiotic healing process where we learn to let
horses *be,* not just for us, but for themselves, teaching us in turn to be well
by simply being. Interspecies empathy is not just about us. Or more
precisely, it is not so much about feeling the horse is like us but that we
are like the horse. It goes both ways: a feeling with (*ein-pathein*).

Myth and folklore also teach us much about the healing power of
horses. Ancient legends can tap into a perennial unconscious imaginary—
une pensée sauvage as Lévi-Strauss calls it—which has never fully dis-
appeared and can be triggered at any moment. The first legendary horse
figure I came across as a student was the winged Pegasus, son of Medusa
and Poseidon, God of the sea, who made rivers of poetic inspiration flow
by striking his hooves on the sides of mountains (the famous Parnassus of
the muses was dedicated to the "flying horse"). Another was Chiron, the
quadruped wounded healer, who was half horse (his lower shanks and
legs) and half-human (torso and head). Then from Celtic legend I learned
of magic horses known as *pucaí* or pookas, who transported people from
one state of consciousness to another. The fact that in Gaelic, *pucaí* is also
the term for magic mushrooms adds a further dimension to the story of
psychic transformation. And this heritage finds echoes in the practice of
equine healing through a symbiotic mirroring of mind and matter and a
triggering of genetic habits of empathy—in both horses and humans.
Anacarnation as anamnesis: a mutual reignition of instincts. Horses, like
humans, have long carnal memories, stretching back to the beginning
of time.

The reciprocating power of the non-human extends, many believe,
beyond animals to trees and mountains—often considered sacred in great
wisdom traditions and indigenous cultures. The Australian Aborigines,
for example, claim that people belong to the land as much as the land
belongs to people. They hold that we are hosted by the earth as much as
we host it. And are constantly receiving its gifts. "How might we think
like a mountain?" asks Brian Treanor in his essay in this volume. And the
answer, he suggests, is by letting it be, again and again. By embracing its
eco-ontological power of anacarnation—the transtemporal potency inhabiting its concrete existence here and now. There is a mysticism of
mountains that invites a contemplative attitude of stillness. As the
ancient adage reminds us: "be still and know that I am God." A lesson

promulgated by the "panentheism" of Irish philosopher John Scotus Eriugena with his notion of the "running god" (*deus currens*)—a sacred life force flowing through all created things.[18] But whether one turns to theology here or not, the fact remains that each human being—regardless of religious faith—can experience a basic everyday connectedness with the being of beings, human and non-human. We experience deep connection when we let things be in their interbeing here and now.[19]

Epilogue: The Dolphin's Way

Seamus Heaney has a poetic dream where the phantom of James Joyce enjoins him to heed the wisdom of the dolphin. "Community is the dolphin's way: swim / out on your own and fill the element / with signatures on your own frequency," he writes. "Echo-soundings, searches, probes, allurements, / elver-gleams in the dark of the whole sea" (Heaney 1982, 76). The way of the dolphin is to be singularly itself while attuned to its communal pod and other surrounding beings—whales, birds, humans. Dolphins are a living emblem of shared interbeing without compromising the unique "frequency" of each one's signature. Joyce's transgenerational call to Heaney is in turn passed on to the reader summoning each one of us to anacarnate the voice as our own—to refigure the text each time in the body of our lives, in our own sufferings and actions. This emits a protean succession of frequencies, from one being to the next. "Don't be so earnest ..." Joyce tells Heaney. "Let go, let fly ... Swim." (75). And Heaney's response is to feel liberated into a future always already there for him, holding and enfolding him in a play of widening circles: "It was as if I had stepped free into space / alone with nothing that I had not known already" (76). That is the way of the dolphin, to be one and many, oneself as another in the great ocean of existence.

My mother taught our family to love dolphins at an early age, during regular boat trips to the islands of West Cork—Brigid's Island and High Island in particular. She often spoke of the legendary hospitality of dolphins, how they were said to reach out to us as we reached out to them, teaching us to connect in new ways and saving souls at sea, guiding them back to life and land. When she died in 2004 she told all her children gathered at her bedside, how grateful she was to have lived on this earth and she promised—with a characteristic smile—to come back and visit us each time we saw a dolphin at sea. Mirabile dictu, when we made annual trips to the islands around her anniversary we would invariably meet dolphins, and return a knowing glance.[20] "I see the sea and the sea sees me."

Experiencing such moments of anacarnation, I often asked myself what it meant. Was it mere fantasy or truth? Phenomenologically, it seemed to me that if I was someone seeing the dolphin through (*dia*) my mother and vice versa, the double vision signaled not just a metaphorical seeing-as but also some kind of carnal connection in that unique chiasmic moment—a fleeting epiphany where non-finite time brushed a finite instant and something happened. A particular sentient being (here the dolphin) was momentarily "maternalised" by my intention to resonate with my mother's memory; just as I was simultaneously summoned by the dolphin's gaze, charged in that instant with the triggering of my mother's promise: "I will be with you if you are with the dolphin. I will see you if you see me through the dolphin." And I repeat, this was not just *seeing-as* but a seeing-with, a seeing-in, a seeing-through. Diaphany. The dolphin ancarnated my mother without ceasing to be a dolphin and vice versa. It worked both ways—in a mutual crossing of waves where neither forfeited their unique being.[21]

To be clear: I am not claiming that my mother became a dolphin or that a dolphin became my mother. I am neither a literalist nor a lunatic. Though I admit I am sometimes something of a nature mystic, in the sense of respecting the sacred interplay of living beings.[22] And, in this respect, I am partial to the line in Matthew 25 suggesting Christ anacarnates in every stranger who asks for water. A sentiment captured in Hopkins' verse—"Christ plays in ten thousand places / lovely in eyes, and lovely in limbs not his / to the father through the features of men's faces" (Hopkins 2012). But, note, only if we see it, recognize it, co-intend it. It is all a matter of relational alertness. Deep attention of body and soul.

So I ask: Is it not possible to believe that departed ones might revisit us—metaphorically and carnally—in the fleeting features of faces. Albeit with the rider, "lovely in eyes and lovely in limbs *not his*" (Hopkins 2012).[23] The uniqueness of each living being—human or animal—is not evacuated by the visitation of a lost one returning. Each retains its ontological singularity. Anacarnation is no takeover of one being by another. It is not a matter of abduction. We are not hijacked or possessed by the visitation of another, be it lower case (the least of these) or higher case (Gods in sheep's clothing). In sum, we are not emptied of our carnality by some transcendental spirit; we retain every atom of our finite thisness (*haecceitas*)— "counter original spare and strange" (Hopkins)—even as we acknowledge our interconnectedness with living beings. This basic sentiment of interdependence is epitomized in the testimonies of many nature mystics and poets throughout the ages and in the classic invocation of indigenous peoples concerning the intergenerational and interspecies heritage of our common life together on this earth: "all my mothers, all my relations."[24]

So, we return to that special deeper sense of space (anamorphic) and time (anachronic)—a time out of time across time. What Walter Benjamin called the *Jetzzeit*, where eternity crosses the instant and we feel suddenly transfigured and alive. Anacarnation is the eternal becoming of being through beings. Each time reembodied, sometimes renewed, and always a surprise.

Notes

1 Hans Moravec, cited by Challenger (2021, 260) and discussed by Gray (2021).
2 Giulio Prisco, cited by Challenger (2021) and discussed by Gray (2021). See also the attempts by cyber engineers like Kurzweil (2005) to interface the brain with computers in order to reverse ageing and other carnal imperfections by means of the technological enhancement of organisms. Such attempts at techno-excarnation often go by the name of posthumanism. But they remain within the dream of the Anthropocene. Instead, I would argue for a form of ana-humanism that reaffirms the human in the form of an interspecies commons of the body, where the digital and the animal may collaborate in critical and creative ways. See also Kearney (2021).
3 See my essay on the Proteus chapter of Ulysses in *The Book about Everything* (Kiberd, Terrinoni and Wilsdon 2022, 50). See also Emmanuel Levinas' notion of anachrony/diachrony—immemorial and unforeseeable—which signals an ana-eschatology of messianic time as a "paradox of posterior anteriority" (time before and after time). A paradox one finds in such enigmatic biblical phrases as "I am who is still to come" (Exodus 3:15) or "Before Abraham was I am" (John 8: 48).
4 See Ricoeur (1984) and Huizinga's *Homo Ludens* (1998).
5 Jean-Luc Marion offers an interesting reading of anamorphosis in *Being Given* where he describes the "saturated phenomena" as an experience of reversibility between the self seeing an icon that dazzles and overflows its subjective intentions (2002). See also James Taylor's essay on "anaskesis" in this volume, inspired by Michel Foucault's genealogical work on the body.
6 See my discussion of this cathartic process in "Writing Trauma" and "The Hermeneutics of Wounds" in *Imagination Now* (Kearney 2020a and 2020b) and in part I of *Radical Hospitality* (Kearney and Fitzpatrick 2021).
7 See also "Dostoevsky and His Demons" (Morson 2021, 47).
8 See our readings of anacarnal epiphany in Joyce, Proust, and Woolf in *Anatheism* (2011, chapter 5). See also Freud's concepts of *Nachträglichkeit* and *Unheimlichkeit* which express the logic of unconscious time as "repetition"—pathological or therapeutic—involving a return of the past in the present. If it is therapeutic-cathartic, this living back again may take the form of a healing living forward, turning melancholy into mourning. It is interesting to compare Freud's therapeutics of unconscious time with what Kierkegaard calls "repetition forward" or kairological time.
9 See in particular Husserl's description of tactile and visual empathy in *Ideas II* (1989) and Merleau-Ponty's analysis of our embodied being with others in *Phenomenology of Perception* (2002). Merleau-Ponty gestures beyond modern anthropocentrism to a recognition of an interspecies chiasmus, based on recursive empathy—or "co-naissance"—between the human and non-human. This double sensation of inter-being (*l'entre-deux* between self and other, human and non-human) is developed by David Abrams in his remarkable works, *The Spell of the Sensuous* (1997) and *Becoming Animal* (2010). See also Oele (2020) and McGrath's *Thinking Nature* (2019) and Edward Casey on affectivity and atmosphere (2021). For an artistic application of these phenomenological insights, see Rufo (2022). For a contrasting view see Emmanuel Levinas critique of Husserl's and Merleau-Ponty's analysis of reciprocal-reversible touch preferring a phenomenology of alterity, asymmetry, and transcendence (Barash, 2006).
10 Wood also cites Heidegger: "Only because the "senses" belong ontologically to a being which has the kind of being attuned to the being in the world, can

they be "touched" and "have a sense" for something so that what touches them shows itself in an affect" (2015, 177). See Heidegger's hermeneutic circle of projection-ejection (*Entwerf-Geworfenheit*) in part I of *Being and Time* (1996).

11 This cosmological phenomenon of reversible perception is echoed in Eckhart's famous observation (Sermon on Sirach 24:30): "The eye with which you will look back at God will be the same eye with which God first looked at you." (Meister Eckhart 1941). See Shesadri: "To think hospitality one must somehow cope with its temporal paradox (as contingent and recursive) ... Whether one speaks arrival or departure, the chance of hospitality implies a necessary openness to a coming (again)—à-venir." (2011, 136). Shesadri offers a deep reading of D.H Lawrence's poem about hospitality towards a snake at an Italian well. See also Jacques Derrida's analysis of hosting the animal in *The Animal that therefore I am*. And one might extend this notion of hospitality to the therapeutic engagement with the repressed "shadow" world of nature which Carl Jung explores in *Man and his Symbols*—a world we ignore at our peril.

12 See also "Indirect Language and the Voices of Silence" (Merleau-Ponty 1993); Julia Kristeva on the somatic-mystical language of Teresa of Avila, articulating her original concept of "semiotics" as a form of carnal expression prior to explicit "symbolic" articulation in verbal language (Kristeva 2015). Wood cites the "sprung rhythm" of Hopkins poetry as an example of tactile semiotics: "What is the 'I' that is touched, moved by Hopkins? It is the 'I' at home with the middle voice, or with a certain creative dwelling at the margin of words. It is essentially liquid, and embodied" (Wood 2015, 179). This raises in turn the question of the relation between human and non-human language. On such interspecies language, see the work of Mary Oliver, Nan Shepherd, and Donna Haraway which informs the reading of Brian Treanor's "Thinking Like a Jaguar" in this volume where he argues that "if the inhuman world "speaks" to us, its "language" is material and we "hear" it bodily—touching, tasting, walking, swimming, climbing, being" (25). Treanor concludes: "The point is not to become a non-human animal but to better understand and empathise with them ... to recognize that empathy with a jaguar or a dog is better served by emphasizing the carnal frame we share rather than the linguistic frame we do not." (24). Treanor extends the hermeneutics of empathy to the non-animal world, asking what it might be like to think like trees and mountains. See also Christina Gschwandner's chapter in this volume on Conrad Martius' carnal hermeneutics of non-human life. Regarding the anacarnate vitality of trees, I am reminded of the extraordinary insights of Peter Wohlleben's *The Hidden Life of Trees*, of Hildegaard of Bingen's liturgy of sacred greening (*viriditas*), and of Patrick Kavanagh's celebration of the trinitarian flowering of a tree: "Yet sometimes when the sun comes through a gap / These men know God the father in a tree / the Holy spirit is the rising sap / and Christ is the January flower that will come again from the sealed and guarded tomb" (Kavanagh 2005). Anacarnation is not a refusal of the earth but a fidelity to it. As an expression of panentheism—for the theologically minded—it carries ethical implications for our ecologically challenged times.

13 See Patrick Hederman's description of these films and others such as *Seabiscuit* and *War Horse* (Hederman 2021).

14 See *The Body Keeps the Score* (van der Kolk 2015) and our discussion of the wounded healer and "trauma therapy" in *Touch* (Kearney 2021, chapters 3 and 4).

15 Belković adds: "I was particularly struck by stories of people who came out of their apartments after 20 years (the infrastructure in Yugoslavia did not provide well for people with disabilities) who spoke both of gaining freedom and a renewed sense of their bodies, which also allowed them to share stories of suffering and trauma of their injuries and their restricted life in a society that often forgot about them. Riding on a horse allowed them not only to regain their bodies but also to find language for their experiences. Many learned later to ride on their own with the aid of additional straps, and there was nothing like seeing their connection to the horse and their confidence."

16 Hederman goes on to praise the legendary powers of horses, from Alexander's Bucephalus (who was born and died on the same day as the king and was said to be descended from Greek gods) to Roy Roger's Trigger (who could walk 50 feet on his hind legs and was house trained to stay in hotels, sit in a chair and sign his name "X" with a pencil) (2021, 195).

17 The Buber passage concludes: "The horse ... very gently raised his massive head, ears flicking, then snorted quietly, as a conspirator gives a signal meant to be recognizable only by this fellow-conspirator; and I was approved" (Hederman 2021, 202).

18 On Eriugena's panentheistic notion of a "running god" see "My Way to Theopoetics through Eriugena" (Kearney 2019a). This notion is consonant with Eriugena's familiarity with Patristic mystical theology including the eschatological notion of the Kingdom as a redemptive "recapitulation" (*anacephalaoisis*) of history—repeating the past forward in a messianic time of love and justice. Whitehead's notion of history as a relational process of divine memory has interesting parallels with the Greek Orthodox notion of "recapitulation" advanced by Irenaeus and others.

19 "We have forgotten what rocks, plants, and animals still know. We have forgotten how to be—to be still, to be ourselves, to be where life is: Here and Now. Whenever you bring your attention to anything natural, anything that has come into existence without human intervention, you step out of the prison of conceptualized thinking and, to some extent, participate in the state of connectedness with Being in which everything natural still exists. To bring your attention to a stone, a tree, or an animal does not mean to think about it, but simply to perceive it, to hold it in your awareness. Something of its essence then transmits itself to you. You can sense how still it is, and in doing so the same stillness arises within you. You sense how deeply it rests in being—completely at one with what it is and where it is. In realizing this, you too come to a place of rest deep within yourself" (Tolle 2003, 77–78). Carl Jung goes even further in his reflections on our essential eco-connection with nature which is crucial for a healthy physic and physical existence, endangered in our techno-consumerist Anthropocene: "Man feels himself isolated in the cosmos, because he is no longer involved in nature and has lost his emotional 'unconscious identity' with natural phenomena ... No voices now speak to man from stones, plants, and animals, nor does he speak to them believing they can hear. His contact with nature is gone, and with it the profound emotional energy that this symbolic connection supplied" (Jung 1978, 85). Anacarnation expresses the desire to reconnect with such an eco-symbiosis of "unconscious identity."

20 Recently, my daughter Sarah Kearney made a film (*Súitú*) of one such sea trip when dozens of dolphins leaped and swirled across our bows turning their agile bodies to look us in the eye. Witnessing the dolphin's way continues across generations (see "#HostingEarth," https://guestbookproject.org/).

21 Incidentally my father called my mother Ana, and my wife Anne tells me I wouldn't have married her if she was called by any other name. Regarding dolphins, the fact that my mother kept a wooden dolphin by her bedside, carved by her brother Maurice, and loved Greek legends of dolphins returning as humans and gods, added to my own hermeneutic memory. As it happened, my mother loved all sea creatures and felt for the pain of lobsters when boiled alive in water. I confess that whenever I performed the culinary ritual I found myself saying "Sorry mum"—visceral empathy reinforced by a recent reading of *The Secret Life of Lobsters* (Corson 2005). Maybe the phenomenology of anacarnation will make me a vegetarian one day. Yet I believe that a grateful and ceremonial partaking of meat and fish can be a very sacred thing. The first act of divine hospitality in many wisdom traditions is the gift of food (meat and milk in the story of Abraham feeding strangers in Genesis). The first Sanskrit word for God is food—Anna. As Gandhi put it: "There are people in the world so hungry, that God cannot appear to them except in the form of bread." If Christ comes in the form of bread, why not meat and fish (one of his earliest symbols)? And in Celtic mythology Ana is the most ancient name for Mother Earth, thought to be the same God that Hindus worship as Ama or Danu (Magan 2020, 112). But it is important when writing of empathy for non-human creatures like lobsters, horses, dogs, and dolphins to avoid sentimentalism. Not every animal, insect, crustacean, or molluscum is eligible for "friendship" (though *My Octopus Teacher* suggests otherwise). We should be chary of anthropomorphism, especially when it concerns domestic animals. Not every dog is Lassie, not every dolphin is Flipper and not every gelding is Mr. Ed, the Talking Horse. That is the stuff of Hollywood and Disneyworld. A critical hermeneutics of suspicion is in order when speaking of both human and non-human relations.

22 See Barbara Holmes on panentheist mystical contemplation as a critical response to our climate crisis: "When the ordinary isn't ordinary anymore and the crisis is upon us, the self can center in this refuge that I am calling "crisis contemplation" … Mysticism reminds us that the boundaries between this life and the life beyond are permeable, and that our power is not seeded in what is bestowed by politicians and society, but to everyone willing and ready to recognize the moves of an active Holy Spirit" (2021, 56).

23 The line occurs in the final verse of Hopkins' poem "As Kingfishers Catch Fire, Dragonflies Draw Flame" (Hopkins 2012). See our "Epiphanies and Hopkins" (Kearney 2019b). But in addition to identifying such serial Christological anacarnations in humans—like the humble porter, Alphonsus Rodriguez, or the suffering nun on the shipwrecked Hesperus—Hopkins' theopoetics often extends to other-than-human creatures: kingfishers, peregrine falcons or stippled trout. (See his "Windhover" or "Pied Beauty"). Hopkins' panentheist poetics draws from both the Scotist univocity of Being and the Pauline notion of the cosmological Christ alive in all beings—the view of Christ as a new creation or "second Adam" who anacarnates potentially in any creature open to new life ("no longer me but Christ in me"—*en Christo*). But if Christ plays in ten thousand places, he does so, for Hopkins, by visiting us in eyes and limbs "not his" but ours. If all are one in Christ, it is because each person celebrates the Christic sacredness of unique "haecceity" (from *haec* meaning thisness and *ecce* meaning to behold)—a cosmic oneness-in-difference epitomized in the Christic inscape of each particular being, in turn articulated in the "instress" of poetic language (sprung rhythm). Hopkins' theopoetics of unity-in-singularity expresses the legacy of Christian kenosis as

serial anacarnation. See Matthew 10-11: "whoever receives you receives me, and whoever receives me receives the one who sent me" and Matthew 25: "whoever gives even a cup of cold water to one of these little ones gives it to me." See also here Rohr (2021): "Until we can experience each thing in its specific "thisness" as artists so often do, we will not easily experience the joy and freedom of divine presence ... Beholding happens when we stop trying to "hold" and allow ourselves to "be held" by the other. We are completely enchanted by something outside and beyond ourselves." Barbara Holmes applies this contemplative double sensation to fishing: "One of the ways I practice contemplation in my life is through fishing. It's the place and the space where I find a real connection through the ocean, the waves, the sound of the water, the birds diving ... the fish." (Center for Action and Contemplation 2021). See the description of Navajo sweat lodge rituals, with panentheist invocations of the "elements," in my dialogue with Catherine Keller (Kearney and Zimmermann 2015). In various wisdom traditions, anatheism expresses itself as panentheism—God in all things but not God as all things (namely, pantheism, which runs the risk of theodicy, justifying evil as part of God's will). Such invocations are consonant with the panentheism of Celtic mystics like Eriugena and Pelagius who wrote that God is present in all that has life, meaning not just fellow humans but other-than-human life forms that surround us. "When our love is directed towards an animal or even a tree," wrote Pelagius, "We are participating in the fullness of God's love" (quoted in Van de Weyer 1995, 36). The nature mystics of Celtic and Eastern Christianity were in tune with the Pauline claim that in Christ "all things hold together ... For in him all the fullness of God was pleased to dwell, and through him God was pleased to reconcile to himself all things, whether on earth or in heaven" (Colossians 1:15–20). "All things" comprise both the human and non-human. See Delio (2020) and Keller (2018).

24 Several insights of mystical panentheism—along with those of aboriginal wisdom teachings on nature—have been confirmed by the scientific research of quantum physicists like David Bohm and eco-scientists like Suzanne Simard, whose contemporary work on the eco-system of trees (paper birches, Douglas firs and red cedars in British Columbia), documents a whole mycorrhizal network of mycelium communications for the sharing of carbon, hydrogen, and other nutrients. Through a process of endosymbiosis mother trees collaborate with understory seedlings allowing them to flourish and grow rather than merely compete and survive. The underground ecosystem of fungal links and nodes constitutes a form of natural interdependency which Simard and other eco-scientists are suggesting may serve as a positive model for human collaboration in our age of climate emergency (Simard 2021).

References

Abram, David. 1997. *The Spell of the Sensuous: Perception and Language in a More-Than-Human World*. New York: Vintage Boks.

Abram, David. 2010. *Becoming Animal: An Earthly Cosmology*. New York: Vintage Books.

Aristotle. 1996. *Poetics*. Translated by Malcolm Heath. London: Penguin Books.

Aristotle. 1931. *De Anima*. Translated by J.A. Smith. Oxford: Clarendon Press.

Barash, Jeffrey. 2006. "Le Corps de L'autre: Levinas Lecteur de Merleau-Ponty." *Études Phénoménologiques* vol. 22, no. 43/44: 5–18.

Barbier, Dominique and Maria Katsamanis. 2018. *The Alchemy of Lightness: What Happens Between Horse and Rider on a Molecular Level and How It Helps Achieve the Ultimate Connection.* Vermont: Trafalgar Square.

Beckett, Samuel. 1999. "Proust." In *Proust and Three Dialogues with Georges Duthuit*, 9–93. London: John Calder Publishers.

Bohm, David. 2002. *Wholeness and the Implicate Order.* London: Routledge.

Casey, Edward S. 2021. *Turning Emotion Inside Out: Affective Life beyond the Subject.* Evanston: Northwestern University Press.

Center for Action and Contemplation. 2021. "Living inside God's Great Story: Weekly Summary." *Posted in Daily Meditations.* September 4. https://cac.org/living-inside-gods-great-story-weekly-summary-2021-09-04/

Challenger, Melanie. 2021. *How to Be Animal: A New History of What It Means to Be Human.* London: Penguin Books.

Compact Oxford English Dictionary: Complete Text Reproduced Micrographically. 1991. Oxford: Clarendon Press.

Corson, Trevor. 2005. *The Secret Life of Lobsters: How Fishermen and Scientists Are Unraveling the Mysteries of Our Favorite Crustacean.* New York: Harper Perennial.

Delia, Ilio. 2020. *Re-Enchanting the Earth: Why AI Needs Religion.* Maryknoll: Orbis Books.

Dostoyevsky, Fyodor. 2003. *The Brothers Karamazov.* Translated by David McDuff. London: Penguin Books.

Flower, Robin. 1993. *"Pangur Bán" in Poems and Translations.* Dublin: Lilliput Press.

Frank, Joseph. 2021. *Lectures on Dostoevsky.* New Jersey: Princeton University Press.

Freud, Sigmund. 2003. *The Uncanny.* Translated by David McLintock. London: Penguin Books.

Freud, Sigmund. 2015. *Beyond the Pleasure Principle.* Dover Thrift Editions. New York: Dover Publications.

Gray, John. 2021. "The Mind's Body Problem." *Review of How to Be Animal: A New History of What It Means to Be Human (book), by Melanie Challenger.* New York Review. December 2, 2021. https://www.nybooks.com/articles/2021/12/02/the-minds-body-problem/

Heaney, Seamus. 1982. "Leaving the Island." In *James Joyce and Modern Literature*, edited by W.J. McCormack and Alistair Stead, 74–76. London: Routledge & Kegan Paul.

Hederman, Mark Patrick. 2021. *Crimson and Gold: Life as a Limerick.* Dublin: Columba Books.

Heidegger, Martin. 1996. *Being and Time.* Translated by Joan Stambaugh. Albany: Suny Press.

Holmes, Barbara. 2021. *Crisis Contemplation: Healing the Global Village.* Sheridan: CAC Publishing.

Hopkins, Gerard Manley. 2012. *The Complete Poems.* Edited by Robert Bridges. Kindle Edition. Long Beach: Lexico Publishing.

Huizinga, Johan. 1998. *Homo Ludens: A Study of the Play-Element in Culture.* London: Routledge.

Husserl, Edmund. 1964. *Phenomenology of Internal Time Consciousness*. Edited by Martin Heidegger and translated by James S. Churchill. Bloomington: Indiana University Press.

Husserl, Edmund. 1989. *Ideas Pertaining to a Pure Phenomenology and to a Phenomenological Philosophy. Second Book Studies in the Phenomenology of Constitution*. Dordrecht: Kluwer Academic Publishers.

Joyce, James. 2000. *Ulysses*. London: Penguin Books.

Jung, Carl G., ed. 1978. *Man and His Symbol*. London: Picador.

Kavanagh, Patrick. 2005. "The Great Hunger." In *Collected Poems*, edited by Antoinette Quinn. London: Penguin Books.

Kearney, Richard. 2011. *Anatheism: Returning to God After God*. New York: Columbia.

Kearney, Richard. 2019a. "My Way to Theopoetics through Eriugena." *Literature and Theology* vol. 33, no. 3, (September): 233–240.

Kearney, Richard. 2019b. "Epiphanies and Hopkins." In *Ciphers of Transcendence: Essays in Philosophy of Religion in Honour of Patrick Masterson*, edited by Fran O'Rourke, 181–192. Newbridge: Irish Academic Press.

Kearney, Richard. 2020a. "The Hermeneutics of Wounds." In *Imagination Now: A Richard Kearney Reader*, edited by Murray E. Littlejohn, 125–136. Lanham: Rowman and Littlefield.

Kearney, Richard. 2020b. "Writing Trauma. Narrative Catharsis in Homer, Shakespeare and Joyce." In *Imagination Now: A Richard Kearney Reader*, edited by Murray E. Littlejohn, 137–148. Lanham: Rowman and Littlefield.

Kearney, Richard. 2021. *Touch: Recovering Our Most Vital Sense*. New York: Columbia University Press.

Kearney, Richard, and Melissa Fitzpatrick. 2021. *Radical Hospitality: From Thought to Action*. New York: Fordham University Press.

Kearney, Richard, and Jens Zimmermann, eds. 2015. *Reimagining the Sacred: Richard Kearney Debates God*. New York: Columbia University Press.

Keller, Catherine. 2018. *Political Theology of the Earth: Our Planetary Emergency and the Struggle for a New Public*. New York: Columbia University Press.

Kiberd, Declan, Enrico Terrinoni, and Catherine Wilsdon, eds. 2022. *The Book about Everything*. London: Head of Zeus.

Kristeva, Julia. 2015. "The Passion According to Teresa of Avila." In *Carnal Hermeneutics*, edited by Richard Kearney and Brian Treanor, 115–127. New York: Fordham University Press.

Kurzweil, Ray. 2005. *The Singularity Is Near: When Humans Transcend Biology*. London: Penguin Books.

Magan, Manchán. 2020. *Thirty-Two Words for Field: Lost Words of the Irish Landscape*. Dublin: Gill Books.

Meister Eckhart. 1941. "The Defense." In *Meister Eckhart – A Modern Translation*, translated by Raymond Bernard Blakney. New York: Harper & Row.

Marion, Jean-Luc. 2002. *Being Given: Toward a Phenomenology of Givenness*. Translated by Jeffrey L. Kosky. Stanford: Stanford University Press.

McGrath, Sean J. 2019. *Thinking Nature: An Essay in Negative Ecology*. Edinburgh: Edinburgh University Press.

Merleau-Ponty, Maurice. 1993. "Indirect Language and the Voices of Silence." In *Merleau-Ponty Aesthetics Reader: Philosophy and Painting*, edited by Galen A. Johnson, 76–119. Evanston: Northwestern University Press.

Merleau-Ponty, Maurice. 2002. *Phenomenology of Perception*. Translated by Colin Smith. London: Routledge.

Morson, Gary Saul. 2021. "Dostoevsky and His Demons." *New York Review*. June 16, 2021.

Oele, Marjolein. 2020. *E-Co-Affectivity: Exploring Pathos at Life's Material Interfaces*. Albany: Suny Press.

Oliver, Mary. 1986. "Wild Geese." In *Dream Work*, 14. New York: Atlantic Monthly Press.

Pangur Bán. Translated by Seamus Heaney. Published in *Poetry* (The Translation Issue), Volume 88 (1), April 2006.

Proust, Marcel. 1981. *Remembrance of Things Past*. New York: Random House.

Rashid, Raphael. 2021. "South Korea Cuts Human Interaction in Push to Build 'Untact' Society." *Guardian (international edition)*, December 10, 2021. https://www.theguardian.com/world/2021/dec/10/south-korea-cuts-human-interaction-in-push-to-build-untact-society

Ricoeur, Paul. 1984. "Time and Narrative: Threefold Mimesis." In *Time and Narrative*, Volume 1. Translated by Kathleen McLaughlin and David Pellauer, 52–89. Chicago: The University of Chicago Press.

Rohr, Richard. 2021. "An Appreciation for Art." *Center for Action and Contemplation*. August 15, 2021. https://cac.org/an-appreciation-for-art-2021-08-15/

Rufo, Raffaele. 2022. "Sensing with Trees: Explorations in the Reciprocity of Perception." *Venti Journal: Air, Experience, Aesthetics*. For the special issue on Senses. Spring 2022.

Sartre, Jean-Paul. 1978. *Being and Nothingness: A Phenomenological Essay on Ontology*. Translated byHazel Estella Barnes. New York: Pocket Books.

Seshadri, Kalpana Rahita. 2011. "The Time of Hospitality—Again." In *Phenomenologies of the Stranger: Between Hostility and Hospitality*, edited by Richard Kearney and Kascha Semonovitch, 126–143. New York: Fordham University Press.

Simard, Suzanne. 2021. *Finding the Mother Tree: Discovering the Wisdom of the Forest*. New York: Alfred A. Knopf.

Tolle, Eckhart. 2003. *Stillness Speaks*. Novato: New World Library.

van der Kolk, Bessel. 2015. *The Body Keeps the Score*. London: Penguin Books.

Van De Weyer, Robert, ed. 1995. *The Letters of Pelagius: Celtic Soul Friend*. Evesham: Arthur James.

Wood, David. 2015. "Touched by Touching." In *Carnal Hermeneutics*, edited by Richard Kearney and Brian Treanor, 173–181. New York: Fordham University Press.

Woolf, Virginia. 2020. *Mrs. Dalloway*. London: Penguin Books.

Yeats, William Butler. 1987. "Lapis Lazuli." In *The Variorum Edition of the Poems*, edited by Peter Allt and Russell King Alspach, 565. New York: Macmillan.

Index

Note: *Italicized* page numbers refer to figures, **bold** page numbers refer to tables

For Product Safety Concerns and Information please contact our EU
representative GPSR@taylorandfrancis.com
Taylor & Francis Verlag GmbH, Kaufingerstraße 24, 80331 München, Germany

www.ingramcontent.com/pod-product-compliance
Lightning Source LLC
Chambersburg PA
CBHW050633280326
41932CB00015B/2634

* 9 7 8 1 0 3 2 2 5 9 1 9 2 *